THOMAS HOOD: HIS LIFE AND TIMES.

THOMAS HOOD:
HIS LIFE AND TIMES

BY

WALTER JERROLD

HASKELL HOUSE PUBLISHERS Ltd.
Publishers of Scarce Scholarly Books
NEW YORK, N. Y. 10012
1968

R7006904   PR
4798
J5
1968

First Published 1907

HASKELL HOUSE PUBLISHERS Ltd.
Publishers of Scarce Scholarly Books
280 LAFAYETTE STREET
NEW YORK, N. Y. 10012

Library of Congress Catalog Card Number: 68-24911

Haskell House Catalogue Item # 209

Printed in the United States of America

To

AUSTIN DOBSON,

In Homage.

PREFACE.

THOMAS HOOD has been dead for over sixty years; by common consent of competent critics he occupies a notable place among our nineteenth-century poets, by popular acclaim he is a writer whose comic verse stands far above that of all competitors, by all who have studied it his life - story is recognised as an interesting chapter in the history of modern letters, and his personality as an attractive and loveable one. Though all these things are true of him there has up to the present been but one attempt to tell the story of Thomas Hood's life with any fulness, and that was in the "Memorials of Thomas Hood," prepared by his son and daughter, and published in two volumes in 1860. Ten years later a single-volume edition was issued, with some portions excised and one or two fresh letters inserted.

The "Memorials" served their purpose: they told something of Hood's life-history, showed him as a hard worker, as a light-hearted fighter against ill-health, and as the idolised head of a household; but though the "Memorials" did all this, the work was sadly incomplete and necessarily uncritical. The authors—who were but children of ten and fifteen when he died—sought chiefly to show their father as they knew him; they can have paid but

Preface.

little attention to research, and were satisfied with dismissing, even in the second edition, the first thirty-five of his forty-six years in sixty-seven pages while devoting four hundred pages to the remaining eleven years. Brief as is the story of his early life there given it is marked by many inaccuracies, by many surmises where facts were ascertainable, and by the almost total ignoring of interesting points in the poet's youth and early manhood, in his work and in his friendships. Of that earlier period I have been able to recover some particulars which cannot fail to interest all who like to follow the story of a notable man's life during the important formative years, and I have further been able to draw upon much material which was not available to the writers of the "Memorials," to give a number of letters that have hitherto remained unpublished, and to draw upon the collection of documents made more than twenty years ago by Mr. Alexander Elliot, of Dundee, when he prepared his volume on "Hood in Scotland." To Mr. Elliot my cordial thanks are rendered for permitting me to make unrestricted use of his materials in preparing this fuller biography of Thomas Hood.

The poet has been fated to have slight errors about his life stated and repeated over and over again. The date of his birth long remained a matter of doubt, and the date of his marriage is given in many works of reference a year earlier than it should be; his marriage has been said to have been in opposition to the wishes of his wife's family—opposition wholly disproved by a series of letters which I am enabled to give. It is true that some of these errors

Preface.

are merely copied from the "Memorials," but the fact that such errors can occur in such a should-be authoritative work only lends plausibility to the suggestion which has been made that the lives of all notable persons should be re-written for each new generation of readers.

To many kindly helpers I am indebted for the loan of letters or other material, or for otherwise aiding me in this attempt to present something in the nature of a complete biography of Thomas Hood. I am especially indebted, as I have said, to Mr. Alexander Elliot, to Mr. W. A. Longmore, nephew of Jane Hood, and the only man who knew the poet with whom I have come in touch, to Sir Charles W. Dilke, Bart., to Mr. John Fulleylove, R.I., to Mr. A. H. Millar, F.S.A. (Scot.), to Major S. Butterworth, R.A.M.C., to Mr. Bertram Dobell, and to Mr. E. J. Collings for drawing my attention to the portrait of Hood as a young man and for allowing me to reproduce that portrait here.

W. J.

1907.

CONTENTS.

ILLUSTRATIONS.

NOTE.—*The tail-pieces on pp.* 11, 60, 91, 122, 201, 310, 337 *are selected from Thomas Hood's comic drawings.*

THOMAS HOOD:

HIS LIFE AND TIMES.

CHAPTER I.

HIS FORBEARS.

THOUGH the eighteenth century had yet nineteen months to complete its tale of years the literary renascence of the nineteenth century may be said already to have begun at the time of the birth of Thomas Hood. James Boswell had been five, Robert Burns had been three, years dead; William Cowper had but a few more months of clouded life; Sheridan's "Pizarro" was to be produced the next day; Landor and Southey had each published several volumes; Wordsworth and Coleridge had a year earlier placed the "Lyrical Ballads" before a world as yet unresponsive; Charles Lamb had recently published his first independent book, "Rosamund Gray"; Scott, who was about to be made sheriff, had written none of the works that were to immortalise his name; Allan Cunningham was still serving his apprenticeship as a stonemason; Byron and De Quincey were boys at school; Shelley was a child of seven, and Keats and Carlyle were children in the fourth year of childhood—when Thomas Hood was born in the City of London in the spring of 1799.

Thomas Hood :

It is a curious fact that the man who is by common consent one of the greatest of English humourists of the nineteenth century, though the accident of birth gives him, even within the narrowest interpretation of the legend, the title to be dubbed a Cockney, was by paternal parentage a Scotsman. It is a fact which Scotsmen are nothing loth to ponder. Born "within the sound of Bow Bells," Thomas Hood most assuredly was, but when we enquire into his parentage we have to turn our attention to a place far north of the Tweed. At Errol, an agricultural village in the Carse of Gowrie— that fertile alluvial tract lying along the left bank of the Tay between Perth and Dundee—there was living during the latter half of the eighteenth century the family to which the poet belonged. The name of Hood was common in the district, but the father of the family with which we are here concerned was apparently a farmer in a small way. He and his wife are traditionally said to have been hard-working folk—the father an honest, painstaking man, the mother a woman endowed with considerable humour. These were the grand-parents of the poet. Their family, consisting of five sons and one daughter, were educated at the Errol village school, and most of the sons won their way in the world. It seems indeed to have been just such a family history as is happily common in Scottish annals —a history which shows how from hard-workers on the land have sprung sons and grandsons destined to win success for themselves, to do the State some service, or even to win world-wide fame. In literature it is but necessary to mention in illustration the names of Robert Burns and Thomas Carlyle.

Of the farmer's eldest son, Thomas, it will be necessary to say something later on. The second son, Robert, sought to qualify himself for the ministry and became a tutor in the family of Admiral Duncan (later

His Forbears.

of Camperdown), from whom he received presents long preserved as relics in the Hood family at Dundee. Of the next son, Peter, no records seem available. James became a grocer and George a saddler and butcher in their native village. The last-named was a somewhat eccentric individual of whom various local stories were recalled when thirty years after the poet's death long-delayed enquiries were made about the Errol family; he was described as hallaket (*i.e.*, crazy), but had sufficiently good Scots' sense to be "a gear gatherin' carle, who keepit a gey hard grip o' the bawbees."

Our present interest lies with the eldest of these diverse brothers. Thomas (born in 1759) seems to have shared the studious tastes of his brother Robert, and on completing such education as the Errol dominie could impart went off to Dundee, where he was bound apprentice to a bookseller. As soon as his indentures had expired the young man set out in company with a distant relative to seek his fortunes in London. Of the elder Hood's early life in the metropolis no definite facts seem now to be recoverable. He is supposed to have found employment in one of the large publishing houses for a time before going into business on his own account as partner in the firm of Vernor and Hood. This was apparently an old-established house, for in 1767 Vernor and Chater had a place of business on Ludgate Hill, and twelve years later we find the publishing house of Vernor in Fore Street. When Hood joined the firm its place of business was in Birchin Lane, but some time before the summer of 1798 it was removed to 31, Poultry.

A propos of the elder Hood's business and place of business I was some time since reminded of the old saying about blind leaders of the blind when reading the information supplied in a popular weekly made up of scraps wherein curious "facts" were supposed to be

Thomas Hood :

given as to the humble origin of great authors. Thomas
Hood's father, having been a publisher whose place of
business stood in the Poultry, was therefore very
naturally described in this popular guide as "a dealer
in poultry and game"—an error which would have
assuredly delighted the "dealer's" famous son.
Nichols, in his " Literary Anecdotes of the Eighteenth
Century," is the main authority for particulars of the
elder Thomas Hood's life, but is not strictly reliable, as
we find by the statement that " he married a sister
of Vernor junior." Hood married—the register of his
son's birth settles that point—Elizabeth, daughter of
James Sands, said to have been an engraver of some
reputation at the time. Of the character of Thomas
Hood the publisher we have slight but definite indications. Nichols, in mentioning his death, refers to him
as a " truly domestic man, and a real man of business,"
while John Britton, the topographer, to give him the title
which he best liked, said " from the year 1799 to 1810
I was in almost constant communication with Mr.
Hood, who was the managing partner, and who was an
active, persevering, punctilious man of business." It
is to be regretted that his son in inheriting his father's
happy taste for the domesticities did not also inherit
something of his aptitude for business.

Some time before July, 1798, as has been said, the
firm moved from Birchin Lane to 31, Poultry, and in
January, 1806—possibly on the death of Vernor—Hood
was joined by a new partner, the style of the firm
becoming Vernor, Hood and Sharpe. It was in the
latter half of 1798 that the firm took over the publication of the *Monthly Mirror*,[1] a capital magazine which

---

[1] Copies of earlier issues of the magazine with Vernor and
Hood's imprint are reprints made necessary by the growing
demand for the periodical.

His Forbears.

devoted no small share of attention to the stage. In putting the periodical in the hands of new publishers, the editor explained that the increasing magnitude of the property had shown "that an alliance with a most valuable and justly-respected body of men would not only promote the interest of the gentlemen concerned in the publication," but tend also to the better accommodation of " subscribers in the remote situations of these kingdoms." The *Mirror*, which had been started at the beginning of 1796, was the property of the eccentric Thomas Hill, and it was edited by Edward Dubois, a wit and miscellany writer of some note in his day, now only to be met with in the limbo of the biographical dictionaries. In its pages James and Horace Smith wrote their " Horace in London "— the " Horace," it may be necessary to explain to the present generation, being the Latin author, not the Smith.

In 1808 Messrs. Vernor, Hood and Sharpe published a clever *jeu d'esprit* by Edward Dubois, entitled " My Pocket Book, or Hints for a Ryghte Merrie and Conceited Tour, in 4to, to be called ' The Stranger in Ireland in 1805, by a Knight Errant, and dedicated to the paper-makers.'" This little satire was directed against Sir John Carr, who had been an occasional contributor to the *Mirror* and was known as one who wrote travel-books on the slightest excuse. Sir John brought an action for libel against Messrs. Hood and Sharpe, presumably the only two members of the firm. The case was tried before Lord Ellenborough at Guildhall, August 1, 1808, when the judge summed up strongly in favour of the publishers, and they won the day. Plaintiff and defendant each issued an account of the trial, that for the latter being prepared by Thomas Hood himself and a summary of it being given in the *Monthly Mirror*. The report of that

5

Thomas Hood :

which was said in Court had been taken by a short-hand writer, and the variations in the two pamphlets accorded with the different points of view of their editors. Hood's additions—foot-notes signed " H."—are not such as to allow us to gauge his literary quality, though in the same notes the poet's father shows himself possessed of the pen of a ready writer. Sir Richard Phillips was a publisher—Christopher North's "dirty little Jacobin"—who was called as a witness on behalf of the plaintiff, and in the course of the evidence he declared that he never read reviews. On this Hood asked, " Did he not compel Long-man & Co. to cancel a leaf of the *Edinburgh Review* for an attack on his immaculate character ? Did he not advertise ' Turnbull's Voyage ' with a long extract from the *Edinburgh Review ?*—No, no ; he *never read* reviews. He *never* gets authors to review their own books. He has *no interest* in ' Collins's Account of Books ' which contains panegyrics on all his own works. And he has *no concern* in his ' Own Life,' published by Mr. Hughes, of Tottenham Court Road—which contains many letters that *no one* else could *furnish.*" But enough of this long-forgotten squabble in the book-world.

Having exhausted Ireland, Scotland, the Baltic, and the nearer parts of the Continent, Sir John Carr went further afield. He met Lord Byron at Cadiz, and the poet begged " not to be put down in black and white " ; but, in case he should receive that doubtful honour, he wrote of " Green Erin's Knight and Europe's wander-ing star " in some suppressed stanzas of " Childe Harold." As Carr was a Devonshire man, it looks as though Byron had not forgotten Dubois' skit of a few years earlier.

We have seen that Hood the publisher was also something of a writer ; many years later, his celebrated son, accounting for his own bent, said : " There was a

His Forbears.

dash of ink in my blood.   My father wrote two novels."
These works of fiction I have unfortunately not been
able to trace; they were probably issued under an
unidentifiable pseudonym, but, as Mr. W. M. Rossetti
has put it, " for the sake of the son rather than the
father, one would like to see some account, with
adequate specimens, of these long-forgotten tales."
Whether the novels were written when Hood was
learning his business as a publisher, or whether he
published as well as wrote them during his maturity,
has not yet been revealed to research, though I am in
hopes that some accident will some day bring them to
light to satisfy our curiosity.   A close search through
the pages of the *Monthly Mirror* does not reveal that
the publisher was also a contributor, unless some
unremarkable lines signed " T. H.," in February, 1809,
were his.   But " T. H." were the initials of the proprietor of the magazine and of Theodore Hook, who
in this very year made himself notorious as perpetrator
of the Berners Street hoax.   As possibly being the
work of Hood the publisher the verses may be quoted.
They are entitled " Lines, written on a Stone Statue
representing a Lady, in a Garden at Peckham " :—

> " This lady, blest with ev'ry grace,
>   And form'd in beauty's mould,
> Though charms supreme adorn her face,
>   Her heart as *stone* is cold.
>
> For her should lovers pine and sigh,
>   Their sighs she'd not regard,
> Though pity beams in either eye,
>   Her heart as *stone* is hard.
>
> Though in her face some smiles appear,
>   The hapless author's moan,
> Could ne'er beguile her of a tear,
>   She's merciless as *stone*.

7

Thomas Hood :

I dare be sworn a maid she'll die,
    Yet could I have my will,
I'd choose her, shall I tell you why ?
    Her tongue as *stone* lies still ! "

Although these lines *may* be by the publisher Thomas
Hood, I am more inclined to ascribe them to Theodore
Hook. Thomas Hill, the worthy drysalter of Queen-
hithe, did not, so far as I am aware, contribute to the
publication which he owned. This Hill, who lived to
a great age, is a familiar figure in the literary annals of
the early nineteenth century. He is persistently said to
have been the original of the inquisitive, despite Poole's
disclaimer, and if small in size and not witty himself,
he certainly had the Falstaffian quality of being the cause
that wit is in other men. One friend declared that
Hill's age could never be definitely ascertained because
the parish register had been destroyed in the Great Fire
of London ; while another ridiculed the suggestion with
a " Pooh, pooh ! he is one of the little Hills that are
spoken of as skipping in the Psalms ! " Hill imagined
himself, it was said, as a kind of " Thames Street
Mæcenas," and used to be fond of inviting literary folk
to his snug villa at Sydenham ; he knew something of
everybody ; and James Smith declared that " if he stood
at Charing Cross he would tell the names of all the
passengers."

The only letter of Thomas Hood the publisher that
I have recovered is addressed to Hill, and interesting as
a trivial indication of character, suggesting that something of the poet's brightness of spirit was inherited
from the father too early lost :—

"9 *Aug.*, 1809.

" DEAR SIR,—If you have any room in your private
night coach for Brighton, Friday night, I am the fellow
to fill the corner. If you don't like me to go, say so, I

His Forbears.

shall not be offended, but tuck myself into some other
vehicle and pursue my lonely way.

" Thos. Hood.

" To The Rough Burglar.
" To Thomas Hill, Esq., Queen Hithe."

The two words which I have transcribed "rough
burglar " are very illegible, and are just as like " sought
burglar "—they probably refer to some understood joke
between the correspondents.

Thomas Hood is described as one of the " Associated
Booksellers who selected valuable old books for re-
printing," and he is said, further, to have been the first
who opened up the book trade with America, a fact
which should entitle him to the grateful consideration of
some authors of to-day.   It has been mentioned that
the publisher married Elizabeth, the daughter of James
Sands, and sister of Robert Sands, an engraver of considerable repute during the early part of the past
century, though he is curiously ignored by the art
dictionaries.[1]   The family of Thomas and Elizabeth
Hood is said to have been a large one, though but two
sons and four daughters—James, Thomas, Elizabeth,
Anne, Jessie and Catherine—survived beyond early
childhood.   Several members of the family seem to
have inherited something from their father of a taste
for art and literature.   James was looked upon as the
clever one of the young family, though, unfortunately,
his promise was to be cut short by an early death.   He
was, it may be gathered, some years older than Thomas,
who wrote of him later, " my brother was decidedly of
a literary turn, to the great disquietude for a time of an
anxious parent.   She suspected him, on the strength

---

[1] Robert Sands was a much-occupied engraver.   Many
examples of his work are to be seen in Neale's " Views," etc.

of several amatory poems, of a very despondent cast, of being the victim of a hopeless attachment; so he was caught, closeted and catechised, and after a deal of delicate and tender sounding, not with the anticipated sighs and tears, but a very unexpected burst of laughter, that he had been guilty of translating some fragments of Petrarch." James is said further to have been a good linguist, and to have had, as also had two of the sisters, a talent for drawing.

Of the members of this family circle we have, indeed, but scanty knowledge. If it were from their father—and the circumstances of their environment—that the young Hoods got their early leaning towards art and letters, it was from their mother, apparently, that they inherited the fatal scourge of consumption. Several members of the family fell victims to this disease. James, the youth of promise, became very ill, and was sent away to the healthful climate of Sandhurst, in Berkshire, where his uncle, Robert Sands, lived. There, in the summer of 1811, he was visited by his father, who, on the return journey to town, took a severe cold, described as "the effects of the night air in travelling," and died of a resultant "malignant fever" on August 20 of that year. The early story of the poet's life, few as are the ascertainable facts, has been rendered more or less intricate by the variety of misstatements or misunderstandings that have been given in various authorities. The late Canon Ainger—a most sympathetic writer on Hood—stated that after the publisher's death his widow removed to Islington, but the removal from the Poultry must have been made at some earlier date, for the death in question is stated both by Nichols and by more immediately contemporary records to have occurred at Islington. The father's death was soon followed by that of the eldest son, for from the *Gentleman's Magazine* we learn of the decease on December 10,

His Forbears.

1811, of " James, eldest son of Mrs. Hood, Lower Street, Islington."

The survivors—the family appear to have continued occupying the Lower Street house for a dozen years— were Thomas Hood, his mother, and four sisters. Mrs. Hood survived her husband for some years, she and her daughter Anne both, it is said, dying of consumption. One sister certainly, two probably, survived the poet, through whom they have for us a certain reflected interest, as we shall learn when we come to the end of his story. It is said, but without any convincing evidence, to have been the death of his sister Anne that inspired Thomas Hood with his beautiful poem, " The Death Bed," with its oft-quoted lines—

> "We thought her dying when she slept,
> And sleeping when she died."

THE LADY OF "OUR VILLAGE."

11

CHAPTER II.

Thomas Hood, the second son of Thomas Hood, bookseller and publisher, was born on May 23, 1799, at 31, Poultry, in the parish of St. Mildred's, in the City of London. For many years there was a doubt as to the actual year of his birth—1798 being commonly given in works of reference—the parish registers for the closing years of the eighteenth century and the opening years of the nineteenth having been searched in vain. At length the difficulty was finally solved by the discovery that the birth was not registered until the "infant" concerned was in the nineteenth year of his age—when the matter may have had to be settled in connection with his apprenticeship. The witnesses to the registration—which was made " at Dr. Williams' Library, Red Cross Street, near Cripplegate, London," thus showing that the elder Hoods were Nonconformists—were Ruth Sands and Jane Cunlee, both of whom certified that they were present at the birth of " Thomas Hood, son of Thomas Hood and Elizabeth Hood, his wife, who was daughter of James Sands," on " the Twenty-third day of May, in the year One Thousand Seven Hundred and Ninety-nine." From a reference in one of Hood's letters to his aunts " Ruth and Cunlee,"[1] I imagine that these were sisters of his mother, though, of course, the Ruth Sands of the registration may well have been his maternal grandmother instead of his aunt.

[1] In the " Memorials" we find it given "Cundee," which is demonstrably wrong.

Birth and Boyhood.

Hood was never sure of the place of his birth, for he described himself as "a native of the Poultry, or Birchin Lane, I forget which, and in truth am not particularly anxious to be more certainly acquainted with my parish. It was a metropolitan one, however, which is recorded without the slightest repugnance; firstly, for that, practically, I had no choice in the matter; and secondly, because, theoretically, I would as lief have been a native of London as of Stoke Pogis or Little Pedlington. If such local prejudices be of any worth, the balance ought to be in favour of the capital. The Dragon of Bow Church, or Gresham's Grasshopper, is as good a terrestrial sign to be born under as the dunghill cock or a village steeple. Next to being a citizen of the world, it must be the best thing to be born a citizen of the world's greatest city. To a lover of his kind, it should be a welcome dispensation that cast his nativity amidst the greatest congregation of his species; but a literary man should exult rather than otherwise that he first saw the light—or perhaps the fog—in the same metropolis as Milton, Gray, De Foe, Pope, Byron, Lamb, and other town-born authors, whose fame has nevertheless triumphed over the Bills of Mortality. In such a goodly company I cheerfully take up my livery; and especially as Cockneyism, properly so called, appears to be confined to no particular locality or station in life. Sir Walter Scott has given a splendid instance of it in an Orcadian, who prayed to the Lord to bless his own tiny ait, 'not forgetting the neighbouring island of Great Britain'; and the most recent example of the style I have met with was in the 'Memoirs of Sir William Knighton,' being an account of sea perils and sufferings during a passage across the Irish Channel by the 'First Gentleman in Europe.'"

The City of London at the time of Thomas Hood's

Thomas Hood :

birth was still largely used as a place of residence by men whose business was transacted in its thoroughfares, men who found no reproach in living " over the shop," but who, like a certain John Gilpin, of Cheapside, took pleasure in attending to customers up to the very moment of setting out on a holiday jaunt. The Hoods, there can be little doubt, lived for some years at the place of business in the Poultry, and therefore the poet's earliest years—apart from such time as he spent as boarder at an academy for young gentlemen—were apparently passed within the City limits. While he was still a child, however, the family removed to Islington, though the place of business remained at 31, Poultry, certainly up to 1811, when the *Monthly Mirror* ceased to be published. It was perhaps not long before that time that the home was transferred to Islington, for we have it on Hood's own authority that he received his first schooling within the City bounds at a dame's school in Tokenhouse Yard. For acquiring a knowledge of the alphabet, and so being " placed on a par with the Learned Pig " he went, he tells us, to an establishment kept by two learned ladies who suffered under the patronymic of Hogsflesh. " The circumstance would be scarcely worth mentioning, but that, being a day-boarder and taking my dinner with the family, I became aware of a Baconian brother, who was never mentioned except by his initial, and was probably the prototype of the sensitive Mr. H. in Lamb's unfortunate farce."

Of Thomas Hood as a child we have the scantiest record. The only personal reminiscences recoverable appear to be coloured by his after-reputation; one of these from a friend of his father, with whom he himself came into intimate relations in later years, said that the impression which he made was that of " a singular child, silent and retired, with much quiet humours and

Birth and Boyhood.

apparently delicate in health." It is worthy of note that Hessey's words would be applicable to the poet at every stage of his life, even, it is sad to have to recognise, those referring to his apparent delicacy. Another old friend recalled years later that Hood, "when a boy, was continually making shrewd and pointed remarks upon topics of which he was presumed to know nothing." That his quiet humour was not altogether averse from the more boisterous form implied in practical joking is shown in an anecdote of his early childhood, telling how he smoked a "demon" on the staircase ceiling near to their bedroom door that he might frighten his brother, only to be hoist with his own petard, for, having forgotten his mischievous achievement, it was he when going-to-bed time came who was greatly terrified, while James passed without even noticing the insubstantial bogey. In later life the simple hoax seems ever to have pleased him.

Those who undertake research into the records of the early years of a man who becomes famous must often lament that coming events do not always cast their shadows before, and that the individual who was marked out from his fellows in manhood should have been more or less ignored in childhood. Conjecture and surmise piled upon surmise and conjecture render it very difficult after the lapse of years to disentangle historic truth from the accretions upon it. In the case of Thomas Hood matters are rendered additionally difficult by the fact that the principal authority—the "Memorials" prepared with loving piety by his son and daughter—were written fifteen years after his death, and that the authors of it were too young at the time of that death to have become the depositaries of much family lore. Those same "Memorials," too, have discrepancies, among which it is not easy to pick a way. One such discrepancy encounters us when we try to

Thomas Hood :

trace the record of Hood's schooling. We find it stated that he went to school at "Prospect House Academy" at Clapham, the locality of the school being fixed by his familiar "Ode on a Distant Prospect of Clapham Academy." Another authority says that "he received his education at Dr. Wanostrocht's school at Clapham"—here it is obvious that the information was taken from the second edition of the "Memorials," where there is a curious slip in a foot-note supplied by the poet's son. In the original edition that foot-note began, "This school was either at Clapham or Camberwell—I can remember my father pointing it out to me while we were living at the latter place." In the ill-amended note of the later edition the "either" and "or Camberwell" are omitted, and it is added that the school was kept by Dr. Wanostrocht—the father of the well-known cricketer Felix. Accepting that amendment in part the matter becomes simple, for Nicholas Wanostrocht kept the Alfred House Academy near Camberwell Green at a spot which, according to a flowery prospectus preserved in the British Museum (dated 1795), was very convenient on account of the coaches going to and from London every hour. At the foot of this prospectus is a hint that is more businesslike than elegant :—

"N.B.—Three months' notice before any young gentleman leaves the school, or pay a quarter ; and no allowance made for absence."

Wanostrocht, who died in 1812, was great-uncle, not father, of " N. Felix " the cricketer. Seeing that Hood, when living at Camberwell, pointed the house out to his son, and that the son gives the master's name, it may safely be assumed that when the poet wrote his " Ode " he purposely changed the locality to Clapham because the Alfred House Academy was then still flourishing.

16

Birth and Boyhood.

The cricketer succeeded his relative as proprietor of the school, and half-a-dozen years later removed the Academy to Blackheath, that suburb then apparently offering a more promising " pitch." Further indirect evidence in favour of Hood having gone to Wanostrocht's establishment may be gathered from the fact that when correcting certain misstatements in a brief biography written by S. C. Hall (in 1838) he did not comment on the name of his school.

In continuing his reminiscences of his own early days, Hood did not give any attention to the details of his schooling, but wrote amusingly in a generalising fashion :—

" Having alluded to my first steps on the ladder of learning, it may not be amiss in this place to correct an assertion of my biographer in the Book of Gems, who states, that my education was finished at a certain sub-urban Academy. In this ignorant world, where we pro-verbially live and learn, we may indeed leave off school, but our education only terminates with life itself. But even in a more limited sense, instead of my education being finished, my own impression is, that it never so much as progressed towards so desirable a consummation at any such establishment, although much invaluable time was spent at some of those institutions where young gentlemen are literally boarded, lodged, and *done for*. My very first essay was at one of those places, improperly called *semi*-naries, because they do not half teach anything ; the principal being probably aware that little boys are as often consigned to them to be ' out of a mother's way,' as for anything else. Accordingly, my memory presents but a very dim image of a pedagogical powdered head, amidst a more vivid group of females of a more composite charter-part dry-nurse, part house-maid and part governess—with a matronly figure in the background, very like Mrs. S., allegorically representing,

Thomas Hood :

as Milton says, 'our universal mother.' But there
is no glimpse of Minerva. Of those pleasant associations
with early school days, of which so much has been said
and sung, there is little among my retrospections,
excepting, perhaps, some sports which, like charity,
might have been enjoyed at home, without the drawback of sundry strokes, neither apoplectic nor paralytic,
periodical physic, and other unwelcome extras. I am
not sure whether an invincible repugnance to early
rising may not be attributable to our precocious wintry
summonses from a warm bed into a dim damp schoolroom
to play at filling our heads on an empty stomach; and
perhaps I owe my decided sedentary habits to the disgust
at our monotonous walks, or rather processions, or may
be to the suffering of those longer excursions of big
and little, where a pair of compasses had to pace as far
and as fast as a pair of tongs. Nevertheless, I yet recall,
with wonder, the occasional visits of grown-up ex-
scholars to their old school, all in a flutter of gratitude
and sensibility at recognising the spot where they had
been caned, horsed, and flogged and fagged, and brim-
stoned-and-treacled, and blackdosed and stickjawed and
kibed and fined—where they had caught the measles and
the mumps, and had been overtasked and undertaught—
and then, by way of climax, sentimentally offering a presentation snuff-box to their revered preceptor, with an
inscription, ten to one, in dog Latin on the lid!

" For my own part, were I to revisit such a haunt of
my youth, it would give me the greatest pleasure, out
of mere regard to the rising generation, to find Prospect
House turned into a floorcloth manufactory, and the
playground converted to a bleachfield. The *tabatière*
is out of the question. In the way of learning, I carried
off nothing in exchange for my knife and fork, and spoon,
but a prize for Latin without knowing the Latin for
prize and a belief which I had afterwards to unbelieve

Birth and Boyhood.

again, that a block of marble could be cut in two with a razor.

"To be classical, as Ducrow would say, the Athenians, the day before the Festival of Theseus, their founder, gratefully sacrificed a ram, in memory of Corridas the schoolmaster, who had been his instructor: but in the present day, were such offerings in fashion, how frequently would the appropriate animal be a donkey, and especially too big a donkey to get over the Pons Asinorum!

"From the preparatory school, I was transplanted in due time to what is called by courtesy, a finishing one, where I was immediately set to begin everything again at the beginning. As this was but a backward way of coming forward, there seemed little chance of my ever becoming what Mrs. Malaprop calls 'a progeny of learning'; indeed my education was pursued very much after the plan laid down by that feminine authority. I had nothing to do with Hebrew, or Algebra, or Simony, or Fluxions, or Paradoxes, or such inflammatory branches; but I obtained a supercilious knowledge of accounts, with enough of geometry to make me acquainted with the contagious countries. Moreover, I became fluent enough in some unknown tongue to protect me from the French Mark; and I was sufficiently at home (during the vacations) in the quibbles of English grammar to bore all my parents, relations, friends, and acquaintances, by a pedantical mending of their ' cakeology.' Such was the sum total of my acquirements; being, probably, quite as much as I should have learned at a charity school, with the exception of the parochial accomplishment of hallooing and singing of anthems."

In these discursive reminiscences the poet was rather supplying an urgent demand for copy than attempting to give an authentic record of his early years, though

Thomas Hood :

there is no reason for supposing that the facts are not substantially as he stated them. When his father died in August, 1811, we may, I think, accept it that Thomas Hood, a boy just over twelve years of age, was a pupil at that Alfred House Academy which was so conveniently situated in the matter of coaches; we have a hint of it when he comes to tell of the unpretentious place at which, so far as his memory went, he did really acquire knowledge: "I did go ahead at another guess sort of academy, a reference to which will be little flattering to those Houses which claim Socrates, Aristotle, *Alfred* and other *Learnedissimi Worthii* as their Sponsors and Patron Saints. The school that really schooled me being comparatively of a very humble order—without sign—without prospectus—without ushers—without ample and commodious premises—in short without pretention, and consequently, almost without custom." The change to this humbler place was necessitated by his father's death, which had brought about a melancholy revolution in his position and prospects. That the family circumstances must have been considerably altered there can be little doubt, so that the change from a boarding "academy" to a humbler day school was probably prompted by prudence as well as by the bereaved wife's very natural desire to have her son at home. Of this unobtrusive school Hood was reminiscently enthusiastic, affording at the same time a curious glimpse of the transforming of a boy's school into a school for young ladies, owing to the aged pedagogue desiring to pass the establishment over to the control of his daughter. Of the change made necessary by his father's death Hood wrote that his mother:—

"did not however neglect my future interest, or persuade herself by any maternal vanity that a boy of twelve years old could have precociously finished his

20

Birth and Boyhood.

education; and accordingly the next spring found me at what might have been called a High School, in reference to its distance from the ground.

"In a house formerly a suburban seat of the unfortunate Earl of Essex—over a grocer's shop—up two pair of stairs, there was a very select day school kept by a decayed Dominie, as he would have have been called in his native land. In his better days, when my brother was his pupil, he had been master of one of those wholesale concerns in which so many ignorant men have made fortunes by favour of high terms, low ushers, gullible parents, and victimised little boys. As our worthy Dominie, on the contrary, had failed to realise even a competence, it may be inferred, logically, that he had done better by his pupils than by himself; and my own experience certainly went to prove that he attended to the interests of his scholars, however he might have neglected his own. Indeed, he less resembled, even in externals, the modern worldly trading Schoolmaster, than the good, honest, earnest, olden Pedagogue—a pedant, perchance, but a learned one, with whom teaching was a 'labour of love,' one who had a proper sense of the dignity and importance of his calling, and was content to find a main portion of his reward in the honourable proficiency of his disciples. Small as was our College, its Principal maintained his state, and walked gowned and covered. His cap was of faded velvet, of black, or blue or purple, or sad green, or as it seemed, of all together with a *nuance* of brown. His robe, of crimson damask, lined with the national tartan. A quaint, carved, highbacked, elbowed article, looking like an *émigré* from a set that had been at home in an aristocratical drawing-room, under the *ancien régime*, was his Professional Chair, which with his desk was appropriately elevated on a daïs, some inches above the common floor. From this moral and material eminence, he cast a vigilant yet kindly eye over some dozen of youngsters; for adversity, sharpened by habits of authority, had not soured him, nor mingled a single tinge of bile with the peculiar red-streak complexion, so common to the healthier natives of the North. On one solitary occasion, within my memory, was he seriously yet characteristically discomposed, and that was by his own daughter, whom he accused of 'forgetting all regard for common decorum,' because, forgetting that he was a Dominie as well as a parent, she had heedlessly addressed him in public as ' Father,' instead of ' Papa.' The mere provoking contrariety of a dunce never stirred his spleen, but rather spurred his endeavour, in spite of the axiom, to make Nihil fit for anything. He loved teaching for teaching's sake; his kill-horse happened to be his hobby; and doubtless, if he had met with a penniless boy on the road to learning, he would have given him a lift, like the charitable Waggoner to Dick Whittington—for love. I recall, therefore, with pleasure, the cheerful alacrity with which I used to step up to recite my lesson, constantly forewarned—for every true schoolmaster has his stock joke—not to 'stand in my own light.' It was impossible not to take an interest in learning what he seemed so interested in teaching; and in a few months my education progressed infinitely farther than it had done in as many years under the listless superintendence of B.A., and LL.D. and Assistants. I picked up *some* Latin, was a tolerable English Grammarian, and so good a French scholar, that I earned a few guineas—my first literary fee—by revising a new edition of ' Paul et Virginie' for the press. Moreover, as an accountant, I could work a *summum bonum—i.e.* a good sum.

" In the meantime,—so generally unfortunate is the courtship of that bashful undertoned wooer, Modest

Birth and Boyhood.

Merit, to that loud, brazen masculine, worldly heiress, Success—the school did not prosper. The number of scholars diminished rather than increased. At least no new boys came—but one fine morning, about nine o'clock, a great ' she gal ' of fifteen or sixteen, but so remarkably well grown that she might have been ' any of our mothers,' made her unexpected appearance with bag and books. The sensation which she excited is not to be described! The apparition of a Governess, with a proclamation of Gynecocracy, could not have been more astounding! Of course SHE instantly formed a class; and had any form SHE might prefer to herself:—the most of us being just old enough to resent what was considered as an affront on the corduroy sex, and just young enough to be beneath any gallantry to the silken one. The truth was, *sub rosa*, that there was a plan for translating us, and turning the unsuccessful Boys' School into a Ladies' Academy; to be conducted by the Dominie's eldest daughter—but it had been thought prudent to be well on with the new set before being off with the old. A brief period only had elapsed, when, lo! a leash of female school *Fellows*—three sisters, like the Degrees of Comparison personified, Big, Bigger, and Biggest, made their unwelcome appearance, and threatened to push us from our stools. They were greeted, accordingly, with all the annoyance that juvenile malice could suggest. It is amusing, yet humiliating to remember the nuisances the sex endured at the hands of those who were thereafter to honour the shadow of its shoe-tie—to groan, moan, sigh, and sicken for its smiles,—to become poetical, prosaical, nonsensical, lack-a-daisical, and perhaps even melodramatical for its sake. Numberless were the desk-quakes, the ink-spouts, the book-bolts, the pea-showers, and other unregistered phenomena, which likened the studies of those four

Thomas Hood :

unlucky maidens to the 'Pursuit of Knowledge under Difficulties,'—so that it glads me to reflect, that I was in a very small minority against the persecution; having already begun to read poetry, and even to write something which was egregiously mistaken for something of the same nature. The final result of the struggle in the academic nest—whether hen cuckoos succeeded in ousting the cock-sparrows, or *vice-versâ*—is beyond my record."

In concluding the necessarily vague story of Thomas Hood's schooling, it may be added that he has stated that the severest punishment which he ever received was, curiously enough, for being "too fond of his book"—but then the volume happened to be "Robinson Crusoe," when it should have been a lesson book! He also said whimsically in after-life, after quoting a Latin phrase in one of his letters, "I believe that's something like the Latin for it, but I forget, *for I had a Latin prize at school!*" Later, too, he affirmed that in spite of the hundreds of persons with whom he had been associated, it had never happened to him amongst the many distinguished names connected with science or literature to recognise one belonging to a schoolfellow.

How long the boy remained at the Dominie's "high" school is uncertain, but at some undetermined date between 1812 and 1815 he had his first start in life. His mother was apparently left with somewhat straitened means, but not, as some accounts of Hood's life would make us believe, in poverty, for the family continued after the elder Hood's death to occupy the house by Islington Green, and there they remained for a number of years. It was, however, only natural that the lad should set about contributing to his own support. Whether he had as yet shown any strong bent towards art or literature cannot be stated with any degree of certainty; but that he had already given evidence of a turn for

24

Birth and Boyhood.

versifying we know from himself, and also that he acted as a boy-editor of some unidentified issue of Saint Pierre's sentimental novelette, so that the pen must have been thought of as a possible means to a livelihood, and not unnaturally with the son of a publisher and bookseller who had also been something of an author himself. Then, too, his leaning towards draughtsmanship was probably suggested by the fact— children being ever imitative—that his uncle was a well-known engraver, while other members of the family had also some artistic abilities. It is probable—though there is little but surmise to go upon in hazarding the suggestion — that James Hood was apprenticed to Robert Sands. He was older (how much older is not known) than Thomas, and he is reported to have had a distinct talent for drawing.

As other men of genius before him, Thomas Hood was not to be afforded such a beginning as best suited his capacities. When the time came for him to leave the Dominie " to be introduced into that Universal School where, as in the preparatory ones, we have very unequal shares in the flogging, the fagging, the task-work, and the pocket-money," the boy had to take the work which offered, not that which he might have chosen. Thus it was that Thomas Hood somewhere about the age of fourteen became something in the City, thanks to the kindly offices of a friend of the family who had taken a fancy to him. As he put it, "like another Frank Osbaldistone, I found myself planted on a counting-house stool, which nevertheless served occasionally for a Pegasus on three legs, every foot of course being a dactyl or a spondee."

The authority that we have for this is Hood's own, and, though in writing the " Memorials " his son and daughter ignored the matter, there can be little doubt

Thomas Hood :

that the poet was recording an autobiographical fact while setting it forth in the playful fashion which his readers had come to expect. The firm was apparently one of merchants or shippers engaged in the Russian trade, but Hood did not remain with it long ; as he put it, "my commercial career was a brief one, and deserved only a sonnet in commemoration." That sonnet—an unusual measure into which to run humour—is the following :—

> " Time was, I sat upon a lofty stool,
>   At lofty desk, and with a clerkly pen
>   Began each morning, at the stroke of ten
>   To write in Bell & Co.'s commercial school :
>   In Warnford Court, a shady nook and cool,
>   The favourite retreat of merchant men ;
>   Yet would my quill turn vagrant even then,
>   And take stray dips in the Castalian pool.
>   Now double entry—now a flowery trope—
>   Mingling poetic honey with trade wax—
>   Blogg Brothers—Milton—Grote and Prescott—Pope—
>   Bristles—and Hogg—Glyn Mills and Halifax—
>   Rogers—and Towgood—Hemp—the Bard of Hope—
>   Barilla—Byron—Tallow—Burns—and Flax ! "

Hood's stay in the counting-house was but a brief one, but, as he put it, "the fault lay not with the muses," adding, "To commit poetry indeed is a crime ranking next to forgery in the counting-house code ; and an Ode or a song dated Copthall Court, would be as certainly noted and protested as a dishonoured bill. I have even heard of an unfortunate clerk who lost his situation through being tempted by the jingle to subscribe under an account current

> ' Excepted all errors
> Made by John Ferrers,'

his employers emphatically declaring that Poetry and Logwood could never co-exist in the same head. The principal of our firm on the contrary had a turn for the

Birth and Boyhood.

Belles Lettres, and would have winked with both eyes at verses which did not intrude into an invoice or confuse their figures with those of the Ledger." It would be pleasant to ascertain who was that principal of the firm who had "a turn for the Belles Lettres"—it is easy to believe, remembering the fourth line of the sonnet, that the writer was merely punning on the name of Bell.

It was a breakdown in health that made an early change of occupation necessary. Turning once more to Hood's fancifully-written record of facts, we learn: "My constitution though far from venerable had begun to show symptoms of decay; my appetite failed, and its principal creditor, the stomach, received only an ounce in the pound. My spirits daily became a shade lower —my flesh was held less and less firmly—in short, in the language of the price current it was expected that I must 'submit to a decline.' The Doctors who were called in, declared imperatively that a mercantile life would be the death of me—that by so much sitting, I was hatching a whole brood of complaints, and that no Physician would insure me as a merchantman from the Port of London to the next Spring. The exchange, they said, was against me, and as the exchange itself used to ring with ' Life let us Cherish,' there was no resisting the advice. I was ordered to abstain from ashes, bristles, and Petersburg yellow candles, and to indulge in a more generous diet—to take regular country exercise instead of the Russia Walk, and to go to bed early even on Foreign Post nights."

After this brief experience in a City office Thomas Hood began to work at the engraver's craft, and presumably advanced some way in it, for we know from a letter written some years later to his uncle-engraver that he had been working on blocks before he went to Scotland, though it has sometimes been assumed that it was after his return from the North that he was

Thomas Hood :

apprenticed to his uncle. It seems likely—and the supposition is borne out by Hessey's recollection—that on its being found that the confined work of the counting-house disagreed with him, he left the merchant's office and took up occasional work at engraving. Writing to his uncle, Robert Sands, shortly after his return from the North he said : " I did some things for Mr. Harris before I went to Scotland with which he was very well pleased, but have had no proofs, as I did them while he was busy on the Battle of Waterloo, and could not prove for me." It was under this Harris that Hood no doubt began his work as engraver, and the reference shows conclusively that Hood did not go to Scotland before July, 1815 ; it was probably in the following month.

We have a glimpse of Thomas Hood as a boy of fifteen afforded in a letter written many years after by John Wilson (author of " The Antiquities of Clerkenwell "). The mothers seem to have been on terms of intimacy, and, recalling this in his old age, Wilson wrote :—

" In 1814 my mother said to me, ' We will go up to Mrs. Hood's and see her. She lived at Islington Green, in an old brick house, Queen Anne's, quite a day's journey for us. Found Mrs. H. and Master Thomas at home. I fancy he was sketching. I was not much of a judge then—but nine years of age."

The Hoods' house evades exact identification. The family was at Lower Street, Islington—" somewhere near Islington Church "—in 1811, and they were at the same vaguely exact place a dozen years later. It was a house with a garden, and, as the above extract tells us, an old red brick Queen Anne's house—before " Queen Anne style " had been devised. A print of Islington Green in Hughson's " Description of London " (1808) shows that that suburb in Hood's day still retained something of the aspect of a rustic village.

CHAPTER III.

STAY IN SCOTLAND (1815—1817).

THE difficulties and discrepancies which occur in
the various records of Thomas Hood's early life, his
schooling and his first essays in business, continue in
no less marked a fashion when we come to follow him
on his first visit to the land of his fathers. Of that
visit he wrote entertainingly enough in his brief literary
reminiscences, but he wrote without any particularity
as to dates and names, so that, though he affords bright
reading on the subject, he does not supply us with such
exact data as we should like; I have therefore thought
it as well to tell the story of the two years' stay in
Dundee so far as it can be recovered and to follow it with
Hood's own reminiscential discursiveness.

It is now more than twenty years ago since Dundee
wakened to the fact of its association with one of the
most individual of the literary geniuses of the nineteenth
century. This awakening was due to the fact that Mr.
Alexander Elliot—a prominent citizen of the town—
published the result of long and patient investigation
in his volume "Hood in Scotland." Mr. Elliot made
plain many matters which had been slurred or ignored
in the "Memorials," and was able to recover various
letters written by the poet to friends made during his
sojourn in the North—valuable aids to us in forming
our estimate of him as a young man, in trying to
elucidate the story of his early life and in learning
something of his youthful interests.

It is commonly stated that Hood went to Scotland

Thomas Hood :

in 1814. Though the actual date does not seem now recoverable, it seems fairly certain that he set out in the following year, some time between the day on which the Battle of Waterloo was fought—so much seems to be established by a subsequent letter—and the middle of September, the date of the first of his recovered letters written from Dundee, so that we get the time of his journey north with an approximate exactness denied to earlier writers on Hood. Tidings of the final overthrow of Napoleon on the field of Waterloo had been hailed as glorious news by the vast majority of English people, while it had been received with qualified enthusiasm by a few, such as Leigh Hunt, and with a sense of irretrievable disaster by fewer still, such as William Hazlitt, who, as Mr. Birrell has put it, staggered under the blow. The youth Thomas Hood was, it may be imagined, one of the vast majority who were thrilled with enthusiasm at the final overthrow of the Corsican and the removal of the bogey "Boney" to an islet instead of France, a scanty plot of ground instead of an empire.

It was while England was yet thrilling with the news, while shiploads of wounded soldiers from the Belgian battlefield were being brought home, that young Hood set out from London for Scotland by sea. It is possible that the trading smack *Union*, as she sailed down the estuary of the Thames with the youth of sixteen going out into the world, may have passed His Majesty's brig *Ernest* bringing wounded men from the Continent and counting among her officers Midshipman Douglas Jerrold, not yet thirteen years of age. The child officer and the young exile on account of health were to become friends in after years when each had won an acknowledged place in the world of letters.

The state of Thomas Hood's health may well have been watched with unusually anxious care by the

30

Stay in Scotland.

members of his family, and therefore when continued application to a sedentary occupation, whether the clerk's quill or the engraver's tool, was found to be harmful, it may well have occurred to his mother that the boy should visit his paternal relatives in the neighbourhood of Dundee. What exactly was the trouble under which he was suffering cannot now be determined; he was probably in a poor state of health generally, and may even have shown already signs of pulmonary weakness. After his return, in proof of the good which his stay in Scotland had done him, he stated that his neck was altogether healed and his leg had gained strength. Whatever the trouble may have been, change of air was recommended, "and in particular the bracing breezes of the North." His father's relatives at Dundee were communicated with, and Scots hospitality was, we may readily believe, at once proffered.

Dundee may not at the present time impress the casual visitor with any idea of its importance as a health resort. It has developed greatly as a commercial and manufacturing centre during the past ninety years; but even now it shares with Scotland's other great centres one important characteristic—we like it the better, and the remark is meant in no invidious sense—in that we can so soon get out of it; can get out of it among the varied and beautiful scenery by the noble Tay, along to the coast or into the fertile Carse of Gowrie, the kindly soil of which supported many generations of the forbears of the youth who in the late summer of 1815 paid his first visit to Scotland. Dundee was, at the time of Hood's arrival, a quiet enough place, far smaller in extent than it is at present; the many factories had not then heavily traced their trade-mark in smoke upon the sky, the small jute trade had not migrated from the banks of the Thames

Thomas Hood :

to wax gigantic on the banks of the Tay—as Mr. Elliot
put it, " the weaver's shuttle had not given place to the
whir of machinery, and the town lay in undisturbed
and monotonous repose." There were no railways in
those days, there was no Tay Bridge connecting the
coasts of Forfar and Fife, and coasting smacks probably
represented the greater portion of the shipping, which,
however, must have been considerable, judging by the
shipping lists of the early issues of the now venerable
Dundee Advertiser.

Despite close and zealous inquiry into the circumstances attending Hood's stay in Dundee, there are
matters that cannot finally be settled, for the reminiscences of the old folks whom Mr. Elliot interrogated
clash with Hood's own recollections written in 1839.
While allowing for humoristic exaggeration, it is impossible to accept the suggestion that the poet's memory
was in the very prime of his life so impaired that he
believed that which he wrote to be true while there
was no truth in it whatever. After all, Hood when he
wrote of his Scottish experiences was writing of that
which had befallen himself a quarter of a century earlier,
whereas the people who are quoted in disproof of his
statements were relying upon memory or tradition for
matters concerning other people that had occurred over
sixty years before. There can be no question as to
which is the better evidence, though it is only natural
that there should be some resentment shown at the
slight cast on Dundonian hospitality.

The youth went to Scotland—his letters show as
much—merely for a holiday trip, and it is quite likely
that that holiday was spent with the relatives to whom
he was "shipped as per advice." After his arrival it
was soon arranged that he should stay over Christmas.
By then it may be assumed that his health had so
greatly benefited that he determined to stay on

longer, and I fancy that the aunt who wished to return
him to London may have done so when he first resolved
to stay on, and not immediately upon his arrival.
This at least partially reconciles contradictory statements. Hood's own reminiscences are contradicted by
a letter written at the time, and written some months
before the date which he later recalled as that of his
stay in Dundee. For a while we may take it that he
did stay with his aunt, Mrs. Keay, in her home in the
Nethergate. His son and daughter give a scrap of
family tradition in support of it, for they describe his
aunt as a rigid Sabbatarian—no rarity in old Dundee—
and tell how on one occasion being prevented from
going herself by indisposition, she found entertainment in getting her nephew to watch the people walking
to church and describe them to her. Already the sense
of humour, the spirit of mischief, were awake in the
youth, and:
"something like the following dialogue would
ensue—

"'Tammie, my man, keek out,—wha's that?'

"'That's Bailie So-and-So's daughter, aunt, and isn't
she making desperate love to young Somebody, who's
walking by her side!'

"'The graceless hizzie! I'd wauk her, gin _I_ were
her mammie! Keek out again, Tam.'

"'There's Mrs. Blank, aunt, and she's got on a grand
silk gown, and such a velvet mantle!'

"'Set us up, laddie! She, indeed! the sillie wastrife
bodie—she'd far better pay a' she's owing. Wha's
neist?'

"And so they would go on, the crabbed auld Scotchwoman little suspecting half the 'stour' proceeded from
the active imagination of her 'nevvy,' to heighten the
fun and draw her out."

This house in which Hood stayed stood in the

Thomas Hood :

Nethergate, opposite the famous Old Steeple, but was long since pulled down to make way for newer buildings and shops. How long the boy remained there must be matter for conjecture, unless further letters should come to light. The only known portion of his correspondence written from Scotland consists of two letters, both of them written to aunts in London. From his aunt's place in the Nethergate he went to a boarding-house in the Overgate, kept by a Mrs. Butterworth.

Mrs. Butterworth's tenement was up a winding, or " buckie " stair, which is still standing, though the building has obviously seen its best days. From its present aspect the visitor with imagination can picture the place as it must have been about ninety years ago. It may be mentioned that a " buckie " is in the language of the neighbourhood a winkle, and from its spiral form the stairway, which starts directly from the street, takes its name. It was presumably during his stay at this Overgate boarding-house that the two earliest of Hood's letters that remain to us were written. The first it appears must have been written from Mrs. Butterworth's, for Hood would scarcely have described his aunt as his " landlady," though Mr. Elliot's investigations went to show that the unflattering description might have been more applicable to Mrs. Keay than to Mrs. Butterworth. It is possible of course, that he changed his lodgings more than once, and that the brogue and unprepossessing appearance belonged to some lady unknown, even though the oldest inhabitant interviewed by Mr. Elliot failed to recall the fact. This earlier letter is dated " September, 1815," and begins :—

" I again take the pen for a double purpose to amuse both you and myself by a description of whatever attracts my notice. I am principally diverted here

34

with the singular characters that come to lodge here in succession. When I first came we had a kind of itinerant minister, who loved his bottle.

> ' And oft would rehearse
> In defence of his custom this scriptural verse,—
> " Take a little wine for thy stomach's sake,"
> But in practice the little, but jolly divine,
> Would oft substitute whisky instead of the wine ! '

Since then we have been enlivened by a French captain who possessed in an eminent degree the gaiety and politeness peculiar to that nation; and I have been peculiarly amused with a pedantic Perth schoolmaster, who went up to London during the vacation and resided a fortnight in *Wapping*—in order to improve himself in English ! and said he was ' vary sure he wadna be takken for a Scotsman.' At present we have a Swiss who appears to be an agreeable man, but I do not know how he may be on further acquaintance. The study of character (I mean of amusing ones) I enjoy exceedingly, and have had an ample field for speculation, for, independent of originality of character, their ideas are also frequently of the same stamp, as in the case of our hostess, who thinks that fresh beef will keep better than that which is salted—but you will perhaps think this notion took its rise in economy and not in originality of idea."

He goes on to discuss a local lottery, the scene at the drawing for which was worthy of Hogarth's pencil—it is curious to get this in Hood's first letter seeing that in another ten years he was himself to be described as our new Hogarth by Charles Lamb; he indicates a love of music by saying that nearly every night he goes to "the beautiful promenade before the barracks," where the fine band of the 77th played every evening; "walking, swimming, drawing," he concludes, constitute his principal employment during his " banishment." In a postscript he says :—

" The smack I intended to send this by is detained, so that I have yet time to send more. As I am to remain and take my Christmas in the Land of Cakes, you will perhaps expect me to return a complete Scot, but to tell you the truth, I approach it as yet but in a small degree. I sicken with disgust at the sight of a singed sheep's head, and notwithstanding the arguments of Lismahago and the preference of the mouse, which I admit is some support of them, I cannot bring myself to endure oatmeal, which I think harsh, dry, and insipid. The only time I ever took it with any kind of relish was one day on a trouting party, when I was hungry enough to eat anything. As to their dialect, I have acquired rather more than I could wish, through the broad brogue of our landlady, whose blunders would do credit to an Hibernian."

The next letter is dated December, 1815, and in it young Hood thanks his aunts for a " handsome present," which it is not unreasonable to suppose may have been a monetary contribution towards the expenses of his " banishment " in search of health. The letter is particularly interesting as affording us our first glimpse of the writer as literary aspirant :—

" As you seem to have some fear of submitting your letters to my criticism, I must assure you that you need be under no apprehensions on that head, my own epistolary style being very indifferent, and I should fear by criticising to lose the pleasure of receiving your letters."

He goes on to say that instead of a regular description of the irregular town of Dundee he will give them some extracts from a note book in which he is endeavouring to describe the town in the way in which the Blunderhead family dealt with Bath in Christopher

Stay in Scotland.

Anstey's long-celebrated "New Bath Guide." These extracts show that he had already got on well with his projected work, for he cites no fewer than one hundred and sixteen lines. As the earliest example of Hood's literary achievements which we possess these bits of a lost "Guide" are interesting; they suggest a fund of good spirits, and they show the author possessed of that ready facility in the false galop of verses which is not only requisite for such an undertaking, but which is also something of a promise of the poetry to come when it is already at the command of an imaginative and observant youth in his mid 'teens :—

"The town is ill-built and is dirty beside
For with water it's scantily, badly supplied
By wells, where the servants, in filling their pails,
Stand for hours, spreading scandal and falsehood and tales.
And abounds so in smells that a stranger supposes
The people are very deficient in noses.
Their buildings, as though they'd been scanty of ground,
Are crammed into corners that cannot be found.
Or as though so ill-built and contrived they had been,
That the town were ashamed they should ever be seen.
And their rooted dislike and aversion to waste
Is suffer'd sometimes to encroach on their taste,
For beneath a theatre or chapel they'll pop
A sale-room, a warehouse, or mean little shop,
Whose windows, or rather no windows at all,
Are more like to so many holes in the wall.
And four churches together, with only one steeple,
Is an emblem quite apt of the thrift of the people. . . .

Like a fish out of water, you'll think me my dear,
When our manner of living at present you hear;
Here, by ten in the morning our breakfast is done,
When in town I ne'er think about rising till one:
And at three, oh, how vulgar, we sit down and dine,
And at six we take tea and our supper at nine,
And then soberly go to our beds by eleven,
And as soberly rise the next morning by seven.

37

Thomas Hood :

How unlike our great city of London, you'll say,
Where day's turned into night, and the night into day.
But indeed to these hours I'm obliged to attend,
There's so very few ways any leisure to spend,
For they ne'er play at cards, commerce, ombre or loo,
Though they often are carding of wool, it is true.
And instead of 'pianys,' Italian, sonatas,
At their spinning wheels sitting, they whistle like carters. . . .

Some large markets for cattle or fairs are held here,
On a moor near the town, about thrice in a year.
So I went to the last, found it full, to my thinking,
Of whisky, and porter, of smoking and drinking.
But to picture the scene there presented, indeed,
The bold pencil and touches of Hogarth would need.
Here you'd perhaps see a man upon quarrelling bent
In short serpentine curves wheeling out of a tent,
(For at least so they call blankets raised upon poles,
Well enlightened and aired by the numerous holes),
Or some hobbling old wife just as drunk as a sow,
Having spent all the money she got for her cow.
Perhaps some yet unsold, when the market has ceased
You may then see a novelty, beast leading beast!"

The different letters into which the "Guide" was
presumably divided were evidently written by quasi-
fashionable Londoners, but the work was lost a few
years later, and, presumably, never reached the publicity
of print until the passages (of which the above scraps
are a portion), quoted in Hood's letter to his aunt, were
given with that letter in the second edition of the
"Memorials." It is interesting to pause thus over these
lines, because they show the writer's leaning towards
literature at a time when he was still regarding himself
as a budding engraver, was still varying his holiday occupations with the exercise of the burin. His instinct
was, there can be little doubt, to express himself through
the medium of the pen. He was in his seventeenth
year when he essayed this guide in the manner of
Anstey, and though the play of it gives no hint of the

Stay in Scotland.

"transcendent" puns of ten years later, yet it may, in the light of its author's after fame, be recognised as one of the straws indicating the direction of the wind.

Hood's stay in Scotland is interesting in that I fancy we may trace to it the final determination of his bent towards literature, though he probably still looked upon writing in the light of a pleasure to be cultivated rather than that of a future profession. Here was a lad left more or less to his own devices—a boy at the Nore of life left dependent on his own pilotage for a safe voyage to the Isle of Man, to use his own illustration. He read with avidity whatever books, good, bad, or indifferent, came within his reach, and recalled with regret that he had not secured then as a literary curiosity, "a collection of halfpenny ballads, the property of a grocer's apprentice, and which contained, amongst other matters, a new version of 'Chevy Chase,' wherein the victory was transferred to the Scots." Nature, as he said, had gifted him with a taste for reading, that precious taste valuable to any, but trebly valuable to one forced by any circumstances to lead a more or less sedentary life. Whatever may have been the health troubles which necessitated Hood's happy stay in Scotland, he appears to have got about a good deal, to have enjoyed walking and fishing in the neighbourhood of Dundee with friends of kindred tastes. These friends included George Rollo, Andrew Wyllie, and a young Swiss named Messieux, with whom he may well have improved his knowledge of French and whom he visited at St. Andrews during the latter part of his stay. The circle of friends was apparently a small one; with them or alone his round of recreations and occupations seems to have been reading and writing, sketching and engraving, playing chess and fishing, with, perhaps, a turn at music. In the summer, according

39

Thomas Hood :

to local tradition, he spent some time in his father's native village of Errol, living in the one-room dwelling of his grandmother, with occasional visits to other friends in the district, notably the Gardiners of Errol Grange Farm, relatives of that Patrick Gardiner who had accompanied the elder Thomas Hood on his fortune-seeking journey to the south, and Patrick Matthew, a young man who had visited the Hoods in London. With these friends he went fishing and walking, and in after years when he had become famous—as after men have become famous such things will be remembered—it was recalled that he was notable for his humour. It is to be regretted that the letters which the youth must have written home from Dundee and the Carse have not been preserved, or if preserved have not yet come to light. We should like to know what the keenly observant boy, with his native sense of fun and humour, had to tell of his life in the north, to the family circle in the Islington home. More or less vague reminiscences of those searching their memories in age, for matters which occurred in their youths and which had no special cause for making strong impressions, form but a poor substitute. That Hood enjoyed himself in Dundee there can be no doubt, that he greatly benefited by his stay we know; indeed, it was owing to the improvement in his health that the holiday visit of a few weeks which was first planned was prolonged to a banishment (or voluntary exile) of two years.

Seeing that Hood was definitely engaged in engraving before he left London, it is more than likely that he continued to exercise the art while in Dundee. One of his companions recalled many years later that he had been engaged in office work while in Dundee, and this is probably the explanation. We have seen that he made an essay at writing, evidently with an eye to future publication—what youth in his 'teens ever dipped

Stay in Scotland.

his pen to write a verse without having his mind's eye intent upon the printed page? Hood, however, went further than the writing stage; he made his appearance in all the dignity of print with an unidentified "quizzing letter" to the editor of a Dundee newspaper, and shortly after with a contribution to the *Dundee Magazine.* In Mr. Elliot's interesting volume a letter dated April 24th, 1815, signed "Juvenis," is cited as being probably Hood's first printed work, but then, as I have shown, Hood was certainly not in Dundee until some months later. To the contribution to the magazine selected as being perhaps Hood's, the same fatal objection applies; it appeared but two months after the letter, that is to say, some time in June, 1815, some days, perhaps weeks, before Hood could have reached Dundee.

Thinking it possible that Hood's reference to the paper might not be the accurate one, I have referred to various Dundee periodicals of the time, but have not been able to ascertain anything definite as to the poet's first appearance in print. There is, however, in the first number of the quarterly *Independent* (Dundee, April, 1816), a letter which I am inclined to ascribe to Hood, firstly, because it tallies with the period that he had been in the town, and, secondly, because its closing sentence has a humorous turn that seems very characteristic of his whimsical manner of looking at things. It is possible that some of the young friends which he made in the Forfar seaport were connected with the new venture, and he may have written other things in it, things that can only be conjecturally associated with him. Some quaint verses on *The Metamorphosis* in the number for September are suggestive of his later vein. The letter referred to is the following—the signature is curiously enough the same as that to the letter which Mr. Elliot gives from the *Advertiser*, but Juvenis was one of the most popular of pseudonyms, as anyone who explores the periodical literature of the time will readily recognise.

" Sir,—I have been more than six months in Dundee, and I am now more a stranger than I was on my arrival. For some time, I made one of every party, and shared in every feast; but now nobody invites me, and very few speak to me. Is it not cruel thus to entice a stranger to the height of society, apparently for no other purpose than that of throwing him down into the gulf of neglect ? How long must one remain here to be totally forgotten ?

" JUVENIS."

" *Wednesday evening.*"

To this communication the editor of the *Independent* (or the correspondent himself) appended the following note :

" Juvenis must be young indeed, not to know that he was invited merely for the *éclat* of having the stranger. Were we to attempt a more philosophical solution of his problem, we might say that external attention is a kind of electric energy—it attracts a stranger just as the prime conductor does a cork ball; and when he is saturated, it repels him with equal violence."

" Stout and original Scotland "—to use the phrase which seems to have tickled his fancy—worked wonders in bettering of the health of the boy. It is recorded that when the slim and delicate-looking youth was introduced to a Perthshire relative, she exclaimed, " Losh! woman ! what are ye daein' bringing that laddie up here to dee!" His two-years' stay seems to have set him up thoroughly, to have introduced him to new friends of kindred tastes, to have given him his first appearance in all the dignity of print, and thus to have materially influenced the colouring and filling up of his future life. While he was in Scotland he had a scrap book in which he wrote his verses and made his sketches, and this he left with some of his Dundee relatives. It was probably not prized to its worth after he had returned south, and was, it is believed, ultimately destroyed. Besides portions of his rhymed satirical "Guide," however, one other of his early exercises in verse has been preserved, and this may most fittingly be mentioned here, as it was probably written during the Scotch visit. The poet was still trying his wings in the time-honoured manner of young writers—that is, by following the literary idols of his youth.

As he put it, "all monkeys are imitators, and all young authors are monkeys," and thus it was that he wrote *The Bandit*. It is a melodramatic story in about eight hundred lines of rhymed verse, with some of the gloomy romance of Byron, some of the manner of Scott, and more than a hint of the didacticism of the eighteenth century poets. The story is of a Scots nobleman who was exiled, became head of a robber band, returned to find his lady love about to marry his friend, and sought to frustrate the union by breaking in upon the marriage feast with his robber band. He comes to slay, but stays to bless. His bandit-lieutenant turns traitor and Glenallan is captured and doomed to die, and then on the day fixed upon for his execution stabs himself fatally just as the cry of pardon is heard. It is such a story as the time was rich in, and though for the most part told in easy couplets it contains some halting lines which betray the immaturity of the writer, and a "cockney" rhyme of the worst kind in "worse" and "us." There is little that is poetical in the rendering, and a few lines from the second canto will suffice to give a taste of the youth's quality. The sixth line is one of the rare instances in which throughout the piece he deviates from mere description or conversation :—

> " Through Arden's pile the lighted tapers blazed,
> The sound of mirth and revelry was raised,
> And in the mazy dance, light bounding feet
> The sprightly measure of the music beat,
> The song, the jest, the laugh, the bowl flew fast,
> And grey-haired Time smiled gaily as he passed ;
> And ' joy to Arden and his bonny bride ! '
> Was hymned by joyous tongues on every side ;
> And oft they pledged the fair in sparkling wine,
> Inspiring wit that better seemed to shine.
> And there were lovely maids that blushed to hear
> The grateful praises whispered in their ear ; .
> And undisguised, love mingled with the rest,—
> A welcome, nor an uninvited guest ;
> And there were beating hearts with rapture filled,
> And throbbing pulses that with pleasure thrilled,
> And eyes that shone with flames they could not veil,
> And tongues and lips that oft confirmed the tale,
> Or strove the avowal but in vain to shun,
> And all were happy—pleasing—pleased—but one ! "

One line in this extract—

> " A welcome, nor an uninvited guest,"

seems to have stuck in the author's mind with peculiar persistence, for he used it twice afterwards—in one *Address* which he never published, and in another, part of which he published as *The Departure of Summer*, where love is described as

> " A welcome—nor unbidden guest."

Before going on with the story of Thomas Hood's life after his return to London, it cannot be uninteresting to present his own recollections of the visit to Scotland, recollections which may, I think, be taken as substantially true, even though some of the details do not entirely accord with ascertained facts. They are written it must be remembered in 1839. Wanting fuller

Stay in Scotland.

immediately contemporary evidence in the way of letters, etc., it is impossible to avoid this repetition unless we contented ourselves with hazarding suppositions, accepting now the reminiscences of the poet himself, and now the traditions and piecing them together into a single connected narrative. Such a course would give us the excellence of continuity, but in the state of the evidence we should have to be more or less arbitrary in our selection and rejection, and so the result could have but small biographical value. After humorously describing his unfitness for a commercial career in London, Hood went on :

" Above all I was recommended change of air, and in particular the bracing breezes of the north. Accordingly I was soon shipped, as per advice, in a Scotch smack, which *smacked* through ' the breeze ' as Dibdin sings so merrily, that on the fourth morning we were in sight of the prominent old steeple of ' Bonny Dundee!' . . . . We have made the harbour of Dundee, and it is time to step ashore in 'stout and original Scotland,' as it is called by Doctor Adolphus Wagner, in his German edition of Burns.[1]

[1] The Baron Dupotet de Sennevoy and Doctor Elliotson will doubtless be glad to be informed, that the inspired Scottish poet was a believer in their magnetismal mysteries—at least in the article of reading a book behind the back. In a letter to Mr. Robert Ainslie, is the following passage in proof:—" I have no doubt but scholarcraft may be caught, as a Scotchman catches the itch—by friction. How else can you account for it that born blockheads, by mere dint of *handling* books, grow so wise that even they themselves are equally convinced of and surprised at their own parts ? I once carried that philosophy to that degree, that in a knot of country folks, who had a library amongst them, and who, to the honour of their good sense, made me factotum in the business ; one of our members, a little wiselook, squat, upright, jabbering body of a tailor, I advised him instead of turning over the leaves, *to bind the book on his back.* Johnnie took the hint, and as our meetings were every fourth Saturday, and

45

Thomas Hood :

"Like other shipments, I had been regularly addressed to the care of a consignee ;—but the latter, not anxious, probably, to take charge of a hobbledehoy, yet at the same time unwilling to incur the reproach of having a relative in the same town and not under the same roof, peremptorily declined the office. Nay, more, she pronounced against me a capital sentence, so far as returning to the place from whence I came, and even proceeded to bespeak my passage and reship my luggage. Judging from such vigorous measures the temper of my customer, instead of remonstrating, I affected resignation, and went with a grave face through the farce of a formal leave-taking; I even went on board, but it was in company with a stout fellow who relanded my baggage ; and thus, whilst my transporter imagined, good easy soul ! that the rejected article was sailing round St. Abb's Head, or rolling off the Bass, he was actually safe and snug in Dundee, quietly laughing in his sleeve with the Law at his back. I have a confused recollection of meeting, some three or four days afterwards, a female cousin on her road to school, who at sight of me suddenly turned round, and galloped off towards home with the speed of a scared heifer.

"My first concern was now to look out for some comfortable roof, under which 'for a consideration' one would be treated as one of the family. I entered

Pricklouse having a good Scots mile to walk in coming, and of course another in returning, Bodkin was sure to lay his hand on some heavy quarto or ponderous folio; with and under which, wrapt up in his grey plaid, he grew wise as he grew weary all the way home. He carried this so far, that an old musty Hebrew Concordance, which we had in a present from a neighbouring priest, *by mere dint of applying it as doctors do a blistering plaster, between his shoulders*, Stitch, in a dozen pilgrimages, acquired as much rational theology as the said priest had done by forty years' perusal of its pages."

46

Stay in Scotland.

accordingly into a treaty with a respectable widower, who had no sons of his own, but in spite of the most undeniable references, and a general accordance as to terms, there occurred a mysterious hitch in the arrangement, arising from a whimsical prepossession which only came afterwards to my knowledge—namely, that an English laddie, instead of supping parritch, would inevitably require a rump-steak to his breakfast! My next essay was more successful; and ended in my being regularly installed in a boarding-house, kept by a Scotchwoman, who was not so sure of my being a beefeater. She was a sort of widow, with a seafaring husband 'as good as dead,' and in her appearance not unlike a personification of *rouge et noir*, with her red eyes, her red face, her yellow teeth, and her black velvet cap. The first day of my term happened to be also the first day of the new year, and on stepping from my bed-room, I encountered our hostess—like a witch and her familiar spirit—with a huge bottle of whiskey in one hand, and a glass in the other. It was impossible to decline the dram she pressed upon me, and very good it proved, and undoubtedly strong, seeing that for some time I could only muse its praise in expressive silence, and indeed, I was only able to speak with 'a *small still* voice' for several minutes afterwards. Such was my characteristic introduction to the Land of Cakes, where I was destined to spend the greater part of two years, under circumstances likely to materially influence the colouring and filling up of my future life.

"To properly estimate the dangers of my position, imagine a boy of fifteen, at the Nore, as it were, of life, thus left dependent on his own pilotage for a safe voyage to the Isle of Man; or conceive a juvenile Telemachus, without a Mentor, brought suddenly into the perilous neighbourhood of Calypso and her enchantments. It will hardly be expected, that from some half-dozen of

47

Thomas Hood :

young bachelors, there came forth any solemn voice didactically warning me in the strain of the sage Imlac to the Prince of Abyssinia. In fact, I recollect receiving but one solitary serious admonition, and that was from a she cousin of ten years old, that the *Spectator* I was reading on a Sunday morning, "was no the Bible." For there was still much of this pious rigour extant in Scotland, though a gentleman was no longer committed to Tolboothia Infelix for an unseasonable promenade during church time. It was once, however, my fortune to witness a sample of the *ancien régime* at an evening party composed chiefly of young and rather fashionable persons, when lo ! like an Anachronism confounding times past with times present, there came out of some corner an antique figure, with quaintly cut blue suit and three-cornered hat, not unlike a very old Greenwich pensioner, who taking his stand in front of the circle, deliberately asked a blessing of formidable length on the thin bread and butter, the short cake, the marmalade, and the Pekoe tea. And here, *en passant,* it may be worth while to remark, for the benefit of our Agnews and Plumtres, as illustrating the intrinsic value of such sanctimonious pretension, that the elder Scotland, so renowned for armlong graces, and redundant preachments, and abundant psalm-singing, has yet bequeathed to posterity a singularly liberal collection of songs, the reverse of Divine and Moral, such as " can only be sung when the punch-bowl has done its work and the wild wit is set free."[1]

" To return to my boarding-house, which, with all its chairs, had none appropriated to a Professor of Moral Philosophy. In the absence of such a monitor, Nature, fortunately for myself, had gifted me with a taste for reading, which the languor of ill-health, inclining

[1] A. Cunningham.

48

me to sedentary habits, helped materially to encourage. Whatever books, good, bad, or indifferent, happened to come within my reach, were perused with the greatest avidity, and however indiscriminate the course, the balance of the impressions thence derived was decidedly in favour of the allegorical lady so wisely preferred by Hercules when he had to make his election between Virtue and Vice. Of the material that ministered to this appetite, I shall always regret that I did not secure, as a literary curiosity, a collection of halfpenny Ballads, the property of a grocer's apprentice, and which contained, amongst other matters, a new version of Chevy Chase, wherein the victory was transferred to the Scots. In the meantime this bookishness acquired for me a sort of reputation for scholarship amongst my comrades, and in consequence my pen was sometimes called into requisition in divers and sometimes delicate cases. Thus for one party, whom the gods had not made poetical, I composed a love-letter in verse; for another, whose education had been neglected, I carried on a correspondence with reference to a tobacco manufactory in which he was a sleeping partner; whilst, on a graver occasion, the hand now peacefully setting down these reminiscences, was employed in penning a most horrible peremptory invitation to pistols and twelve paces, till one was nicked. The facts were briefly these. A spicy-tempered captain of Artillery, in a dispute with a superior officer, had rashly cashiered himself by either throwing up or tearing up his commission. In this dilemma he arrived at Dundee, to assume a post in the Customs, which had been procured for him by the interest of his friends. To his infinite indignation, however, he found that instead of a lucrative surveyorship, he had been appointed a simple tide-waiter! and magnificent was the rage with which he tore, trampled and danced on the little official paper book wherein he

had been set to tick off, bale by bale, a cargo of
'infernal hemp.' Unluckily, on the very day of this
revelation, a forgery was perpetrated on the local
Bank, and those sapient Dogberries, the town officers,
saw fit to take up our persecuted ex-captain, on the
simple ground that he was the last stranger who had
entered the town. Rendered almost frantic by this
second insult, nothing would serve him in his paroxysm
but calling somebody out, and he pitched at once on
the cashier of the defrauded Bank. As the state of his
nerves would not permit him to write, he entreated me
earnestly to draw up a defiance, which I performed, at
the expense of an agony of suppressed laughter, merely
to imagine the effect of such a missive on the man of
business—a respectable, powdered, bald, pudgy, pacific
little body, with no more idea of 'going out' than a
cow in a field of clover. I forget the precise result—
but certainly there was no duel.

"To do justice to the climate of 'stout and original
Scotland,' it promised to act kindly by the constitution
committed to its care. The air evidently agreed with
the natives ; and auld Robin Grays and John Andersons
were plenty as blackberries, and Auld Lang Syne himself seemed to walk, bonneted amongst these patriarchal
figures in the likeness of an old man covered with a
mantle. The effect on myself was rather curious—for
I seemed to have come amongst a generation that
scarcely belonged to my era ; mature spinsters, waning
bachelors, very motherly matrons, and experienced
fathers, that I should have set down as uncles and
aunts, called themselves my cousins; reverend personages, apparently grandfathers and grandmothers,
were simply great uncles and aunts: and finally I
enjoyed an interview with a relative oftener heard of
traditionally, than encountered in the body—a great-
great-grandmother—still a tall woman and a tolerable

pedestrian, going indeed down the hill, but with the wheel well locked. It was like coming amongst the Struldbrugs; and truly, for any knowledge to the contrary, many of these Old Mortalities are still living, enjoying their sneeshing, their toddy, their cracks, and particular reminiscences. The very phrase of being 'Scotch'd but not killed,' seems to refer to this Caledonian tenacity of life, of which the well-known Walking Stewart was an example: he was an annuitant in the County Office, and as the actuaries would say, died very hard. It must be difficult for the teatotallers to reconcile this longevity with the imputed enormous consumption of ardent spirits beyond the Tweed. Scotia, according to the evidence of Mr. Buckingham's committee, is an especially drouthie bodie, who drinks whiskey at christenings, and at buryings, and on all possible occasions besides. Her sons drink not by the hour or by the day, but by the week,—witness Souter Johnny:—

> " 'Tam lo'ed him like a vera brither,
> They had been fou for weeks thegither.'

Swallowing no thin washy potation, but a strong overproof spirit, with a smack of smoke—and 'where there is smoke there is fire,' yet without flashing off, according to temperance theories, by spontaneous combustion. On the contrary, the canny northerns are noted for soundness of constitution and clearness of head, with such a strong principle of vitality as to justify the poetical prediction of C——, that the world's longest liver, or Last Man, will be a Scotchman.

"All these favourable signs I duly noted; and prophetically refrained from delivering the letter of introduction to Doctor C——, which was to place me under his medical care. As the sick man said, when he went into the gin-shop instead of the hospital, I 'trusted to

natur.' Whenever the weather permitted, therefore,
which was generally when there were no new books to
the fore, I haunted the banks and braes, or paid flying
visits to the burns, with a rod intended to punish that
rising generation amongst fishes called trout. But I
whipped in vain. Trout there were in plenty, but like
obstinate double teeth, with a bad operator, they would
neither be pulled out nor come out of themselves. Still
the sport, if so it might be called, had its own attrac-
tions, as, the catching excepted, the whole of the
Waltonish enjoyments were at my command, the contemplative quiet, the sweet wholesome country air, and
the picturesque scenery—not to forget the relishing the
homely repast at the shealing or the mill ; sometimes I
went alone, but often we were a company, and then we
had for our attendant a journeyman tobacco-spinner,
an original, and literary withal, for he had a reel in his
head, whence ever and anon he unwound a line of
Allan Ramsay, or Beattie, or Burns. Methinks I still
listen, trudging homewards in the gloaming, to the
recitation of that appropriate stanza, beginning—

   " ' At the close of the day when the hamlet was still,'

delivered with a gusto perhaps only to be felt by a day-
labouring mechanic, who had ' nothing but his evenings
to himself.' Methinks I still sympathise with the zest
with which he dwelt on the pastoral images and dreams
so rarely realised, when a chance holiday gave him the
fresh-breathing fragrance of the living flower in lieu of
the stale odour of the Indian weed : and philosophically
I can now understand why poetry, with its lofty aspirations and sublimed feelings, seemed to sound so gratefully to the ear from the lips of a ' squire of low degree.'
There is something painful and humiliating to humanity
in the abjectness of mind, that too often accompanies

Stay in Scotland.

the sordid condition of the working classes; whereas it is soothing and consolatory to find the mind of the poor man rising superior to his estate, and compensating by intellectual enjoyment for the physical pains and privation that belong to his humble lot. Whatever raises him above the level of the ox in the garner, or the horse in the mill, ought to be acceptable to the pride, if not to the charity of the fellow creature that calls him brother; for instance, music and dancing, but against which innocent unbendings some of our magistracy persist in setting their faces, as if resolved that a low neighbourhood should enjoy no dance but St. Vitus's, and no fiddle but the Scotch.

"To these open-air pursuits, sailing was afterwards added, bringing me acquainted with the boatmen and fishermen of The Craig, a hardy race, rough and ready-witted, from whom perchance was first derived my partiality for all marine bipeds and sea-craft, from Flag Admirals down to Jack Junk, the proud first-rate to the humble boatie that 'wins the bairns' bread.' The Tay at Dundee is a broad noble river, with a racing tide, which, when it differs with a contrary wind, will get up '*jars*' (*Anglicé*, waves) quite equal to those of a family manufacture. It was at least a good preparatory school for learning the rudiments of boat craft; whereof I acquired enough to be able at need to take the helm without either going too near the wind or too distant from the port. Not without some boyish pride I occasionally found myself intrusted with the guidance of the Coach-Boat—so called from its carrying the passengers by the Edinburgh Mail—particularly in a calm, when the utmost exertions of the crew, four old man-of-war's-men, were required at the oars. It not unfrequently happened, however, that 'the laddie' was unceremoniously ousted by the unanimous vote, and sometimes by the united strength, of the ladies, who

invariably pitched upon the oldest old gentleman in the
vessel to

> " ' *Steer* her up and haud her gaun.'

The consequence being the landing with all the baggage,
some half-mile above or below the town—and a too late
conviction, that the *Elder* Brethren of our Trinity House
were not the best Pilots.

"It was during one of these brief voyages, that I
witnessed a serio-comic accident, at which the reader
will smile or sigh according to his connexion with the
Corporation of London. I forget on what unconscious
pilgrimage it was bound, but amongst the other
passengers one day, there was that stock-dove of a
gourmand's affection, a fine lively turtle. Rich and
rare as it was, it did not travel unprotected like Moore's
heroine, but was under the care of a vigilant guardian,
who seemed as jealous of the eyes that looked amorously
at his charge, as if the latter had been a ward in
Chancery. So far—namely, as far as the middle of
the Tay—so good; when the spirit of mischief, or
curiosity, or humanity, suggested the convenience of a
sea-bath, and the refreshment the creature might derive
from a taste of its native element. Accordingly, Testudo
was lifted over the side, and indulged with a dip and a
wallop in the wave, which actually revived it so powerfully, that from a playful flapping with its fore-fins it
soon began to struggle most vigorously, like a giant
refreshed with brine. In fact, it paddled with a power
which, added to its weight, left no alternative to its
guardian but to go with it, or without it. The event
soon came off. The man tumbled backward into the
boat, and the turtle plunged forward into the deep.
There was a splash—a momentary glimpse of the broad
back-shell—the waters closed, and all was over—or at
least under! In vain one of the boatmen aimed a

Stay in Scotland.

lunge with his boat-hook, at the fatal spot in particular
—in vain another made a blow with his oar at the Tay
in general—whilst a third, in his confusion, heaved a
coil of rope, as he would, could, should, might, or
ought to have done to a drowning Christian.   The
Amphibious was beyond their reach, and no doubt,
making westward and homeward with all its might,
with an instinctive feeling that

> " ' The world was all before it where to choose
> Its place of rest, and Providence its guide.'

" Never shall I forget, whilst capable of reminiscences,
the face of that mourning mate thus suddenly bereaved
of his turtle! The unfortunate shepherd, Ding-dong,
in Rabelais, could hardly have looked more utterly and
unutterably dozed, crazed, mizmazed, and flabbergasted,
when his whole flock and stock of golden-fleeced sheep
suicidically sheepwashed themselves to death, by wilfully
leaping overboard! He said little in words, but more
eloquently clapped his hands to his waistcoat, as if
the loss, as the nurses say, had literally 'flown to his
stomach.' And truly, after promising it both callipash
and callipee, with the delicious green fat to boot, what
cold comfort could well be colder than the miserable
chilling reflection that there was

> " ' Cauld kail in Aberdeen ? '

" My first acquaintance with the press—a memorable
event in an author's experience—took place in Scotland.
Amongst the temporary sojourners at our boarding-
house, there came a legal antiquarian who had been
sent for from Edinburgh, expressly to make some
unprofitable researches amongst the mustiest of the
civic records. It was my humour to think, that in
Political as well as Domestic Economy, it must be
better to sweep the Present than to dust the Past; and

55

Thomas Hood :

certain new brooms were recommended to the Town Council in a quizzing letter, which the then editor of the *Dundee Advertiser* or *Chronicle* thought fit to favour with a prominent place in his columns. ' 'Tis pleasant sure,' sings Lord Byron, 'to see one's self in print,' and according to the popular notion I ought to have been quite up in my stirrups, if not standing on the saddle, at thus seeing myself, for the first strange time, set up in type. Memory recals, however, but a very moderate share of exaltation, which was totally eclipsed, moreover, by the exuberant transports of an accessary before the fact, whom, methinks, I still see in my mind's eye, rushing out of the printing-office with the wet sheet steaming in his hand, and fluttering all along the High Street, to announce breathlessly that 'we were in.' But G. was an indifferent scholar, even in English, and therefore thought the more highly of this literary feat. It was this defective education, and the want of a proper vent for his abundant love nonsense in prose or verse, that probably led to the wound he subsequently inflicted on his own throat, but which was luckily remedied by 'a stitch in time.' The failure of a tragedy is very apt to produce something like a comedy, and few afterpieces have amused me more than the behaviour of this Amicus Redivivus, when, thus dramatising the saying of 'cut and come again,' he made what ought to have been a posthumous appearance amongst his friends. In fact, and he was ludicrously alive to it, he had placed himself for all his supplementary days in a false position. Like the old man in the fable, after formally calling upon Death to execute a general release, he had quietly resumed his fardel, which he bore about, with exactly the uneasy ridiculous air of a would-be fine gentleman, who is sensitively conscious that he is carrying a bundle. For the sake of our native sentimentalists who profess

Stay in Scotland.

dying for love, as well as the foreign romanticists who affect a love for dying, it may not be amiss to give a slight sketch of the bearing of a traveller who had gone through half the journey. I had been absent some months, and was consequently ignorant of the affair, when lo! on my return to the town, the very first person who accosted me in the market-place was our *felo-de-se;* and truly, no Bashful Man, 'with all his blushing honours thick upon him,' in the presence of a damp stranger, could have been more divertingly sheepish, and awkwardly backward in coming forward as to manner and address. Indeed, something of the embarrassment of a fresh introduction might naturally be felt by an individual, thus beginning again, as the lawyers say, *de novo*, and renewing ties he had virtually cast off. The guilty hand was as dubiously extended to me as if it had been a dyer's—its fellow meanwhile performing sundry involuntary motions and manipulations about his cravat, as if nervously mistrusting the correctness of the ties or the stability of a buckle. As for his face, there was a foolish, deprecatory smile upon it that would have puzzled the pencil of Wilkie; and even Liston himself could scarcely have parodied the indescribable croak with which, conscious of an unlucky notoriety, he inquired 'if I had heard'—here, a short husky cough—'of anything particular?'

"'Not a word,' was the answer.

"'Then you don't know'—(more fidgetting about the neck, the smile rather sillier, the voice more guttural, and the cough worse than ever)—'then you don't know'—but, like Macbeth's amen, the confession literally stuck in the culprit's throat; and I was left to learn, an hour afterwards, and from another source, that 'Jemmy G—— had *fought a duel with himself,* and cut his own weazand, about a lady.'

"For my own part, with the above figure, with all its

Thomas Hood :

foolish features vividly imprinted on my memory, I do not think that I could ever seriously attempt 'what Cato did, and Addison approved,' in my own person. On the contrary, it seems to me that the English moralist gave but an Irish illustration of 'a brave man struggling with the storms of fate,' by representing him as wilfully scuttling his own hold, and going at once to the bottom. As for the Censor, he plainly laid himself open to censure, when he used a naked sword as a stomachic—a very sorry way, by the way, when weary of conjectures, of enjoying the benefit of the doubt, and for which, were I tasked to select an inscription for his cenotaph, it should be the exclamation of Thisby, in the ' Midsummer Night's Dream '—

> " ' This is old Ninny's tomb.'

" *Mais revenons à nos moutons*, as the wolf said to her cubs. The reception of my letter in the Dundee Newspaper encouraged me to forward a contribution to the *Dundee Magazine*, the Editor of which was kind enough, as Winifred Jenkins says, to ' wrap my bit of nonsense under his Honour's Kiver,' without charging anything for its insertion. Here was success sufficient to turn a young author at once into ' a scribbling miller,' and make him sell himself, body and soul, after the German fashion, to that minor Mephistophiles, the Printer's Devil! Nevertheless, it was not till years afterwards, and the lapse of term equal to an ordinary apprenticeship, that the Imp in question became really my Familiar. In the meantime, I continued to compose occasionally, and, like the literary performances of Mr. Weller Senior, my lucubrations were generally committed to paper, not in what is commonly called written hand, but an imitation of print. Such a course hints suspiciously of type and antetype, and a longing eye to the Row, whereas, it was adopted simply to

Stay in Scotland.

make the reading more easy, and thus enable me the more readily to form a judgment of the effect of my little efforts. It is more difficult than may be supposed to decide on the value of a work in MS., and especially when the handwriting presents only a swell mob of bad characters, that must be severally examined and re-examined to arrive at the merits or demerits of the case. Print settles it, as Coleridge used to say; and to be candid, I have more than once reversed, or greatly modified, a previous verdict, on seeing a rough proof from the press. But, as Editors too well know, it is next to impossible to retain the tune of a stanza, or the drift of an argument, whilst the mind has to scramble through a patch of scribble scrabble, as stiff as a gorse cover. The beauties of the piece will as naturally appear to disadvantage through such a medium, as the features of a pretty woman through a bad pane of glass; and without doubt, many a tolerable article has been consigned hand over head to the Balaam Box for want of a fair copy. Wherefore, O ye Poets and Prosers, who aspire to write in Miscellanies, and above all, O ye palpitating Untried, who meditate the offer of your maiden essays to established periodicals, take care, pray ye take care, to cultivate a good, plain, bold, round text. Set up Tomkins as well as Pope or Dryden for a model, and have an eye to your pothooks. Some persons hold that the best writers are those who write the best hands, and I have known the conductor of a magazine to be converted by a crabbed MS. to the same opinion. Of all things, therefore, be legible; and to that end, practise in penmanship. If you have never learned, take six lessons of Mr. Carstairs. Be sure to buy the best paper, the best ink, the best pens, and then sit down and do the best you can; as the schoolboys do—put out your tongue, and take pains. So shall ye haply

Thomas Hood.

escape the rash rejection of a jaded editor; so, having got in your hand, it is possible that your head may follow; and so, last not least, ye may fortunately avert those awful mistakes of the press which sometimes ruin a poet's sublimest effusion, by pantomimically transforming his roses into noses, his angels into angles, and all his happiness into pappiness."

A SECOND COURSE.

CHAPTER IV.

AS ENGRAVER (1817—1821).

It was in the autumn of 1817 that Thomas Hood reinvigorated left his new-found relatives and his new-made friends in Scotland and returned to his mother's house in Lower Street, Islington. He had left London as a boy but returned to it a young man, full of hope, it would appear, with regard to work in his chosen profession, and already, we may imagine, fired with literary ambitions. He had begun work as an engraver before going to Dundee, and it was as an engraver that he took up the occupation of life on returning to the metropolis. Whether he had been definitely apprenticed to Mr. Harris and had had his indentures cancelled we have no means of knowing, but it was probably after his return that steps were taken for his definite apprenticeship—either to his uncle Robert Sands or to one of the Le Keux—and then it was that the belated registration of his birth was made on November 27, 1817. Robert Sands was living at Sandhurst, in Berkshire, where with his work as engraver he was apparently doubling that of farmer, as we learn from an undated letter from his nephew written shortly after the return to London. In the course of this letter, which was apparently written after paying a visit to Sandhurst, Hood says :

" I have the pleasure of informing you that my voyage to Scotland has done wonders for me, as, since my return, my neck has altogether healed, and my leg has gained so much strength that I have been enabled to walk several times to the West End and back without any injury, and I certainly feel and look better than I have done for years. I now hope to be able to look after business a little, and to do well, both in that and in health. I did some things for Mr. Harris before I went to Scotland with which he was very well pleased, but have had no proofs, as I did them while H. was busy on the Battle of Waterloo, and could not prove for me. I desired him to send you a proof I did in Spring, which I suppose you have had. We had the pleasure of Mrs. Le Keux's company to dinner while she was in town, and I was happy to see that she looked much better than when I left the country."

The reference to the proof sent in the spring seems to show that Hood continued his work as engraver while in Dundee. In a postscript to this letter he expresses a hope that his uncle's farm is in a thriving condition. Mrs. Le Keux was probably the wife of John, the elder of the two celebrated brothers, and may have lived in Sands' neighbourhood.

The Thomas Hood whom we find as an engraver seems at once a lively and a serious-minded young man. His sedentary occupation he varied with the diversions of the book-lover. He read, he wrote, he played chess, and he practised on the flute, and of all these occupations and accomplishments we get notes in his few early letters. It is curious that his son declared that the poet had no ear and no taste for music. In his very earliest letter, as we have seen, there is mention of his taste for it, and in his 'teens he took the trouble necessary to master an instrument—the flute, the playing of which as an amateur accomplishment has long since ceased to be, as it once was, common.

Hood for a time kept up his Scots friendships, and corresponded freely with George Rollo, a young lawyer of Dundee, Robert Miln, a young man of tastes and

As Engraver (1817—1821).

aspirations somewhat similar to his own, and Samuel Messieux, a Swiss teacher of languages, who settled first at Dundee and later at St. Andrews, and is the only one of Hood's early associates who qualified for inclusion in the *Dictionary of National Biography*.[1] Two or three of his letters to the first two of these friends are preserved, but, unfortunately, none of those to Messieux has so far proved recoverable. The few letters that we have are interesting for the light which they throw upon the development of the poet. This is the first of the brief series :—

"Somewhere near Islington Church,
" *Sometime about 7th February*, [1820].

"Dear George,—I received your obliging letter per Mr. Wyllie, and am grateful to you for the great pleasure it afforded me.

"I promised Mr. W. to call on him and try his strength at chess, which I have yet been unable to do, for Christmas brought me no vacation, and this, I trust, will excuse and account with you for my delay in answering your letter.

"I have the pleasure in being able to tell you that the improvement in my health leaves me now little to wish for on that head, added to which my business and connection gradually extend. In short, that I succeed as well as I can reasonably expect in these days of universal depression. The little crosses and vexations, and the chicaneries of business in general, are now less new to me, and I can meet them with comparative

---

[1] In 1832 Messieux was appointed Master of Modern Languages in Madras, and held the appointment for nearly thirty years, when he retired owing to failure of eyesight, but only survived his retirement by about two years. He was described by a colleague in the warmest fashion : " In conversation, manner, and address, he was as nearly perfect as I have known—a warm friend, both witty and wise."

calmness, so that in another year I hope to be tolerably settled.

"I have made an alteration in the nature of my amusements, and flatter myself that they have now a more useful tendency, and may in the end be of benefit both to myself and others. I sometimes devote an hour to little mechanical inventions connected with my pursuits, and sometime ago completed a little instrument which I deem would be serviceable in copying drawings, etc. I sent it to the Society of Arts, and had the honour of explaining it before the Society's Committee on Mechanics, but found they were in possession of a similar one for the same purpose I had never seen. This was rather unlucky, but I have another one in progress which may succeed better. At any rate I lose nothing.

"I am at present trying to perfect an instrument for drawing lines to meet in a point at any distance, as used in perspective, in order to be able to draw them without going beyond the margin of your drawing, and thus obviating the inconvenience of having to rule so far.

"Since writing the above I have had the pleasure of seeing Mr. Wyllie, who called to inquire the reason of my not seeing him, and I have returned his visit, and have, moreover, engaged him at chess, gaining five battles out of six. But one trial, of course, is not sufficient to determine the mastery. I must confess that I was afraid my want of practice would have served me worse, but, after leaving your country *unconquered*, I was resolved not to be beaten by your countryman on my own ground if I could help it. I shall now provide myself with a set, which I have hitherto been without for mere want of somebody to play with. It is true that a young lady within a few doors of us desires me to teach her to play at chess, but to learn it requires so

As Engraver (1817—1821).

much patience that I am not anxious to attempt the task, recollecting that Job was not a woman.

"I should much like to know if Messieux has returned, and to have his address at St. Andrews, if you could procure it for me. He called here when I was with you, but I have not heard of or from him since. If ever you see him in Dundee I wish you would tell him to send it himself, or come with it himself,—whichever may be most convenient.

"With respect to what you are pleased to call my poem, you may delay it till any convenient time, as it is of no other use to me but to show of what has been the nature of my amusements. I cannot now find time for anything of the kind, except a few short bagatelles as New Year compliments, etc., etc. And, let me here, in adverting to those compliments, present you with my sincere wishes for that happiness which one friend should wish to another, and which it is customary to offer rather earlier; but, I assure you, they have not lost in strength like some things by long keeping, and therefore still are fit for me to present to you for yours and your brother's acceptance—only that I regret to be thus obliged to send them wrapped up in paper!

"I have said that I cannot find time to write such things now—and, indeed, after the study and close application necessary in engraving, it would cease to be any relaxation. But, independent of this employment, I have to keep my books (not my *ledger*, for that is kept too easily), but my note and plate books, in which I keep account of any hints, occurrences, discoveries, instructions, etc., etc., relative to the art, together with a journal of my own operations and transactions— history of my plates, my own comments and those of others, difficulties, failures, successes, etc., etc., so that I have enough to do in that way. Altogether, these compose rather a medlied history, and one, perhaps, that will afford me more pleasure to peruse hereafter than it does at present.

" In fact, I am now obliged to turn the amusing, if I can, into the *profitable*, not that I am ambitious, or of a very money-loving disposition, but I am obliged to be so. Otherwise, I believe, if left to myself, I should be content with a very moderate station, for, like you, I believe I am of a ' domestic indolent turn.' But this is all speculative reasoning, perhaps; and I might find —that summit attained—that the content was as far off as ever, increasing by a kind of arithmetical pro- gression. Thus, when seen from the valley, the summit of the mountain appears to touch the skies; but when we have ascended and reached its top, we seem, and no doubt are, as far from heaven as ever![1]

" The most provoking part of my profession is that the fame and the profit are so connected that those who wish to decrease the price can only do it by depre- ciating the merit and withholding that fame which is, in fact, part of the price. This is all so much the worse for me, now that I have grown so wise, that if they took away the former I could philosophically console myself with the latter. I find that I am not yet quite *sharp* enough to cope with veteran men of business, but suppose every rub they give me will make my wit much keener. I am now tolerably content with what I pay

---

[1] In " I remember, I remember," half a dozen years later, the poet used something of the same idea in the lines :—

> " I remember, I remember,
> The fir trees dark and high;
> I used to think their slender tops
> Were close against the sky.
> It was a childish ignorance,
> But now 'tis little joy
> To know I'm farther off from Heav'n
> Than when I was a boy."

for my experience, considering I have just concluded my first year's apprenticeship to the world.

" I hope you will decipher this, for I see it is vilely scrawled ; but deeming it more friendly to meet you *en dèshabillé* than to deny myself to you, I send it with this one request that you will put those stops which I cannot stop to put.

" Remember me kindly to your brother and all friends, and believe me, dear George, yours very truly,

" THOMAS-HOOD.

" P.S.—I do not know anybody through whom you may send anything except Wyllie, unless Captain Lyon would bring it here."

This letter Mr. Elliot conjecturally dated 1819, but I had thought that it must belong to the following year, when it would better fit in with the story of the lost manuscript, and have established that fact from the clue which is afforded by the reference to the instrument which Hood submitted to the Society of Arts. Thanks to the kindness of Sir Henry Trueman Wood, I am enabled to give the following extract from the manuscript Minutes of the Society's Committee on Mechanics. At a meeting on January 26, 1820, it is recorded that the members of that committee—

"Took into consideration a communication from Mr. T. Hood, Lower Street, Islington, dated December 9, 1819, on an indicator. The candidate attended to exhibit and explain the use of the instrument. Mr. Hood's indicator is constructed for the purpose of transferring points from a drawing, etc., to paper, the scale of the original and of the intended copy being the same. It consists of three legs united by one of their extremities. The legs move freely upon the pin or rivet, and the instrument is to be used precisely in

the same manner as the three-legged or triangular compasses, of which very convenient instrument the one in
question is a rude resemblance.

"The candidate, on being asked by the Chairman
(T. Gill, Esq.), stated that he had never seen the
triangular compasses.

"Resolved—It appears to this Committee that Mr.
Hood's indicator is not equal to other instruments now
in use for similar purposes; they cannot therefore
recommend it to the further attention of the Society."

Apparently the second instrument on which Hood
was at work had no better fate than the first, for
we hear no more of it. He was, however, it may be
mentioned, always interested in little mechanical con-
trivances, though the ingenuity which might with
encouragement have been devoted more regularly to
such was diverted from things to words.

That while in Dundee Hood had set about a satirical
guide to that town we learned from an earlier letter,
and there can be little doubt that the "poem" which
had already lost value in his eyes was probably this same
work which crops up again in each of the following
letters belonging to this period. The "Mr. Wyllie"
was Andrew Wyllie, son of a Dundee merchant, of
whom Hood appears to have seen much during these
days in London, though but slight references to their
intercourse have been recovered. The letter seems to
give indications at once of the serious and playful sides
of the writer's nature, and is interesting for its auto-
biographic touch in the modesty of the writer's ambition, and in his acceptance of the description of himself
as of a "domestic indolent turn"—though indolence is
by no means suggested by a record of twelve hours a
day at the engraving table.

Hood's Dundee friend Miln evidently wrote enquiring about the fate of the satirical "guide," as he had

As Engraver (1817—1821).

some idea of obtaining its insertion in the *Dundee Advertiser*, or some other weekly periodical. After this point the manuscript mysteriously disappears. The young engraver-author replied in a letter, dated from Lower Street, May, 1820, saying :—

" I have sent to my friend Rollo—who will hand you this letter—the book which you have requested me to send to you—the *Dundee Guide*—and which I have been unable to procure till lately.

" Upon looking it over I think that many of the subjects to which it refers will now be out of date, and particularly that part of it beginning—

" ' And the French jockey hat is now worn in this town,'

and ending at—

" ' He without her consent would not steal e'en a kiss,'

which I have marked for you to print in case you should make that use of it which was proposed. It would be better, I presume, to send a few of the letters together instead of a single one at first, in order that the editor might see the design of them ; and I shall endeavour to send a preface addressed to that gentleman, in case you should think proper, on conference with Mr. R., to make use of them.

" I have numbered the letters in the order which I should wish them to follow, and marked some omissions in pencil.

" I fear they are not worth the trouble of your writing out, and I cannot forget that *lawyers* are not fond of writing for nothing.

" I have now no news, but, hoping for at least as many lines in return, I am, dear Bob, yours truly,

" THOS. HOOD.

" P.S.—I write, as you will perceive, in great haste."

69

Thomas Hood :

Despite the haste in which he wrote, the young satirist found time to sketch the proposed prefatory note to the editor of the periodical in which it was hoped that the *Guide* was to make its appearance. This preface is written on the fly-leaf of the letter :—

" Sir,—Although it is well known that Bath and Cheltenham have been visited by the celebrated Blunderhead family, it has hitherto been unknown that some of their descendants have visited the town of Dundee in strict incognito. This fact is, however, confirmed by some letters which have fallen into my hands, which I have arranged, and with the permission of the author, now send to be inserted, if you think fit in your weekly paper.

" Some subjects to which they refer may now be partially out of date, as they were written in 1815, but some remarks may still be applicable. I am, sir, yours, &c.

" Thos. Hood."

It has been taken for granted that the " Mr. R." referred to stands for Rintoul, who was then editor of the *Dundee Advertiser*, but I think it represents Rollo, with whom the young lawyer was quite likely to have a conference on the subject when talking over the manuscript to submit it to the editor. Within the next few months the *Guide* mysteriously disappeared ; as we have not the letter in which Rollo gave an account of its disappearance we cannot join with the young author in laughing over his loss. Whether Miln submitted it to Rintoul who refused to make use of it in the *Advertiser*, whether it actually appeared somewhere later, whether it was used to light a fire like Coleridge's *Watchman*, or accidentally destroyed like Newton's essay, we shall

As Engraver (1817—1821).

apparently never know.   The manuscript seems to have
got back to the hands of Rollo and when in his charge
to have vanished.   It would have been interesting could
we have read the *Guide* in its entirety, though the loss
can have no effect in lessening the poet's fame.   The
recovery of a writer's early work has been known to
have that effect.

Hood's next letter, in which he touches upon the theme,
suggests that any idea of the immediate publication of
the *Guide* had been abandoned, in that he could "if
necessary" write it out from memory.   This letter is
important as showing that it was to the burin that he
was looking as his fixed professional implement, while
keeping up his interest in the pen as a source of recreation; it is dated "Lower Street, January sometime,
1820," and at the foot "February 20, 1821," but the
first date must have been such a slip of the pen
as most of us are liable to at the beginning of a
New Year, and it should be "January sometime
1821."   In May, 1820, the *Guide* had recently been
sent to Rollo and was to be handed over to Miln,
so that the following letter must have been written
some months later.   Even as a busy young engraver
Hood seems to have been gifted with the pen of
a ready letter-writer, as he assuredly was during his
busiest period as author.   It is to be regretted
that we cannot build up the story of his early life
from his correspondence as we can that of his
maturity.   Such letters as remain from his youth
and early manhood are the more interesting in that
they suggest something of those many letters that have
been lost, letters in which he must have described his
Scotch experiences for the home circle at Islington, or
those in which he must have enlarged, as he does
in the following one, upon his entrance into the
world of business.   This long letter to George Rollo,

71

Thomas Hood :

of Lochie, shows us the young engraver at his busiest.

"DEAR GEORGE,—Mr. Wyllie, in bringing me your welcome letter, found me very busy upon a plate from a drawing of a gentleman's seat which I told you, I think, nearly a year ago, I was endeavouring to obtain. I have just got it, and, as it is for a very fine work, I am obliged to pay very close attention to it, working from ten morning till ten or eleven o'clock at night for these last three weeks, so that the Christmas season has brought me no holidays. But as I had been more idle before, hunting for business rather than doing it (a general case now), I sit down to it cheerfully, and especially as it shall open to me, if I succeed, a new and wider path. I have done so far as to form some idea of how it will be, and am induced to hope favourably.

"From the midst of all this I write in order to ease your mind on the subject of a disaster, which in vexing you one hour has vexed you more than it has me, for I assure you your description of it had no other effect than that of making me laugh. The sudden and mysterious disappearance of the *Dundee Guide* has in it something so romantic as to make a very fine sequel to its history, by leading one to imagine that Apollo— or one of the Nine Muses, perhaps—had taken possession of it. I will tell you, too, a secret for your comfort, that the loss, even if great, would not be irreparable, for I could, if necessary, write afresh from memory, and nearly verbatim. It is the same with nearly all the rest of my effusions, some of which I shall hereafter send for your perusal, to show you that I do not consider you the 'careless friend' you represent yourself to be. I continue to receive much pleasure from our literary society, and from my own pursuits in

As Engraver (1817—1821).

that way—in which, considering my little time, I am very industrious—that is to say, I spoil a deal of paper. My last is a mock heroic love tale of 600 lines,[1] with notes critical and explanatory, which I have lately finished after many intervals, independent of two poetical addresses to the society on closing and opening a fresh session with various pieces, chiefly amatory. The society only costs me a page or two once in three months or so, but I join in their discussions every fortnight, if able. I receive few visits, and I pay still fewer, and thus my time wears away.

" I am very happy, however, when I have time, to pay my visits on paper, as I now do, because I am sure of a greater pleasure in its being returned, not that I mean to stand on ceremonies with you more than Wyllie, for as we do not regularly balance visit against visit, so if it comes into my head to send you two letters for one, I shall not stick at it, and if you do the same, I shall not feel offended by such a breach of punctilio.

" I have had no letter from Messieux, and feel obliged to you for your offer to him that you would forward any letter to me. I shall write to him ere long, and, as I know not where to find him, I shall perhaps give you the trouble of directing it and forwarding it to him. I learned from the newspaper the dreadful accident to which you have carried my attention in your letter, and have no doubt of its being an inexpressible shock to Mrs. Brown. If you recollect, there was a pistol with which Messieux and I used to amuse ourselves, and is, I daresay, the one which has proved fatal to poor Henry.

" I am the more anxious to open, or, rather, renew, a correspondence with M., because—and I am sorry to say it—I see no prospect of seeing you or him next

[1] Possibly " Lalla Crow," see p. 77.

summer, not that I could make any trip more agreeable, but that I shall be able to make no trips at all. I find that I shall have so much to do to establish myself in business properly, and to attain to proficiency in an art which has made so great a progress towards excellence, that I shall have no time at my command, unless I should be able to get a long plate, and do it down with you; and, indeed, if I were engraving there you would have so little of my company as to make it of little or no consequence whether I were there or in London. I shall therefore defer my visit till I can make a thorough holiday of it, and enjoy the company of my friends without interruption.

" I should like very much to make with you the tour you propose to make next summer. I could there find first-rate subjects for my pencil; and I wonder that so many persons who can or will travel do not first visit those places in their own country and neighbourhood which could afford them so fine scenery and so great hospitality as the Highlands of Scotland. These, and the western lakes in Cumberland and Westmoreland I would rather visit, and next to these the romantic and wild scenery of Switzerland.

" I hope that Sylvester's translation to Glasgow will be a step towards advancement and happiness. You will, no doubt, regret that he should have to go there while you are stationary; but I hope that, nevertheless, they will not be prevented from coming to you where you are, lest when I go to Dundee I should have to look in vain for you, who are amongst my last friends there.

" Grey called on me here some months ago. He came only *en passant*, and was not long enough for me to learn what brought him to London. I was not very desirous of inviting him to an intimacy, for reasons you will readily guess, and I have not seen him again. But

As Engraver (1817—1821).

with Wyllie I am very thick as you call it, and we have a duo at flutes and a duel at chess with great pleasure. He told you, no doubt, of his success at the latter, and I begin to doubt if I shall ever regain those laurels I once wore. But I am not cowed, and in a few days I hope to open a fresh campaign with greater success. He drank tea here together with Bailie Thoms' son, who is also a player at chess, but as yet untried by me. I would not advise him to attack me now, for Wyllie has worked me up so, that like an urchin that has been thumped, I am ready to wreak my revenge upon anyone I meet—even though it should be yourself.

" Since writing the preceding I have been waiting for a call from Wyllie to send it, but he has stayed away longer than usual, and I have been unable to call on him, as his business is on the other side of the city to where my business lies. I have also had more business on my hands these last six weeks than I ever had before; for, besides the plate I mentioned, I have three others all in hand at once, which I am obliged to superintend. I have been successful in the plate which has cost me so much anxiety, and the result of four years' learning and experience in the art will appear in a work along with those of my former master, and of others who have generally served apprenticeships of seven years. I was but two years old in engraving when I set up for myself, and have been two more on my own fingers; and, as some of my friends seemed doubtful as to the success of such an experiment, I am very happy and somewhat proud of this result, in which I have obtained the one object of my ambition.

" I shall send you with this or hereafter an impression of my plate for your acceptance, as a thing of no value, but as a token of my regard and esteem. I find that I shall not be able to send my poems to you for some time, as they are in the hands of an intelligent

Thomas Hood :

bookseller, a friend of mine, who wishes to look them over. He says that they are worth publishing, but I doubt very much if he would give me any proof of his opinion or I should indulge in the hope of sending them to you in a more durable shape.

"Wyllie has called, but I have been so busy—sometimes till two and three in the morning—that I could not really finish this. Besides the four plates, I have had two others as soon as I could finish two of the first, so that I am just where I was. I have not been able, therefore, to call on Wyllie till the date of this. I send, however, the engraving, and something for Messieux, which I will trouble you and thank you to forward at your convenience. I do not know his address, but, if you take charge of it, I have no doubt of its reaching him. I hope to write more at leisure next time, and am, dear George, yours truly,

"THOS. HOOD.

"*Feb. 20th*, 1821."

From this long letter we learn that the young engraver was getting work of some importance to do with his four plates in hand, one of which was to appear in a work along with that of his former master.[1] More interesting still, in view of his special talents, is the quiet indication that he has in the hands of an intelligent bookseller sufficient poems to make a volume. The arrangements for publishing such a volume were apparently never completed, and it is not now ascertainable which of the poems were written thus early,

[1] The plate referred to I have identified. It is a view of the mansion of St. Clerons, Galway, "engraved by T. Hood," and duly appeared, dated April, 1821, in the sixth volume of J. P. Neale's "Views of Seats." The other plates to which Hood refers have not so far been traced. The "former master" may have been Le Keux, who had general control of the engraving for Neale's famous work, or it may have been his uncle, Robert Sands, who engraved several of the plates.

As Engraver (1817—1821).

though it is likely that among them were some of those which appeared during the following two or three years in the pages of the *London Magazine*. Connected with this is the reference to " our literary society." This was the Social Literary Society, a coterie the members of which fortnightly met at each others' houses to read papers and otherwise entertain themselves in the manner of young men and women wishful of imping their wings when preparing for literary flights. In his brief reminiscences of many years later Hood spoke jestingly of this society as follows :—

" Though working in *aqua fortis*, I still played with Castaly, now writing—all monkeys are imitators, and all young authors are monkeys—now writing a Bandit,[1] to match the Corsair, and anon, hatching a Lalla Crow, by way of companion to Lalla Rookh. Moreover, about this time I became a member of a private select Literary Society that ' waited on Ladies and Gentlemen at their own houses.' Our Minerva, allegorically speaking, was a motley personage, in blue stockings, a flounced gown, Quaker cap, and kerchief, French flowers and a man's hat. She held a fan in one hand, and a blowpipe in the other. Her votaries were of both sexes, old and young, married and single, assenters, dissenters, High Church, Low Church, No Church; Doctors in Physics and Apothecaries in Metaphysics, dabblers in Logic, Chemistry, Casuistry, Sophistry, Natural and Unnatural History, Phrenology, Geology, Conchology, Demonology; in short, all kinds of Colledgy-Knowledgy-Ology, including ' Cakeology,' and tea and coffee. Like other Societies, we had one President—a sort of Speaker who never spoke, at least within my experience he never unbosomed himself of anything but a portentous shirt frill. According to the usual order of the entertainment, there was — first, Tea and Small Talk;

1 Referred to fully in the preceding chapter.

Thomas Hood :

secondly, an original Essay, which should have been followed, thirdly, by a discussion, or Great Talk; but nine times in ten, it chanced, or rather mumchanced, that between those who did not know what to think, and others who did not know how to deliver what they thought, there ensued a dead silence, so 'very dead indeed' as Apollo Belvi says, that it seemed buried into the bargain. To make this awkward pause more awkward, some misgiving voice, between a whisper and a croak, would stammer out some allusion to a Quakers' Meeting, answered from right to left by a running titter, the speaker having innocently, or perhaps wilfully, forgotten, that one or two friends in the drab coats, and as many in slate-coloured gowns, were sitting thumb-twiddling, in the circle. Not that the Friends contented themselves with playing *dumby* at our discussions. They often spoke, and very characteristically, to the matter in hand. For instance, their favourite doctrine of non-resistance was once pushed—if Quakers ever push—a little 'beyond beyond.' By way of clencher, one fair, meek, sleek Quakeress, in dove colour, gravely told a melodramatical story of a conscientious Friend, who rather than lift even his little finger against a Foe, passively, yea, lamblike, suffered himself to be butchered in bed by an assassin, and died consistently, as he thought, with Fox principles, very like a goose. As regards my own share in the Essays and Arguments, it misgives me that they no more satisfied our decidedly serious members, than they now propitiate Mr. Rae Wilson. At least one Society night, in escorting a female Fellow towards her home, she suddenly stopped me, taking advantage perhaps of the awful locality and its associations, just in front of our chief criminal prison, and looking earnestly in my face, by the light of a Newgate lamp, inquired somewhat abruptly, 'Mr. Hood! are you not an infidel?'"

As Engraver (1817—1821).

Elsewhere in commenting on a woman's meeting which had been held to protest against the Poor Laws, Hood recalled something of this Literary Society to point out that its women members were never moved to take part in the debates:—

"In my MS. days—and like many bookish bachelors of the same standing—I was a member of a private literary society with a name whereof I only remember that it began in Greek and ended in English. This re-union was framed on the usual plan of such institutions; except that the gallantry of the founders had ruled that half the members might be of the female sex, and accordingly amongst our 'intellectual legs,' we numbered a fair proportion of the hose that are metaphorically blue. We assembled weekly[1] at the house of some Fellow that had a house, where an original essay was first read by the author, and then submitted to discussion, much as a schoolboy first spins his top and then lays it down to be pegged at by the rest of the company. The subjects, like Sir Roger de Coverley's picture, generally left a great deal to be said on both sides, nor were there wanting choppers, not to say hackers of logic to avail themselves of the circumstance; and as we possessed, amongst others, a brace of Irish barristers, a Quaker, a dissenter to everything, an author who spoke volumes, a geologist who could find sermons in stones, and one old man eloquent, surnamed for his discursiveness the rambler, we had usually what Bubb Doddington has called a 'multiplicity of talk.'"

If it was an Islington society, some of its members must have come from a distance, but its exact title is forgotten, and but for Thomas Hood's membership the society itself would seemingly have left no record, though two other of its members subsequently took what he described as "type-us fever," and are known as

[1] This is an error. The meetings appear to have been fortnightly.

Thomas Hood :

authors of books of some repute in their day.   One of these was Miss Hannah Lawrance, author of a " History of the Queens of England," and of a " History of Woman in England."

The two poetical addresses referred to in the lengthy letter to Rollo were sent by Miss Lawrance to Tom Hood when he was preparing the second edition of the " Memorials."   The first of these, which was delivered on the closing of the session in July, 1820, opens with a line that might have suggested to Oliver Wendell Holmes his " Evening—by a Tailor "—

> " Nature, like man, her summer coat puts on."

The address is about two hundred lines in length, and deals with the themes of holiday-making distant or near.   Already the insistent pun is finding its way into the author's lighter verse.

> " Some, sick of London and of smoke, agree
> To go to Margate—and be sick at sea ! "

And again—

> " All Cockney beauties are to Cockneys sweet,
> So Canonbury seems a country seat . . . .
> But if in town predestin'd to remain,
> To sigh, ' Oh, Rus,' but sigh, alas ! in vain,
> The Cit invests a sum in Purple Stocks,
> And from his window hangs his Country Box.
> There strives the smell of London to forget,
> Snuffing the fragrance of the Mignonette,
> And revelling in Fancy's airy food,
> Enjoys a garden—in his hanging wood ! "

At the close of the address the poet looks forward to the autumn—

> " When jolly farmers their October brew—
> Then, this Society shall meet anew.
> Then Social Harmony shall take the chair,
> And Learning's votaries be welcome there,
> And smiling Mirth shall mingle with the rest
> A welcome, nor an uninvited guest."

As Engraver (1817—1821).

and he goes on to name some of the characteristics of fellow members. When holidays were over, for those who were able to travel far afield as well as for those who picknicked in the neighbourhood of cockneydom, the members of the society gathered at each others' houses once more, and again the laureate of the coterie had an address ready for the occasion. If in the earlier he gave evidence of a developing readiness in happy play upon words, in the latter he certainly showed poetical improvement. A large part of this second address was revised and published a few months afterwards as " The Departure of Summer," but from the portion which was too personal for general publication we can gather some idea of the variety of subjects over which the members of the society ranged in their discussions. It is indeed possible that the subjects hit off in the following lines were those down for discussion in the ensuing session of the society :—

> " 'Tis theirs to ask if one may trace
> The mind, the heart, within the face ?
> Or whether Satire's venom'd sting
> From Envy and ill-nature spring ?
> If people fill the planets bright ?
> And whence their life, and heat, and light ?
> Then leave the skies to ask, and show
> The springs from whence ideas flow.
> Or cut vile Prejudice in shreds,
> To analyse the Hydra's heads.
> And what is taste ? and does the stage
> Or pulpit most to mend the age ;
> Or musing o'er the olden time,
> Talk o'er its chivalry sublime,
> Or turn to Chymistry's deep page—
> Then last, not least, they wisely ask,
> What man himself—his moral nature ?
> Or view their country's laws and task,
> The flaws in Civil Judicature.
> Happy are those who thus can meet

Thomas Hood :

And find such conversations sweet !
Happy are those who thus can chuse
Such blameless themes, that oft amuse,
And oft improve."

It suggests such a programme as has been gone through by many mutual improvement societies. How long Hood continued an active member of the society cannot now be said; probably not much longer than he needed it as a relaxation from his work as engraver, for when he came to depend upon writing it would probably be too like a continuation of his regular work to hold his interest.

Before we proceed to this change, however, there are two further letters remaining of those which he wrote to his Scots friends, both of which belong to this year of change when the engraver's implements were laid aside, half reluctantly it may be imagined, though the pen was probably taken up with unalloyed pleasure. The first of these two letters—both of which are addressed to Rollo—suggests that the writer was feeling something of that fever for work which it has been observed sometimes attends on the consumptive. Despite his new literary undertaking, he wishes—writing on June 17, 1821—to commence a kind of mutual improvement correspondence with his Dundee friend.

" DEAR GEORGE,—You are a pretty fellow to send me such a short letter, and, if it were not for fear of falling short myself, I should scold you. But I heartily forgive you for hastening it, even in its infant state, or half-grown, that I might sooner have the benefit of the enclosures.

" That must, indeed, be your excuse for me, for I would have heard of no other. Your town, I know, is barren of news, and ours is all sent you by the papers; but I can feed upon very slight food, and the description

As Engraver (1817—1821).

of even a fishing excursion or anything of that kind would be very agreeable; or if you were to sketch me any odd character who may fall in your way, or any odd sayings or stories. I know that you once dealt in such things, and I have not lost my relish for them.

"As for me, I am just scribbling a Cockney's sentimental journey from Islington to Waterloo Bridge —about three miles—so what a letter you ought to be able to give me by and by about your excursion to the Highlands with kilts and Ben-Somethings and Loch-Somethings, and I know not what!

"I wish I could go with you, and so do you, and so does R. Miln—but I have told the latter why I cannot. I have a literary engagement which will occupy my leisure time (that is to say, what I have heretofore devoted to scribbling), so that I shall not only write now for Pleasure but for Profit, and I begin to have hopes that what I have scribbled in verse will make its appearance in a little volume, and, should that be decided on, I shall necessarily have a great addition to my occupation in arranging, correcting, etc., etc., but I expect that they will, in that case, be out by Christmas.

"I do not think my health will suffer, for I shall be obliged to go out rather more than I perhaps should do voluntarily, and you may mention this to R. M. for his comfort. He says he supposes I am making my fortune, but he is out there, and consequently, as I could not leave him anything if I were to die to-morrow, he may wish for my long life most sincerely.

"I have written to him that I would rather the *Dundee Guide* should remain unknown, *for I think I can do better things;* and as for the other things (this 'Bandit' I believe) it is yours if you like it.

"I see our friend Wyllie as often as possible. We went together to an exhibition of paintings, some time since, and last Thursday he went with me to our

Thomas Hood:

Society, where I gave an essay on Poetry to close the Session. But chess I must resign, my head is now so much occupied. Methinks I hear you say, what an altered being I must be to give up chess, and that, too, when I have been beaten! But, from the cause just mentioned, I have ceased to find any amusement in it, and therefore there is no hope of retrieving my laurels. Even my flute I must use but sparingly, although it delights me with my own music when I can get no better. But Health! health!—(show this to R. Miln)— I sacrifice them both to health! And as for my paper concerns, I can take them into a garden (and luckily we have one), so that I shall not want for fresh air.

"I received very great joy from M. Messieux's letter, being only the second since our separation, and have answered it as you will perceive. I do not know whether I may not be giving you great trouble to forward them to him; but, if not, I shall feel obliged by your becoming the medium of communication. There is never anything in my letters that will cool by waiting, so that you can take any opportunity of himself or his friend being in Dundee to forward them; but pray let me know how the matter stands.

"I know not how it is that I find more time to write, now that I have more to do; but it may be that I am more settled, and have got into more of a routine; and perhaps, above all, I am oftener in the mood for writing. At any rate, I am happy, on looking back to find that I can keep it on so well, all things considered.

"I confess that I want subject more than inclination generally, for I am sick, and you will be too, of eternally writing about Self. But we may sometimes start some interesting subject of controversy and inquiry, and then we shall go on better. And as those who challenge give the choice of weapons, so I, who propose, give you the choice of subjects; and I hope in your next you

As Engraver (1817—1821).

will give me some such things as I have mentioned in the beginning to comment upon. What think you of a discussion upon Angling, which I know you are fond of? Pray give me some description of its pleasures, etc., etc., etc., and I will reply all that I can *pro* and *con*. Having paved the way, as I imagine, for long letters, I shall end this; and though I have only occupied a page more than yours, yet, taking my dwarf hand into account, I really think that I have given you '*two for one!*'—I am, dear George, yours very truly,

"THOS. HOOD.

"P.S.—It has been said that an angling rod and line hath a fool at one end and a worm at the other. I do not believe this, and want your vindication."

Chess and the flute have both to be sacrificed for the sake of health. It is a sad note for a young man of two-and-twenty to have to strike, but there is no tone of despondency or repining.

About a month or so after that letter was written Hood's mother died, probably still in the prime of life, though, unfortunately, beyond her name no particulars of her are recoverable. That the poet was deeply attached to the only parent he had known from early boyhood is certain, and it was sad indeed that he should lose her just when his prospects were improving and he was getting his first firm footing in the literary world by his appointment on the staff of the *London Magazine*. From the fact that after Mrs. Hood's death the family still stayed on in the Islington house, it is not unlikely that the place had been bought by the poet's father.

If there is no note of repining or despondency over his own ill-health in the letter of June, neither is there in that of nearly four months later, when his mother's

Thomas Hood :

recent death has left him in charge of a household of four sisters.

"LOWER STREET, ISLINGTON, *October* 11, 1821.

"DEAR GEORGE,—I write to you for several reasons, viz. :—First, because my sister is going to Dundee; second, because I have not heard of you for a long time; and third, to give you a troublesome commission. My youngest sister is going on a visit to her aunt, Mrs. Keay, and will forward this to you in order that you may provide me with a plaid against my winter campaign. There are such things to be got here, but I apprehend not so good; and I shall be sure to fancy it more for coming *bonâ fide* from Scotland, as it is such a national article. And moreover, when I shall be lapped in it I may fancy that I am in Dundee. Therefore you will oblige me by choosing me one, and ordering it to be made as follows. To tell you the truth, I have fallen in love with our friend Wyllie's, and should like one of the same family—a twin—that is to say, a Stuart, and if that should be troublesome to get I will put up with a Kyd, or a —— (I have forgot this name; but I will ask Wyllie, and write it outside). But I should prefer the Royal Stuart, on account of the romantic and poetical associations connected with it. The collar, red shag (or green if there be green, if not, red); the body without sleeves, like Andrew's, but not lined; and a large loose cape lined with green —— (I must write this outside too); and—and —and—that is all, except have the goodness to pay for it, for which purpose I enclose £2, which Andrew tells me was about the price of his; but at all events, we shall settle that. And now about the size. I am about five feet nine inches high, and as thick as a rushlight, and I hope that will be measure sufficient. I think Wyllie calls his a rachan, or some such name, which I cannot

As Engraver (1817—1821).

pronounce upon paper : but I hope you will know what I want, and how large it ought to be. I think, as I have described it, that it covers a page of paper, so enough of it. I trust it will not be a very troublesome commission, in which hope I send it ; but if it is at all likely to be so I beg that you will not take it upon you, and let me give up the idea of Scottish fancies and associations.

" Bless me, Geordie, what's come owre ye, man, that ye canna w-write. I hope your hand is not rheumatised! I do nothing but write, write, day and night ; but I cannot resist a letter now and then, and if my present fit continues this is likely to be a long letter. I was told, or else I dreamt, that a large trout (as muckle as a saumont !) had put both your wrists out, and that you were past scribbling, and consequently could not write to me a letter upon the Pleasures of Fishing, as I had proposed you to do. If it be true, then write upon some other subject, and you will forget your disaster. If you cannot use your fingers, tak' your taes til't, and I shall not mind the handwriting. Write at all events, whether you can or not. If you have nothing to say, say so. Perhaps, if the truth must be told, you are waiting for Messieux ; but if the horses were to wait for the coach to move, the mail would stand still. I shall perchance enclose a letter for that gentleman, to be forwarded at your leisure.

" Perhaps you will ask what I am doing. Why, truly, I am T. Hood, *scripsit et sculpsit.* I am engraving and writing prose and poetry by turns. I have some papers coming forth in next month's *London Magazine*, signed incog., and in the meantime I am busy extending and correcting my long poem and other pieces—perhaps for publication. I have a good deal to do now—more than ever. I have got my affairs into more regularity, and therefore go on more smoothly to what I did. But I

87

Thomas Hood :

have sustained a very severe and irreparable loss in the
death of my dear mother, about three months since, by
which event a serious charge has devolved upon me ;
and I have all the concern of a household and a family
of four sisters—a charge which can never be a light
one. I have suffered an inexpressible anguish of mind
in parting with my only parent, and but for the consolations which I have had I should have sunk under it.
I have now recovered a great deal of my cheerfulness,
and though such an event will be a cloud upon all my
happiness, my other prospects are brighter, and enable
me to look forward with a pleasure which I cannot
have, however, without a sigh whilst I look behind.
The writing for the *London* is a very agreeable employment for my mind, and prevents my thoughts from
preying upon me as they otherwise would do.

"There appears now a prospect of my seeing you,
as should my sister stay through the winter I shall most
probably fetch her. In this I anticipate much pleasure,
as I shall be able to reach Lochee ; yea, and much
further, and perhaps see more of Scotland. But I
must hush upon that subject, as it is too long for any
prudent man to look forward.

"After a long interval I have attacked our friend
again at chess, and with better success, for our meetings
stand thus :—

Hood.	Wyllie.
1	—
2	—

1 drawn,

but I had a balance against me in our last campaign of
40 or 30, which I do not expect to pay off.

"Last Sunday we (Andrew and I) went to a very
fine garden, etc., and if you are at all a botanist I shall
regret that you were not with us. There were a

greenhouse, 500 feet long, full of camellias, and a hot-house 40 feet high, the whole warmed by steam carried in two miles of pipe. The latter house was a great wonder, being full of African and other plants of the gigantic kind. Palm trees 30 feet high, extremely beautiful; screw-palm, fan-palm; bread-fruit; cinnamon; clove; all-spice; and specimens of very rare and beautiful plants. There was also a contrivance by which they were watered by an artificial rain in small drops, or rather a dew, by turning a few cocks. There was a beautiful papiflora, and the wonderful pitcher-plant, each leaf containing about a tablespoonful of clear water —mimosa, and other curiosities. I just mention this subject because, if I recollect right, you are a gardener or a botanist, neither of which am I. But, say you, why go on Sunday? Truly because we could not on any other day. But W. and I went to chapel in the evening, and heard a rather ridiculous sermon. W. has twice taken me to chapel when I otherwise would not have gone, and this was the second.

"And now the end of my paper gives me warning to end. I am writing to you with my head in my night-cap, and my legs and lower half in bed. My watch says half-past twelve, and I am very dozy, or I would take a fresh sheet. I shall be writing another against yours arrives, with a packet for Messieux.—I am, dear George, yours very truly,

"THOS. HOOD."

"Five feet nine inches in height and as thick as a rushlight." There we have the young poet's outer man limned for us in a few words. He describes himself as "*scripsit et sculpsit*," but of his later engraving work nothing has been identified, and it may be assumed that his connection with the *London Magazine* was the turning point in his career, that the pen became

Thomas Hood :

month by month more assuredly the tool on the exercise of which, as he himself expressed it, the lively Hood depended for a livelihood.

These years during which the poet was feeling his way to his rightful profession were busy ones in the world of letters. In 1817—the year of Hood's return from Dundee —John Keats published his first volume of " Poems," followed in 1818 by "Endymion," and in 1820 by "Lamia," and on February 23, 1821, he died. These dates are significant in connection with Hood's life; great on him was, as we shall have occasion to notice, the influence of that marvellous youth who, though he perished in his third decade, had enriched his country's poetical literature with much of imperishable beauty. The four years during which we may consider Thomas Hood as professionally an engraver with a leaning towards letters were indeed remarkably rich in literature—so rich that, looking back, we cannot help envying the folk who within so short a period had so much that was to be recognised as classic put before them as current literature. When Hood returned to London from his sojourn in Scotland, Shelley's " Revolt of Islam," Coleridge's " Biographia Literaria "and " Sibylline Leaves," Hazlitt's " Characters of Shakespeare's Plays," and Moore's " Lalla Rookh " were new to the world; in the following year came the concluding cantos of Byron's " Childe Harold," the two precious volumes of Charles Lamb's " Works," Scott's " Rob Roy " and " Heart of Midlothian," and Mrs. Shelley's " Frankenstein "; 1819 saw Byron's " Don Juan " begin, saw Shelley's " Cenci " and " Prometheus Unbound," Scott's " Bride of Lammermoor," Hazlitt's " Lectures on the Comic Poets," and Wordsworth's " Waggoner " and " Peter Bell " (to say nothing of John Hamilton Reynolds' " runaway peal " in the way of his forestalling parody of that poem); then came Words-worth's " River Duddon," Shelley's " Epipsychidion,"

As Engraver (1817—1821).

and Scott's "Monastery" and "Abbot," and other works scarcely less notable. It may be doubted whether any other four consecutive years of the century gave so much of classic stamp to English prose and poetry. To apply the lines which Wordsworth wrote of an earlier period, it might be said that for anyone endowed with any share of the poetic spirit, with any deep love of letters :—

> "Bliss was it at that time to be alive,
> But to be young was very heaven."

It is worth recalling, too, that it was in January, 1817, that the *Literary Gazette*—the first weekly literary review—started on a career of prosperity which remained unchallenged until the *Athenæum* superseded it more than a dozen years later.

"SARE, I AM AT WHERE ?—"
"WELL, I KNOW YOU BE !"

CHAPTER V.

PERHAPS the most significant period in the life of Thomas Hood was that in which he assisted in the editing of and regularly contributed to the *London Magazine;* it was significant as marking the change of career from that of engraver to that of author, it was significant as introducing him directly to some of the most remarkable writers of the day, and it was significant as introducing him indirectly to the woman who was to be his life-companion. The very name of that remarkable periodical of the third decade of the nineteenth century conjures up memories of its extraordinary band of contributors—Charles Lamb, William Hazlitt, Allan Cunningham, and the three Thomases—De Quincey, Carlyle, and Hood. A reader of the present time, turning over the pages and coming now upon the "Confessions of an English Opium Eater," now on "Dream Children," or "A Dissertation upon Roast Pig," then on "The Life of Schiller," or "Lycus the Centaur," or "Fair Ines," cannot help wondering whether the readers of the magazine when it first came out were fully aware of the rare excellence of that which was being placed before them. The *London Magazine* was adding true riches to the body of English literature month by month in a way which puts it far ahead of its contemporaries in the affection of book lovers. It had, however, but a short life of brilliance. It began in 1820, but had paled into insignificance some time before George the Fourth's brief reign had come to an end.

The London Magazine (1821—1824).

Early in 1821, when the magazine was in its third volume, certain recriminations which had been going on for some time between the *London Magazine* and *Blackwood's Magazine*, led to a duel between John Scott, the capable editor of the former periodical, and Jonathan Henry Christie, a friend of John Gibson Lockhart, who was editor of *Blackwood's*. The circumstances of the duel do not belong to Hood's life story, and, having been repeated many times, need not be detailed here. The meeting ended in the death of Scott, and shortly afterwards the readers of the magazine were apprised that "arrangements have been completed for the future Editorship of the *London Magazine*, which enable us to promise an interesting accession to the valuable contributions of our old friends and regular correspondents." Change of proprietors followed close upon the inevitable change of editors. At first the magazine had been issued by Messrs. Baldwin, Cradock and Joy, but from the number for July, 1821, it became the property of Messrs. Taylor and Hessey, and with the new proprietors came Thomas Hood's opportunity. Himself, as we have seen, the son of a publisher who had died nearly ten years earlier, Hood had shown during his short career as engraver a strong bent towards writing. His own account of the change runs thus :—

"In the mean time, whilst thus playing at Literature, an event was ripening which was to introduce me to Authorship in earnest, and make the Muse, with whom I had only flirted, my companion for life. It had often occurred to me that a striking, romantical, necromantical, metaphysical melodramatical, Germanish story might be composed, the interest of which should turn on the mysterious influence of the fate of A over the destiny of B, the said parties having no more natural or apparent connexion with each other than Tenterden

Thomas Hood :

Steeple and the Goodwin Sands. An instance of this occult contingency occurred in my own case; for I did not even know by sight the unfortunate gentleman on whose untimely exit depended my entrance on the literary stage. In the beginning of the year 1821 a remarkable duel, originating in a pen-and-ink quarrel, took place at Chalk Farm, and terminated in the death of Mr. John Scott, the able editor of the *London Magazine*. The melancholy result excited great interest, in which I fully participated, little dreaming that his catastrophe involved any consequences of importance to myself. But on the loss of its conductor the Periodical passed into other hands. The new Proprietors were my friends, they sent for me, and after some preliminaries, I was duly installed as a sort of sub-Editor of the *London Magazine*.

" It would be affectation to say, that engraving was resigned with regret. There is always something mechanical about the art—moreover, it is as unwholesome as wearisome to sit copper-fastened to a board, with a cantle scooped out to accommodate your stomach, if you have one, painfully ruling, ruling, and still ruling lines straight or crooked, by the long hundred to the square inch, at the doubly hazardous risk which Wordsworth so deprecates of 'growing double.' So farewell Woollett! Strange! Bartolozzi! I have said, my vanity did not rashly plunge me into authorship; but no sooner was there a legitimate opening than I jumped at it à la Grimaldi, head foremost, and was speedily behind the scenes.

" To judge by my zeal and delight in my new pursuit, the bowl had at last found its natural bias. Not content with taking articles, like candidates for holy orders—with rejecting articles, like the Belgians—I dreamt articles, thought articles, wrote articles, which were all inserted by the editor, of course with the

EARLY PORTRAIT OF THOMAS HOOD.

[*To face p.* 94.

The London Magazine (1821—1824).

concurrence of his deputy. The more irksome parts of authorship, such as the correction of the press, were to me labours of love. I received a revise from Mr. Baldwin's Mr. Parker, as if it had been a proof of his regard; forgave him all his slips, and really thought that printers' devils were not so black as they are painted. But my top-gallant story was in ' Our Contributors!' How I used to look forward to Elia! and backward for Hazlitt, and all round for Edward Herbert, and how I used to look up to Allan Cunningham! for at that time the *London* had a goodly list of writers—a rare company. It is now defunct, and perhaps no ex-periodical might so appropriately be apostrophized with the Irish funereal question—' Arrah, honey, why did you die?' Had you not an editor, and elegant prose writers, and beautiful poets, and broths of boys for criticism and classics, and wits and humorists —Elia, Cary, Procter, Cunningham, Bowring, Barton, Hazlitt, Elton, Hartley Coleridge, Talfourd, Soane, Horace Smith, Reynolds, Poole, Clare, and Thomas Benyon, with a power besides. Hadn't you Lion's Heads with Traditional Tales? Hadn't you an Opium-Eater, and a Dwarf, and a Giant, and a Learned Lamb, and a Green Man? Had not you a regular Drama, and a Musical Report, and a Report of Agriculture, and an Obituary, and a Price Current, and a current price of only half-a-crown? Arrah, why did you die? Why, somehow the contributors fell away— the concern went into other hands—worst of all, a new editor tried to put the Belles Lettres in Utilitarian envelopes; whereupon the circulation of the Miscellany, like that of poor Le Fevre,[1] got slower, slower, slower—and slower still—and then stopped for ever! It was a sorry scattering of those old Londoners! Some went out of the country; one (Clare) went

[1] " Tristram Shandy," Book VI., chap. X.

Thomas Hood :

into it. Lamb retreated to Colebrooke. Mr. Cary presented himself to the British Museum. Reynolds and Barry took to engrossing when they should pen a stanza, and Thomas Benyon gave up literature."

It was, indeed, a brilliant band in which Hood, as a young man of twenty-two, found himself enrolled—a band of men of the most varied genius, the most varied attainments and the most varied characters, all brought together by the literary nexus, and Hood, running over the list of names, omits those of Thomas Carlyle, who had not then come into his own, and of Thomas Griffiths Wainewright, forger and murderer. The *London Magazine* might well be the theme of a treatise by itself, were the scattered portions of its history brought together; that history forms a chapter—a highly important chapter—in the life of Charles Lamb; it forms a chapter in the unwritten life of Keats's friend, John Hamilton Reynolds; a chapter in the life of Allan Cunningham and of Thomas Hood, while bits of it are embedded in the biographies of half a score of more or less notable men of letters. The magazine was indeed, from the literary point of view, as good as it could be. John Scott, who had earlier earned distinction in the journalistic field, was an ideal editor, and had got together a splendid band of contributors at the time of his tragic end, and it is a sufficiently remarkable thing that his successor kept the magazine going without any falling off in spirit or quality. The new publishers seem to have kept the actual editorial control in their own hands, while Hood acted, as he put it, as a sort of sub-editor, which, though it sounds a sufficiently vague description, probably describes the position fairly accurately. The publishers—the actual editor being Taylor[1]—kept control of the conduct of the periodical, while upon the young poet, whom

[1] John Taylor (1781—1864).

The London Magazine (1821—1824).

they had called in to assist them, devolved the duties of examining and adjudicating upon the manuscripts submitted for consideration by would-be contributors. In the first line of the first number of the magazine published under the new conditions we seem to recognise the hand of Hood. Each monthly number opened with notices to correspondents under the title of the Lion's Head—a custom that John Scott had started a year earlier—and the July one opens with "The Lion's Head is determined on having a paw in the Coronation." Hood apparently had charge of this department, and we find his hand again and again in amusing comments on prose and verse sent in. The style of these suggests that he had studied the *Mirror*, which had been published by his father, for in that earlier magazine there were similar notices, in which the editor, Dubois, scored, as the saying puts it, off some of his aspiring contributors. The following three specimens from the *Mirror* notices to correspondents will indicate the extent to which Hood followed a similar method :—

"Jaques asks our opinion of his *imitation* of Shakespeare. We never saw anything like it."

" We are surprised that *Incognito* should complain of being 'in the dark'—It is the place he has chosen."

" A Mr. Jamieson has sent us a sort of advertisement, describing a middle-aged lady who is lost. All we can say to it is, that we have not found her, and that if we do we shall certainly not *keep* her."

Month after month in the " Lion's Head " the blow of " declined with thanks " was softened with a pleasantry, frequently embodying criticism. One or two specimens from these earlier numbers may be taken as suggestive of the gusto with which the young author took to his new work :—

" W.'s ' Night ' is too long, for the moon rises twice in it."

Thomas Hood:

"We look for very light articles from anonymous contributors who forget to pay the postage."

"We really did not know before that 'Juvenile was handed down to posterity as an author much read by the Romans.' He was, no doubt, the Mr. Newbery of their day. For this information we are indebted to Bs., and not less so for his candour in pointing out one fault in our magazine, that 'the *London* is too full of Literature.' We are glad it is no worse, and have no doubt that, with Bs.'s assistance, we shall be able, when necessary, to render it quite otherwise."

"To Y. and Y. No.—A word to the *Y.'s!*"

"J. B. 'On the Management of Harriers' is deferred till the Dog-days; and Homo's 'Sonnet to Eve' is out of date."

"T. T. T.'s lines to '*My* Mary' are not amiss for a lover rising fifteen. We shall be glad to hear from him again upon his coming of age."

"Colin has sent us a Summer Pastoral, and says that he can supply us with one every month.—Has he always got sheep in his *pen*?"

"N. of Margate says he means to send us 'A Marine Subject.'—We hope it will be a Mermaid."

"Napoleon Buonaparte's death will surely be the cause of ours. Will the reader believe that we are up to our middles in mourning verses? What can be said to an ode beginning—

"'High General, Mighty Emperor, Eagle vast!'

Or to lines containing the following :—

"'France's thunder now is *dim!*'

We have elegies enough to paper all the tenements in Saint Helena, and shall be very glad to contract for furnishing linings to any respectable builder of bonnet boxes."

The London Magazine (1821—1824).

"A. A.'s 'Walk from Highgate' may 'go to the place whence it came!'"

"T. T. (not T. T. T., but a more unlettered personage) will never suit us. His poetical portrait of Mr. Kean is the veriest *daub* we ever looked upon. We were sitting at one of his own initials when his packet arrived, and it totally ruined our Bohea."

"T. says his tail is out of his own head: is he a tadpole?"

"Lion's Head feels its temples throb at having to reject the offerings of such kind Correspondents; but the public is remorseless, and is more dainty than even Lion's Head at feeding-time."

From the very first number of the magazine in the production of which he shared, Hood was a contributor of prose or poetry. In the number for July, 1821, appeared his lyric " To Hope " :—

> "O! take, young Seraph, take thy harp,
> And play to me so cheerily."

This was unsigned, and in later numbers he varied his signature in a way that makes the identification of his work extremely difficult. "Incog.," "T. H.," three asterisks, "H.," and other signatures were employed by him, and many others appeared without any name, while yet others were given in the Lion's Head as though sent in by strangers, and were introduced by such words as "We really cannot think of printing the following." Many of the pieces were later collected by the author himself, but there are several others much in his manner which on internal evidence might well be ascribed to him; though the pleasant game of ascription is one in which the wish to make a find may sometimes father the thought that the find has been made. This is not the place in which to go seriatim through the contributions which Hood made to the

Thomas Hood:

London Magazine—the verses, including some of the best known, both serious and comic, will be found in any complete collection of his poems, while some of the prose will be found in the seven or ten-volume edition of his works.

The most consistent signature used by Hood in the magazine was "Incog.," and one unreprinted paper indisputably his is a brief essay signed "Cogin"— obviously a syllabic inversion of the other pen-name. The brief essay—it is but a page and a half of the magazine—is of considerable importance in the story of Hood's literary development, showing, as it seems to do, whence he considered himself to have learned his trick of punning. The latter part of this confession runs:—

"I believe I as seldom repeat myself as most persons, but I may not be assoiled from the charge of a worse and wilful kind of imitation of others, if not in matter, at least in manner. There was one especial occasion (would that I could forget it) when I endeavoured to *supply* my ingenious and respected friend R. Vain thought! As if by becoming, as it were, his material ghost, I could be his joyous, witty, and excellent spirit! When I dined with him, I believe for the first time, at a friend's table, I was delighted with his right merrie conceites, and the happy tone of his conversation; and I wished, which has since been realized, that the born friendship of that night might be of age in somewhat less than twenty-one years. After the cloth was removed, he read to us a copy of verses so lively and humorous, that the very table vibrated to our mirth, and the purple-faced wine, as if in sympathy with our merry cheeks that wrinkled over it, kept

"'verging in successive rings.'

"I think—I am sure I did not envy him these tokens of applause, for there is no genius of the present day

The London Magazine (1821—1824).

whom I more sincerely admire—but I believe I longed for his manner of making so many persons happy.

"That very night I invoked the muses in my night-cap, and at two o'clock in the morning I found myself at the fag-end of five stanzas, each of which was wound up by some inversion of meaning approaching to a pun. I had nothing left, therefore, but to wish for the day—not the dawn—but the day which was to bring me an occasion of repeating *my* verses; and it came, I remember, in less than a fortnight, as if on purpose. It brought me to the same table, and the same party—with the exception of R., or rather of myself; for, on this occasion, I intended to *supply* him. At the same time, that is to say, just after the second circumambulation of the decanters, I pulled forth my paper, and began to read; but, alas! the points were only greeted with meek and melancholy smiles, and if I was indeed like R., I read to other guess sort of people. Perhaps they were too original to laugh twice at the same kind of thing; but they certainly did not at all repeat themselves; and I learned, what I should have known before—that we have more chance of our own than of another man's originality."

The "R." of this essay was, there can be no doubt, John Hamilton Reynolds, one of the contributors to the *London Magazine*; and, if we accept the little story as fact, we may safely assume that the dinners at the same place and with the same company were probably two of those periodical gatherings at Waterloo Place— Messrs. Taylor & Hessey's West End office—where the proprietors of the *London Magazine* gave excellent dinners "and consulted and talked on literary matters, and enlarged their social sympathies."[1]

Reynolds was a young man three years Hood's senior. The two, who met apparently first as fellow

[1] B. W. Procter.

Thomas Hood :

writers for the *London,* soon struck up a firm friendship, and it is certainly interesting to find Hood so frankly expressing himself as imitator. Reynolds had already published several small volumes of serious and humorous verse, and appears to have been a lively and entertaining companion. If it was his example that set Hood on writing verses marked by " some inversion of meaning approaching to a pun," then the pupil—as is not uncommon in the history of the arts —soon outstripped his master. The acquaintance with Reynolds warmed into a strong friendship and introduced Hood to a new circle of people, while he also made other notable friends among the *London Magazine* circle, most notable of all, one whom he was later to term " father," as the young wits of the early seventeenth century termed Ben Jonson their father, was Charles Lamb, whose essays signed " Elia " were at the time giving the *London* an immortal reputation. The story of the meeting of the two, as written by the younger man, has appeared in various biographies of Lamb, but will bear repetition here :—

" I was sitting one morning beside our Editor, busily correcting proofs, when a visitor was announced, whose name, grumbled by a low, ventriloquial voice, like Tom Pipes calling from the hold through the hatchway, did not resound distinctly on my tympanum. However, the door opened, and in came a stranger—a figure remarkable at a glance, with a fine head on a small, spare body, supported by two almost immaterial legs. He was clothed in sables of a by-gone fashion, but there was something wanting, or something present about him, that certified he was neither a divine, nor a physician, nor a schoolmaster : from a certain neatness and sobriety in his dress, coupled with his sedate bearing, he might have been taken, but that such a costume would be anomalous, for a Quaker in black.

The London Magazine (1821—1824).

He looked still more like (what he really was) a literary Modern Antique, a New-Old Author, a living Anachronism contemporary at once with Burton the Elder and Colman the Younger. Meanwhile he advanced with rather a peculiar gait, his walk was plantigrade, and with a cheerful ' How d'ye,' and one of the blandest, sweetest smiles that ever brightened a manly countenance, held out two fingers to the Editor. . . . After the literary business had been settled, the Editor invited his contributor to dinner, adding, ' We shall have a hare——'

" ' And—and—and—and many Friends ? '

" The hesitation in the speech and the readiness of the allusion were alike characteristic of the individual, whom his familiars will perchance have recognised already as the delightful Essayist, the capital Critic, the pleasant Wit and Humorist, the delicate-minded and large-hearted Charles Lamb ! He was shy, like myself, with strangers, so that, despite my yearnings, our first meeting scarcely amounted to an introduction. We were both at dinner, amongst the hare's many friends, but our acquaintance got no farther, in spite of a desperate attempt on my part to attract his notice. His complaint of the Decay of Beggars [1] presented another chance: I wrote on coarse paper, and in ragged English,[2] a letter of thanks to him as if from one of his mendicant clients, but it produced no effect."

Of Hood's association with Lamb we shall see more later on. The dinner which gave rise to Elia's famous

[1] This essay appeared in the *London* for June, 1822, so that Hood must have been there at least a year before he got to know the greatest of the magazine's contributors.

[2] A kind of practical joke of which Hood was rather fond ; he played it on Mrs. Dilke with considerable effect about ten years later.

Thomas Hood :

mot was no doubt one of those gatherings at which Messrs. Taylor & Hessey kept in touch with their contributors, "gatherings of the clan to eat, drink, and be merry," at which Hood came in touch with many kindred souls. At a representative one of these dinners, Lamb would sit on the right hand of the Editor, with, strange contrast indeed, John Clare, the Peasant Poet, in "grass-coloured coat and yellow waistcoat," on his right; next to Clare would be "the Brobdingnagian" Allan Cunningham, and on the Editor's other side Cary, the translator of Dante. Hood himself sat between Barry Cornwall (Bryan Waller Procter) and Thomas De Quincey, with John Hamilton Reynolds opposite. They must have been wonderful gatherings; and it is to be regretted that no one of their number gave us something in the nature of that "Retaliation," in which Goldsmith felicitously hit off the members of the coterie that met at the St. James's Coffee House.

The fullest account that we have of these *London Magazine* dinners is that given in Hood's brief but discursive literary reminiscences contributed to "Hood's Own" more than a dozen years after the gatherings had ceased. From those reminiscences we may cull one or two sketches of famous "Londoners." Clare, we are told, in his finery, shone "verdantly out from the grave-coloured suits of the literati like a patch of turnips amidst stubble and fallow." Little wonder was it "that in wending homewards through the Strand, the Peasant and Elia, *Sylvanus et Urban*, linked comfortably together, there arose the frequent cry of 'Look at Tom and Jerry—there goes Tom and Jerry!' for truly, Clare in his square-cut green coat, and Lamb in his black, were not a little suggestive of Hawthorn and Logic in the plates to 'Life in London.'" When the Peasant Poet first came to London his publishers

The London Magazine (1821—1824).

sent a servant to meet him, and on the servant enquiring "Are you Mr. Clare?" the poet, determined not to be taken in by any City sharps, emphatically responded "No!" Though Clare the Peasant and Elia the Templar—the typical countryman and the typical Londoner of letters—might not seem to have much in common, they found a subject which both delighted to discuss in poetry in general; "and Montgomery's 'Common Lot' in particular, Lamb insisting on the beauty of the tangental sharp turn at 'O! she was fair!' thinking, mayhap, of his own Alice W——, and Clare swearing, 'Dal!' (a clarified d——n) 'Dal! if it isn't like a dead man preaching out of his coffin!'"

"The Brobdingnagian next to Clare, overtopping him by the whole head and shoulders—a physical 'Colossus of Literature,' the grenadier of our corps—is Allan, not Allan Ramsay, 'no, nor Barbara Allen neither,' but Allan Cunningham—'a credit,' quoth Sir Walter Scott (he might have said a long credit), "to Caledonia.' He is often called 'honest Allan,' to distinguish him, perhaps, from one Allan-a-Dale, who was apt to mistake his neighbour's goods for his own— sometimes, between ourselves, yclept the 'C. of Solway,' in allusion to that favourite 'Allan Water,' the Solway Sea. There is something of the true, moody poetical weather observable in the barometer of his face, alternating from variable to showery, from stormy to set fair. At times he looks gloomy and earnest and traditional—a little like a Covenanter—but he suddenly clears up and laughs a hearty laugh that lifts him an inch or two from his chair, for he rises at a joke when he sees one like a trout at a fly, and finishes with a smart rubbing of his ample palms."

The reverend personage by the Editor,—"with the studious brow, deep-set eyes, and bald crown, is the

mild and modest Cary—the same who turned Dante
into Miltonic English blank verse. He is sending his
plate towards the partridges, which he will relish and
digest as though they were the Birds of Aristophanes."
Pity it was, said Hood, that "such a Translator found
no better translation in the Church!" The same jest
was used in another form on the same subject in the
notices in the " Lion's Head." Hazlitt, a regular contributor to the magazine, Hood never met at the
editorial dinner-table, but he recorded his impressions
of two other fellow-diners, the one a leading figure in
the literary history of his time, the other a man who
plays an important part in the life story of Thomas
Hood.

" Procter,—alias Barry Cornwall, formerly of the
Marcian Colonnade, now of some prosaical Inn of
Court—the kindly Procter, one of the foremost to
welcome me into the Brotherhood, with a too-flattering
Dedication (another instance against the jealousy of
authors), is my own left-hand file. But what he says
shall be kept as strictly confidential; for he is whispering
it into my Martineau ear. On my other side, when I
turn that way, I see a profile a shadow of which ever
confronts me on opening my writing-desk,—a sketch
taken from memory, the day after seeing the original.[1]
In opposition to the ' extra man's size' of Cunningham,
the party in question looks almost boyish, partly from
being in bulk somewhat beneath Monsieur Quetelet's
' Average Man,' but still more so from a peculiar delicacy

---

[1] "Unable to make anything ' like a likeness ' of a sitter for the
purpose, I have a sort of Irish faculty for taking faces behind
their backs. But my pencil has not been guilty of half the
personalities attributed to it; amongst others ' a formidable likeness of a Lombard Street banker.' Besides that, one would
rather draw on a banker than at him. I have never seen the
gentleman alluded to, or even a portrait of him, in my life."

The London Magazine (1821—1824).

of complexion and smallness of features, which look all
the smaller from his wearing, in compliment, probably,
to the *Sampsons* of Teutonic Literature, his locks
unshorn.   Nevertheless whoever looks again

" ' Sees more than marks the crowd of common men.'

There is speculation in the eyes, a curl of the lip, and a
general character in the outline, that reminds one of
some portraits of Voltaire.   And a Philosopher he is
every inch.   He looks, thinks, writes, talks and walks,
eats and drinks, and no doubt sleeps philosophically—
i.e., deliberately.   There is nothing abrupt about his
motions,—he goes and comes calmly and quietly—like
the phantom in Hamlet, he is here—he is there—he is
gone !   So it is with his discourse.   He speaks slowly,
clearly, and with very marked emphasis,—the tide of
talk flows like Denham's river, ' strong without rage,
without overflowing, full.'   When it was my frequent
and agreeable duty to call on Mr. De Quincy (being an
uncommon name to remember, the servant associated
it, on the Memoria Technica principle, with a sore throat
and always pronounced it Quinsy), and I have found
him at home, quite at home, in the midst of a German
Ocean of *Literature*, in a storm,—flooding all the floor,
the tables and the chairs,—billows of books, tossing,
tumbling, surging open,—on such occasions I have
willingly listened by the hour whilst the Philosopher,
standing with his eyes fixed on one side of the room,
seemed to be less speaking than reading from a ' handwriting on the wall.'   Now and then he would diverge,
for a Scotch mile or two, to the right or left, till I was
tempted to inquire with Peregrine in John Bull
(Colman's, not Hook's), ' Do you never deviate ? '—but
he always came safely back to the point where he had
left, not lost the scent, and thence hunted his topic to
the end.   But look !—we are in the small hours, and a

Thomas Hood :

change comes o'er the spirit of that 'old familiar face.'
A faint hectic tint leaves the cheek, the eyes are a
degree dimmer, and each is surrounded by a growing
shadow—signs of the waning influence of that Potent
Drug whose stupendous Pleasures and enormous pains
have been so eloquently described by the English Opium
Eater. Marry, I have one of his Confessions with his
own name and mark to it :—an apology for a certain
stain on his MS., the said stain being a large purplish
ring—'Within that circle none durst drink but he,'—
in fact the impression, coloured, of 'a tumbler of
laudanum negus, warm, without sugar.'

"That smart active person opposite with a game-cock-
looking head, and the hair combed smooth, fighter
fashion, over his forehead—with one finger hooked round
a glass of champaigne, not that he requires it to inspirit
him, for his wit bubbles up of itself—is our Edward
Herbert, the Author of that true piece of Biography,
the Life of Peter Corcoran. He is 'good with both
hands,' like that Nonpareil Randall, at a comic verse
or a serious stanza—smart at a repartee—sharp at a
retort,—and not averse to a bit of mischief. 'Twas he
who gave the runaway ring at Wordsworth's Peter Bell.
Generally, his jests, set off by a happy manner, are
only ticklesome, but now and then they are sharp-
flavoured,—like the sharpness of the pineapple. Would
I could give a sample. Alas ! What a pity it is that
so many good things uttered by Poets, and Wits, and
Humorists, at chance times—and they are always the
best and brightest, like sparks struck out by Pegasus'
own hoof, in a curvet amongst the flints—should be
daily and hourly lost to the world for want of a recorder !
But in this Century of Inventions, when a self-acting
drawing-paper has been discovered for copying visible
objects, who knows but that a future Niepce, or
Daguerre, or Herschel, or Fox Talbot, may find out

The London Magazine (1821—1824).

some Boswellish sort of writing-paper to repeat whatever it hears!"

The "Boswellish writing-paper" was to come, before the century ended, in the phonograph, but Hood wrote his words nearly ten years before Thomas Alva Edison was born. Besides the dinners at Waterloo Place the "Londoners" seem to have had occasional outings together, as when they spent a pleasant day with Cary and his family of Caryatides, as Lamb called them, at Chiswick, where "the Interpreter (of the House Beautiful as well as of the Inferno)" occupied the house that had been the residence of Hogarth.

Of those who gave their written good things month by month to the public in the pages of the *London Magazine*, and whose unrecorded spoken good things must have made those periodical gatherings at the publisher-editor's veritable feasts of reason and the best fun, the one whose friendship was to have the greatest influence on the career of Thomas Hood was "our Edward Herbert," whose proper name was John Hamilton Reynolds, and who, though he was but three years older than Hood, had published his first volume of poems as far back as 1814. He used the pen name of John Hamilton as well as that of Edward Herbert—perhaps because, having at about the time that Hood met him been taken into partnership with a solicitor, he may have thought that light literature and the law did not together fit the same name. Reynolds wrote a number of "letters" to friends in the country dealing with notable London events, and these formed some of the best of his recognisable work in the *London Magazine*, although it is probable that he also wrote much anonymously. In 1819 Reynolds gave his "runaway ring" at Wordsworth's "Peter Bell," when he published a skit on the poet under the title of the poem which had only just been published, and he had also published a small

Thomas Hood :

volume of verses, "The Fancy," purporting to be the remains of one Peter Corcoran. He was a man of distinct ability, but wanting apparently in steadiness of character, his reputation being that of a man whose social graces led him to over-indulgence in conviviality and to the neglect of his talents instead of to the exercising and maturing of them. In these early years of the twenties, however, he was a young man full of spirit, and with an evident genius for inspiring friendship in the kindred soul of Thomas Hood, for we soon find them working together, while that their friendship was something more than an inspiring of collaboration is shown by the fact that Hood soon became a welcome visitor at Reynolds' home. Of his friendship with the Reynolds family we shall see more in the next chapter.

Of the personality of John Hamilton Reynolds curiously little seems now ascertainable, though perhaps investigation may reveal more when his writings are collected, as some of them might well be. Though active as a writer in the twenties, he seems later to have devoted himself more exclusively to the law. The only description of him is that by Hood in the passage already quoted describing various members of the staff of the *London*—" that smart active person with a game-cock-looking head, and the hair combed smooth, fighter fashion, over his forehead," seems to fit the poet of pugilism, the writer of the many "Letters" and other papers of Edward Herbert, the writer summed up by Sir Charles Abraham Elton, 'The Idler' of the *London*, in—

> "Hast thou nodded blithe and smiled
> At Herbert's vein?"

"Janus Weathercock"—a writer of whom we may see more before taking leave of the "Londoners"—in

The London Magazine (1821—1824).

some of his gay, racy contributions to the magazine was wont to rally his fellow contributors, and in the number for May, 1822, he appeals to the Editor to keep his men up to the mark—" Clap Elia on the back for such a series of good behaviour. . . . Entreat the lively observant Edward Herbert to keep out of bad company : the influences of Drury Lane green-room had an awful effect on the conclusion of his last, as he himself seemed aware. Give us some good serious poetry (if to be had anywhere :—why is the harp of Coleridge mute ?) and contrast it with some such smart bubbles of wit as ' Please to ring the belle.' " Edward Herbert in his discursive talk of the Covent Garden green-room had concluded with some jingling verses about the Exhibition at Somerset House :—

> " Come, come—I am willing
> To down with my shilling,
> The time to be killing
> With varnish and paint."

" Janus's " appeal for serious poetry contrasted with witty bubbles had surely been forestalled by the sub-editor, as the same number of the magazine contained Hood's " Faithless Sally Brown " and his impressive fragment " The Sea of Death." A few months later, and " Janus " had another article in the magazine rallying the " Londoners " in the same spirit, and on this occasion he addressed Hood in a pointed fashion, which showed that the young poet's quality was recognised by his colleagues. The article was entitled " Janus Weatherbound ; or the Weathercock steadfast for lack of oil," and in it he pretended to take farewell of the magazine for which he had written off and on from the commencement, giving as motto to his

III

Thomas Hood :

"grave epistle" some lines from Milton "slightly altered":—

> " Ear-cracking Fleet-street o'er,
>   And the resounding shore,[1]
>   A voice of weeping heard and loud lament:
>   From the Magazine
>   Clothed in dismal green,
>   The parting Janus[2] is with sighing sent."

After some interesting particulars about his own career the writer proceeds to sum up some of his fellow "Londoners" in an appreciative fashion—the passages on Lamb have been frequently quoted. He has the following about Thomas Hood, addressing him by a nickname which seems to have been fastened on him soon after he had joined the *London Magazine*:—

"Young Theodore[3]! Young in years, not in power! Our new Ovid!—only more imaginative!—Painter to the visible eye—and the inward;—commixture of, what the superficial deem, incongruous elements!—Instructive living proof, how close lie the founts of laughter and tears! Thou fermenting brain—oppressed, as yet, by its own riches. Though melancholy would seem to have touched thy heart with her painful (salutary) hand, yet is thy fancy mercurial—undepressed;—and sparkles and crackles more from the contact—as the northern lights when they near the frozen pole. How! is the fit not on? Still is 'Lycus' without mate!— Who can mate him but thyself? Let not the shallow induce thee to conceal thy depth. Leave ' *Old Seamen*,'

---

[1] " Shore, pro *Strand*."

[2] " Janus, Hibernicè pro Genius."

[3] To this, in his collection of Wainewright's works, Mr. W. Carew Hazlitt appends the amazing footnote, "Theodore Hook, of course." Which, incidentally, illustrates the danger of jumping to conclusions.

The London Magazine (1821—1824).

—the strain thou held'st was of a higher mood; there
are others for your 'Sketches *from* Nature,' (as they
truly call 'em)— * * * * * * * —and such small deer!
As for thy word-gambols, thy humour, thy fantasies, thy
curiously conceited perception of similarity in dis-
similarity, of coherents in incoherents, they are
brilliantly suave, innocuously exhilarating :—but not a
step farther, if thou lovest thy proper peace! Read the
fine of the eleventh, and the whole of the twelfth chapter
of Tristram Shandy; and believe them, dear Theodore,
O most truly. For *others* (not for thee) is the following
paragraph thence quoted: 'Trust me, this unwary
pleasantry of thine will sooner or later bring thee into
scrapes and difficulties which no afterwit can extricate
thee out of. In these sallies, too, oft I see it happens,
that a person laughed at considers himself in the light
of a person injured, with all the rights of such a situation belonging to him; and when thou viewest him in
that light too, and reckonest up his friends, his family,
his kindred and allies,—and musterest up with them
the many recruits which will 'list under him from a
sense of common danger,—'tis no extravagant arithmetic
to say that for every ten jokes thou hast got a hundred
enemies; and till thou hast gone on, and raised a swarm
of wasps about thine ears, and art half stung to death
by them, thou wilt never be convinced it is so.'"

The man who wrote this cordial appreciation of Hood's
talents, who thus warned him of a danger to which for
a time he may be said to have succumbed, the "Janus
Weathercock" of the *London Magazine*, was a man of
whom his associates have recorded but little. The
literary ability of the "Janus Weathercock" of the
twenties came to be eclipsed by the criminal actions of
Thomas Griffiths Wainewright[1] in the following decade.

[1] Thomas Griffiths Wainewright (1794—1852) was a poisoner
and forger, an artist, art critic, and miscellaneous writer, full

Thomas Hood:

Wainewright's career does not concern us here, for beyond the association on the magazine there does not seem to have been any lasting acquaintanceship between him and Hood.

It is not easy to settle the question of why it was that Thomas Hood received his nickname of "Theodore." According to his son the explanation was very simple; it was owing to his using that name as a signature to contributions to the *London*, but the explanation was evidently hazarded without any reference to the magazine. The nickname *may* have arisen from Hood's surname having been confused with that of Theodore Hook, as it was many years later in a notable volume of essays, but I think it is possible that he was the author of a sentimental dramatic sketch in blank verse entitled "Theodore and Bertha," which appeared in the magazine for September, 1821, and that the raillery of friends fastened the name of the hero upon the author. Be the occasion what it may the name was evidently a common one, for not only was Hood written of as Theodore but he used the signature in letters to friends.[1]

There was probably a break in Hood's connection with the *London Magazine*. According to Hessey, recalling the matter many years later, the poet wrote nothing in it after June, 1823, and the volume ending then is the latest one which afforded material for his collected works. At the close of the following year the magazine changed hands. Lamb had lamented in his letters that it was "sadly falling off," that the good men had been leaving it, but under the new control Hood

particulars of whose life and character are to be found in his "Essays and Criticisms," collected and edited by Mr. W. Carew Hazlitt (1880), and in the "D. N. B."

[1] In the *Literary Speculum* for 1822 (p. 488), is a Sonnet to the Moon signed "Theodore."

became once more an occasional contributor. The earlier severing of the connection may have been in consequence of a dispute with the proprietors. Though Hessey does not hint at such, in one of Hood's letters there is a reference to that one of the proprietory which does not suggest cordial relations (see p. 162).

In the summer of 1822 Hood made his first essay on the stage, when an opera entitled " Gil Blas," the joint production of himself and John Hamilton Reynolds, was brought out at the English Opera House. In the magazine for August of that year the monthly article on the Drama ended thus :—

" The following is one of the songs out of the new opera of ' Gil Blas,' which will be undergoing its trial about the time our readers are undergoing our magazine. A printed copy of the songs has been sent to us, and we dip into it at a venture.

> " ' At Evening's close, at Evening's close,
> The ladye-spirit that haunts the rose
> Her fragrant web of slumber weaves,
> And foldeth up her hundred leaves.
>
> At Evening' close, at Evening's close,
> The fairy-ladye, whose repose
> Is in the water-lily's shell,—
> Shuts her white bower, and sleepeth well.
>
> At Evening's close, at Evening's close,
> My heart forsakes the budded rose;
> Forgets the lily's placid breast,
> And wakes and wanders while *they* rest ! ' "

It is known that Hood and Reynolds collaborated in this dramatisation of " Gil Blas," but the son of the former thought that it was produced at Drury Lane Theatre, and put it conjecturally in 1831–32. As both the writers were on the *London,* and as that magazine gave this preliminary matter, then in due course a lengthy notice of the piece, and returned to the theme

Thomas Hood:

a year later, it may well be conjectured that this was their work. Indeed we may go further, and on reading the three column notice of the piece in the *London* may shrewdly guess that one or other of the authors of the opera also penned the criticism. That criticism appeared in the September number of the magazine—the number which contained Elia's " Dissertation upon Roast Pig " and his " Bachelor's Complaint of the Behaviour of Married People "—under the title of the English Opera House, and the first half of it shows the way in which the young authors set about compressing a lengthy romance into a single evening's stage entertainment.

" Two new pieces have been produced at this prolific theatre,—Gordon the Gipsy, a melodrame, and Gil Blas, a *five* act opera, which last now carries Gordon pick-a-back, through the warm summer nights, in the shape of an afterpiece. To speak first of the greater novelty, Gil Blas,—novel in its construction, and taken from Le Sage's novel,—it is indeed an originality, an invention—a Gregorian innovation, wherein the Author, introducing his hero at seventeen, changes his style to twenty-five, and finally dates him at the ripe age of fifty-two. To effect this, two lapses—or leap-years—are supposed between the acts, one of eight, the other of twenty-seven years; and the three ages are personated by Miss Kelly, Mr. Pearman and Mr. Bartley. The attempt was strange, difficult, and dangerous; yet we anticipated that, well managed, it might prove a happy invention, and present an interesting abridgment of the chronology of Gil Blas—a foreshortened picture of his life—with three distances—and lending our imagination to the leap, the transitions really did not shock us. We say this of the time only, for in truth we fancied a gap elsewhere, in the hero himself, who seemed to want some trait, some enduring characteristic to accompany

The London Magazine (1821—1824).

him in his transmigrations, and to show that although so changed, it was still Gil Blas that was altered.

"The Author, with some deviations, has followed the novel in his early incidents. After Gil Blas, parting with his uncle, who blesses him—with a bag of ducats —we have his adventure with Picaro, the false beggar— his first lesson of life at Pennaflor, as the Eighth Wonder of the World—his capture by the banditti,— and his fortunate escape from their cavern, with the sweet warbling Donna Mencia (Miss Carew). In the third act, being eight years older, and so long beloved by the Donna, he is discovered in her father's garden,— fights with and wounds her brother,—and is obliged to fly, but, rescuing her father in an attack of robbers, is rewarded with the hand of the lady; and here the play begins to outgrow the novel. The *Senior* Gil Blas, at fifty-two, is the happy father of Donna Antonia, and minister of state to Philip IV. That monarch, under the disguises of Duke of Lerma, and a knight of Calatrava, thinks proper to tempt his honesty as a father and a minister; and, as a further trial of his constancy, the inflexible Gil Blas is imprisoned, by order of the Duke of Lerma, in the dungeons of Madrid. Here he meets with his old acquaintance, the robber chief, now turned jailor, and is saved from his vengeance and dagger by Picaro, who visits him as a holy father, to the salvation of his body,—the gates are suddenly thrown open—the king enters with Antonia, guards, etc., etc., and the integrity of Gil Blas being formally recognised and lauded, the monarch graciously cedes Antonia to her lover.

"Altogether, the play is sufficiently fruitful of incident, with some interesting situations—for instance, that of Donna Mencia's tying the negro's black leg to his white one, in the cavern—the scenery of which is very in-genious—and the attempted assassination of Gil Blas in

Thomas Hood:

the dungeon. The duration of the piece—its worst novelty—extending itself into the noon of night, was somewhat felt at its first performance, but after the necessary and judicious curtailments, "making it keep better hours," it met with a very favourable reception. We could wish that one song 'With spirits aching,' had been left in for the sake of the words as well as the air—but let that pass."

The notice continues by discussing the way in which the actors bore themselves, with special commendation for Elia's Miss Kelly, to whom both Reynolds and Hood offered the homage of verse. The composer of the opera is not mentioned nor any fuller particulars than those quoted. It would be interesting to know if the "Londoners" made a night of it and helped their colleagues with a hand on the all-important opening night; it would be doubly interesting to know if Charles Lamb was there to see his friends' work, and to recover his record of the evening. There is a suggestion of him in this tribute to Miss Kelly:—

"She was as arch as an angel, and so natural, that if there were not so many Sonnets to Nature already, we would write one to *her*, and desire nothing better than to hear her read it! Her dress too—to step out of our element—was tasteful and elegant; and, if the word were not applied vulgarly, Corinthian, in that crisp, silky foliage on the sleeve, and as for her train—O what a train to 'list in!"

A year later the dramatic critic of the *London* returned to the theme, with a playful reference winding up a notice of a new production with "It is nearly as long as the last year's opera of Gil Blas, which was just twice as long as Hastings' trial."

With Reynolds Hood became a close friend; with Charles Lamb, too, he established a mutual warm regard which continued throughout life, and with one

118

The London Magazine (1821—1824).

other writer on the *London* he was to become intimately acquainted; this was Charles Wentworth Dilke who contributed to the magazine over the pen name of "Thurma." It is not known whether Hood made his acquaintance at this time, though it is probable, but later they became good friends.

Of the pleasant gatherings at Messrs. Taylor and Hessey's West End offices we have but few records. Hood's own recollections of them we have seen, and may finish with Wainewright's few lines evidently inspired by the walk home with Elia and others from the monthly gathering. "The wits," it may be mentioned, was John Clare's collective name for his fellow contributors to the *London Magazine*, and the account suggests that those same wits kept their conviviality going well on into the new day.

"The gas was now waning fast; so were the patrole and watchmen. With creaks, rumbles, *gee-whut's*, and the smell of matting, cabbages, etc., market carts slowly progressed to The Garden! from the delightful villages of Isleworth, Twickenham and Turnham Green. Several *noticeable* men with black silk stockings, were returning from a high court-plenary of literature and French wines —one might see at a glance that they were famous in puns, poetry, philosophy and exalted criticism! Briefly, they were the *wits* of London! One of them 'soaring aloft in the high region of his fancies, with his garlands and singing robes about him,' chaunted in the ringing emptiness of the streets, ' *Diddle, diddle dumpkins.*' "

The "one" was surely Charles Lamb, who chaunted the same inconsequent words to memorable effect when he wanted to "feel the gentleman's bumps " at a gathering into which one of the matter-of-fact men whom he disliked had unhappily strayed. Among these wits Thomas Hood had, as a young man in the early twenties of his age, taken a place, not as yet recognised by the

Thomas Hood :

reading public, but readily welcomed by the fellow spirits among whom he was happily thrown. Already in 1823 one of these fellow spirits had singled out Hood for one of those friendly dedications which belonged to the pleasant literary amenities of the time. One of the pieces in Barry Cornwall's (Bryan Waller Procter's) "The Flood of Thessaly and other Poems" was addressed as follows :—

"To THOMAS HOOD, ESQ.

"MY DEAR SIR,—I offer this fragment to you; partly because ·you are a lover of the mirthful, as well as of the serious; but principally because I am anxious to incite you, by this open acknowledgment of your rare poetical powers, to exercise them for the gratification of the public.

"I would not be thought forward in thus becoming the herald of your reputation; but I am nevertheless desirous of saying (what I have never before said to you) that believing your poetical faculty to be equal to very high accomplishment, I shall venture, in case you enrol your name amongst the living poets, to look forward with confidence to your complete success."

At the beginning of 1823, while still on the staff of the *London Magazine*, Hood seems to have contemplated the preparing of an "annual" or other miscellany volume; whether such was ever completed has not yet proved ascertainable. The only reference to it is in the following hitherto unprinted letter from Bernard Barton. The letter is addressed to "Taylor & Hessey, Booksellers, Fleet Street, London," and from that fact it would appear that they were to be the publishers of the projected volume.

"WOODBRIDGE, 11/2nd, 1823.

"RESPECTED FRIENDS.—I have a little piece of eleven nine-line stanzas, to which I hardly know what

The London Magazine (1821—1824).

title to give, and which, from *personal* grounds of hesitation, I have not yet liked to publish myself, or to put among the pieces I am collecting for a third volume. How far its length might be objectionable to your friend Hood I cannot tell; but I feel quite willing he should judge for himself; so if he will do me the favour to let me know when he really wants it, I will send it to him ; or a shorter piece as he may prefer.

" Perhaps he may have no objection to favour me with a line stating the general length of his contributions, as I should be sorry to take up more room than my betters; and when he expects to bring his volume out.—Yours respectfully,

" B. B.

" P.S.—Your correspondent Allan C. surpasses himself this month.

" Lest it should be thought there is anything amiss in the sentiments of the poem I have alluded to I may state it merely pours out some of the feelings which even so humble a Poet as myself cannot suppress at the uncongeniality of task-work at the desk, with his favourite pursuit—but I copy its first and last stanzas, which may suffice as a specimen.

> " Oh ! for some quiet, blest retreat
>   From Traffic's ceaseless toil ;
> From all the din and strife that meet
>   Where Worldlings gather spoil ;
> Oh ! for some calm obscure abode
> Far from Life's hackney'd, crowded road,
>   On some secluded soil ;—
> Where, loosen'd from this busy world,
> My soul could feel her wings unfurled.

> " Yet mourn I not ! My Spirit bows
>   To Him whose will has given
> To do the best our lot allows,
>   And leave that lot to Heaven.

Thomas Hood :

There is an elevating joy
Defeat itself can not destroy,
　In having nobly striven,
And viewing, though the world deride,
The little done with honest pride ! "

A search through the literary announcements of the time and through Taylor & Hessey's advertisements does not help us to the discovery of the work which Hood evidently contemplated.

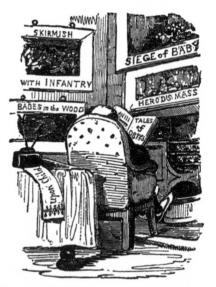

FANCY PORTRAIT—MR. MALTHUS.

CHAPTER VI.

FRIENDSHIPS AND MARRIAGE (1822–1825).

JOHN HAMILTON REYNOLDS, who, as we have seen, was an important contributor to the *London Magazine*, is familiar to all who have followed the story of the life of John Keats. To Reynolds that poet addressed a couple of sonnets and poetical epistles, besides a number of his most characteristic letters. Besides knowing John, Keats established the friendliest relations with the Reynolds family, and among his letters (1817–1820) are many addressed to Mrs. Reynolds, to her eldest daughter, Jane, and her eldest son, John Hamilton. The familiar letters which a man receives are scarcely less important revelations of his character than those that he writes, and if we knew nothing more of the Reynolds family than is revealed to us in Keats's letters it would be clearly a family that it was good to know. To Jane Reynolds the poet subscribed himself as a "brother," and with her sisters as well as with her real brother he was evidently on an affectionate footing.

The father was George H. Reynolds,[1] head writing master at Christ's Hospital, and the children—all of whom were probably born at Shrewsbury—Jane (born November 6, 1794), John Hamilton (born September 9, 1796), Marianne (afterwards Mrs. Green), Eliza (afterwards Mrs. Longmore), and Charlotte (born May 12, 1802, died, unmarried, in 1882). The family lived in Little

---

[1] Died July 29, 1853, at the age of 88.

123

Thomas Hood :

Britain and their pleasant house, presumably attached to Christ's Hospital, was the resort of a circle of friends, several members of which have a lasting interest for us.

Keats left England for the south in the vain search for health in the autumn of 1820 and died at Rome in the following February. There is nothing to show that Thomas Hood made the acquaintance of the Reynoldses before he joined the staff of the *London Magazine* in the summer of 1821, and therefore it is very unlikely that he ever met Keats, though in the *Memorials* young Hood refers to "the talking over of literary matters between my father and Keats." It would be pleasant to know that they had met, for there was much of kinship in their genius, though Keats, who was but four years the elder, had run his course and left us an imperishable body of poetry when Hood, so far as can be ascertained with certainty, had scarcely put pen to paper so far as his living work is concerned. Though we have no means of tracing any acquaintance-ship of Hood with the Reynoldses before the *London Magazine* period, it is quite possible that he might have met them earlier through knowing John Taylor and James Augustus Hessey, for it was Taylor & Hessey who published Keats's poems and Reynolds's "ante-natal Peter," his prophetic skit on Wordsworth's "Peter Bell." Within sixteen months of joining the circle of the "Londoners," Thomas Hood was evidently engaged to Jane Reynolds, and that, as can be shown, with the cordial consent of her family. It has been recorded in the Hood " Memorials " that the Reynolds family opposed the projected marriage, and the statement has been repeated frequently on that authority, but letters to Jane's mother and sister, which I am enabled to publish for the first time, effectually dispose of that tradition. The earliest of these letters, evidently written in the autumn of 1822, was addressed to

124

Friendships and Marriage.

Mrs. Reynolds, who was staying at Upwell, in Norfolk, with her daughter Eliza, the wife of a Dr. Longmore, who had taken a practice in that small village on the Cambridgeshire confines of the county. This letter, which bears eloquent testimony to the way in which the writer had been accepted as one of the family, runs thus :—

" MY DEAR MOTHER, for so I may now call you, with how deep affection do I redeem all that I owe to that blessed name, feeling that I am indeed your son in perfect respect and duty. Only in this can I have deserved to be so dear to you, that you would bestow on me thus willingly an object of so much of your love as our excellent Jane. She is beside me while I pen this, and as I look at her, I know that what I write is a record of one eternal and unchangeable feeling which is to become more and more intense as I approach her great worth. So much the likeness of my wishes,—so worthy of all admiration and affection that I should indeed exceed all others in the measure of my love as she in her virtues is excellent above all. Therefore I have singled her from the world, to be to me its grace and ornament, and its treasure above price, being proud above all things of her favour, and for this once, of my wisdom in this choice. And I desire that you should believe, that it is only for herself that I have loved, and will constantly while this life endures, which she has so blessed, and that in this only I can hold myself at all worthy of her invaluable heart. For I know that there is nothing like it in this world for excellence, and that its affection must of itself be my perfect happiness, whether I live or die, and in this knowledge I look forward with hopeful impatience to the time when I may claim her as mine for ever. And in the meantime I will always remember your exceeding kindness, and rest my everlasting love upon you and yours.

Thomas Hood:

Indeed, I have desired—but could not hope—that my happiness should be nothing but welcome to you, and perfect content,—but you have adopted me into your family in a manner that has made me twice grateful, and before I can forget it—and after—I must be as entirely miserable as I am now otherwise. I could not dream that so many would take me at once to their warm hearts, making me both exult and wonder, but hoped only that I might win such affection hereafter by becoming what you now believe me, and such as your welcome praise will most surely make me. I may thus prove a gratitude, which otherwise will not be expressed but to my own heart, making me distrust all words, and I pray God thus to bless you through me, that I may only be an addition to that happiness which through John has lately visited us. I would not cost a sigh or a tear to any of you, nor a painful thought, so entirely is my love among you, that I would rather die than bring a grief to interfere with your affectionate union with one another. Our good Lizzy, as I have learned to call her, has touched me deeply by her kind words, for I have seen quite enough of her to make me anxious to win her regard, and for this reason I have ever since been most earnest in wishes,—and now drink her birthday health with a brother's affection. I wish Upwell were near Mrs. Butler's,[1] or near anywhere, that I might tell her audibly of this. Do not let her think that Jane, our dear Jane, can make me forget her, for we often mention her among other pleasant matters, such as Lotty, for instance, to whom I am the dear Brother Theodore, that she has so baptized. I will never be otherwise, and would be if I could only a second edition (with alterations) of John, but this is to wish very much indeed, and I know my dear Lotty will so take it. I love Marianne,

[1] Mrs. Butler was, presumably, the mother of Mrs. John Hamilton Reynolds.

Friendships and Marriage.

too, though she is not at Upwell,—indeed, I think I like her rather better because she is not at Kennington. I ought to say much about our other dear Lizzy and John but I write in the midst of distractions.

" Pray forgive me that I have not said this much even at an earlier time—I have longed to write but could not, and feel now how little in this haste I have done justice to my feelings, but I know now that you regard me as what I truly am. God bless you, my dear mother, my dear Lizzy, my dear Lotty, and all that are dear to yo[u], and believe me, one and all, your most affectionate
" THEODO[RE.]"

The letters filled in in brackets have been torn from the original. The reference to " Lizzy and John " is undoubtedly to the recent marriage of Hood's particular friend, who had evidently been married while his mother was away at Upwell.[1] Hood drew up an elaborate and amusing account of the wedding in the form of a parody of the programme of a State procession. The next letter, to Charlotte, was apparently written near the time of the one to her mother just quoted. It is addressed to Upwell, is postmarked October, 1822, and is particularly interesting for the glimpse it affords us of the happy household in Little Britain :—

" MY DEAR LOTTY,—How often have you turned your spiritual eye this way and aimed at us with your mental telescope ? How often has fancy worked us into a piece like a schoolgirl's with double refined cobwebs, till memory came like a great buzzing blue-bottle and tore it into nothings ? How often have you painted Mrs. John Reynolds as faint as water-colours

[1] The " Dictionary of National Biography," in conjecturally dating John Hamilton Reynolds's marriage " at about 1821," is evidently a year out.

Thomas Hood:

thrice drowned and tease your wits to death for the finishing? Surely you must sometimes have felt your mind's eye at work this way in the middle of your forehead like a Cyclops, or as if you had a camera obscura where your brain ought to be. You must have been here, there, and everywhere. Sometimes seeming—in the body—to be playing at draughts with Mr. Longmore or breaking in a grey pony—or tickling the strings of music till it bursts into merry song—or mingling a part of your voice with Eliza's—but in spirit fluttering about like a midge in the sunshine of Little Britain and stealing a tiny taster into the ripe of our happiness. Indeed, your thoughts have been a part of our atmosphere and I have been not unconscious of your presence —using your familar name with all affectionate reverence, and handling the peculiar china with a proper five-fingered fear. For—(I only repeat the family superstition)—the piano has played to me of itself —Jane and Marianne, poor dears, have heard noises —and, above all, Mrs. John R. is said to have felt kisses she knew not wherefrom—but I say, Upwell. I saw her put her hand to her cheek the other evening, and the flies have been long gone. Oh, Lotty, is not she a sweet, kind, unaffected—and didn't John look well!—so merry, and so happy, and so like a fly in a honey-pot, as Rice says—and I'm sure he loves the taste of his wings. And we have been so joyous round him as if he were a common centre of sweets like a sugar cask with all the little loves round it—

"'So many and so many and such glee.'

"You must have been there sometimes. Nor has your good Mother turned the back of her mind upon us altogether. Jane has met her at the cupboard and the carving-knife, and I have seen her in her seat—and doubtless she has been here, not indeed by coach, but

Friendships and Marriage.

drawn by a 'team of little atomies'—to watch our visible enjoyment with invisible eyes. Well Heaven give her some day a good safety coach and horses not given to drink, and we shall see her again—I have such a shake in my hand for her.

"I was quite overjoyed to hear of your safe arrival after the adventurous journey which it proved to be— I shall quite love you if it be only for the perils you have passed, as if of all days in all years you must needs go at the very hour of the opening of the fifty arch bridge at St. Ives, and do for it what the Duke of Wellington did here at Waterloo.[1] I could see that your Mother enjoyed it, putting her so much in mind of the Procession—with that train of people behind her holding themselves up instead of cupids—and then St. Hives and the honeycomb—and that simple Maid of the Inn with her simple congratulation as if you had never opened a bridge before in your lives! It was very pleasant to be sure, and the very affectionate greeting of your head against mine at that sudden jolt when the traces broke,—what a mercy it was not the wheel—and our diverting search after your Mother's glasses among the tangled perplexities of the straw, will long endure in my remembrance, and the more pleasantly as our progress was unattended by any accident to the crowd. That man putting his silly wooden leg like a spoke in our wheel, and that pieman jamming his tarts through the window, made incidents more married to mirth than to misery and if your Mother had been a little less alarmed, the whole would have been extremely amusing.—But what is the use of telling you of what you know, and saw, and heard? I might as well describe Eliza to you or Mr. Longmore and draw a ground plan of Upwell with the water

[1] Waterloo Bridge was opened by the Duke of Wellington in 1817.

Thomas Hood:

before the house, or repeat your own conversation with
the gipsies, telling the story twice over—so stay—and
I will draw you a little picture—as I saw it on Monday
evening in that Blue Beard room of Little Britain,
and so 'tease you out of thought' about us and ours.
You know the place—the folding doors—the tables,
the two windows—the fire-place—the antique china
teapots which if they were hearts, would break themselves for your absence—the sofa—and on it with her
eyes like compressed stars, and her eloquent brows—
but your father will tell you about those—and her
mouth like somebody's you have never seen, and with
her easy grace of manner which Jane will tell you of
—and her smile which herself will show you—sits the
unimaginable reality—the tantalizing mystery—the
still-undiscovered Mrs. Reynolds—Mrs. John—John's
wife—with a great thick misty veil between her and
Upwell—which Jane is trying to fan away with a very
circumstantial sheet of paper—but it won't do—you
must still wish to see her, and then see her to your
wish—as I have done.—Only look at John—what a
talk he makes! With the horns of his mouth upwards
like a fair moon—laughing like a fugleman to let off
our laughters—and lo! that farce brown with the steel
but—and then that—like a footman with—did you ever
see such a—it is impossible to describe it. There—
between me and the teapot—her cheek the very colour
of content, and her eyes how earnest, sits Jane, the
kindly Jane—hugging her own hands for very happiness
—she one side of me—I beside myself—and on the other
hand gentle maid Marianne, making go[od] tea as if
for Robin Hood and smiling as if her heart drank
cream and sugar. How the tea dimples in the cup
and the urn sings for joy! Now if you look through
the urn you will see your father smiling towards the
sofa, and there is Rice smiling towards nine o'clock.

Friendships and Marriage.

How slily the under half of his visage sneers at the upper gravity, as if his nose were Garrick between Tragedy and Comedy, and how his jests come stealing seriously out as if from his sleeve. There is Mrs. Butler with a face that Good Nature might borrow for a year's wear—and there are John Lincoln and William —'my friend,' as it hath been said.—And there in the distance, looking blue as is usual with such objects, is Lotty in the background of Upwell;—peeping perhaps thro' a little opera glass that diminishes us to nothing. This is the picture that I saw on Monday at Little Britain,—with all the drawing-room for its frame—but it will not leave the country and when you come to town therefore you may chance to see it, or one quite as good. So in the meantime comfort yourself at Upwell with your own Eliza,—and remember that happiness hath a home everywhere giving this to that and that to this—we have no poney.

"I ought to tell you that I have been to Kennington where Mrs. Butler grows a great deal of pleasure for the use of her friends, as I found—and indeed I brought mine home with me to keep as a dried flower through the Winter. To-night we all meet at Rice's, and I shall see Mrs. R. for the second time; for which I reserve my intended letter for your good Mother. Pray remember me to her as kindly as you can—and do not let me lose ground in her good graces.—Do say something kind for me to Eliza, that may win her esteem at a jump, and as much elsewhere as may be left to your own generosity. I will redeem it all. And lastly think of me sometimes rather than 'whistle for want of thought' and believe me ever, my dear Lotty, your affectionate Friend,

"THEODORE.

"P.S. [written in pencil]—My pencil desires to be remembered to you and so I have let it speak for itself."

Thomas Hood :

Mrs. Butler of Kennington, John Lincoln, and "my friend" William unfortunately all of them evade identification. We just get this glimpse of them as members of a lively and affectionate circle, and that is all. Rice was the clergyman who was later to officiate at Hood's marriage, and later still to become the headmaster of Christ's Hospital, and as in the July number of the *London Magazine* there appeared Hood's two sonnets "To a Sleeping Child," it may safely be said that they were inspired by the visit to the Rices referred to in this letter. In the manuscript of the sonnets to which I have been able to refer they are entitled, "Sonnets to Mrs. Rice's Little Boy." It must have been shortly before this, though after the poet's engagement to Jane Reynolds, that he made his first essay in this form, for among the Reynolds' papers to which I have had access I found the following, headed "To my dear Marianne, this first Sonnet":—

> " If kindly words could warm th' unkindly air
>   To summer clemency, that there might be
>   A constant atmosphere of love with thee,
> Won by a constancy of tender care,—
> Then thy most delicate cheek should ever wear
>   An exquisite blush, red-ripening to the glee
>   Of cheerful lips ; and my contentment see
> Its wish so recognised and written there :
> So much my bosom clings to thee and feels
>   A painful echo of thy bosom pains ;
> The patient paleness of thy cheek so steals
>   With more than chill of winter to my veins ;
> And conscious sympathy of blood reveals
>   The tender Brother-hood that now obtains !
>   "T. H."

Hood, even as Lamb, was not above punning on his own name. The sonnet further illustrates the fact, abundantly shown in a number of letters, that Thomas Hood in an unusual degree became as one of the family

Friendships and Marriage.

into which he had entered on his engagement to Jane
Reynolds. From the same family papers, too, may be
taken the following amusing fragment in which Hood
has evidently sought to give us through her own lips
something of a sketch of the hospitable, kindly, perhaps
a little fussy, lady—his prospective mother-in-law :—

> " Mary, I believ'd you quick
> But you're as deaf as any beedle ;
> See where you have left the plates,
> You've an eye and so's a needle.
> Why an't Anne behind the door,
> Standing ready with her dishes ?
> No one ever had such maids,
> Always thwarting all my wishes.
> Marianne set up that child,
> And where's her pinafore—call Mary—
> The frock I made her will be spoil'd—
> Now, Lizzy, don't be so contrary,
> Hand round the bread—' Thank God for what ?'
> It's done to rags ! How wrong of Ann now,—
> The dumplings too are hard as lead,
> And plates stone-cold—but that's her plan now—
> Mary, a knock—now, Hood, take that
> Or go without—Why, George, you're wanted,
> Where is that Lottie ? Call her down,
> She knows there's no white wine decanted.
> Put to the door, we always dine
> In public
> Jane take that cover off the greens ;
> Our earthenware they play the deuce to ;
> Here's Mr. Green [1] without a fork—
> And I've no plate—but that I'm used to—"

At the end of July, 1823, Hood went down into
Norfolk to visit the Longmores at Upwell, where Jane
Reynolds was staying, his object being, as he put it, to
pick up a month's health in a fortnight's holiday. In

---

[1] " Mr. [H. G.] Green " married Marianne Reynolds, and
became the father of Charles and Towneley Green, both of whom
won celebrity as artists.

Thomas Hood :

a letter written on August 8 to his sister Betsy, he said
that he had driven fifty miles, "through a most pleasant
country," to Norwich, where Mr. Longmore had been
summoned to the Assizes, and stayed in the city of
churches for four days, attending "A grand Charity
Musical Festival, as fine as an Oratorio," at the
Cathedral, and trying "to find E. G., *alias* Mrs. R.,
but after a long hunt from street to street on the scent,
I came at last to the wrong old Mr. R., who looked
very ill-pleased at being called from his breakfast to a
perfect stranger. I thought it must be his son I wanted,
and told him so. He said he *had* no son, being an old
bachelor. . . . Norwich is a very large place, and E.
does not sit on a steeple, so there was little chance of
finding her without her address."

In the course of this letter, too, Hood mentions that
he has been doing some sketching—"the church for
Mr. L[ongmore],[1] the rectory for ―― ――, and the
house here for Mrs. Reynolds; but if you should be
in Little Britain before I return, be 'mum budget' as
usual on this subject."

There is one mysterious line in this letter on which it
would be pleasant to find light, as it might lead to
a fuller knowledge of the work on which Hood was
engaged at the time that he was contemplating marriage.
"The account of Frankenstein is not mine, but F.'s.
I should have spoken more favourably of it, and Mr.
Peake will take it ill till the matter is explained, that
it is not more kindly treated, for I understand it deserves
no less." While there is presumptive evidence that
Hood took part in the dramatic criticism of the *London
Magazine*, it was in the September number of that
periodical that the notice appeared of Richard Brinsley
Peake's "Presumption, or the Fate of Frankenstein,"

―――――――――
[1] Now in the possession of his son, Mr. W. A. Longmore.

134

Friendships and Marriage.

which had been produced at the English Opera House in July. It looks therefore as though Hood was at this time acting as dramatic critic for some other periodical.

The next letter to Charlotte Reynolds, though undated, evidently belongs to late October or November, 1823, for it was in the former month that Thurtell murdered Weare—a crime which took hold of the popular imagination with peculiar force, and to which the references in contemporary letters and literature are frequent.

"MY DEAR LOTTE,—You say a letter from me will be a charity, and you see I begin it at home. God knows I can sympathise with the dearth of news which must be commonly felt in such a place, and how by this time you must have emptied yourself of talk, and be ready to listen to anyone's letters. The Murder of Mr. Weare must have been a godsend to you;—it kept us a week in conversation, and a hungry person might have lived a day upon our crumbs,—but with you I doubt not it hath been chewed twice over like the Abyssinian sweetmeats. By-the-by, is it thought in your parts that Hunt was personally assistant and abetting in the murder? It is current here, that he stood on the left hand side of the Horse,—with his right hand holding the bridle, within two inches of the bitt that he might not start,—and humming the second part of Hummel's Fanchon, with Cramer's Variations. He was a public singer, you know,—and fond of *humming* as appears in his evidence.

"Talking of murder—we have been much amused by hearing of Mr. Rawngely's falling in love,—and long to know the assassin. He has long looked 'pale with passion'—or bleached white with bleedings, like the animal you wot of, to make his flesh delicate. Oh the she-Shylock! I have seen Mr. Green but once,—it was

Thomas Hood :

a cold day,—and made him look blue and numb ; but you must miss him at Upwell,—for I should think that you would miss the buzz of a fly if it left your Parish.—When I was there I heard the flowers grow—there was so little stirring. If it was not for the noise of Cambridge, half-way, I should think you could listen to us in Little Britain.—But you will have Taylor & Hessey's Magazine to speak for all London, and I envy you, for in your dull parts it must read lively !

" How you must have envied us the debut of Mr. Daniel !—or indeed the first appearance of Mr. Any-one with a new face. Change, in your neighbourhood must be scarce and at a premium—only nineteen shillings and sixpence to the sovereign. You must tire of Mr. Terry's eternal white hat,—and the muddy sluggishness of the river—A barge must be an incident in your lives,—and a fired chimney like a comet in your Calendar. Pray,—last Sunday, exactly at 5 P.M., did you observe a cloud—52″ 20° North and very like a Whale.—It passed directly over my house and disappeared in the horizon.—You must have seen it for it was in broad daylight.—I really wonder what you do (when the Child is asleep) for by this time you must have dissected us all, your friends here, into atoms.—Do you read ?—I have been skimming Boxiana and think you would like it for there are three thick volumes with plates.—Or do you sleep after dinner ? or walk ? I will send you a herbal to help you in your botany. You will find the study very amusing as well as endless ;—and by help of a magnifier—taking care to have one strong enough,—may discover eternal new wonders.— I have heard that the Mosses are more than a man's life would suffice to reckon—and then when they are severally examined, that they will take as much longer to describe.—I am sure I shall be obliged to you for the account of them :—or of any other studies by which you

136

Friendships and Marriage.

may think proper to fill up your leisure. I doubt not you bestow much time and attention on that sweet child your sister's,—and I hope she will prettily show the fruits of such vigilant and indefatigable instruction. —Her Grandma has favoured me with many interesting particulars of her bearing and conduct;—and I feel much pleasure in sending her a little present, whilst she is so unconscious as she must be of the giver to show that my love is quite disinterested, and looks for no return. Pray teach her to carry it in a genteel and ladylike manner,—like her mother—or it may not be amiss to remind her of the carriage of her aunt in London,— Miss Marianne Reynolds, mind and call her Miss Marianne, as it will give the little dear a feeling of her own importance, and say that she—her Aunt Marianne —never soils the pretty pink lining by thrusting into it mutton bones or whatever else she may happen to hold in her ivory fingers.—Pray also give her a kiss for me— but wipe her mouth first—though her mother will call me over nice for it—and then give her the muff—calling it pitty-pitty, or puss-puss, or some other such words adapted to her comprehension, or tickling her little nose with it or bopeeping her eyes,—or creep-mouse, creeping it as your own judgment shall think most expedient.—But I am growing Nurselike!—besides instructing you in your own business.—So, farewell, do not forget my love to Eliza,—and a thousand kind things which I would sooner write to her myself than by commission if my time were not so short. She shall say what she likes for me to G[eorge] and I shall still have to spare for yourself.—Accept then, my dear Lot, my most brotherly love, and believe me in serious and sincere earnest, Your affectionate,

" T. H.

" P.S.—Marianne and Jane have new Bonnets, but I do not know how they fit."

Thomas Hood :

Another of these bright and amusing letters to Charlotte Reynolds which is undated, seems to belong to December of the same year; in it Hood narrates at considerable length a small social adventure which befell him, and shows himself ready to spare no pains as letter writer to please his correspondent. They must have been leisurely days in which a man who was living by his pen could indulge in letter writing at such length. To-day the spirit of gossip by correspondence is a rare thing, our authors having learned to calculate that in the new literary multiplication table one thousand words equals so many guineas, according to the popularity of the pen-driver. This letter is dated from " Islington, Lower Street, Sunday Morning."

"MY DEAR LOTTE,—Once more I write to you out of pity—for I know that the very sight of a letter must make you move your ears like Baby's rabbit,—or as Mr. Darley doth, I have observed, in little twitches before he speaks. But those who listen to him feel as if theirs were turning inside out with impatience—which I hope is not your case with me for I could never hope to fill the double drums of your female curiosity. You must gaze your fill, therefore upon Jane's or Marianne's letters before you venture upon mine; though I do suppose that in your parts, the least scrap is a godsend, and that you lick every word off the butter papers. It must be a comfort to you then to know that here we have Marianne Longmore,[1] and have seen Brides and Brides' groom by pairs, but I will not meddle with these matters. Jane and Marianne will describe their dresses and trimmings to a nicety, with endless quotations, as it were of Mr. Harvey's shop bills,—and I do not expect till you have read these letters twice over

---

[1] Mary Anne Sophia Longmore, only sister of George Longmore. She died unmarried in 1838.

138

Friendships and Marriage.

that you will turn your blue eyes upon mine. Heaven,
however, has kindly blown up something like an incident
for your amusement,—and according to your desire to
draw all the particulars of so extraordinary an occurrence
(as Browne the novelist [1] would begin) tho' indeed you
have expressed no such desire—I commence my Narrative. It was on Wednesday, the 16 inst., at ½ past 6 P.M.,
squally with rain, that I set off for a dance at Hackney,
with my sister and two others—(your sisters were no
party to my party so have this slice of news to myself)
—but the wind was so high that whether we *sailed* or
rode thither I have some doubts.—If it had been a boat
I should have thought we rowed ; but it was in a coach
—Number 1776.—There was a large party when we
arrived—I think it was said there were 16 or 18 ladies
arrived, and the entertainment was given by the *single*
unmarried daughter of Mr. and Mrs. Gouldsmith—
late our neighbours of Islington. She is a young girl
of a very solemn aspect,—giving the lie to the proverb
about old heads and young shoulders—and of a very
pious turn, and when she complains of the most winding
and melancholy voice possible. Then we all had tea
and coffee in the back parlour—I could send you a cut
of the house and grounds like Probert's but for want
of time ;—yet suffice it that there are two large rooms
communicating by folding doors, and both entered
from a large Hall on the left.—I sat in the back room
close to the garden window,—with my feet in the fourth
position—talking of I know not what to a young lady
with very lobster-like eyes.—I only remember that she
said, with a flirt of her fan, that she liked ' the simplicity
of the country,' and I thought of you when she said it.
In the meantime the gale roared without and the

[1] Charles Brockden Brown (1771—1810), American novelist;
author of " Edgar Huntley, or the Memoirs of a Sleepwalker," to
which Hood refers at the close of his poem, " The Fall."

Thomas Hood :

gentlemen came dropping in like windfalls.—And I remember remarking—the only remark I made aloud—that the hurricane without made a most pleasant contrast to the comforts within,—for the wind was making a sort of Pan's pipes of our stack of chimneys, and played such an air in a little ante-chamber behind the hall,—where all the fruit and custards, &c., were laid out, that the grate would hold no fire within its bars. —And now a game of bagatelle was proposed, before dancing,—and all the company adjourned to the front room, except myself, who took that opportunity of examining a picture which hung in the extreme corner. It represented a group in a hayfield during a storm, —watching the sky, as it seemed, in awful expectation of a thunderbolt. When just then, at that very moment,—in the silent pause, just on the eve of the bagatelle,—I heard a most tremendous fall overhead—right on the ceiling—as if a lady in practising her steps upstairs,—some dowager—only as loud as twenty dowagers, had tripped and fallen.—But it was not as I thought a lady, but a whole stack of chimneys that had tumbled—beating through the roof and stamping on the first floor like the very giant of the castle of Otranto. The explosion was tremendous;—and might aptly be compared, yes, most aptly—for this *was* to have been a Ball—to the first awful cannon-shot at Brussells!

> " '—Hackney had gather'd then
> Her beauty and her chivalry all bright,
> And there were well-dressed women and brave men,'

but now—at a blow—the glory of the Ball was demolished for ever!—I looked through the folding doors, and it was like a glimpse of L. fill'd with smoke and darkness palpable, and in the midst moved shapes of Men and Ladies;—demons and soil'd angels,—whilst

140

Friendships and Marriage.

the huge grate continually spit forth its flames in fiery tongues towards the infernal centre. And the soot whirled round and round with the wind and the smoke, like black bandalores,[1]—so that some fled into 'the wide gusty Hall';—and others stopped not until they had reached the forecourt or garden,—where they stood, shaking and blowing out of all shape. Among these I found my sister, planted in the mid-walk, with a white pocket handkerchief pulled round her white face!— 'each lent to each a double charm'—and waiting as if for a tile from above. Then I pulled her into the Hall, and looked round me on the grimly company.—O, how Beauty (if any beauty *was* there) was soil'd and dimmed! What lustres were quenched! What silks were tarnished! What fair faces were *rawncely'd* by filthy smoke and soot!—It was like a May day in high life! —The rich Sweep's Jubilee!—or a revel among the blacks!—Only there was no 'white lass' for Black Man to kiss;—they were all Wowskis.—I looked for the lady with lobster-eyes, whom I had conversed with, but she was run away out of the House, and like De Quincey's Ann—with all my search I could never find her again. I spoke to another, but she only stared and could make no answer, and then the Lady of the Mansion came to me, with her hands flapping up and down with wonder and fright, and asked me which way the wind blew.— Then came a little old Lady from over the way, to offer beds for the family but in reality to slack the quicklime of her own curiosity,—and then came an old gentleman, hastily fetched over by one of the daughters who thought he was a surveyor,—but he turned out to be an old Stockbroker. This is he who would not come,—tho' the young woman said that her ma was dying of terror—till

[1] The bandalore was a toy containing a coiled spring, which caused it, when thrown down, to rise again to the hand by the winding of the string by which it was held.

he had put on his best gaiters. Of course he was of no
service, so he went off with as many of us as lived near,
but some were forced to wait for their coaches. Thus
we stood all about, and for some of the ladies we wiped
chairs—in that little back room you wot of—behind
which perchance we stood like Pompey or Mungo, and
served them with wine and tarts.—I only, owing to my
fortunate station at the time of the fall, showed off
amongst these grimed Othellos like—forgive the comparison—like a swan amongst ravens.—I believe they
would have been glad to smut me out of envy and spite.
—I asked one, a Frenchman, how long he had been
from Africa, but he mistook my drift, and replied he
was not from Africa, but the United States.—Another,
unmannerly, had stood between the ladies and the fire,
and the spurting flames had singed his [   ] pantaloons
to a nice crisp brown ;—but the object of all objects
was the young lady our invitress—who with mingled
soot and disappointment, looked blacker than black,
and in a crow's voice croaked a thousand regrets for
this uncomfortable entertainment.—Then she rated her
brother for stuffing at the tarts and custards when he
might be dusting the chairs, or blowing the soot off the
pictures.—As for the relics of us—the guests—we were
invited to the next house—a Madhouse—till our coaches
came for us, and thither we went, and were formally
introduced [   ] to the Family. We were quite
strangers to each other—but to be sure had we *been*
Friends they could scarcely have known us—and here
we were provided with houseroom, coal and candle
and young ladies till ½ past 11. They did not offer us
any refreshment however,—thinking perhaps that we
had brought our own *grub*—and might sup off each
others faces—but for the rest we were very comfortable, and I met with amusement enough for another
chapter.

Friendships and Marriage.

" II.

" Of the People at the Madhouse : their " Appearance and Behaviour.

" On entering the Madhouse, we were ushered into a very handsome large room, with a fine blazing fire, that seemed to crackle and enjoy its safe and sound chimney. Indeed the fall of ours seemed to have cleared up the weather, which had settled into a fine moonlight ; nevertheless we all sat at a respectful distance from the fireplace, protesting we were not cold, and the corners were occupied by the family. The Lady of the House was a goodly well-grown dame, I guess Welsh,—and opposite to her sat two daughters who took after their mother in size—and might have visited the great Cattle show at Sadler's without any very humiliating sense of their own insignificance. They kept all their conversation in the family, so that I cannot speak of them beyond their looks, but I should take them to be young and good tempered—the first because they had very girlish faces, with sleek combed braided hair, and altogether rather a bread and butter look, and the last because they seemed to thrive so well on their victuals. The father was a very respectable kind of man but rather homely betwixt his nose and chin, and there were three Brothers, one tall, nothing uncommon in appearance except that he wore spectacles, the other ditto except the spectacles, and the third—but of him more anon. We—the Accidentals—were five in number,—myself, two ladies, their brother, the gentleman of the scorched pantaloons— and the Frenchman. The latter—I should tell you— had suffered most in complexion and sat with his grim black face, in most agreeable relief, between the two white busts of Paris, and Canova's Venus, which stood upon the chiffoniéres. He addressed most of his

Thomas Hood :

animated discourse to the mother, and she received it with a most polite and inflexible gravity, in spite of all the smoky workings of his face and fingers, by which he illustrated his meaning. But the consciousness of her stiff crisp immaculate double and triple frills and smooth white-kidlike face, by the side of his dingy flesh and cravat might account for some part of her complacency.—I sat silently watching them, till I believe the Father, thinking I wanted some amusement, sends his youngest son, who anchor'd himself in a seat beside me and began to pour in a regular [flood] of talk, great and small—he had been a sailor and the climate had tanned his face into a mahogany brown which advantageously set off his curly flax-coloured hair. He had too, a strange crooked upper lip to his mouth that twisted and worked whenever he spoke enough to turn all his letters to an S. Of his discourse as well as I can, I will give you a sample. He began with his last voyage to Jamaica. The captain was a Scotchman and pinched his crew very much,—hoped I was not a Scotchman, he was a Welshman. That gentleman opposite (the Frenchman) was talking of Deal boats, so he described the Deal boats. He had been in the Downs in a storm—very bad anchorage in a storm—and the ship ran down another with a cargo of ivory on board, but they had a freight of timber, but the crew of the ivory ship were all ashore but two—what a providence it was.—How should I climb up a mast? Really I could not tell. Why, when he tried, he endeavoured to get up the pole, but it was greased and he slipped down again— you should lay hold of the two backstays and *warp* yourself up, hand over hand. Begged I would excuse his nautical phrases and then explained what a hobbe-de-hoy was. Really *those* black girls (not our ladies) but the negresses in Jamaica, were very humane, he had

Friendships and Marriage.

a deep cut once in his ankle and they healed it. Did I ever wake at a thunderstorm? No; or very seldom. No more should he if it was not for that fellow (pointing to the manservant who came in with coals) who waked him always and said, 'See, sir, what beautiful lightning.' Did I ever see a dolphin? but he forgot they were not by law allowed to be brought into England. What did I think Bill would do for (pointing to his Brother)? I guessed a Doctor—from the spectacles.—No, he was to be a parson. Dick, pointing to the other was a painter and poet, and played on the flute and keyed bugle—and in this very candid ingenuous way he ran on till we parted when he shook my hand and bid God bless me and I parted from one of the most amusing openhearted little Boy-men that ever twaddled about ships and canvas. There! feast upon him in your fancy. I am sure such a mere shadow of a young Tar as I have given you must be a comfort in your country. I wished I could have packed him up and sent him to you per Canal. He would out-talk Mrs. H.!—and make you quite enjoy the Barges.

"We have had Mr. Green here with three of your ribbons in his hat, beating up for recruits to go abroad with him to Upwell—but he can get no one to take your shilling. I have however volunteered some riddles for Mr. Hardwicke which you shall receive per first opportunity, and my next letter will be to Eliza; provided she will from this sample condescend to take it in. If she pleases I will pay the postage. I could write a deal of nursy-pursy for Baby, but I will not take it out of your mouth. I am quite delighted with the accounts I hear of her mimicry—and count her already as clever as Clara Fisher—but as she imitates it behoves you who are so much with her to be very guarded in your own conduct—that she may profit by her pattern. I own I should be sorry to see her, on being paid a compliment by a young gentleman, sidle off, and hold down her head, and shake it, like a poney about to *shy*—or when she begins to talk, to hear her fumbling and poking out her explanations, like broken corks picked piecemeal out of the necks of bottles ;—a comparison which to be candid, I have known to be inspired by yourself. I know you will not be offended at my telling you of all your little faults, since I do it only for that dear child's benefit ;—and I shall not have room in this letter or I would tell you of all the rest which I have observed in you with the affectionate vigilance of a Friend. I would also favour you with a few of her Mother's—if I could just now remember what they were—but I abstain lest they should seem easier invented than recalled. I merely suspect in the meantime that that dirty little trick Miss has, of poking her mutton bones into other people's eyes, must have been learnt of her mother for I do not recollect that you had any such practice when I have sat with you at dinner. If such be the case however much it may divert and entertain you for the present, and tend to her Father's amusement yet I cannot but consider her talent for imitation rather as a *bane* (the Scotch for bone) than as a blessing to her, if it is to lead to such consequences. But I will not school you in your own duty and province—only I must send a kiss thro' you to your little charge—and I wish it were a bullet for your sake. Do give a little hug to her then for my sake, and kiss her mouth—so pretty and little as Rowland Prince says of *his* child 'that it might be covered with a six-pence.' But give her a shilling kiss ! Her aunts have sent her some toys. I did not think she would take to the rabbit ; but perhaps by rubbing it over with a little parsley and butter at the beginning she may be tempted to ~~liek~~ (like) it.—Do, do take care that she doesn't get

Friendships and Marriage.

the ninepins under her little feet and so fall, in which caution I have got the start of her grandmother. I went with Jane for the toys—and our purchases were, oddly enough, as follows,—*Pins* for Baby, *Pegs* for Ma, and *stumps* for Marianne! Can you club together such another set of commissions? I have no news but that I am learning quad——

*　　*　　*　　*　　*

"A parcel-knock at the door and a general skuttle! —Your letter is come, and I have got thus far,—so you must give me credit for writing all in advance of this without being *coaxed*. But I am grieved to hear that our good Eliza is unwell; if anything I could wish would cure her it is entirely hers. I believe I like her better and better, as Baby grows—and you may tell her so for me, and very sincerely. I hope I do not need Jane's or Marianne's affidavits to confirm this assurance, and so venture to offer my simple love to her, and pray present it in your kindest manner. I need but to mention George for I know she will box your ears or mine for forgetting him but as I am out of reach of her gent[le hands] he will receive my remembrances as from reg[ard] more than fear. And now, dear Lotte, accept [my] own love and this long letter in token of my des[ire to] please you, but do not presume upon it, or [presume] upon me by sending up all Mr. Hardwicke's notes [   ] for you. Such a wish is not expressed,—but [I have] guessed it. God bless you. Your affectionate brother,

"Thos. Hood.

" P.S.—*Have the goodness to turn over a new leaf!*"

The postscript is of course but a bantering way of putting the familiar invitation of " please turn over."

Thomas Hood :

"I had nigh forgot to wish a 'Merrie Christmas' to you all my dear good Masters and Mistresses and also the Young Lady from London. So in the name of the Bellman, 'God bless your House and all the wery worthy people as is in it.'—Have you heard the Bellman yet, and what time do your Waits play at Upwell? I do suppose by this, that little Miss has ate up all the plumbs from your pudding. A little dear, to seem to know so naturally what Xmas means!

"So you have been to hear the new Bells for the sake of their tongues. Did you make any conquests among the Triple Bob Majors!"

In the spring of 1824 we have a first account of illness to which Hood was frequently a victim, though his almost indomitable good spirits were such that even out of ill health he could wrest something of amusement. He was still living at Lower Street, Islington, with his sisters, and we have a hint of the suburban character of that now overbuilt neighbourhood in the references which are made to the garden in which he was able to work when convalescent, and the flowers which were being grown there, including roses from Upwell. The next letter to Charlotte is dated March 30, and with it is a fragment of a letter to Jane, evidently torn off by the recipient and sent to her sister for the sake of the riddles on one side of it, evidently those first referred to in the preceding letter. On the other side we have this sole scrap of the letters written by the poet to his future wife during the time of their engagement.

"I always fancy [   ] when I think you will be reading my letters, and shall look over you on Sunday. How delightful it is to please you, dear. I am quite happy to think that I shall fulfil your wish, and would exceed it if I could. It is enough to pay me to know

148

Friendships and Marriage.

that you take delight in my letters, it makes me so proud and so happy, that I can never write enough. There is nothing in the world so dear to me as your pleasure, and that you look for it, and acknowledge it at my hands. My Doctor is just gone and as usual we have had a long literary chat. He says I must expect to feel such days as this—and not to gain much strength till I get out of this room—and he has given me leave to go down the first fine day—I have hopes, after so much rain, that it will happen to-morrow. He says part of what I feel is from the confinement; and want of exercise, and indeed I seem to ache and get cramped with so much sitting. Well is it said—I translate from the Latin—of the poor statue

" ' He sits, and eternally will sit, *unhappy* Theseus.'

" My Doctor's call has been quite a comfort to me,—a little chat is a windfall! You will share in this I know, dear—and wish that you could multiply my visitors. I keep an eye hard fixed on May,—and remember my promise. Think of me then, dear, cheerfully, and let us dream away the interval of each other. I know when that blessed hour comes, with the delight of clasping you again to my heart, I shall think that the pain of separation is all atoned for and that you will try to make me all possible amends for an increased affection if greater can be."

On the other side of this portion of a letter are the jests to which the scrap of paper evidently owes the fact of its preservation.

" I must now put my riddles here—and will find other snug little corners for my kindnesses. Some of them are new.—Mr. Hardwicke must really give you another bunch of vilets when you give them to him—

149

Thomas Hood :

" Why is a farmer like a fowl?—Because he likes a
full crop. Spell a large bird in two letters.—P. N.
Why is a man who hangs himself like a porter?—
Because he finds life a burthen and takes a knot to it.
Why is the wind like fashion?—Because it regulates
the *vane*. Why is the cow a finer animal than a horse?
—Because a horse is a courser. Why is a towel like a
snake?—Because it is a *wiper*. Why are horses like
sentimentalists?—Because they like to indulge in *wo*.
Why does good wine resemble the game of draughts?
—Because an extra draught makes a common man a
king. What is the rudest kind of diction?—Contra-
diction. Why are icicles like listeners?—Because they
are eavesdroppers. Why is a hatter the most respectable of tradesmen?—Because he serves the heads of the
nation. What Judges are all of a bigness?—The
Judges of Assize. Why are rabbits like electors?—
Because they live in *burrows*. Why are fishwomen like
Dr. Faustus?—Because they sell their soles. Why is
a Bow Street officer when heated like a bean?—Because
he's a scarlet runner. Why should secret drops of
sorrow be shed in the sea?—Because that's the place
for private-tears. Why are the children of the Chinese
capital like sickly children?—Because they're Pekin
ones. Why is the sky when the sun's coming out like
the King on his road to the Pavillion?—Because it's
going to *brighten*. There, this fold just embraces
them all."

Presumably the next letter of the series addressed to
Charlotte Reynolds was written immediately after the
one to her sister. It is dated from Lower Street,
Islington, and is postmarked March 30, 1824.

" My dear Lotte,—I have been obliged to make a
long pause in our correspondence and that, too, when
I was your debtor for a very kind and sister-like letter

Friendships and Marriage.

—but I have the good bad excuse of having been ill and you know one cannot write from the inspiration of slops and gruel.—You must look upon this letter then as a bulletin of my recovery,—and it is a pleasure after the restlessness and delirium of a fever to turn my thoughts to you and Upwell,—your fresh budding trees, and cool clear air,—and your crystal canal.—I have had a little relish of such enjoyments to-day—for I have just come out of my garden, and have watched for a change a few tiny clusters of crocus, and my lilies just pushing forth from the mould, tender and red, like vegetable chilblains.   Mr. Hardwicke's seeds make quite a show—or at least the labels,—promising in some instances I know not what for the coming summer,— and the Upwell roses, I am glad to say, are all alive and growing—I hope you will perceive something of the fresh air I have been breathing in this letter,—for it gives a spring to the heart, and makes one twice pleased with everything, which, as I am reading your letter over again, makes it a great enjoyment indeed. —How little cause had you to fear writing to me when you could do justice by your expression, to so much kindness as just then prompted you to overcome that fear of my criticism.   Indeed it was a very pretty letter, earnestly affectionate and unaffected as a country born epistle ought to be—there—I think now you will write to me again ; at least once ! before you come hither, and sadden all the echoes of Upwell.

" Talking of talking—I have indeed been very much delighted with the accounts you have given of the little tricks of Lizzie (Jane says you are her Boswell) and above all with that which described her as coming by your desire to have ' a little chat.'   It was so character-istic.   We all cried ' That is so like Lot ! '—Look here's a *cut* for you.   I call it ' Bid me discourse ! '

[Here comes a rough pen and ink sketch of a lady

Thomas Hood :

and a child seated, with a toy rabbit behind the child's chair.]

"Pray observe how the rabbit pricks up its ears! I am afraid Eliza will not acknowledge her own as I have drawn her—but it is impossible to satisfy a Mother's eye—or even a grandmother's—I leave likenesses to Marianne.

"And now, what next—

"'You have not the book of riddles about you, have you?' No, but reading this enquiry of Slender's in the 'Merry Wives of Windsor' I remembered Mr. Hardwicke, and have given Jane a list of such riddles as I could muster—and if you keep the answers to yourself you may retaliate upon him the puzzlings he has cost you. If any others should occur to me I will send them, but just now I feel very little inclination to tease my brains with such entanglements.—I have found out I believe most of his conundrums on the flow'rs, but there are some still obstinate against solutions.—I am afraid the Sphinx had a hand in them. Perhaps I am dull,—indeed, in one sense I am,—for the time that I spend at home I wish I could spend like a dormouse by sleeping it over. I have so little change and the worst of company—my own. I am almost too impatient and fidgetty to write or read, and have learnt to know all the hours of the day by the street cries.—Those evening bells, the muffin bells are just beginning to ring—and remind me that I have not been able to hear Mr. James Green. I verily believe that my dear Jane's kind visits have kept me alive—by rescuing me from those most tedious letters of the alphabet N U E—(that will make a pozer for Mr. Hardwicke)—Marianne too has been to see me and your mother!—and your father several times,—and both of the Greens—but then the dismal intervals—but I forget—you can no doubt get 'The Diary of an Invalid' at the Wisbeach Circulating

Friendships and Marriage.

Library. I ought not to complain now, for I can get out—by coach—and spent yesterday in Little Britain— I should tell you that in spite of the wearisome sense of restraint and confinement I have read through the Simple Story with an unimpaired interest, and it was the only real pleasure of reading I have enjoyed.—Don't you think Miss Woodley is very like Miss Good? I thought so all the while I was reading it. Miss Fenton is Miss Butler—and the Mistress Hortons are as 'plenty as blackberries'—when they are sour. Don't you respect Mr. Sandford, he is such a monitor? I wish you knew him. Do you think Donif[. . . .] most like [. . . .]erry, or Mr. Townley?

"What does [Mrs. Hard]wicke think of the last [? volume of] St. Ronan's W[ell?] We call it very dry—but in your country that may s[eem] no fault. Do you think she has ever read Herwald de Wake? It is very sleepy. Your good mother, by the way, has turned authoress, and has written a long poem in Miss Acton's album. Her Advice to a Mother by a Grand-mother, has reached a fourth edition, and Longmans are in treaty for the copyright. You know I always thought she wrote it. She asked your father some weeks ago for some blank copy books, and it turns out that she has just completed the Child's First Book,— of course with a reference to little Eliza.—I have mustered, for Eliza, as many as I could of the *Lady's Museum*, to amuse her, when you leave her,—but I am afraid that you have talked at the rate of more than a number a month. Why, it would kill you to publish only twelve times a year. She should have kept G.'s Encyclopædia to go through when you are gone. Poor thing. The moss will grow in her ears! I will write to her out of pity. However, I am almost glad I shall not have to write to you again, which I cannot help doing. I shall be glad to see you;—I understand you are to come the end of March,—or the beginning of Wisbeach—but do not make it late. We cannot do without you on the 1st of April.—We shall have much to say to each other on that day. Wish I *could* fetch you, for it were worth two Jews' eyes to see our good Eliza—large and small—or if you please the diamond edition—and I should like to tell G. how J. Green abused Norwich. I wonder if Mr. Lemon is alive yet? Pray kiss Baby for me again and again; I wish she were here; can't you steal her, with your black hair and eyes and berry face you might pass for a gipsey, or why can't her mother pawn her and send us the Duplicate, or why wasn't she a Twin for her grandmother to cry halves!—but as she is one and indivisible, I suppose it would ossify G.'s pericardium to part with her. Pray tell Eliza to tell her not to spoil her father, —and pray—for I feel like getting up into a corner like Randall against the ropes—pray give my love to them right and left, as hard as you can put it, and believe me, dear Lotte, in very haste.—Your most affectionate brother, "THOS. HOOD."

In the summer of this year his health-seeking holiday was passed at Hastings, as we learn from a letter addressed to him at that pleasant Sussex resort by Charles Lamb. The letter has often been printed, yet deserves to find a place in the life-story of Thomas Hood as serving to show how the acquaintanceship, begun two years earlier, had ripened into friendship. Elia could not have written such a letter to any but one with whom he was on a footing of cordial intimacy. The letter, which Mr. E. V. Lucas, in his " Letters of Charles and Mary Lamb," considers possibly incomplete, is post-marked August 10, 1824, and begins abruptly—

"And what dost thou at the Priory? *Cucullus non facit Monachum.* English me that, and challenge old

Friendships and Marriage.

Lignum Janua to make a better. My old New River has presented no extraordinary novelties lately; but there Hope sits every day, speculating upon traditionary gudgeons. I think she has taken the fisheries. I now know the reason why our forefathers were denominated East and West Angles. Yet is there no lack of spawn; for I wash my hand in fishets that come through the pump every morning thick as motelings.—little things o o o like *that*, that perish untimely and never taste the brook. You do not tell me of those romantic land bays that be as thou goest to Lover's Seat: neither of that little churchling in the midst of a wood (in the opposite direction, nine furlongs from the town), that seems dropped by the Angel that was tired of carrying two packages; marry, with the other he made shift to pick his flight to Loretto. Inquire out and see my little Protestant Loretto. It stands apart from trace of human habitation; yet hath it pulpit, reading-desk, and trim front of massiest marble, as if Robinson Crusoe had reared it to soothe himself with old church-going images. I forget its Christian name, and what she-saint was its gossip.

" You should go also to No. 13, Stangate Street,—a baker, who has the finest collection of marine monsters in ten sea counties,—sea dragons, polypi, mer-people, most fantastic. You have only to name the old gentleman in black (not the Devil) that lodged with him a week (he'll remember) last July, and he will show courtesy. He is by far the foremost of the savans. His wife is the funniest thwarting little animal. They are decidedly the Lions of green Hastings. Well, I have made an end of my say. My epistolary time is gone by when I could have scribbled as long (I will not say as agreeable) as thine was to both of us. I am dwindled to notes and letterets. But, in good earnest, I shall be most happy to hail thy return to the waters of Old Sir

Thomas Hood :

Hugh. There is nothing like inland murmurs, fresh ripples, and our native minnows.

> " ' He sang in meads how sweet the brooklets ran,
>   To the rough ocean and red restless sands.'

I design to give up smoking; but I have not yet fixed upon the equivalent vice. I must have *quid pro quo,* or *pro quo quid,* as Tom Woodgate would correct me. My service to him.

" C. L."

This letter reached Hood apparently when he was leaving Hastings, too late for him to " hunt the ' Lions.' " It would be pleasant to recover the long letter to which it was an Elian reply ; further reference will be made to it when we come to Hood's next visit to Hastings. Tom Woodgate—" Old Lignum Janua "—was a Hastings boatman, to whom both Hood and Lamb seem to have become attached. In the writings of the former he is several times referred to, and some special " stanzas " were addressed to him five years later.

The next recoverable letter was written shortly after Hood's return to London after his brief holiday, probably about the end of August, while Mrs. Reynolds and Charlotte were both at Upwell. It is the last of the series which had been kept by Charlotte, and is further evidence of those very cordial relations of Hood with the family into which he was about to marry to which the first of the series bore no less eloquent testimony.

" MY DEAR MOTHER,—If I had not another line in the world I must write to congratulate you upon so interesting an event as your being made a Grandmother.[1]

[1] George Moody Longmore, the second child and eldest son of George Longmore and Eliza Reynolds, was born at Upwell on August 22, 1824. He died unmarried at Sydney, N.S.W.

MRS. HOOD.

From the Painting in the National Portrait Gallery

[*To face p.* 156.

Friendships and Marriage.

Indeed, I feel Uncle already for if I do not I have not another sister in the world who is married enough to make me one, and besides my dear Jane, looks already as if a sluggard might go to her, as Solomon says, 'and consider her ways and be wise'—not but that in this respect she seems to have had a nephew for ears. I wish I were within fourteen lines of him, and he should have a sonnet for certain,—but if I were now to begin,

> " ' Thy father's eyes, thy mother's lips '

and it should not be like him, I fear he would never grow into his Portrait. I once sowed Marry Golds in my garden and they came up Larkspurs.

" Nevertheless if ' our good Lizzy ' desire it, I will strive to label the sweet son-flower—but at present his god-Father Apollo—(which is only another name for the sun)—will not inspire me, and moreover, somebody is so pressing for her package that, without haste I shall not parcel of it.—Good-bye,—and the hearty blessings of the Gods ' be with you, over you, and round about you,' making your lives longer than this letter, and far happier than the wit of it ; or as a better blessing, Heaven make you all Grand Mothers—but not now —so that I may often wish you joy of nephews or nieces, as it may happen to be.

" Pray accept my love, which is large enough for a longer letter if time allowed me, and believe me how truly, my dear Mother, I am yours, and dear Lizzy's and dear Lotty's, affectionate Son and Brother,

" THEODORE."

" P.S.—We desire our kind thanks to Lotty for her Flour, which were very sweet Smeling and odious ; as if she had picked the Best of them if not all with her one hand. The Roses came safe and went to bits for Joy of it, but we have kept the remains of them to make Essence of Lavender with to wash one's lining in—but I must shut up, for the Porter has got the Box on his ear and we have only time to call after him, our loves to the little boy,—for he won't stop for the kiss as he has not brought his knot with him.—If I had thought of it—hollo !—Here ! we shall drink all your Honourses healths, upon mine, that we shall—to the House of Longmore, root and branch, and there's half-a-pint of small Beer for little Master's Health, till he gets stronger.

" Pray do not forget to express my love to Mr. Longmore and Lizzy and—but I have done it before."

At the foot this letter has the following jumbled up direction, " G. Upwell, Esqre., care of Mrs. Reynolds, Longmore, Norfolk."

It was in February, 1825, that the volume of " Odes and Addresses to Great People " was published—to which we shall refer more fully in the next chapter—and three months later, on Thursday, May 5, 1825, Thomas Hood and Jane Reynolds were married by licence at St. Botolph's, Aldersgate. Hood was described as a bachelor, " of the parish of St. Mary, Islington." The service was conducted by Edward Rice, and the signing witnesses were the bride's father, George Reynolds, John Hamilton Reynolds, James Rice, junior, and Charlotte Reynolds. An error of a year in the date of Hood's birth was long repeated in many works of reference, and the same antedating of his marriage by a year has been continued, and is still frequently done, ever since the error was given in the " Memorials." It is a curiously persistent error, despite the fact that the actual entry of the marriage in St. Botolph's register was made known some years ago. But even apart from that entry the matter stood recorded in the number

Friendships and Marriage.

of the *London Magazine* for June, 1825, where, under
the marriages of the preceding month, is given :—

" May 5th, at St. Botolph's, Aldersgate, Thomas Hood, Esq.,
of Islington, to Jane, eldest daughter of — Reynolds, Esq., of
Christ's Hospital."

The omission of Reynolds' Christian name seems to
accentuate the fact that neither Hood nor J. H.
Reynolds remained on the staff of the magazine in
1825. The Reverend Edward Rice, who officiated,
later became Head Master of Christ's Hospital. Jane
Hood recorded a few days later that " he read the
marriage ceremony so beautifully that we wish to have
it over again."

The young couple proceeded by post-chaise to Hastings to spend their short honeymoon, and one letter of
the bride's, one of the bridegroom's, are all that remain
of any correspondence they may have kept up during
the holiday. Writing on May 10, to her sister-in-law
Betsy, Jane Hood gave some little account of their
" proceedings and adventures."

" Our lodgings are very snug and comfortable, and
Mrs. Fermor is a nice civil little woman. We enjoy
the sea, the air, and our meals with all our might, and
if I go on as I have set out, your brother has got as idle
and gossiping a wife as your will find in the three kingdoms! The day after our arrival here, we went out
for a sail in Tom Woodgate's new boat, and were
invited on board a man-of-war, which had just come
from Calais, where it had just taken the Duke of
Cambridge. I was whipped up in the chair, and we
were conducted over the vessel by as handsome a young
lieutenant as you would wish to see! It was unlucky
I was married, as such an adventure to a single woman
would have been advantageous. . . .

" I am very much pleased with Hastings; we have

had some beautiful walks, and have many more in store. I have not yet reached the Castle, nor Charles Lamb's little church, but the weather is very favourable to our little schemes, and we have no fault to find, but that a week has flown like a day, and we have only another to stay here. Your brother begs I will tell you that the town is empty, and that he is the handsomest man here! For this reason he drags me over the shingle every day, wearing out my shoes, that he may be seen!

" I have heard from home to-day. My mother seems to have been very much fatigued after Thursday, and I am not surprised, as her feelings must have been much tried, and M.'s [? Marianne's] illness rendered the bustle greater than it would have been otherwise. I hope you all found the day as agreeable as such a day could be, for I know what a sister's feelings are upon such an occasion. But I hope that you will all think that I am your sister indeed, ever ready to show you the affection of one, and *eager* to be beloved by you all. The love I bear for one you all love, and the happiness that I experience in being his wife, will always make me look upon you with affection ; and I think I should be very ungrateful if I did not add that your kindness to me will be another motive that I shall love you all. I am getting serious ; but you will forgive me, I hope, for my heart is very full, and if I touch it the happiness will overflow. You will laugh at me, perhaps, and talk about the honey-moon ; but your brother and I have had many seasons of trouble and vexations that have made our present enjoyment greater. I must say to you all, get married as fast as you can ; but don't marry unless you love the man, for then a married state *must* be miserable."

Very sage advice from a young wife of less than a week's experience ! The trouble and vexations may

Friendships and Marriage.

have arisen from the precariousness of Hood's health from time to time, or from the precariousness of his work, for after the determination of his connection with the *London Magazine* we have no record of any regular work on which he was engaged. It is possible that Jane Reynolds' parents, in view of these circumstances, despite their regard for Thomas Hood, may have thought it advisable to propose the further postponement, or even the abandonment, of the projected marriage. Whatever the troubles and vexations may have been, and despite those which followed, it cannot but be recognised that from first to last it was a happy marriage.

Jane having written to her husband's sister, Thomas wrote to Jane's sisters—Marianne and Charlotte—a few days later, after the young couple had made their way to the beautiful little Hollingdon Church of which Lamb wrote so whimsically.

" This is the last of our excursions. We have tried, but in vain, to find out the baker and his wife recommended to us by Lamb as the very lions of green Hastings. There is no such street as he has named throughout the town, and the ovens are singularly numerous. We have given up the search, therefore, but we have discovered the little church in the wood, and it is such a church! It ought to have been our St. Botolph's . . . Such a verdant covert wood Stothard might paint for the haunting of Dioneus, Pamphillus, and Fiammetta as they walk in the novel of Boccace. The ground shadowed with bluebells, even to the formation of a plumb-like bloom upon its little knolls and ridges ; and ever through the dell windeth a little path chequered with the shades of aspens and ashes and the most verdant and lively of all the family of trees. Here a broad, rude stone steppeth over a lazy spring, oozing its way into grass and weeds ; anon a fresh pathway divergeth, you know not whither. Meanwhile the wild blackbird startles across the way and singeth anew in some other shade. To have seen Fiammetta there, stepping in silk attire, like a flower, and the sunlight looking upon her betwixt the branches! I had not walked (in the body) with Romance before. Then suppose so much of a space cleared as maketh a small church *lawn* to be sprinkled with old gravestones, and in the midst the church itself, a small Christian dovecot, such as Lamb has truly described it, like a little temple of Juan Fernandes. I could have been sentimental and wished to lie some day in that place; its calm tenants seeming to come through such quiet ways, through those verdant alleys, to their graves.

"In coming home I killed a viper in our serpentine path, and Mrs. Fermor says I am by that token to overcome an enemy. Is Taylor or Hessey dead? The reptile was dark and dull, his blood being yet sluggish from the cold; howbeit, he tried to bite, till I cut him in two with a stone. I thought of Hessey's long backbone when I did it.

"They are called *adders*, tell your father, because two and two of them together make four."

Here again we seem to get a hint of trouble with the proprietors of the *London Magazine*, but there is nothing definite. The considerable success which had attended the "Odes and Addresses" during this spring of 1825 made the Hoods' married life begin under the happiest auspices. The time was one when a popular writer could find a ready market for his wares in the magazines and annuals which were so marked a feature of the literature of the day, while it is probable that Hood had, from time to time, connection with one or other of the many journalistic ventures of the period.

CHAPTER VII.

EARLY COMIC WRITINGS (1825—1827).

HAVING followed Hood up to the time of the commencement of his happy married life we may pause to consider the position which he occupied at the time. It has been shown that his talents were early recognised on the *London Magazine*, that he had been honoured with the tribute of a dedication by Barry Cornwall, but to the wider public—the public on whose favour the penman is dependent for his bread and cheese—the name of Hood was but little known until after the publication in February, 1825, of the "Odes and Addresses to Great People." The little book was evidently projected by Hood in the autumn of 1824. He had inserted an amusing "Ode to Dr. Kitchener" in the *London* as one of his first contributions, and had happily thought of singling out various notabilities and notorieties for a like honour. The subject had evidently been discussed with John Hamilton Reynolds, and his co-operation invited, when Hood wrote the following undated letter from Lower Street, Islington :—

"MY DEAR REYNOLDS,—I send you the Ode on Martin, which, with those on Graham and Kitchener, makes three completed.

"These are the names I have thought of to choose from,—Elliston you would make a rich one,—and then there's Pierce Egan or Tom Cribb—ditto—Mr. Bodkin —Mr. McAdam—Mrs. Fry—Hy. Hunt—Sir R. Birnie —Joseph Grimaldi, sen.—The Great Unknown—Mr.

Thomas Hood :

Malthus—Mr. Irving—Mr. Wilberforce—Prince Hohen-
lohe—Capt. Parry—Dr. Combe—Mr. Accum—The
Washing Company—Sir W. Congreve—Bish—Cubitt
on the Treadmill — Tattersall — Owen of Lanark—
Bridgman, on the Iron Coffins—W. Savage Landor,
on the use of cork armour and bows and arrows—
Fitzgerald on Literature—Dymoke. I think the thing
is likely to be a hit—but if *you* do some, I shall expect
it to run like wildfire. Let's keep it snug.—Pray,
remembrances to Rice—and in the kindliest at Home.
—I am, dear Reynolds, yours very truly,

"T. Hood."

Reynolds did co-operate, and the book certainly
made a hit, though it cannot but be recognised that
it was Hood's work which was the richer in fun, in
satire, and in that wonderful play upon words which
in this first of his " comic " books he raised to a fine
art. Of the fifteen odes and addresses nine were by
Hood, five by Reynolds, and one was written in collaboration, and all of the subjects with the exception
of three were taken from this list suggested by the
former.[1] In the *London Magazine* for January, 1825,
there appeared an " Ode to George Colman the
Younger," which there can be little doubt was by
one of the collaborators, and most probably by Hood.
It was it is likely written after the others were already
in the publisher's hands, and its appearance in the
London may have marked the beginning of a temporary

[1] Mr. W. A. Longmore has in his possession two copies of the
" Odes and Addresses to Great People," one given to himself by
Hood, and the other given to a member of the Reynolds family
by Reynolds. In the first-mentioned Hood put the author's
initials against each piece, while in the other Reynolds initialled
those for which he was responsible—and their markings tally in

Early Comic Writings (1825—1827).

renewal of Hood's connection with the magazine. The latest of his acknowledged writings to appear there was the poem "To a Cold Beauty," which had been published in the number for June, 1823. At the beginning of 1825 the *London* started a new series, raising its price from half-a-crown to three shillings and sixpence, and may also have started a new editorial *régime*, for Charles Wentworth Dilke "appears also about this time to have been the editor of the *London Magazine*, in which he wrote, as did at the same time, Lamb, Hood, Reynolds."[1] Hood had probably met Dilke during his own connection with the editorial side of the magazine—indeed their acquaintance is said to have dated from some years earlier—and that he made a reappearance in its pages in the number for February, 1825, is fairly conclusively shown by the

every respect. The allocation of their respective shares is as follows :—

> Ode to Mrs. Graham. T. H.
> Ode to Mr. M'Adam. J. H. R.
> A Friendly Epistle to Mrs. Fry. T. H.
> Ode to Richard Martin. T. H.
> Ode to the Great Unknown. T. H.
> To Mr. Dymoke. J. H. R.
> Ode to Joseph Grimaldi. T. H.
> To Sylvanus Urban. J. H. R.
> An Address to the Steam Washing Co. T. H.
> Ode to Captain Parry. T. H.
> Ode to R. W. Elliston. J. H. R.
> Address to Maria Darlington. Both.
> Ode to W. Kitchener. T. H.
> Address to the Dean and Chapter. J. H. R.
> Ode to Mr. Bodkin. T. H.

[1] "Papers of a Critic: selected from the writings of the late Charles Wentworth Dilke: with a Biographical Sketch by his grandson, Sir Charles Wentworth Dilke, Bart.," p. 16. Dilke had been an occasional contributor to the *London* over the signature "Thurma."

Thomas Hood :

twenty-fifth stanza of the "Ode to Mr. Graham," which runs—

> "*My* name is Tims.—I am the man
> That North's unseen, diminish'd clan
>   So scurvily abused!
> I am the very P. A. Z.,
> The London Lion's small pin's head
>   So often hath refused!"

On looking through the magazine for February we find that an article with those unusual initials had been accepted; it was "The Art of Advertising Made Easy," giving some examples of the florid advertising of the day, with one or two sly digs at Colburn, the publisher, who was considered a master of the art of puffing, and with whom Hood was later to have business relations. There is something of a modern note about the writer's reference to a periodical almost killed by the art of advertising, and he certainly piques curiosity when he tells us that—

"It is pretty well known that a celebrated prose writer of the present day was induced by Bish to try his hand at those little corner delicacies of a newspaper —the Lottery puffs, and that his productions were returned upon his hands as being too modest for use. Poor soul! He thought he could write; and florid Mr. Atkinson, with a pen dipped in his own curling fluid, wrote a flourishing paragraph that put him quite beside himself."

It would be interesting to identify that "celebrated prose writer." Of the "Ode to George Colman," which preceded the volume of "Odes and Addresses," the opening and two closing of its fourteen stanzas may be quoted with some confidence as the work of Hood. Colman, it may be mentioned, had been appointed "Deputy Licenser of Plays" about a year

Early Comic Writings (1825—1827).

earlier, and had roused the wrath of many playwrights by his excision of any strong expressions from pieces submitted to his ridiculously squeamish attention. The Ode makes continuous fun of this trait.

"Come, Colman! Mrs. Gibbs's chum!
Virtue's protector! Come, George, come,—
Sit down beside this beech
That flourisheth in Fulham road;
And let me all my heart unload
Of levity,—and preach!

"Thou'rt alter'd, George, since thy young days
Of wicked verse and heedless plays,
With double meanings cramm'd;
'White for the harvest' is thine age,
Thou chief curse-cutter for the stage
And scourger of the damn'd! . . .

"Poor Farce! her mourning now may put on!
And Comedy's as dead as mutton!
(No sheep must have a *dam*).
Farewell to Tragedy! her knell
And neck are wrung at once,—farewell
The Drama!—(dele *dram*) . . .

"Good-bye to Godby[1]! (dele *God!*)
Methinks I see all curtains nod
To one sad final fall!
Stages must sink from bad to *worser*,—
The sad precursor (dele *cursor*)
Of ruin frowns on all!

"Who, George—Oh, who that hath of wit
A grain, his fancies will submit
To nonsense and to Thee?—
What!—come, to be 'run through,' and then
Give sovereigns to reward the pen
That cuts us?—
"U. B. D.!"

This foretaste of the work having appeared in the *London* for January, the duodecimo volume "Odes and

[1] A celebrated theatrical carpenter.

Thomas Hood :

Addresses to Great People" was published by Messrs. Baldwin, Cradock & Joy in the following month. Its reception was immediately gratifying, so much so that before the summer was well advanced a second edition had to be prepared. The *London Magazine* hurriedly produced its meed of praise, devoting more than five pages (largely extracts, it is true) to the work; pointing out that wit, gaiety, good nature, and truth would ensure the work a very extensive popularity, drawing attention to the fact that the satire was a *moral* rather than a personal or political one, and finding that "the vice and a great part of the virtue of the book, both lie in its *puns*." This instant review may have meant that the authors had still a friend at court, if they were themselves no longer attached to the periodical. Other papers followed suit, and Charles Lamb, ever the kindly, helpful friend, wrote a brief review in the *New Times*, and in doing so happily differentiated the various kinds of pun, showing where, in his view, the pun was a permissible and good thing, and where it was a blot. In the South Kensington Museum is a copy of this review with the follow manuscript note on the margin. "The papers are to be sent you daily from us you returning all but those which concern you, *e.g. this*, any containing your writing &c. C. Lamb." That note was evidently addressed to Hood, who, living at Lower Street, Islington, was thus a near neighour of Lamb's during his tenancy of the house in Colebrook Row.

Though the little book was received with enthusiasm and achieved popularity there were not wanting critics who saw that there was a danger for the author in thus courting public applause by "light verse" when he had shown himself capable of higher things. Wainewright had implored, a couple of years earlier, "let not the shallow induce thee to conceal thy depth." Bryan Waller Procter wrote to a friend shortly after the volume was published to this effect, and showed that the secret of its authorship was known in literary circles.

"Have you read the "Odes and Addresses to Great People"?—It is a joint production by that united Beaumont and Fletcher brotherhood—Reynolds and Hood. What a pity it is that Hood should have given up serious poetry for the sake of cracking the shells of jokes which have not always a kernel!"

Barry Cornwall was too well circumstanced to remember that a man who has to get his living out of an inkpot has to devise some means of hitting the popular taste rather than sit down and write only such things as he wishes; has to sacrifice to the Lares and Penates as well as to the Graces. Sir Walter Scott, to whom a copy of the book was sent, wrote a kindly acknowledgment, wishing "the unknown author good health and good fortune and whatever other good things can best support and encourage his lively vein of inoffensive and humorous satire." A copy sent to Canning did not elicit an acknowledgment.

The success of the volume must have been a source of considerable gratification to Thomas Hood and his wife during their "half-honeymoon" holiday in May, though it was after their return that they received from Charles Lamb the following letter which had been sent him from Samuel Taylor Coleridge. Hood had met Coleridge once at the Lambs' but his silent habit in general company would not have suggested his latent abilities, so that the elder poet was little like to think of him as the author of the arriding book.

"My dear Charles,—This afternoon, a little, thin, mean-looking sort of a foolscap, sub-octavo of poems, printed on very dingy outsides, lay on the table, which the cover informed me was circulating in our book-club, so

Thomas Hood :

very Grub Streetish in all its appearance, internal as well as external, that I cannot explain by what accident of impulse (assuredly there was no *motive* in play) I came to look into it. Least of all, the title, Odes and Addresses to Great Men, which connected itself in my head with Rejected Addresses, and all the Smith and Theodore Hook squad. But, my dear Charles, it was certainly written by you, or under you, or *una cum* you. I know none of your frequent visitors capacious and assimilative enough of your converse to have reproduced you so honestly, supposing you had left yourself in pledge in his lock-up house. Gillman, to whom I read the spirited parody on the introduction to Peter Bell, the Ode to the Great Unknown, and to Mrs. Fry; he speaks doubtfully of Reynolds and Hood. But here come Irving and Basil Montagu.

"*Thursday night,* 10 *o'clock.*—No! Charles, it is *you.* I have read them over again, and I understand why you have *anon'd* the book. The puns are nine in ten good —many excellent—the *Newgatory* transcendent. And then the *exemplum sine exemplo* of a volume of personalities and contemporaneities, without a single line that could inflict the infinitesimal of an unpleasance on any man in his senses; saving and except perhaps in the envy-addled brain of the despiser of your *Lays.* If not a triumph over him, it is at least an *ovation.* Then, moreover, and besides, to speak with becoming modesty, excepting my own self, who is there but you who could write the musical lines and stanzas that are intermixed?

"Here Gillman, come up to my garret, and driven back by the guardian spirits of four huge flower-holders of omnigenous roses and honeysuckles— (Lord have mercy on his hysterical olfactories! what will he do in Paradise? I must have a pair or two of nostril-plugs, or nose-goggles, laid in his coffin)—stands at the door,

Early Comic Writings (1825—1827).

reading that to M'Adam, and the washerwoman's letter, and he admits *the facts*. You are found *in the manner*, as the lawyers say! so, Mr. Charles! hang yourself up, and send me a line, by way of token and acknowledgment. My dear love to Mary. God bless you and your Unshamabramizer.

" S. T. COLERIDGE."

Coleridge's confident ascription of the book to Lamb was soon shown to him to be wrong, for his old friend of many years and Hood's new one of a few replied on July 2—

" The Odes are 4-5ths done by Hood, a silentish young man you met at Islington one day, an invalid. The rest are Reynolds's, whose sister H. has recently married. I have not had a broken finger in them.

" They are hearty good-natured things,[1] and I would put my name to 'em chearfully, if I could as honestly. I complimented them in a Newspaper, with an abatement for those puns you laud so. They are generally an excess. A Pun is a thing of too much consequence to be thrown in as a make-weight. You shall read one of the addresses over, and miss the puns, and it shall be quite as good and better than when you discover 'em. A Pun is a Noble Thing per se ; O never lug it in as an accessory. A Pun is a sole object for reflection (vide *my* aids to that recessment from a savage state) —it is entire, it fills the mind : it is perfect as a sonnet, better. It limps asham'd in the train and retinue of Humour : it knows it should have an establishment of its own. The one, for instance, I made the other day ; I forget what it was.

[1] That they were on the whole taken in good part by those be-oded we know from Hood himself, for he has recorded that " the once celebrated Mr. Hunt presented to the authors a bottle of his best 'permanent ink,' and the eccentric Doctor Kitchiner sent an invitation to dinner."

Thomas Hood :

" Hood will be gratify'd as much as I am by your mistake. I liked 'Grimaldi' the best; it is true painting of abstract Clownery, and that precious concrete of a Clown; and the rich succession of images and words almost such, in the first half of the Mag. Ignotum."

The last reference is, of course, to the ode to the " Great Unknown," Sir Walter Scott. Despite the views of Lamb and some other critics, it was largely by virtue of the puns and the amazing dexterity both intellectual and verbal at the back of them that these odes and addresses achieved and maintained their popularity. It is sometimes objected at the present day that the poems, being topical, require a large machinery of annotation to make them understandable, but such criticism, while true of parts, is certainly untrue of the whole. It would not be possible to take up any similar body of topical work and find so much of it requiring no such elucidation. The book was hailed at the time of its publication as "one of the wittiest and pleasantest little books since Rejected Addresses," and some later critics have attempted to institute a comparison, but no such comparison is really possible. Each stands *sui generis*: each was something new in literature, and each has had no successor. It is a curious fact that both of these works should have been produced in collaboration. Where Horace and James Smith sought to deal with a single theme as it might have been dealt with by various distinguished writers, and in imitating their various styles added that lightest touch of exaggeration which turned mere imitation into amazingly clever parody, Hood and Reynolds had quite other ends in view. They took the idea of laudatory odes to notable people and converted laudation into satire of a ticklesome and

Early Comic Writings (1825—1827).

always good humoured character, and in the expression of that satire utilised the pun in a way hitherto unexampled. Samuel Rogers later declared that as a punster Hood was equal to Swift, and fell short of justice in saying so. And on this point Coleridge is surely a truer critic than is Lamb ; Coleridge, whom it is difficult to realise appreciating a pun in any other than a spirit of tolerance, than Lamb, who has himself been described as a prince of punsters. To Lamb, however, the pun was a light and airy thing to be used for proper effect in the give and take of familiar talk, and not to be put down in cold type. Hood thought otherwise. To him the pun was a very useful and helpful thing, and certainly its use adds new point to his satire again and again. The " Odes and Addresses " are obtainable to-day in a dozen editions, so that it is not necessary to cite them. In writing prefaces to the second and third editions—which were called for within a year of the book's appearance—the authors dealt whimsically with some of their critics who had objected to the puns, saying firstly—

" To the universal objection,—that the Book is over-run with puns,—the Author can only say, he has searched every page without being able to detect a thing of the kind. He can only promise therefore, that if any respectable Reviewer will point the *vermin* out, they shall be carefully trapped and thankfully destroyed."

In the third edition they said no alterations had been made " with the exception of the introduction of a few new commas, which the lovers of punctuation will immediately detect and duly appreciate ; — and the omission of the three puns, which, in the opinion of all friends and reviewers were detrimental to the

correct humour of the publication."[1] Hood, it has
to be recognised, lifted the pun from its position of
disrepute to literature.   One of the silliest things ever
said by a great man was said by Dr. Johnson, when he
declared that the man who would make a pun would
pick a pocket.   The common pun, the mere twisting
of the sound of one word so that to the ear it suggests
another is of course extremely silly, but the pun in the
hands of Hood is quite another matter.   The pun, as
most of us use it, is merely a mechanical trick; as
Hood uses it, it comes as a sort of surprise, as though
the double meaning was a mere accident in the saying
of an inevitable thing.

If there were not wanting people who for one reason
or another disliked the odes, because of the puns or
because they recognised Hood's qualities as a serious
poet and thought that his flirtation with the comic
muse might prove more than temporary, there was
cordial congratulation for him on many hands. Another
of the old *London* contributors whose letter has been
preserved, is Allan Cunningham, who wrote :—

" DEAR HOOD,—Had I behaved honestly to my own
heart, this note would have been with you long ago;
for much have I laughed over your little book, and
often have I silently vowed to compel my sluggish
nature to tell you how much I liked it. There was
enough of wit visible at first reading to ensure a second,
and at the second so many new points appeared that I
ventured on a third, and with the fourth I suppose I
shall go on discovering and laughing. I was an early
admirer of your verses. I admired them for other and
higher qualities than what you have displayed in your

---

[1] Hood's son, in editing his father's works, does not seem to
have recognised the humour of the preface, but gravely comments
on this : " I have read, and had the two editions read repeatedly,
but have failed to detect any of these omissions."

Early Comic Writings (1825—1827).

odes; but I believe a smile carries a higher market price than a sigh, and that a laugh brings more money than deeper emotion. Even on your own terms I am glad to see you publicly. I think you might mingle those higher qualities with your wit, your learning, and your humour, and give us still more pleasing odes than them that you have done. But, ' ilka man wears his ain belt his ain gait.'

" Give my respects to Mrs. Hood. I shall have the honour of personally assuring her that I esteem her for her own sake, as well as for that of her facetious husband, when I can make my escape from the bondage of a romance which at present employs all my leisure hours. I remain, dear Hood, your faithful friend,

" ALLAN CUNNINGHAM."

The success of the " Odes and Addresses " may well have given such promise of future work as to have made Hood's marriage in May possible; it certainly was such as to open up many periodicals to his pen. In the following year (1826) he had a new volume ready, and this he published under the title of " Whims and Oddities in Prose and Verse." The volume, which was published by Lupton Relfe, of Cornhill, is notable as being the first illustrated by Hood himself, for it contained forty of those comical cuts with which for many years the author added pictorial point to many of his jests. These comic cuts proved popular, but have at times met with severe criticism, some writers having regarded Hood's pictorial efforts with smiling toleration, hinting that though he was a master of fun he " could not draw." It is therefore interesting to find that an acknowledged critic has spoken most highly of the odd fancies with which the author's pencil varied and newly pointed the work of his pen.

" It sometimes happens that there are great virtues

Thomas Hood :

in the work of amateurs which are prevented from receiving due recognition because the amateur is not a master of form. The pen-sketches of Hood, the poet and humourist, were admirably sound in manner, far sounder and better than many laboured attempts by accomplished painters; and yet, as it was evident that Hood's knowledge of form was quite unscientific, it was thought that his sketches had no higher quality than that of making people laugh. Not only was his line very expressive, but his management of the means at his command in lights and darks was always exceedingly judicious. For example, in the scene where four expectant negroes are roasting a white man, he uses positive black on the negroes with the most artistic reserve, it is kept for the two nearest, and only used, even on them, for the deepest shades; the receding distances of the others are expressed by three shades of grey; finally, the white man, who is suspended over the fire, is drawn in very thin outline without any shading whatever, that we may clearly perceive his whiteness. Rembrandt himself could not have arranged the subject better."[1]

The "Whims and Oddities" consisted in part of miscellaneous pieces which had been contributed to various periodicals during the preceding four years, and included "The Ballad of Sally Brown and Ben the Carpenter," one of the earliest written and one of the most widely known of Hood's purely comic poems. This had appeared in the "Lion's Head" of the *London Magazine* in March, 1822, and that it had achieved considerable success may be seen from the note with which the author prefaced it on first printing it as his own:

"I have never been vainer of any verses than of my part in the following Ballad. Dr. Watts, amongst

[1] P. G. Hamerton's *Graphic Arts*, Chap. X. (1882).

evangelical muses, has an enviable renown—and Campbell's Ballads enjoy a snug genteel popularity. ' Sally Brown' has been favoured, perhaps, with as wide a patronage as the ' Moral Songs,' though its circle may not have been of so select a class as the friends of ' Hohenlinden.' But I do not desire to see it amongst what are called Elegant Extracts. The lamented Emery, drest as Tom Tug, sang it at his last mortal Benefit at Covent Garden;—and, ever since, it has been a great favourite with the watermen of Thames, who time their oars to it, as the wherrymen of Venice time theirs to the lines of Tasso. With the watermen, it went naturally to Vauxhall:—and, overland, to Sadler's Wells. The Guards, not the mail coach, but the Life Guards,—picked it out from a fluttering hundred of others—all going to one air—against the dead wall at Knightsbridge. Cheap printers of Shoe-lane, and Cow-cross, (all pirates !) disputed about the Copyright, and published their own editions,—and, in the meantime, the Authors, to have made bread of their song, (it was poor old Homer's hard ancient case !) must have sung it about the streets. Such is the lot of Literature! the profits of ' Sally Brown ' were divided by the Ballad-Mongers :—it has cost, but has never brought me, a halfpenny."

Hood's reference to his " part " in the verses, and his allusion to " the Authors," suggests that the ballad was not entirely his own, and it is quite possible that it may have been early fruit of collaboration with Reynolds. The success of the earlier topical volume was repeated with the new miscellany, and though in his preface the author made known that he was resolved upon publishing some things of a more serious tone and purpose, yet with this book he may be said to have clinched his reputation, with those whose approval

Thomas Hood :

means popularity, as a humorous writer. The next
volume to be published was the serious one here hinted
at, but it was immediately followed by " Whims and
Oddities : Second Series," a volume similar in every way
to the first, and, like it, containing some of Hood's
most characteristic work in a comic vein, and, in " The
Demon Ship," the first of those remarkable poems in
which he wrought his readers up to a pitch of excite-
ment only to make them break out in laughter at a
ridiculous anti-climax. In the preface, too, he made
one of his various whimsical defences of the pun when
he said " Let me suggest, however, that a pun is somewhat like a cherry : though there may be a slight
outward indication of partition—of duplicity of meaning—yet no gentleman need make two bites at it against
his own pleasure."

In these two volumes of the " Whims and Oddities "
Hood gave the world a number of his most characteristic
pieces. Here were the punning ballads of " Sally
Brown," " Nelly Gray," " Tim Turpin," " Mary's
Ghost," and " Death's Ramble," and those other examples of his playing with the gruesome in " Jack Hall,"
and " The Last Man " ; also " The Irish Schoolmaster."
Most of these pieces and many of the others are
reprinted in every selection from Hood's works. They
show his peculiar genius as a verbal humorist when it
was at its very height, when, like Lamb, he was largely
punning for the fun of the thing, and often with a
felicity that is simply amazing to the reader. There is
nothing of that forced punning which in the later days
of H. J. Byron and the pantomime pun reduced the
playing with words to contempt. With Hood in these
early years of his literary success it seems as though he
must have used words with a double meaning almost
unconsciously, so easy is it to read his words with their
single significance and only by a kind of second sight

to see that they bear a further meaning. Stanzas might be taken from any of the pieces mentioned in illustration of this remarkable quality. Here are two from "Death's Ramble," a poem which, as Canon Ainger has said, is ablaze with wit and real imagination :—

> " He met a coachman driving his coach
> So slow, that his fare grew sick ;
> But he let him stray on his tedious way,
> For Death only wars on the quick. . . .
>
> " Death saw two players playing at cards,
> But the game wasn't worth a dump,
> For he quickly laid them flat with a spade
> To wait for the final trump."

Here is another verse, with the same happy use of single words with double meanings, from the " Mermaid of Margate " :—

> " And Christians love in the turf to lie
> Not in watery graves to be ;
> Nay, the very fishes would sooner die
> On the land than in the sea."

Examples might be multiplied to show once more that Hood's puns are not word-twistings of the kind that Oliver Wendell Holmes inveighed against in his remarks on what he happily termed verbicide. It is rare, indeed, that there is any wresting of the form or meaning of a word with Hood ; he just allows the word with two meanings to fall pat, so that either meaning may be attached and yet his sentence read logically. And not only do the sentences read logically, but the poems to which they belong are frequently characterised by a richness of fancy and imagination which makes them remarkable quite apart from the verbal wit with which they are marked. At times, indeed, though the manner may be that of the humorist and pun-maker, the matter is essentially that of the poet. In the " Last Man," for example, there is a sense of tragedy and a grimness of humour in combination that remove it quite out of the range of comic verse, and place it by some of his later writings in which these qualities were again blent.

Reference has been made to the impressive story of " The Demon Ship " in these volumes. Though it is generally reputed as a self-sufficing narrative, telling how a man in a boat was wrecked in a storm off the Wash and on being picked up by a collier, coming to surrounded by grimy men thought himself in the nether world. In " Whims and Oddities" the verse is prefaced by a prose passage. This the author concludes by saying, " The spectre-ship, bound to Deadman's Isle, is almost as awful a craft as the skeleton bark of the Ancient Mariner ; but they are both fictions, and have not the advantage of being realities, like the dreary vessel with its dreary crew in the following story, which records an adventure that befell even unto myself." The closing words are sufficiently explicit, but when and where the adventure befell cannot be said, though it may be recalled that Hood was never so pleased when recreating himself as when he had an opportunity of going out in a boat either alone or with some such congenial sailorman as old Tom Woodgate of Hastings.

Though it is chiefly by the verse included in them that the two series of " Whims and Oddities " are now remembered, the prose sketches interspersed deserve some mention, for Hood continued such diversifying of his work up to the end. Sometimes these prose sketches are slight stories of a humorous kind, essays, or anecdotes, with accompanying illustrations by the

Early Comic Writings (1825—1827).

author. Here is the closing portion of a couple of pages on " The Popular Cupid," with a woodcut of an unhealthily chubby little god of love :—

" I can believe in his dwelling alone in the heart—seeing that he must occupy it to repletion ;—in his constancy, because he looks sedentary and not apt to roam. That he is given to melt—from his great pinguitude. That he burneth with a flame, for so all fat burneth—and hath languishings—like other bodies of his tonnage. That he sighs—from his size.—I dispute not his kneeling at ladies' feet—since it is the posture of elephants,—nor his promise that the homage shall remain eternal. I doubt not of his dying,—being of a corpulent habit, and a short neck.—But for his lodging in Belinda's blue eye, my whole faith is heretic —*for she hath never a sty in it.*"

Sometimes in these short essays in prose Hood exhibited something of the qualities of his friend Elia, but through most of them ran evidence of his " impertinent custom of punning ; " in them, though dealing with varied themes in lightest fashion, there was frequently that vein of serious philosophising usually characteristic of the true humorist. One of these prose bits, entitled " Walton Redivivus : a New River Eclogue," is prefaced by some lines " from a Letter of C. Lamb "—that letter addressed to Hood when at Hastings (see p. 154). Piscator and Viator are engaged in the recreation of the contemplative man in the New River, " near the Sir Hugh Middleton's Head," and here is a scrap of their dialogue :—

" *Via.* What, are there no dace or perch ?—

" *Pis.* I doubt not but there have been such fish here in former ages. But now-a-days there is nothing of that size. They are gone extinct, like the mammoths.

" *Via.* There was always such a fishing at 'em.

Thomas Hood:

Where there was one Angler in former times, there is now a hundred.

" *Pis.* A murrain on 'em!—A New-River fish now-a-days, cannot take his common swimming exercise without hitching on a hook.

" *Via.* It is the natural course of things, for man's populousness to terminate other breeds. As the proverb says, ' The more Scotchmen the fewer herrings.' It is curious to consider the family of whales growing thinner according to the propagation of parish lamps.

" *Pis.* Aye, and withall, how the race of man, who is a terrestrial animal, should have been in the greatest jeopardy of extinction by the element of water ; whereas the whales, living in the ocean, are most liable to be burnt out.

" *Via.* It is a pleasant speculation. But how is this ? I thought to have brought my gentles comfortably in an old snuff box and they are all stark dead !

" *Pis.* The odour hath killed them., There is nothing more mortal than tobacco, to all kinds of vermin. Wherefore, a new box will be indispensable, though for my own practice, I prefer my waistcoat pockets for their carrying. Pray mark this :—and in the meantime I will lend you some worms."

In *Blackwood's Magazine* the work was hailed in an amusing and appreciative fashion in a sixteen page notice which began with " for three years past have we been pining away for the appearance of a new Cockney." Maga with a flourishing knout ready for use was looking out for a Cockney: " But what a bitter disappoint-ment ! Thomas Hood, so far from deserving to be knouted to death, or sent with his stripes into Siberian silence, turns out to be a most admirable fellow—quite of the right kidney—with a warm heart—a sound head—a humour quaint and original — a disposition amiable and facetious—a boon companion, worthy to be carried

Early Comic Writings (1825—1827).

by proclamation or storm — an honorary member of the Nox-Ambrosial club." There was a passing regret at there being no opportunity of using the knout — " three stripes to a Hunt — four to a Hazlitt ! the Cockney is not who could sustain a dozen and live " — and then came a full and appreciative account of the contents of the volume. A writer like Hood, declared the critic, may do some service even to the morality of the rising generation, by his playful muse. One of his prose sketches — the droll " Fancies on a Teacup " is said to be pleasingly reminiscent of Addison, Goldsmith, Elia, and North — " and yet original and Thomas Hoodish." " The Last Man " is picked out for special laudation as " worth fifty of Byron's ' darkness ' (a mere daub), a hundred and fifty of Campbell's Last Man, and five hundred of Mrs. Shelley's abortion."

The two series of " Whims and Oddities " met with considerable success and were reproduced in new editions during the next few years. Their production had, however, a definite effect in establishing the author in the popular regard as a comic writer, and so had an important result in forcing him more or less closely to continue, as he put it, to " breathe his comic vein." Though it is idle to speculate over might-have-beens, it may be believed that could Hood at this moment have taken some editorial appointment which, while ensuring him a living wage, would have left him free to express his genius in his own way, we might have had more of his best and less of that journeyman work which he had to go on producing to earn a livelihood. At the time, however, nothing of this was evident. He had taken his place in the front rank of the funny men of his day, and the audience insisted that he must continue to be funny, and henceforward, with some notable exceptions, it was in the comic way that he had to keep. The success of these three books opened many new channels for his work in magazines and in the annuals which were so prominent a feature of the literature of the time. During the closing years of the third decade of his life his contributions to such miscellanies were many, and met with so cordial a reception as to augur well for the future. Henceforward, too, his writings were often accompanied by his drawings, for though his mastery of the pictorial art may have been small, his little cuts were irresistibly droll and therefore widely appreciated. In prefacing the first of his books which he had thus ornamented he showed that he had no illusions as to his work as comic draughtsman :

" It will be seen from the illustrations of the present work, that the Inventor is no artist ;—in fact he was never ' meant to draw '—any more than the tape-tied curtains mentioned by Mr. Pope. Those who look at his designs, with Ovid's Love of Art, will therefore be disappointed. . . . The designer is quite aware of their defects : but when Raphael has bestowed seven odd legs upon four Apostles, and Fuseli has stuck in a great goggle head without an owner, when Michael Angelo has set on a foot the wrong way, and Hogarth has painted in defiance of all the laws of nature and perspective, he has hope that his own little enormities may be forgiven—that his sketches may look interesting like Lord Byron's Sleeper—' with all their errors.' "

As Thackeray was shortly to be doing, Hood seems ever to have been ready to sketch anything comical that he saw or fancied, and if the work of both of them in this medium sinned against the canons of art, yet it may be said for them that they possessed qualities which make them attractive when the work of many of their more canonical contemporaries has long ceased to interest us. The pencil seems to have been a perpetual source of recreation to Thomas Hood, and as

Early Comic Writings (1825—1827).

though the verbal possibilities were not sufficient for his ever alert fancy he invented the pictorial pun.

It was apparently after the publication of the second series of " Whims and Oddities" that Hood received an appeal for an autograph which is interesting as showing how the persistence of an autograph hunter provided the inspiration for a remarkable piece of verse. The letter evidently tickled the recipient, and was carefully preserved by him, but has not hitherto been printed to throw amusing light on the " Lines to a Lady on Her Departure for India." The letter is dated from " 22, Hans Place. Thursday, Nov. 8, [1827 ?]," and runs—

" Miss Roberts feels quite ashamed of importuning Mr. Hood for favours to which she is aware she possesses no legitimate claim, yet as she is so soon to leave England and perchance forever, she cannot avoid making another appeal to Mr. Hood's generosity, and not a little shocked by the surprising boldness of her former request now only ventures to ask for one of the original drawings from which his last most mirth-exciting Whims and Oddities were engraved. Mr. Hood may estimate the value which Miss Roberts attaches to such a contribution to her album by the extraordinary, and, as she fears, unjustifiable exertion she has made to procure it ; she is more shocked than she can express at her pertinacity, yet notwithstanding persists in her solicitations, stimulated by the hope of being the sole and fortunate person who on the banks of the Ganges can boast of possessing a souvenir from the gentleman to whom the laughter-loving portion of the community are indebted for so much delight, and in whose works all those who dwell in every civilized quarter of the globe take so lively an interest. In the hope of hearing soon and satisfactorily from Mr. Hood, Miss Roberts takes leave with the sincerest wishes that

Thomas Hood:

his health and prosperity may be ever equal to his popularity." [1]

The writer of this persuasive letter was evidently successful in her appeal to Hood. The surmise that the "Lines" referred to above were sent her in response is proved to be accurate by the fact that the manuscript [2] is entitled " Lines Addressed to Miss Roberts on Her Departure for India." The verses, which are a parody of a song by John Hamilton Reynolds, " Go where the water glideth gently ever," are in Hood's happiest comic vein, and include a triumphant pun in one of the two stanzas added before the piece was published—

> " Go where the maiden on a marriage plan goes
> Consign'd for wedlock to Calcutta's quay,
> Where woman goes for mart, the same as mangoes,
> And think of me ! "

India was then a happy ground for marriageable young ladies, but Miss Roberts, despite the poet's sly hint as to the purpose of her voyage, did not marry. In the facsimile of the original draught of the poem the refrain is " And think of we."

The instant popularity of Hood's early comic writings may be gauged by the way in which his work was imitated and commented upon by rivals and lesser masters of fun. In his " Absurdities " (1827), A. Crowquill addressed the following quatrain " to Thomas Hood, Esq."—

> " Wits may now lay aside their pens,
> Their sallies being no good;
> Till thou art *dead* they cannot hope
> To—*urn a lively Hood.*"

[1] The Miss Roberts of this persuasive letter was Emma Roberts (1794 ?—1840), writer of four books in verse and prose dealing with Indian subjects, and other volumes. In 1828 she went to India with her sister, who had married a military officer in the East India Company's service.

[2] Of which a facsimile is given in *Pen and Pencil*, by Mary Balmanno, 1858.

186

Early Comic Writings (1825—1827).

The little book in which that compliment was given was described as "perhaps too direct a copy, and is certainly far off from the merits of the original." In the *Literary Gazette* of March 15, 1827, appeared, over the signature of " Sam Wildfire," " A Free and Friendly Address, to the Author of ' Odes and Addresses, &c.' " This ran to a dozen stanzas, of which the opening two and the closing one are as follows :—

> " Oh Thomas Hood ! Thou soul of fun,
>   I know not one in London
> Better than thee to make a pun,
>   Or better to be punn'd on !

> " Would that I knew thee !—come—reveal !
>   Art honest Tom, and good ?
> Dost thou a pun now never steal
>   And turn a Robbin' Hood ? . . .

> " Oh Tom ! how much and oft I've longed
>   That then you kindly would
> Leave me the mantle that belonged
>   To such a funny Hood ! "

In the following week's issue the editor inserted a specimen of a reply to the Address, of which these three verses are less than half, signed " Timothy P. Hunter,"—

> "O Wildfire ! I would not be thee
>   For a miser's store of riches ;
> Though thou in Hood's mantle fain would be
>   I would not be in thy b———s !

> " For Hood will punish thy bold pun
>   That him accused of thieving ;
> And make thee in future a pun to shun
>   By thee in a pun-cheon leaving. . . .

> " But do not thou his mantle wear—
>   Mind well what thou'rt about ;
> The prying world will lay thee bare
>   And find the false-Hood out."

CHAPTER VIII.

THE PLEA OF THE MIDSUMMER FAIRIES, AND OTHER POEMS (1827).

"Delightful bard! what praises meet are thine,
  More than my verse can sound to thee belong;
Well hast thou pleaded with a tongue divine,
  In this thy sweet and newly breathed song,
  Where, like the stream, smooth numbers gliding throng
Gather'd, methinks I see the elfin race,
  With the *Immortal* standing them among,
Smiling benign with more than courtly grace;
Rescued I see them,—all their gambols trace,
  With their fair queen Titania in her bower,
And all their avocations small embrace,
  Pictur'd by thee with a Shakespearean power—
O when the time shall come thy soul must flee,
Then may some hidden spirit *plead* for thee."
                                    EDWARD MOXON.

WHILE Thomas Hood was still engaged in practising the art of the engraver, as we have seen, he had written enough verse to justify the contemplation of publishing a volume. We know that with that end in view he submitted his poems to a publisher, but beyond that we know nothing. Whether the manuscript volume was lost, or whether the friendly bookseller was not sufficiently friendly to venture upon publication cannot be said. It is certainly conceivable. Shortly after the episode Hood joined the staff of the *London Magazine*, in the pages of which he published several of his poems, and it may be that some of these were taken from the projected collection. Sub-editorial activities combined with continuous writing—and the pleasant interlude of

188

The Plea of the Midsummer Fairies.

courtship—and then the success of the comic books may
have caused the postponement of the projected volume.
But, be the cause what it may, it remains that though
a volume of serious poems was projected in 1821, such
was not published until 1827, when Messrs. Longmans,
Rees, Orme, Brown & Green issued "' The Plea of the
Midsummer Fairies, Hero and Leander, Lycus the
Centaur, and Other Poems,' by Thomas Hood, Author
of 'Whims and Oddities,' etc., etc." It was pointed
out that there was a tactical error on the part of the
poet (or his publishers) in accentuating on the title
page the fact that he who now came before the public
with higher matters was the writer of the popular
comicalities. The objection came of recognition of the
common idea that the shoemaker must stick to his last:
that the man who has been applauded for doing one
thing well must not attempt to win applause by doing
something other. The story runs that the book was so
much of a failure that the author had to buy the edition
from the publishers to avoid its being utilised on the
counter of the butter-merchant. That a fair number
of copies must have passed into circulation is proved
by the fact that now—eighty years later—copies of the
volume, generally priced at a moderate figure, are by
no means rare in second-hand bookdealers' lists.[1] The
book certainly cannot have had an extensive sale, and
the author's disappointment over its fate may well
have led him to the exaggeration as to the butter-
shop. By the smaller circle—and it is frequently the
verdict of the smaller contemporary circle which
becomes that of posterity—of poetry lovers, by those
friends of Hood's who had recognised his quality from

---

[1] My own copy of the work—the last book to be "snapped
up" by me in the old Booksellers' Row—cost me but a single
shilling.

the first, the book was hailed with pleasure for many excellencies.

The chief critical journal of the day, William Jerdan's *Literary Gazette*, in a notice of some length acknowledged that "Lycus the Centaur" boasted a number of passages "which would do honour to any poet, age, or country," but by way of general criticism thought Hood showed "too great a leaning, in parts, to those dainty simplicities which are admired in the productions of Lloyd, Lamb, Reynolds, and others of that school; but which we can never consider otherwise than an affectation of imitating the elder bards such as Crashaw, and, in some of his pieces, perhaps, Michael Drayton." Though the reviewer thus found fault with a "school" of writers for going back to our early poets, he was most enthusiastic about Hood's volume as a whole, and likened it to "a lovely summer day, sunny, not scorching; placid, enchanting, its airs balmy and refreshing, its various aspects delicious and even its clouds delightful; so that all minister to enjoyment."

The volume is indeed a remarkable one, and goes far to justify Mary Russell Mitford's claim that Hood was the greatest poet of his age—an age between that of Wordsworth, Shelley, Keats, Byron, and Coleridge (the first and last of these, the only survivors, produced but little poetry after the mid-twenties)—and that of Tennyson and the Brownings. It is worth recalling, perhaps, that Hood's volume appeared in the same year as the Tennysons' "Poems by Two Brothers."

The chief poems of the collection were separately dedicated to Charles Lamb, to S. T. Coleridge, and to J. H. Reynolds,—dedications which are interesting as showing at once the course of the author's friendships and the trend of his literary admiration. The dedicatory letter prefixed to "The Plea of the Midsummer Fairies" may be quoted, both as illustration of Hood's friendship

The Plea of the Midsummer Fairies.

with Charles Lamb and as indicating the nature of
the poem :—

" My dear Friend,—I thank my literary fortune
that I am not reduced, like many better wits, to barter
dedications, for the hope or promise of patronage, with
some nominally great man ; but that where true affection
points, and honest respect, I am free to gratify my
head and heart by a sincere inscription. An intimacy
and dearness, worthy of a much earlier date than our
acquaintance can refer to, direct me at once to your
name : and with this acknowledgment of your ever
kind feeling towards me, I desire to record a respect
and admiration for you as a writer, which no one
acquainted with our literature, save Elia himself, will
think disproportionate or misplaced. If I had not these
better reasons to govern me, I should be guided to the
same selection by your intense yet critical relish for the
works of our great Dramatist, and for that favourite
play in particular which has furnished the subject of
my verses.

" It is my design, in the following Poem, to celebrate,
by an allegory, that immortality which Shakspeare has
conferred on the Fairy mythology by his Midsummer
Night's Dream. But for him, those pretty children of
our childhood would leave barely their names to our
maturer years ; they belong, as the mites upon the
plumb, to the bloom of fancy, a thing generally too
frail and beautiful to withstand the rude handling of
time : but the Poet has made this most perishable part
of the mind's creation equal to the most enduring ; he
has so entwined the Elfins with human sympathies,
and linked them by so many delightful associations
with the productions of nature, that they are as real to
the mind's eye, as their green magical circles to the
outer sense.

Thomas Hood:

"It would have been a pity for such a race to go extinct, even though they were but as the butterflies that hover about the leaves and blossoms of the visible world. I am, my dear Friend, Yours most truly,

"T. Hood."

Beautifully is the allegory told, rich in such happy phrasings as are characteristic of our older poets of whom Hood was evidently a loving reader. He pictures a gathering of all the powers of fairydom under Queen Titania holding debate with Father Time.

"And lo! upon my fix'd delighted ken
 Appear'd the loyal Fays.—Some by degrees
 Crept from the primrose buds that open'd then,
 And some from bell-shap'd blossoms like the bees,
 Some from the dewy meads, and rushy leas,
 Flew up like chafers when the rustics pass;
 Some from the rivers, others from tall trees
 Dropp'd, like shed blossoms, silent to the grass,
 Spirits and elfins small, of every class.

"Peri and Pixy, and quaint Puck the Antic,
 Brought Robin Goodfellow, that merry swain;
 And stealthy Mab, queen of old realms romantic,
 Came too, from distance, in her tiny wain,
 Fresh dripping from a cloud—some bloomy rain,
 Then circling the bright Moon, had washed her car,
 And still bedew'd it with a various stain:
 Lastly came Ariel, shooting from a star,
 Who bears all fairy embassies afar."

The devourer of all things has resolved that the fairies must go the way of the Titan and the Mammoth, and raises his scythe to make away with them when—

"Just at need a timely apparition
 Steps in between."

The apparition is that of Shakespeare, who, in "The

The Plea of the Midsummer Fairies.

Midsummer Night's Dream," has conferred a time-defying immortality on

> " King Oberon, and all his merry crew
> The darling puppets of romance's view
> Fairies and sprites and goblin elves."

Time fails in his encounter with "that immortal Shade," and Titania bids her elves do all service to the gracious bard to whom they owe their continued existence—

> " Goodly it was to see the elfin brood
> Contend for kisses of his gentle hand,
> That had their mortal enemy withstood,
> And stay'd their lives, fast ebbing with the sand.
> Long while this strife engag'd the pretty band;
> But now bold Chanticleer, from farm to farm,
> Challeng'd the dawn creeping o'er eastern land,
> And well the fairies knew that shrill alarm,
> Which sounds the knell of every elfish charm.

> " And soon the rolling mist, that 'gan arise
> From plashy mead and undiscover'd stream,
> Earth's morning incense to the early skies,
> Crept o'er the failing landscape of my dream.
> Soon faded then the Phantom of my theme—
> A shapeless shade, that fancy disavow'd,
> And shrank to nothing in the mist extreme.
> Then flew Titania,—and her little crowd,
> Like flocking linnets, vanish'd in a cloud."

The whole poem, of upwards of eleven hundred lines, is instinct with beauty and imagination, and in the parleying between the destroyer and those whom he would destroy are some lines of happiest description—such as the closing couplet in the above extract—and of neatest expression, as when, Time boasting that he has destroyed the Titans, a timid fairy retorts—

> " Great giants work great wrongs,—but we are small,
> For love goes lowly."

T.H.   193   O

Thomas Hood:

The whole poem is a beautiful gem of the imagination fittingly shaped by the poet, a lovely piece of allegory, rich in such happy phrasings as are most frequently found in the writings of our older poets, yet full of a sweet and original freshness. That Lamb appreciated the poem we know. He wrote a brief prose paraphrase which, under the title of "The Defeat of Time; or a Tale of the Fairies," he contributed to Hone's "Table Book," concluding thus :—

"What particular endearments passed between the Fairies and their Poet, passes my pencil to delineate; but if you are curious to be informed, I must refer you, gentle reader, to the 'Plea of the Fairies,' a most agreeable Poem, lately put forth by my friend, Thomas Hood: of the first half of which the above is nothing but a meagre and a harsh prose-abstract.

"*The words of Mercury are harsh after the songs of Apollo.*"

In the very choice of his theme for the poem which follows the "Plea," Hood challenged comparison with earlier poets of distinction. But though he took a subject which had already been dealt with in successful fashion he dealt with it himself with a new success. It is a re-presenting of that ancient romance which has proved fascinating to a long succession of generations, the story of Leander—

> "Who was nightly wont
> (What maid will not the tale remember?)
> To cross thy stream, broad Hellespont."

Adopting with every appropriateness the six-line stanza of Shakespeare's "Venus and Adonis," Hood began his poem, and at the very outset struck that true Elizabethan note which rings through the whole :—

> "Oh Bards of old! what sorrows have ye sung,
> And tragic stories, chronicled in stone,—

194

The Plea of the Midsummer Fairies.

> Sad Philomel restor'd her ravish'd tongue,
> And transformed Niobe in dumbness shown ;
> Sweet Sappho on her love for ever calls,
> And Hero on the drown'd Leander falls ! "

In his version of the legend the poet makes a sea-maid enamoured of the spent Leander drag him down to her home beneath the waves, only to find him dead when she reaches it :—

> " Down and still downward through the dusky green
> She bore her treasure, with a face too nigh
> To mark how life was alter'd in its mien,
> Or how the light grew torpid in his eye,
> Or how his pearly breath unprison'd there,
> Flew up to join the universal air."

The poem gives a succession of beautiful pictures illustrating the parting of the lovers, the fears of Hero, the struggling of Leander, torn by the necessity of swimming away from her and the desire of staying. Then comes the time when he was enfeebled by his struggling with the waters—

> " His face was pallid, but the hectic morn
> Had hung a lying crimson on his cheeks,
> And slanderous sparkles in his eyes forlorn ;
> So death lies ambush'd in consumptive streaks ;
> But inward grief was writhing o'er its task,
> As heart-sick jesters weep behind the mask."

The closing line of that stanza suggests that the author may already have been rebelling against the call made upon him as jester. To the worn-out swimmer there suddenly appears a sea-maid, painted in words that appropriately suggest without any attempt at definition something elusively beautiful—

> " She's all too bright, too argent, and too pale,
> To be a woman ;—but a woman's double,
> Reflected on the wave so faint and frail,
> She tops the billows like an air-blown bubble ;
> Or dim creation of a morning dream,
> Fair as the wave-bleach'd lily of the stream."

Thomas Hood:

The whole story is beautifully told up to its tragic close, with a delicacy of imagination, a fineness of imagery, a grace of language, that no other poet writing at the time could have bettered.

"Lycus the Centaur" is the tragic story of a man half turned into a horse by a Circean spell. Written as early as 1822, when Hood was worshipping at the shrine of Keats and gradually feeling his way to a more individual way of expressing the poetry that was in him, this poem is perhaps more derivative than those of its companions just noticed. It is however a masterly conception, unequal in treatment, it is true, but containing some magnificent passages descriptive of the emotions of a half brutalised man shunned at once by humanity because he is half brute and by the beasts because he is half man. It starts with the awful experiences of the newly metamorphosed imagined with an impressive grimness of horror :—

"And I gave me to slumber, as if from one dream
To another—each horrid—and drank of the stream
Like a first taste of blood, lest as water I quaff'd
Swift poison, and never should breathe from the draught,—
Such drink as her own monarch husband drain'd up
When he pledg'd her, and Fate clos'd his eyes in the cup.
And I pluck'd of the fruit with held breath, and a fear
That the branch would start back and scream out in my
  ear;
For once, at my suppering, I pluck'd in the dusk
An apple, juice-gushing and fragrant of musk;
But by daylight my fingers were crimson'd with gore,
And the half-eaten fragment was flesh at the core;
And once—only once—for the love of its blush,
I broke a bloom bough, but there came such a gush
On my hand, that it fainted away in weak fright,
While the leaf-hidden woodpecker shriek'd at the sight;
And oh! such an agony thrill'd in that note,
That my soul, startling up, beat its wings in my throat,
As it long'd to be free of a body whose hand
Was doom'd to work torments a Fury had plann'd;

The Plea of the Midsummer Fairies.

"There I stood without stir, yet how willing to flee,
As if rooted and horror-turned into a tree,—
Oh ! for innocent death,—and to suddenly win it,
I drank of the stream, but no poison was in it ;
I plung'd in its waters, but ere I could sink,
Some invisible fate pull'd me back to the brink ;
I sprang from the rock, from its pinnacle height,
But fell on the grass with a grasshopper's flight ;
I ran at my fears—they were fears and no more,
For the bear would not mangle my limbs, nor the boar,
But moan'd,—all their brutalized flesh could not smother,
The horrible truth,—we were kin to each other ! "

Writing to the author a few years later, Hartley Coleridge said, " I am not a graduate in the Academy of Compliment, but I think ' Lycus ' a work absolutely unique in its line, such as no man has written, or could have written, but yourself." John Clare, on the other hand, candidly confessed to the author that he could not understand a word of " Lycus."

The volume in which these three poems were published is not a large one, but it contained besides "The Two Peacocks of Bedfont," and seventy pages of " Minor Poems "—the adjective was then used as applicable to length, and had not come to be used in a derogatory sense as implying something less than excellence in quality. Among these shorter pieces was Hood's most exquisite lyrical outpouring in the half-dozen stanzas of " Fair Ines," the poem which made so profound an impression upon Edgar Allan Poe that after reading it he described the author as the most singularly fanciful of modern poets. The critic used " fanciful " of course in the sense of being rich in poetic Fancy, not with its narrower colloquial signification. Like " Kubla Khan," this song might be employed as a standing test of any reader's capacity for appreciating poetry. In it we have musical rhythm, beautiful words, and that rich suggestiveness of a story which lifts it to the realm of

Thomas Hood :

pure fancy. Poem after poem might be cited to prove Hood's just title to a place among our truest poets, despite the popular verdict which has ever inclined to throne him supreme among the funny men of our literature. In the handful of pieces at the close of this volume are several of his best-remembered poems— "A Retrospective Review," "Ruth," "I remember, I remember," etc. There can, it may be said, have been little of the autobiographical in the last-named poem, for the description would scarcely apply to the business premises in the Poultry ; it is, however, quite likely that the description may have applied to the house at the then fairly countrified Islington Green, whither the Hood family may have removed while the poet was still in the early and impressionable years of childhood. Of this poem Bernard Barton said, " I would rather be the author of those lines than of almost any modern volume of poetry published during the last ten years. This may seem extravagant, but I know it is written in no complimentary mood."

Among the miscellaneous pieces of this volume are several which show that even in early manhood the poet was, as men of true humour so frequently are, particularly felicitous when dealing with subjects impinging upon the domain of decay and death. There are striking pieces in this vein, showing at once the richness of his fancy and the felicity of his diction. Here, for example, is a magnificent prosopopœia—

> " I saw old Autumn in the misty morn
> Stand shadowless like Silence, listening
> To silence, for no lonely bird would sing
> Into his hollow ear from woods forlorn,
> Nor lowly hedge nor solitary thorn ;—
> Shaking his languid locks all dewy bright
> With tangled gossamer that fell by night,
> Pearling his coronet of golden corn."

The Plea of the Midsummer Fairies.

Another piece, worthy of Coleridge, is an impressive fragment entitled " The Sea of Death," with closing lines which may indeed be described as poetically perfect—

> " So lay they garmented in torpid light,
> Under the pall of a transparent night,
> Like solemn apparitions lull'd sublime
> To everlasting rest,—and with them Time
> Slept, as he sleeps upon the silent face
> Of a dark dial in a sunless place."

One more passage may be cited from these " minor poems," showing again how the poet had realised that, as Shelley had put it, " our sweetest songs are those that tell of saddest thought," how humour and sadness are ever more or less closely allied—

> " All things are touch'd with Melancholy,
> Born of the secret soul's mistrust,
> To feel her fair ethereal wings
> Weigh'd down with vile degraded dust;
> Even the bright extremes of joy
> Bring on conclusions of disgust
> Like the sweet blossoms of the May,
> Whose fragrance ends in must.
> O give her, then, her tribute just,
> Her sighs and tears, and musings holy!
> There is no music in the life
> That sounds with idiot laughter solely;
> There's not a string attun'd to mirth,
> But has its chord in Melancholy."

Even here it will be seen, as Canon Ainger has pointed out, how extraordinarily felicitous was Hood in utilising the pun. How many readers must have passed over those lines without realising the poignant double meaning which they convey—

> " Like the sweet blossoms of the *May*,
> Whose fragrance ends in *must*."

In the same way his lighter pieces are often shot through with threads of deeper thought.

In concluding this notice of this, the only volume by

which Hood challenged the verdict of his contemporaries as a serious poet, it may be well to cite a couple of his sonnets further to illustrate the mastery of his materials—

> " It is not death that sometime in a sigh
> This eloquent breath shall take its speechless flight ;
> That sometime these bright stars, that now reply
> In sunlight to the sun, shall set in night ;
> That this warm conscious flesh shall perish quite,
> And all life's ruddy springs forget to flow ;
> That thoughts shall cease, and the immortal spright
> Be lapp'd in alien clay and laid below ;
> It is not death to know this, but to know
> That pious thoughts, which visit at new graves
> In tender pilgrimage, will cease to go
> So duly and so oft,—and when grass waves
> Over the past-away, there may be then
> No resurrection in the minds of men."

Here we have the thought expressed which, forty years later, George Eliot was to re-render in her better-known verse, "O may I join the choir invisible." The other sonnet, " To Silence," is, perhaps, in the form of its opening lines, a little reminiscent of the stanza in " Childe Harold " beginning " There is a pleasure in the pathless woods "—

> " There is a silence where hath been no sound,
> There is a silence where no sound may be,
> In the cold grave—under the deep deep sea,
> Or in wide desert where no life is found,
> Which hath been mute, and still must sleep profound ;
> No voice is hush'd—no life treads silently,
> But clouds and cloudy shadows wander free,
> That never spoke, over the idle ground :
> But in green ruins, in the desolate walls
> Of antique palaces, where Man hath been,
> Though the dun fox, or wild hyena, calls,
> And owls, that flit continually between,
> Shriek to the echo, and the low winds moan,
> There the true Silence is, self-conscious and alone."

The Plea of the Midsummer Fairies.

This is not the place to deal at length with the characteristics of Hood's poetry. Enough has been said perhaps to show that by the publication of this volume in 1827 he had definitely fixed his place among contemporary writers. It is true that " The Plea of the Midsummer Fairies " was not a commercial success, but if it was more or less ignored by book-buyers of the day later generations have found in it much of that by which they remember the author, and in a survey of his life as a whole it is seen to have an important place, indicating by its excellence the quality of his genius as a poet, and showing by its reception how he was more or less strongly compelled to turn his attention to the producing works which in another art would be described as pot-boilers.

" WHAT MUST BE—MUST."

CHAPTER IX.

EARLY HOME LIFE (1825—1829).

> " I have heard one who was well fitted by his intimacy to judge of Hood's social qualities speak of the beauty of his domestic life. We had a mutual admiration of his humour and his pathos, and above all could appreciate that exquisite sensibility which made Hood touch the sore places of the wretched with such a tender and delicate hand. That one was Douglas Jerrold."
>
> CHARLES KNIGHT.

WE have seen that the volume of "Odes and Addresses," published on the eve of Thomas Hood's marriage with Jane Reynolds, was followed within the next two years or so by the publication of two further volumes of comicalities and the long-delayed volume of serious poetry, but there were also two volumes of prose stories, so that the young author must have been kept very busy on first receiving the great encouragement of success. That he was happy too in his friends we may gather from the few letters of his which have come down to us representing this period.

According to the "Memorials," when the newly married couple returned from their honeymoon they took up their residence in the Adelphi, but the statement does not seem to be accurate. It would appear that Hood and his bride returned to his old home at Lower Street, Islington, and presumably they lived there for about a year and a half before removing to the neighbourhood of the Strand. In November, 1826, Mrs. Reynolds was with her daughter, the wife of Dr. Longmore, at Watford, whither they had removed from Upwell, and on

Early Home Life (1825—1829).

November 9, at the end of a long letter from Jane Hood to her mother, Thomas Hood had occasion to write fresh congratulations.

" My Dear Mother,—It has been my fault that this did not go into the post yesterday,—but the time went by whilst I was over my picture. You who are an artist know [how] difficult it is to leave off whilst you have all your subject in your mind's eye. The drawing (as they say of the lottery) will be over to-day, and I am very well satisfied—such is my vanity—with its effect.

" We have imagined you in a rare bustle as tho'·a babe[1] had been dropped from the clouds. I wish the new one may be as gentle and fine a boy as the other whom I was disappointed not to see. I always look upon him as half a god-child. Does he seem to feel his being made a Ward of ? Has it hurt his appetite ? or encreased his relish for books ? Liz and I are the best of friends and perhaps the best children in the world—for our years. I am quite a father to her—so let her parents be easy on her account. I never saw any child so sensible beyond her years, and yet so childish as she is— to which you would add, bless her heart I have taken pains with her indeed. However, out of so many grandchildren as you have now you must expect a bad one to turn out—which I hope will not be the Watford cadet—in spite of all our congratulations. I think I hear you in your rash way pronouncing that he is like Eliza, without your spectacles :—and refusing to entrust him with your accustomed vigilance even to the experienced arms of Mrs. Dyson. But I shall drop this subject (as gently as I can without hurting him) lest you should think me more of a gossip than I wish to be thought—only let me suggest that if the parents have not thought of a name and are not particular, that

---

[1] William A. Longmore, born November 7, 1825.

Thomas Hood :

Aminadab is soft, and well-sounding, and he might be
called ' Dab ' for shortness.

" It was Jane's birthday on Sunday which of course
you did not forget—we remembered yours on the 5th
and burnt you in effigy to the infinite amusement of your
granddaughter who could hardly be restrained from playing with the fire. It is fine to-day—for the Lord Mayor's
Show—but Jane and I have agreed not to take Liz to
see it for fear it should give her a taste for gaudy and
vulgar fripperies.

" Lamb called the other day and brought us a delicious hen pheasant which is reckoned the genteelest of
presents—not excepting *epergnes*. His sister is no better.
Marianne still mends but Mr. R[eynolds] like a lonely
turtle is pining in proportion. Mr. and Mrs. H[ood]
are quite well and united afresh in love to each other
and to you.—My best congratulations to Eliza and
Longmore on the advent of their little Unknown—
and believe me my dear Mother very truly your
affectionate son,

"T. Hood."

In the autumn of this year Hood's Dundee friend
Andrew Wyllie died from an illness brought on by
injudicious bathing in the Tay, but so far as his letters
have been recovered it does not seem that he kept up any
correspondence with his Scottish friends as late as this.
His busy literary and journalistic life and new interests
had necessarily led to the curtailing of such letters as
marked the first few years of his return to London.
During this autumn Hood was no doubt putting together
the prose and verse for his first series of " Whims
and Oddities." But he was also apparently engaged
at the same time on his large satirical etching " The
Progress of Cant," for to that it would seem he refers
in the above letter to Mrs. Reynolds. This plate was

Early Home Life (1825—1829).

published by Maclean at the close of 1825 and was very well received. In the *New Monthly Magazine* there was a capital description of it, presumably by Charles Lamb, who was then contributing his "Popular Fallacies" and *Eliacal* essays to that periodical. This summary description of the plate may be quoted, as it happily indicates the nature of this work, the only one of the kind which Hood undertook. The etching, which was entitled "The Progress of Cant," may well have been designed originally as a frontispiece to the little volume of "Odes and Addresses"; it was described as "designed and executed by one of the Authors of the Odes and Addresses to Great People." Says the critic of the *New Monthly* :—

"A wicked wag has produced a caricature under this title in which he marshalleth all the projected improvements of the age, and maketh them take their fantastic progress before the eyes of the scorner. It is a spirited etching, almost as abundant in meaning as in figures, and hath a reprobate eye to a corner — an Hogarthian vivification of post and placard. Priests, anti-priests, architects, politicians, reformers, flaming loyalty-men, high and low, rich and poor, one with another, all go on progressing, as the Americans say. Life goes on, at any rate ; and there is so much merriment on all sides, that for our parts, inclined to improvements as we are, we should be willing enough to join in the laugh throughout, if the world were as merry as the artist. The houses are as much to the purpose as the pedestrians. There is the office of the Peruvian Mining Company in dismal, dilapidated condition; a barber's shop, with 'Nobody to be shaved during divine service,' the *h* worn out; two boarding schools for young ladies and gentlemen, very neighbourly ; and the public house, called the Angel and Punch-Bowl, by T. Moore. Among the crowd

Thomas Hood :

is a jolly, but vehement, reverend person holding a flag, inscribed, 'The Church in anger,' the *D* for danger being hidden by another flag, inscribed, 'Converted Jews.' Then there is the Caledonian Chap (*el* being obstructed in the same way), who holds a pennon, crying out 'No Theatre!' Purity of Election, with a bludgeon, very drunk; and, above all, a petty fellow called the Great Unknown, with his hat over his eyes, and a constable's staff peeping out of his pocket. Some of the faces and figures are very clever, particularly the Barber; the Saving-banks man; the Jew-Boy picking the pocket; the Charity Boy and the Beadle. The Beadle is rich from head to foot. Nathless, we like not to see Mrs. Fry so roasted : we are at a loss to know why the Blacks deserve to be made Black Devils; and are not aware that the proposal of an University in London has occasioned, or is likely to occasion, any sort of cant. However, there is no harm done where a cause can afford a joke; and where it cannot, the more it is joked at the better."

It was in the month that that notice of the etching was written that Lamb, in a note to Charles K. Ollier, said, "We will get Hood, that half-Hogarth, to meet you." The Hogarthian spirit of his picture was recognised on all hands. In the January number of his old *London Magazine* two pages were devoted to an appreciation of the work in which the writer confidently anticipated that it would attract very considerable notice from its singular and happy humour of design and felicity of execution. "We can fearlessly say, that we know of no production so nearly approaching to the admirable works of Hogarth, in their forcible delineations of nature and their comic and pungent satire, as this etching of the 'Progress of Cant,' and we can safely recommend it to our readers as a work well deserving their *perusal*. Someone has said, and said truly, that 'Hogarth's

Early Home Life (1825—1829).

pictures we read.'[1] We may say the same of the picture before us. A mere look at it will be utterly insufficient; for there is enough to delight and amuse the *reader* for hours." After describing some of the features of the plate the same critic concluded: "Considering that it has been planned, drawn, and etched, by the same person, we confess we do not a little admire the patience, genius and skill of the author." Over three pages of Hone's " Every Day Book " were given up to a description of the etching, introduced by an enlargement of the " jewel of a beadle," and a brief appropriate bit about that worthy from the pen of Lamb. The writer of Hone's notice looked forward to Hood's further work in the same kind, but henceforth as draughtsman he seems to have mostly limited himself to making little " cuts " to accompany his own comic verses and sketches.

With Charles Lamb and his sister at this time the Hoods were on the friendliest footing, and several allusions to the fact are made in the letters of Lamb. " Hood sups with me to-night. Can you come and eat grouse ? 'Tis not often I offer at delicacies." Ollier, to whom that invitation was addressed, evidently could not accept, for there follows another Elian note to him :—

" We lamented your absence last night. The grouse were piquant, the backs incomparable. You must come in to cold mutton and oysters some evening. Name your evening; though I have qualms at the distance. Do you never leave early ? My head is very queerish and indisposed for much company; but we will get Hood, that half Hogarth, to meet you."

A little later, Lamb, writing to Bernard Barton, said that he was so deaf with cold that he seemed too deaf to see what he read, and described one of Hood's little

[1] See Lamb's essay "On the Genius and Character of Hogarth."

Thomas Hood :

pencil sketches, entitled " Very Deaf Indeed ! " " of a good-natured stupid-looking old gentleman, whom a footpad has stopt, but for his extreme deafness cannot make him understand what he wants ; the unconscious old gentleman is extending his ear-trumpet very complacently, and the fellow is firing a pistol into it to make him hear, but the ball will pierce his skull sooner than the report reach his sensorium." [1]

During many of the years of their friendship Hood and Lamb were such near neighbours that they probably saw much of each other and had little occasion to correspond, so that Lamb's rich correspondence comprises but few letters to the man who described him as " one whom, were such literary adoptions in modern use, I might well name, as Cotton called Walton, my father." At Colebrooke Cottage Thomas Hood met Wordsworth, Coleridge, and other of the notable people who were proud to number Elia among their friends. In such gatherings, judging from the personal accounts on which we can base an opinion, Hood was generally the " silentish young man " of the company ; he was probably always more or less shy with people whom he did not know well, though with those whom he did he was the liveliest and most boyish of companions.

On May 21, 1826, there was started the *Atlas*, a new London Sunday " general newspaper and journal of literature," which proudly boasted that it was " nearly double the size of *The Times*," and " the largest newspaper ever printed." Robert Stephen Rintoul, who had come to London from the *Dundee Advertiser*, was on the staff for a time, but left the *Atlas* to become first editor of the *Spectator* in 1828 ; Robert Bell, afterwards to become celebrated as a miscellaneous writer and editor of a series of British poets, became editor,

---

[1] The sketch appeared this year in the first series of " Whims and Oddities."

Early Home Life (1825—1829).

and Thomas Hood was appointed dramatic critic. I have been unable to consult a file of this journal, and cannot say how long it was that Hood remained its dramatic critic, but in the appendix to the ten-volume edition of his works are given several passages from his criticisms, and there we learn, too, that in this paper the dramatic critic occasionally dropped into verse with odes and addresses to certain actors and actresses— Wrench, Miss Kelly, " Paul Pry," etc. The attitude which Hood adopted in this work may be gathered from the opening address to his readers, in which he indulged on taking up his new *rôle*:—" We come unbiassed by any stage connections, and resolute to perform our office without fear or favour.

" Our delight in Miss Kelly does not hinder us from seeing what is pleasant in Mrs. Farlowe. Our partiality for Mr. Wrench does not blind us to the merits of Mr. Bennet. There are other persons who never value any talents till they are gone by, and therefore could not say a good word for Munden till after his retirement. But although we have been happy enough to have seen Mrs. Jordan and Mrs. Siddons, and the great Kemble, our praises will not be of that retrospective kind. The living actors and actresses who shall deserve them, may expect our hearty commendations, in prose and verse,— the faulty will be treated, of course, with a wholesome severity. In the first row of the pit—the critic's proper place, though he cannot always get to it—we shall take our seat, and from thence keep a wary eye upon both play-wrights and players."

The critic then proceeded, in not very good taste, it must be admitted, to make fun of Elliston's last appearance at Drury Lane, when the " Great Lessee," as Falstaff, fell, in some kind of fit, says his biographer —from being overtaken by drink, recorded the *Atlas*, and that seems to have been the opinion of the audience, where "there were forty laughing like one." Apostrophising the fallen dictator, the critic proceeded—

"Thy fault is, after all, venial—a gentlemanly frailty—though the fit was ill-timed. To drink is human; but we dread the effect of such high, flagrant example upon the universal establishment. If, hereafter, a Hamlet come in maudlin, who shall reprove it? Canst thou fine Lear for being only in his cups? In our mind's eye we see a groggy Macbeth. The three over-taken witches are tumbling into their own cauldron. The figurantes dance reels bacchanalian. The scene-shifters are misjoining fragments of land and sea—ill-painted blotches, for Stanfield has dipped his brush into a full rummer."

The biographer's account of Elliston's fall may have been but euphemistically meant, for there are other stories of the Great Lessee's liking for strong drink. A young dramatist, whose work brought back some-thing of the tide of success to the manager three or four years later at the Surrey Theatre, on hearing an irate caller declare that he could see a prime minister or duke any time in the morning, but could never see Elliston, promptly broke in with:—"There's one comfort, if Elliston is invisible in the morning, he'll do the handsome thing any afternoon, by seeing you twice—for at that time of day he invariably sees double."

It cannot now be ascertained how long Hood con-tinued to act as dramatic critic of the *Atlas*, but it may be surmised that it was the holding of some similar appointment which made him contemplate removal from Islington to a place nearer the theatres. The next letter of his, dated October 10, but obviously belonging to this year, refers to the *Atlas*—and to Rintoul—in no very complimentary terms. It is written

Early Home Life (1825—1829).

from Lower Street, and is addressed to Alaric A. Watts [1]—

"MY DEAR SIR,—My best thanks for the 'Souvenir.' We, I and my wife, have read together your poem of the 'First-Born' and admire it exceedingly. I hope this will please you, as I have been pleased and gratified by the praises of Mrs. Watts. I return the proof of 'A Retrospective Review,' with additions, which you will please return or not as you please. I am glad you like the thing so much, for I was really anxious to do something worthy of your book. The other thing I wrote, and rejected, for you will help me through a sheet of the 'Whims and Oddities.' I saw M—— for a moment yesterday, which sufficed for his telling me in so many words, that the book will not suit him. As I had a handsome letter of introduction to him, I think he might have treated me with a little more courtesy than poor FitzAdam. But I am obliged to him for a hint, that there is a capital subject which I had not set down in my list, for the next of my 'Odes and Addresses to Great People.'

"I observed, in a certain last Sunday's paper, a malicious attack on your *Literary Magnet*. The editor of this Sunday news-waggon is a Scotchman, heretofore Editor of a Dundee newspaper. To my mind it shows no signs of editorship, and is but a hulking lubber of a paper; but it serves to wrap up twice as many parcels as any other. It plumes itself chiefly on its size, as though the mere superficial extent of paper and print ensured the *spread* of intelligence. A large sheet quotha,—a patchwork quilt rather! Twice as big as a daily without being any better, like

[1] Alaric A. Watts (1797—1867), a minor poet of his day, editor of " The Literary Souvenir," and other miscellanies.

Thomas Hood :

a spread-eagle to an eagle *au naturel !* A little intelligence going a great way, like a puddle overflowing a Lincolnshire level. Poor in matter but prodigious, like Bankruptcy enlarged! A Gog among newspapers,— and as wooden.

"Pray give my respects and remembrances to Mrs. Watts, and believe me, very truly yours,

"T. Hood."

From this letter we gather that Hood and his wife were still living at Lower Street, Islington, eighteen months after their marriage. We also find that he was either still projecting a second volume of odes and addresses, or was contributing a series of such to some periodical. Who M—— was, evidently a publisher or member of a publishing firm, cannot be said; it may have been Murray, or it may have been Marshall, who two years later undertook "The Gem,"—Moxon was yet a few years off setting up as publisher. The *Literary Magnet* was a miscellany, a kind of tit-bits of literature, in which were gathered passages in prose and verse from many sources. (In September of the year following it was to give Hood's "Fair Ines" without a word of acknowledgment.) The Sunday journal out of the size of which Hood makes so much fun was of course the *Atlas,* to which reference has just been made, and the tenour of his remarks suggests either that he had not found working for the paper pleasant occupation, or that his son was wrong in ascribing his connection with the paper to its commencement. It is possible that it was after Robert Bell joined the paper —presumably in 1828—that Hood became dramatic critic, for it was to Bell's recollections that we owe the knowledge of Hood's connection with the journal at all. Access to a file of the paper—a copy of which is

Early Home Life (1825—1829).

not in the British Museum—would be necessary to establish the point.

It was at the close of 1826, or early in 1827, that the Hoods moved from Lower Street, Islington, to No. 2, Robert Street, Adelphi, "over against the Society of Arts," and here they continued to live for a couple of years or so, near neighbours of John Hamilton Reynolds, who had a house in another of the Adelphi streets. The only letter of Hood's that is extant written from here is a brief and studiedly formal note addressed to " Mrs. Hamerton, care of Mrs. Reynolds, Little Britain " :—

" MADAM,—I have the pleasure of enclosing to you £15 on acct. of Mrs. Hamerton on whose behalf I have this day signed an agreement.

" Mr. Tilt requests that the lady aforesaid will provide a new title for the work without delay as the presses are standing idle. I am, Madam, your most obedient

" THOS. HOOD."

The book referred to was a very pleasant little volume for young readers, entitled " Mrs. Leslie and Her Grandchildren," by Mrs. Hamerton, and that name was the pseudonym of Mrs. Reynolds herself. The story would perhaps meet with the favour of present-day children were it made newly available. That it met with Charles Lamb's approval is shown by a brief note written by him to Hood about this time, and probably taken to the Adelphi by Emma Isola, Lamb's adopted daughter :—

" DEAR H.,—Emma has a favour, besides a bed, to ask of Mrs. Hood. Your parcel was gratifying. We have all been pleased with Mrs. Leslie ; I speak it most sincerely. There is much manly sense with a feminine expression, which is my definition of ladies' writing."

Thomas Hood :

In May, 1827, there was born to the Hoods, only to die at once, their first child, a girl. Many years later, when Thomas Hood himself lay dead, there was found in his desk a tiny scrap of golden hair enclosed in a piece of paper, on which was written—

> "Little eyes that scarce did see
> Little lips that never smiled ;
> Alas ! my little dear dead child,
> Death is thy father, and not me,
> I but embraced thee, soon as he."

The blow must have been a painful one to the young father and mother—the destruction of all their hopes at the very moment of apparent fulfilment—for both were great lovers of home and all that home stands for, the greatest part of which is formed by the children. The birth of the child might have been premature, for a note of Lamb's written at the time suggests that they had arranged for a visit from friends :—

" DEAREST HOOD,—Your news has spoil'd us a merry meeting. Miss Kelly and we were coming, but your letter elicited a flood of tears from Mary, and I saw she was not fit for a party. God bless you and the mother (or should-be mother) of your sweet girl that should have been. I have won sexpence of Moxon by the *sex* of the dear gone one. Yours most truly and hers."

Lamb has recorded somewhere that he always wished to laugh at a funeral and cry at a wedding, and here the poor pun was doubtless more a hiding of feelings than the tasteless levity which an unknowing reader might consider it. Shortly after, Lamb wrote for Jane Hood those exquisite verses of his, " On an Infant dying as soon as born," beginning—

> " I saw where in the shroud did lurk
> A curious frame of Nature's work.
> A flow'ret crushed in the bud
> A nameless piece of Babyhood."

Early Home Life (1825—1829).

In the summer of this year the Lambs went to Enfield to stay (taking with them Hood's dog, Dash, for whom it may well be believed a house in the Adelphi was not a happy place), and in the autumn they finally removed there from Islington, a removal which Hood records and apropos of which he jotted down some pleasant recollections of Elia which may well find a place here. Of Elia, for whom and for whose memory he retained a life-long affection, keeping always with him to the end, ever hanging in his study, in his successive homes, a portrait of his " literary father."

On his removal Lamb wrote the following pleasant letter to " the Hoods "—

" DEAR HOOD,—If I have anything in my head I will send it to Mr. Watts. Strictly speaking he should have had my Album verses, but a very intimate friend importuned me for the trifles, and I believe I forgot Mr. Watts, or lost sight at the time of his similar Souvenir. Jamieson conveyed the farce from me to Mrs. C. Kemble, *he* will not be in town before the 27th. Give our kind loves to all at Highgate, and tell them that we have finally torn ourselves out right away from Colebrooke, where I had *no* health, and are about to domiciliate for good at Enfield, where I have experienced *good.*

> " ' Lord what good hours do we keep !
> How quietly we sleep ! '

" See the rest in the Complete Angler. We have got our books into our new house. I am a drayhorse if I was not asham'd of the indigested dirty lumber as I toppled 'em out of the cart, and blest Becky that came with 'em for her having an unstuff'd brain with such rubbish. We shall get in by Michael's mass. 'Twas with some pain we were evuls'd from Colebrooke. You

215

Thomas Hood :

may find some of our flesh sticking to the door posts.
To change habitations is to die to them, and in my time
I have died seven deaths. But I don't know whether
every such change does not bring with it a rejuvenes-
cence. 'Tis an enterprise, and shoves back the sense of
death's approximating, which tho' not terrible to me, is
at all times particular distasteful. My house-deaths have
generally been periodical, recurring after seven years,
but this last is premature by half that time. Cut off in
the flower of Colebrooke. The Middletonian stream and
all its echoes mourn. Even minnows dwindle. *A parvis
fiunt MINIMI.* I fear to invite Mrs. Hood to our new
mansion, lest she envy it and rote us. But when we
are fairly in, I hope she will come and try it. I heard
she and you were made uncomfortable by some unworthy
to be cared for attacks, and have tried to set up a feeble
counteraction through the Table Book of last Saturday.
Has it not reach'd you, that you are silent about it ?
Our new domicile is no manor house, but new, and
externally not inviting, but furnish'd within with every
convenience. Capital new locks to every door, capital
grates in every room, with nothing to pay for incoming
and the rent £10 less than the Islington one. It was
built a few years since at £1,100 expense, they tell me,
and I perfectly believe it. And I get it for £35 exclusive
of moderate taxes. We think ourselves most lucky.
It is not our intention to abandon Regent Street, and
West End perambulations (monastic and terrible
thought !) but occasionally to breathe the FRESHER AIR
of the metropolis. We shall put up a bedroom or two
(all we want) for occasional ex-rustication, where we
shall visit, not be visited. Plays too we'll see—perhaps
our own. Urbani Sylvani, and Sylvan Urbanuses in
turns. Courtiers for a spurt, then philosophers. Old
homely tell-truths and learn-truths in the virtuous shades
of Enfield. Liars again and mocking gibers in the

216

Early Home Life (1825—1829).

coffee-houses and resorts of London. What can a mortal desire more for his bi-parted nature?

"O the curds and cream you shall eat with us here!
O the turtle soup and lobster sallads we shall devour with you there!
O the old books we shall peruse here!
O the new nonsense we shall trifle with over there!
O Sir T. Browne!—here.
O Mr. Hood and Mr. Jerdan there!
    thine, C(urbanus) L(sylvanus) (ELIA ambo)—

"Inclos'd are verses which Emma sat down to write, her first, on the eve after your departure. Of course they are only for Mrs. H.'s perusal. They will shew you at least that one of our party is not willing to cut old friends. What to call 'em I don't know. Blank verse they are not, because of the rhymes.—Rhimes they are not, because of the blank verse. Heroics they are not, because they are lyric, lyric they are not, because of the Heroic measure. They must be called EMMAICS.—"

Lamb's reference to "unworthy to be cared for attacks" was probably to the *London Weekly Review*, in which appeared the statement that "Mr. Hood bestows his tediousness on that most sage and chaste of periodicals (the *Literary Gazette*), where he celebrates David Laing or any other blacksmith that may happen to die." Laing was the wed-lock-smith of Gretna Green to whose memory Hood had dedicated an amusing ode. In the *Literary Gazette* he addressed the editor of that journal in another ode, in which he severely handled his critic and even condemned him out of his own mouth by quoting the deadly parallel of the public words from the *London Weekly Review* along with the following words from a private note from the editor of the same periodical: "The editor would be sorry indeed to part with Mr. Hood's occasional contributions, if he could possibly secure them."

217

Thomas Hood:

It was not long before Hood journeyed out for Enfield "curds and cream," and some of his reminiscences, jotted down a dozen years later, may well find a place here in further illustration of a pleasant friendship.

"From Colebrooke, Lamb removed to Enfield Chase, —a painful operation at all times, for as he feelingly misapplied Wordsworth, 'the moving accident was not his trade.' As soon as he was settled, I called upon him, and found him in a bald-looking yellowish house, with a bit of a garden, and a wasp's nest convanient, as the Irish say, for one stung my pony as he stood at the door. Lamb laughed at the fun; but, as the clown says, the whirligig of time brought round its revenges. He was one day bantering my wife on her dread of wasps, when all at once he uttered a horrible shout,—a wounded specimen of the species had slily crawled up the leg of the table, and stung him in the thumb. I told him it was a refutation well put in, like Smollett's timely snowball. 'Yes,' said he, 'and a stinging commentary on Macbeth—

> "'By the pricking of my thumbs
> Something wicked this way comes.'

"There were no pastoral yearnings in this Enfield removal. There is no doubt which of Captain Morris's town and country songs would have been most to Lamb's taste. 'The sweet shady side of Pall-Mall,' would have carried it hollow. In courtesy to a friend, he would select a green lane for a ramble, but left to himself, he took the turnpike road, as often as otherwise. 'Scott,' says Cunningham, 'was a stout walker.' Lamb was a porter one. He calculated distances, not by Long Measure, but by Beer and Ale Measure. 'Now I have walked a pint.' Many a time I have accompanied him in these matches against Meux, not without sharing in

Early Home Life (1825—1829).

the stake, and then, what fearful and profitable talk! For instance, he once delivered to me aurally the substance of the essay on the Defects of Imagination in Modern Artists, subsequently printed in the *Athenaeum*. But besides the criticism, there were snatches of old poems, golden lines and sentences culled from rare books, and anecdotes of men of note. Marry, it was like going a ramble with gentle Izaak Walton, minus the fishing.

"To make these excursions more delightful to one of my temperament, Lamb never affected any spurious gravity. Neither did he ever act the grand senior. He did not exact that common copy-book respect, which some asinine persons would fain command on account of the mere length of their years. As if, forsooth, what is bad in itself, could be the better for keeping; as if intellects already *mothery*, got anything but *grandmothery* by lapse of time! In this particular, he was opposed to Southey or rather (for Southey has been opposed to himself) to his poem on the Holly Tree.

> "So serious should my youth appear among
> The thoughtless throng;
> So would I seem among the young and gay
> *More grave than they.*

"There was nothing of Sir Oracle about Lamb. On the contrary, at sight of a solemn visage that 'creamed and mantled like the standing pool,' he was the first to pitch a mischievous stone to disturb the duck-weed. 'He was a boy-man,' as he truly said of Elia; 'and his manners lagged behind his years.' He liked to herd with people younger than himself. Perhaps, in his fine generalising way, he thought that, in relation to eternity, we are all contemporaries. However, without reckoning birthdays, it was always 'Hail fellow, well met,' and although he was my elder by a quarter of a

219

Thomas Hood :

century, he never made me feel, in our excursions, that
I was 'taking a walk with the schoolmaster.' I
remember, in one of our strolls, being called to account,
very pompously, by the proprietor of an Enfield Villa,
who asserted that my dog Dash, who never hunted
anything in his dog-days, had chased the sheep; whereupon, Elia, taking the dog's part, said very emphatically, ' Hunt *Lambs*, sir? Why he has never hunted
me !' But he was always ready for fun, intellectual or
practical—now helping to pelt D [aniel], a modern
Dennis, with puns; and then to persuade his sister,
God bless her! by a vox et preterea nihil, that she was as
deaf as an adder. In the same spirit, being requested
by a young schoolmaster to take charge of his flock for
a day, ' during the unavoidable absence of the principal,'
he willingly undertook the charge, but made no other
use of his brief authority than to give the boys a whole
holiday."

Hood's dog, Dash, makes several appearances in
Lamb's correspondence, and is always provocative of
many pleasantries. Dash was with the Patmores (the
parents of Coventry Patmore) for a time, but whether
on a visit or not is not clear, and later seems to have
been given to Edward Moxon. Writing to Patmore in
September, 1827, Lamb, making fun of a mad-dog scare,
suggested that " if the slightest suspicion arises in your
breast that all is not right with him (Dash), muzzle him
and lead him in a string (common pack-thread will do;
he don't care for twist) to Hood's, his quondam master,
and he'll take him in at any time. You may mention
your suspicions or not, as you like, or as you think, it
may wound or not Mr. H.'s feelings. Hood, I know,
will wink at a few follies in Dash, in consideration of
his former sense. Besides, Hood is deaf, and if you
hinted anything, ten to one he would not hear you.
Besides, you will have discharged your conscience, and

Early Home Life (1825—1829).

laid the child at the right door, as they say. . . . I send my love in a —— to Dash." On the outside of this letter Lamb wrote :—" Seriously I wish you would call upon Hood when you are that way. He's a capital fellow. I sent him a couple of poems—one ordered by his wife, and written to order ; and 'tis a week since, and I've not heard from him. I fear something is the matter."

It is quite likely that something was the matter, for towards the close of this year—1827—Hood had a severe attack of rheumatic fever, and on his recovery was ordered to Brighton to recruit his health. He had, it is likely, been overworking himself, for besides publishing the second series of "Whims and Oddities" and "The Plea of the Midsummer Fairies" he had also produced early in the same year two volumes of "National Tales" in prose.[1] These tales, which were published by Harrison Ainsworth, during his brief term as publisher, before he had himself turned wholly author, show considerable invention in the devising of tragical situations, but are, as a whole, the poorest books which Hood published. They belong to the artificial style of narration of which the early years of the nineteenth century gave so many examples. The author seems so resolutely to have set himself to being serious that he is sometimes dull, for the stories lack that spontaneity which makes his serious poetry or his earnest satire successful, and suggest that though he could write fun when he was feeling grave it was foreign to his nature to write romantic tales. His preface may be cited, for it seems to have been penned as something in the nature of a protest against the common belief that a funny man is incapable of being serious.

[1] In the collected works of Thomas Hood these "National Tales" are incorrectly said to have been published at the end of 1827 or beginning of 1828.

Thomas Hood :

"It has been decided by the learned Malthusians of our century, that there is too great an influx of new books into this reading world. An apology seems therefore to be required of me, for increasing my family in this kind; and by twin volumes, instead of the single octavos which have hitherto been my issue. But I concede not to that modern doctrine, which supposes a world on short allowance, or a generation without a ration. There is no mentionable overgrowth likely to happen in life or literature. Wholesome checks are appointed against over-fecundity in any species. Thus the whale thins the myriads of herrings, the teeming rabbit makes Thyestean family dinners on her own offspring, and the hyenas devour themselves. Death is never backward when the human race wants hoeing; nor the critic to thin the propagation of the press. The surplus children, that would encumber the earth, are thrown back in the grave—the superfluous works, into the coffins prepared for them by the trunkmaker. Nature provides thus equally against scarcity or repletion. There are a thousand blossoms for the one fruit that ripens, and numberless buds for every prosperous flower. Those for which there is no space or sustenance drop early from the bough; and even so these leaves of mine will pass away, if there be not patronage extant, and to spare, that may endow them with a longer date.

"I make, therefore, no excuses for this production, since it is a venture at my own peril. The serious character of the generality of the stories, is a deviation from my former attempts, and I have received advice enough, on that account, to make me present them with some misgiving. But because I have jested elsewhere, it does not follow that I am incompetent for gravity, of which any owl is capable; or proof against melancholy, which besets even the ass. Those who can be touched

Early Home Life (1825—1829).

by neither of these moods rank lower indeed than both of these creatures. It is from none of the player's ambition, which has led the buffoon by a rash step into the tragic buskin, that I assume the sadder humour, but because I know from certain passages that such affections are not foreign to my nature. During my short lifetime, I have often been as 'sad as night,' and not like the young gentlemen of France, merely from wantonness. It is the contrast of such leaden and golden fits that lends a double relish to our days. A life of mere laughter is like music without its bass; or a picture (conceive it) of vague unmitigated light; whereas the occasional melancholy, like those grand rich glooms of old Rembrandt, produces an incomparable effect and a very grateful relief."

The author went on to say that he had other stories by him "which I keep at home like the younger Benjamin, till I know the treatment of their elder brethren, whom I have sent forth (to buy corn for me) into Egypt." The treatment was not, it is to be feared, very encouraging. In *Blackwood's* "Noctes Ambrosianae" in April, 1827—and *Maga*, as we have seen, was whole-hearted in its expressions of admiration over the "Whims and Oddities" in the January number— the Shepherd says :—" What for did ye no send out to me Altrive Hood's National Tales ? Yon Whims and Oddities o' his were maist ingenious and divertin'. Are the National Tales gude ? " To which North replies, "Some of them are excellent, and few are without the impress of originality. I am glad to see that they are published by Mr. Ainsworth, to whom I wish all success in his new profession. He is himself a young gentleman of talents, and his Sir John Chiverton is a spirited and romantic performance." The "National Tales," which were thus damned with faint praise as being good—in parts—were not successful, and though they have been reprinted during the past few years with other of Hood's prose writings, they remain among the least known—and the least deserving to be known—of his works.

In 1827, too, it is recorded that a miscellany publication issued at Glasgow under the title of the "Ant" was dedicated to Hood, which suggests—with *Maga's* treatment—that he was early appreciated in the land of his family origin. The "Ant" was in two parts, original and selected; only the former is in the British Museum, and that is dedicated to Thomas Campbell.

A brief note written to Ackerman, the publisher of the "Forget-me-Not," towards the end of 1827 shows that the contributors to those fashionable miscellanies had often to write their fancies to such inspiration as they could find in the plates which were to accompany them—even Sir Walter Scott did so— and it hints also something of the illness which befell Hood about this time. He writes: "I have the pleasure of sending you 'The Logicians.' It being rather a crabbed subject, and myself not overwell, I have been longer about it than I promised. The other subject is in progress, and you shall have it in proper *trim*, I hope, in two days." That "other subject" was a picture from "Tristram Shandy," showing Corporal Trim giving his illustration of the uncertainty of human life. "'Are we not here now?' continued the corporal (striking the end of his stick perpendicularly on the floor, so as to give an air of health and stability)—'and are we not' (dropping his hat upon the ground) 'gone? —In a moment!'" From this sprang Hood's verses of "Death in the Kitchen."

The illness from which Hood suffered towards the close of 1827 and in the early part of the following year necessitated change of air, and when he was sufficiently convalescent he and his wife went to Brighton, which

Early Home Life (1825—1829).

afterwards shared with Hastings his holiday affections. On setting out he is said to have been so weak that he had to be lifted into the coach, but the sea air at once effected an improvement, and the very next day it is recorded that his love of fun made him play off a trick on his wife. The anecdote would seem to belong to the honeymoon trip to Hastings rather than to this visit, for Jane Hood would scarcely have allowed herself, after nearly three years of housekeeping experience, to be so quietly taken in. The family tradition, however, attaches to this visit, and is told as follows :—" At breakfast Hood offered to give his wife a few hints on the buying of fish, on account of his superior experience of the sea. 'Above all things, Jane,' he said, 'as they will endeavour to impose upon your inexperience, let nothing induce you to buy a plaice that has any appearance of red or orange spots, as they are sure signs of an advanced stage of decomposition.' My mother promised faithful compliance in the innocence of her heart, and accordingly, when the fishwoman came to the door, she descended to show off her newly acquired information. As it happened, the woman had very little except plaice, and these she turned over and over, praising their size and freshness. But the obnoxious red spots on every one of them still greeted my mother's dissatisfied eyes. On her hinting a doubt of their freshness, she was met by the assertion that they were not long out of the water, having been caught that morning. This shook the housewife's doubts, but only for a moment, and remembering Hood's account of the fishwomen's ways she shook her head, saying, 'My good woman, it may be as you say, but I could not think of buying any plaice with those very unpleasant red spots!' The woman's answer was a short, 'Lord bless your eyes, mum! Who ever seed any without 'em ?' A suppressed giggle on the stairs betrayed the perpetrator of the joke."

Hood was fond of these mild practical jokes, and his wife, by her enjoyment of them, allowed herself to be made a willing victim. A lady friend who saw a good deal of "the Hoods," as they were commonly called, in recording some such episode, has added: "Sometimes, perhaps, the jest was pointed a *little* too heavily, but never did the sweet face or gentle voice of Mrs. Hood betray anything like a cloud or exasperation even when put to tests that would have proved eminently trying to the female patience of many modern Griseldas ! "

It was in the latter half of March that the Hoods set out for Brighton. The sea air, however, worked a rapid change, as we learn from a letter which he wrote to a friend a day or two later. The friend in question was Robert Balmanno, secretary to the Artists' Benevolent Fund, and a neighbour of the Hoods, living as he did in Craven Street, Strand. He and his wife emigrated to New York some years later. The following two characteristic letters, which show at once that Hood was rapidly recovering his health and spirits, were addressed from 25, King's Road, Brighton, the first being dated March 21, 1828 :—

" MY DEAR FRIEND,—We got down here safe, but heartily tired—I think Jane the most fatigued of the two —and took up our quarters for the night at the Norfolk. The next morning to my own astonishment and my wife's, I got out and walked about a mile on the shingles, partly, and against a strong wind which now and then had the best of me. Here we are now settled in a nice lively lodging—the sea fretting about 20 yards in front, and our *side* window looking down the road westward and along the beach, where, at about 100

Early Home Life (1825—1829).

yards lies the wreck of a poor sloop that came ashore the night we arrived—nobody lost. She looks somewhat like the 'atomies' in Surgeon's Hall, with her bare ribs and backbone, and the waves come and spit at her, with incurable spite. We have had one warm beautiful day quite like summer with flies (the hackflies) all about too; but to-day is cold—squally, with rain. The effect of the sea upon me is almost incredible, I have found some strength and much appetite already, though I have but sniffed the brine a single time. The warm bath has removed all my stiffness—an effect I anticipated from something that occurred in the coach. The approach to the coast, even at half-way, had such an effect on the claret-jelly that it took away all *its stiffness*, and let it loose in Mrs. Hood's bag. ' The regal purple stream' has caused some odd results. Made my watch a stop-watch by gum-ming up the works, glued Jane's pocket book together, and fuddled a letter to Dr. Yates in such a style that I'm ashamed to deliver it. Pray don't let Mrs. Balmanno take any reproach to herself for the misconduct of her jelly—I suspect it was so glad to get off it didn't know whether it stood on its head or its heels. I rather think it was placed for safety bottom uppermost; I forgot to say that the jelly got into her purse and made all the money stick to it, an effect I shan't object to, if it prove permanent. Jane is delighted with Brighton, and wishes we could live there, regretting almost that I am not a boatman instead of an author. Perhaps when my pen breaks down I may retire here and set up a circulating library like Horace Smith's.[1] I shall deliver your credentials to that gentleman to-morrow.

" So far was written yesterday. I got up to-day, ate a monstrous breakfast and took a walk, but could not

[1] This alludes to Smith's numerous publications.

Thomas Hood :

fetch up Horace Smith's, for I set out along the beach, which being *shingle* the fatigue was *double*. As yet I don't think I have any ankles. I don't bore myself yet with writing (don't tell Yates this) but amuse myself with watching the waves, or a seagull, or the progress of a fishing boat, matters trifling enough, but they afford speculation seemingly to a score old smocked, glazed hatted, blue-breeched boatmen or fishermen before my windows, and why not to me? There is great pleasure in letting a busy restless mind lie fallow a little, and mine takes to its idleness very complacently. Jane murmurs, and want books (scandal). *Her* mind is so used to be idle it requires a change. She takes to her victuals as well as I do, and has *such* a colour, particularly on her *chin*! Here is a look out of our window,[1] raging main and all—Jane made me draw it in my best style for your satisfaction. I leave to her the scraps to write upon, and subscribe myself with best regards to Mrs. Balmanno and yourself, my dear friend, yours very truly,

"Thos. Hood.

"P.S.—Mind and put on your hat when reading near the open window!"

The sheet of paper was then filled out by a note from Jane Hood to Mrs. Balmanno, in which she said that Hood had gained strength already far beyond her hopes at the time of setting out. "Tell our kind friend Mr. Balmanno that my worst half is getting as impertinent as he is when he is quite well, and treats me with as much flippancy and scorn as Jenny Wren used to Cock Robin when she got well and 'stood upon her feet.'"

[1] Here, in the original, is a drawing of a large French window, opening on a balcony with a view of the sea.

Early Home Life (1825—1829).

Three days later and to the same correspondent Hood wrote again:—

" Many thanks my dear Balmanno for your very welcome letter—a treat even when letters are numerous, for almost every house has a *bill* on the window. Along with yours came a lot of others like an Archangel mail just *thawed*—and they served very much to relish my breakfast. *Literary Gazette*, too, was a God-send, particularly as we afterwards exchanged it, or the reading of it, for the perusal of the *Times*, with our fellow-lodger. I had among the rest an epistle from W. Cooke, and one from Ackermann, recommending me to try Mahomet's vapour baths here—that damn'd C. Croker certainly put him up to it. But I trust I know better than to trust my carcase to the Infidel. I might get into his hot-well and come out a *Muscle-man*. The hot brine of the *Artillery* Baths (so-called, I suppose, because they heat water for Perkins and his steam guns) has done more good for me; taken the stiffness out of my limbs, but my ankles still suffer from a very *strong weakness*. Thank God, I have found out that I have a stomach; from the former state of my appetite I seem to have *three*, like a camel; and when the loaf comes up I take a very large *impression*. For example, I have eaten to-day for dinner, a turbot, a tart, and a tough old fowl that nothing but a coast appetite would venture on. But on the beach you may munch anything, even an old superannuated fisherman. I called on Horace Smith yesterday, but he was out; to-day I have had better luck, though he was out still, for we met at his door, and I gave him your letter on the steps. I was delighted with him and with *her*. He was all that is kind and gentlemanly, and I shall break through my resolution and take a family dinner with them, though I had vowed to accept no such invitations.

229

Thomas Hood:

I hope that he and I are to be quite thick ere I leave—if such a stick as I may be *thick* with any one. Mrs. Smith is an invalid on the sofa, and she and I regard each other, I believe, with fellow interest on that account; I was taken with her very much, and with the little girl too, who seems destined to make hearts ache hereafter. She has all the blossom of a beauty about her. There were some grown-up misses making a call, so that we had not our visit all to ourselves, but Smith and I contrived to gossip; he calls here to-morrow. I should have liked to make one at Green's. Your account of it is very amusing. Your meeting with Reynolds pleases me much, and your liking of him, which I find is reciprocated on his part. I trust you will sometimes meet in Robert Street, if there still be such a place. We are to be up at the Golden Square party, or rather I am to be up to everything on Thursday, and we shall meet in the evening of that day. Don't you think a crowded assembly may have all the effect of a *hot-air bath* ? But the real thing is Brighton. C[rofton] C[roker] did not give it a fair trial, he was only sham-shampooed and dived not into the bath, but the bathos. The fact is, he mistakes his complaint—he keeps his room and calls it room-atism; no man who pretends to such an affliction should lay claim to Fairy Leg-ends. I am much amused with a squad of mer-men before the window—I observe they never walk more than eight paces on end—and then 'back again,' all things by *turns* and nothing *long*. They seem like old duellists, so accustomed to that measure of ground that they can't help it. To-day has been beautifully fine; sunshine and a fresh breeze; luckily all the winds have been from South and West—great *points* in my favour and quite 'equal to bespoke.' I watch over the ex-panses, and Jane over the expenses, so that I am more careless than cureless, and enjoy myself as though there

230

were no *Tilts*[1] in being. I hear the waves constantly
like 'woodpeckers tapping' the hollow beach. Jane
says there is something solemn and religious in its
music, and to be sure, the sea is the *Psalter* element.
Besides my warm baths, in hobbling along the beach a
great surge gave me an extempore *foam*entation of the
feet and ankles, so that I have tried the cold bath also.
But we have not had any Elizabethan sea, that is in
the *ruff* state, though we have violently desired to see a
storm, and a wreck, a pleasure admirably described by
Lucretius—

> "'Tis sweet to stand by good dry land surrounded,
> And see a dozen of poor seamen drownded.'

In the meanwhile Jane has picked up three oyster shells
and a drowned nettle as marine curiosities—also a
jelly-fish, but she fears it will melt in her bag and spoil
more watches. She enjoys everything akin to the sea,
even our little *moreen* curtains, and swears that Ossian's
poems are nothing to *Ocean's*. She is only astonished
to find *sheep* in the *Downs* instead of ships. With great
labour I have taught her to know a sloop from a frigate,
but she still calls masts *masks*. Pray tell Mrs. B. that
Mrs. H. will write to her to-morrow if the tide comes
in—it is at present low water with her ideas. The fact
is she gets fat and *idle*, but she always was *idol*ized.
The 'Fairy Legends' she has perused (borrowed of
Moxon), but don't send her any books here, as it will be
more kindness thrown away. I have offered to get
Whims and Oddities for her at the Library, but she
says she wishes for something lighter and newer. She
has over-fed herself like the bullfinch, and I am persuaded can't read. Pray give my kind regards to Mrs.
Balmanno with my best thanks for all her good wishes,

---

[1] His publisher.

Thomas Hood:

though she may suffer by the fulfilment, as I am re-
gaining my impertinence; the tide is coming in, and the
post going out, so I must shorten sail. It is lucky for
you we stay but a week, or you would find our *post*
quite an *impost*. Thanks for the *frank*ness of yours, we
don't hold them *cheaply* notwithstanding. I am, my
dear Balmanno, yours very sincerely,

" THOMAS HOOD."

It seems strange, Horace Smith having been a frequent
contributor to the *London*, that Hood should not have
met him earlier. It may have been during this visit that
Hood wrote his verses " I'm not a single man" in the
album of Horace Smith's daughter. Smith and he
evidently found much in common, and Hood no doubt
took the opportunity of enlisting Smith's interest in a new
annual which he had been asked to edit. It may be that
the editing of this miscellany had been arranged during
his brief holiday, for writing from Brighton to Ackerman,
who had asked him to contribute to the next year's
" Forget-me-not," he replied that he would be happy to
do so, " but this year it will not depend upon myself.
I have an annual under my own Editorship, and am
bound not to write for the others."

Some time in the spring the Hoods returned to the
Adelphi and on "Sunday 4th of the 5th" received the
following invitation from the friends of whom they seem
to have seen much about this time :—

" ESTEEMED FRIEND,—If thou and thy help mate be
not engaged in any rational recreation this evening,
wilt thou think of we ? Thy assured friends,

" ROBERT AND MARY BROADBRIM."

The signatories of this note—written on the half-sheet
of one from Lord Lansdowne regretting his inability to

Early Home Life (1825—1829).

be present at the anniversary dinner of the Artists' Benevolent Fund—were of course Robert Balmanno and his
wife. Balmanno was a member of the Society of Arts
and evidently an expert in handwriting, for the following
letter is copied from the original, written in beautiful
imitation of a seventeenth-century hand. It is
addressed " To my very loving friend, Maister Thomas
Hoode, author of Whimms and Oddytys Dwelling at
No. 2 Robert Street Over against the Society of Arts
in the Adelphi.

" Please to deliver these With Respect.

" MY VERY LOVEING FREND,—I hartely begge thy
pardon and hope for thy forgiveness, for the longe delay
which hath taken place, in forwarding thee the little poem
called the Exyle, which I promysed to send thee longe
agoe and which I have nowe enclosed herein.

" It is written by a very worthy divine, one maister
Thomas Dale, an ornament of the Churche and a great
and goode pulpit oratour. It sholde have come to thy
hande when thou wert on a visit to thy respected friend
atte Enfield, fully believing it might have humoured
both him and thee, but I was idly inclined.

" I pray thee of thy good nature to informe me,
whether when thou wert at Enfield, thou heardest any
thing of one Maister Gylpyn who hath retired there, he
was sometyme a draper in the Ward of Chepe. Maister
Gylpyn was my very good frend, and I would that I
had made thee acquainted, as Mistress Gylpyn maketh
surpassing goode cheese, and is righte merrie in her
house, and keepeth store of goode wine in grete stone
bottles which she nowise stinteth. I holde that wine
was made from the beginning to make men glad, and
not for drunckennes, but measurablie taken and in tyme
causeth a chearfull countenaunce and comforteth mans
heart, but immoderatlie received powreth in errours,

233

sendeth in forgettfullnes, dulleth the braine, & bringeth forth sluggishnes.

" I pray thee present my own and my wifes heartie commendacions to thy excellent good Lady : We greatly long to see ye bothe, for tis merrie when gossips meet.

" In all chearfullness of heart, I remain, my very loveing friend

" Thy truly affecionate humble servant to command,

" ROBERT BALMANNO, F.S.A.

" From my House in Craven Streete in the Strand this 29th of August 1628."

The poem, " The Exile," was by the Rev. Thomas Dale, afterwards Dean of Rochester, a voluminous writer and contributor to periodicals; and in asking to see a proof before the piece appeared in the new annual, the author said : " I should be glad to have the opportunity of correcting it as my trifles have been more than once marred by typographical errors. The 'Friendship's Offering ' metamorphosed a ' child ' into a ' shield,' and my friend Mr. Watts, by reading ' vernal' for 'genial ' identified *Spring* with *Summer*." The reverend poet was less hardly used than a later verse-writer who in an impassioned sonnet in one of the weekly reviews was made to say " music peeled forth."

Before Hood received that old-style epistle from Balmanno he had had much work to do on the forthcoming annual, and had also in July or August gone with his wife on a visit to the Lambs at Enfield. Charles Cowden Clarke and his bride, Mary Victoria Novello, honeymooning in the neighhourhood in the former month, called on the Lambs and learned of the coming visit of the Hoods and the grand preparations that were to be made for the entertainment, Lamb

Early Home Life (1825—1829).

proposing that one of the dishes should be bubble and squeak!

In the summer of 1828, too, Hood wrote an address for Joseph Grimaldi, the famous clown, to deliver at one of his farewell performances, but neither of the addresses given in the memoirs of Grimaldi reads at all like Hood's work. He had addressed the inimitable clown in one of the " Odes and Addresses," and has left an entertaining account of a visit from Grimaldi in "A Serio-Comic Reminiscence " in " Hood's Own," when the great Pan of Pantomime called to plead that the farewell address might be a brief one. On Grimaldi's behalf Hood wrote the following to the *Literary Gazette*:—" Pray publish in your Gazette that on Friday, the 27th inst. [June], this inimitable clown will take his leave of the boards at Drury Lane Theatre, in character. After that night the red and white features of Joe Grimaldi will belong only to tradition! Thenceforth he will be dead to his vocation,—but the pleasant recollections of his admirable fooling will still live with childhood, with manhood, and with—T. Hood."

We have seen that early in the year (1828), Hood, who had been well represented in the current annuals, had been asked to bring one out under his own editorship. Charles Lamb, Barry Cornwall, Hartley Coleridge, Bernard Barton, Miss Mitford and other popular writers of the day promised assistance, and an appeal to Sir Walter Scott met with a ready response, first in the shape of the following cordial letter, and later in his verses on "The Death of Keeldar."

" My dear Mr. Hood,—It was very ungracious in me to leave you in a day's doubt whether I was gratified or otherwise with the honour you did me to inscribe your whims and oddities to me. I received with great pleasure this new mark of your kindness and it was

Thomas Hood :

only my leaving your volume and letter in the country which delayed my answer as I forgot the address.

"I was favoured with Mr. Cooper's beautiful sketch of the heart-piercing incident of the dead greyhound which is executed with a force and fancy which I flatter myself that I who was in my younger days and in part still am a great lover of dogs and horses and an accurate observer of their habits can appreciate. I intend the instant our term ends to send a few verses if I can make any at my years in acknowledgment. I will get a day's leisure for this purpose next week when I expect to be in the country. Pray inform Mr. Cooper of my intention, though I fear I will be unable to do anything deserving of the subject. I am very truly your obliged humble servant

"WALTER SCOTT.

"EDINBURGH 4 *March*."

In quoting this letter in his scraps of literary reminiscence, Hood recorded that the first time he saw Scott was at the private view of Martin's picture "Nineveh," "when, by a striking coincidence, one of our most celebrated women, and one of our greatest men, Mrs. Siddons and Sir Walter Scott, walked simultaneously up opposite sides of the room, and met and shook hands in front of the painting," a meeting that is not recorded in Lockhart's voluminous biography of Scott. It was some time after his return from Brighton that Hood had an opportunity of meeting Sir Walter, being asked to call upon him on May 19, in Sussex Place, where he was staying.

"The number of the house had escaped my memory; but seeing a fine dog down an area, I knocked without hesitation at the door. It happened, however, to be the wrong one. I afterwards mentioned the circumstance

Early Home Life (1825—1829).

to Sir Walter. It was not a bad point, he said, for he was very fond of dogs; but he did not care to have his own animals with him, about London, 'for fear he should be taken for Bill Gibbons.' I then told him I had lately been reading the Fair Maid of Perth, which had reminded me of a very pleasant day spent many years before, beside the Linn of Campsie, the scene of Conachar's catastrophe. Perhaps he divined what had really occurred to me,—that the Linn, as a cataract, had greatly disappointed me; for he smiled, and shook his head archly, and said he had since seen it himself, and was rather ashamed of it. ' But I fear, Mr. Hood, I have done worse than that before now, in finding a Monastery where there was none to be found; though there was plenty (here he smiled again) of Carduus Benedictus, or Holy Thistle.'

"In the mean time he was finishing his toilet, in order to dine at the Duchess of Kent's; and before he put on his cravat I had an opportunity of noticing the fine massive proportions of his bust. It served to confirm me in my theory that such mighty men are, and must be, physically, as well as intellectually, gifted beyond ordinary mortals; that their strong minds must be backed by strong bodies. Remembering all that Sir Walter Scott had done, and all that he had suffered, methought he had been in more than one sense 'A Giant in the Land.' After some more conversation, in the course of which he asked me if I ever came to Scotland, and kindly said he should be glad to see me at Abbotsford, I took my leave, with flattering dreams in my head that never were, and now, alas! never can be, realised!"

The annual to which Scott so readily contributed duly came out at the end of that year, under the title of the "Gem," with sixteen plates in the approved fashion of the

237

Thomas Hood:

day, and with contributions from a large number of writers. Lamb, despite his expressed objection to the fashionable miscellanies, promised, besides his verses " On an Infant Dying as Soon as Born," a contribution to accompany a plate entitled " The Widow." He being unwell, Mary Lamb suggested that Hood should write something in Lamb's name, which he did, and " A Widow,—by C. Lamb, Esq.," duly found its place among the contents of the annual. That Lamb, as Hood recorded, took the forgery in good part may be seen from the notelet in which he reversed their names:—

" DEAR LAMB,—You are an impudent varlet, but I will keep your secret. We dine at Ayrton's on Thursday, and shall try to find Sarah and her two spare beds for that night only. Miss M. and her Tragedy may be d——d, so may *not* you and your rib. Health attend you.—Yours,

" T. HOOD, ESQ.

" ENFIELD.

" Miss Bridget Hood sends love."

It is not necessary to discuss the contents of the " Gem " in detail; in it was first published Keats' sonnet " On a Picture of Leander," probably from a manu-script in the possession of a member of the Reynolds family, and the editor himself was represented by some comic verses on the same theme, by " Birthday Verses," " The Farewell," " A May-Day," in prose, and above all, by " The Dream of Eugene Aram," by far the most remarkable thing in the little volume. This poem made a deep impression at once. The *Literary Gazette* quoted the " Dream " entirely, recognising its value, but criticising—surely with scant justice—its closing stanzas. " Were it not that the end is rather feeble (one verse or two verses more might perfect it), we

Early Home Life (1825—1829).

would say that this is one of the most remarkable poems in our modern literature, and one that will be as such remembered." Bernard Barton, writing to Hood, said: "Thy own Poem of 'Eugene Aram' is the gem of the 'Gem'; and alone worth the price of the book. I thank the *Gazette* critic for quoting that entire, as I shall cut it out and save it"—a somewhat naïve conclusion. Sir John Bowring, another contributor to the "Gem," said: "I have read that Aram story, which I will put by the side of the very grandest productions of poetical conception." "The Dream of Eugene Aram," which has taken its place among our masterpieces of narrative poetry, was separately issued two years later as a booklet, with a series of appropriate illustrations by the poet's friend, William Harvey.

Though the "Gem" met with a very cordial reception Hood did not continue his editorship after the first issue. He was probably not fitted for the work of beating up contributors to such a miscellany, work which was much better left in the hands of Frederick Shoberl and Alaric A. Watts and such men. It may be that he was too much occupied to continue that kind of task, for he was evidently busy in many ways, or it may be that he did not find himself properly treated by his publisher. "They infallibly cheat you," said Lamb, on this very subject. Hood seems to have had a happy knack of entering into arrangements with publishers who for one reason or another proved unsatisfactory colleagues, and it may have been so in this case; there is nothing but surmise.

A further and hitherto unpublished note of Lamb's (postmarked September 25, 1828), addressed to Robert Street, runs:—

"DEAR MRS. HOOD,—Mary begs me to say for her that we are very desirous to hear from you, how you

Thomas Hood:

both are, what Hood is about, your probable move-
ments. We have given up our idea of coming again to
town for some little time, having been very much
accompanied—M. Burney, his sister and Husbd,
Coleridge, &c.—and think it would not add to our
quiet yet awhile. Believe me, ever yours affectionately,

"C. LAMB."

Presumably one of the Hoods replied as to what he
was " about," for Lamb, writing to Bernard Barton a
fortnight later, was able to give some particulars :—

" What a fertile genius (and a quiet good soul withal)
is Hood. He has 50 things in hand, farces to supply
the Adelphi for the season, a comedy for one of the
great theatres, just ready, a whole entertainment by
himself for Mathews and Yates to figure in, a meditated
Comic Annual for next year, to be nearly done by himself.
—You'd like him very much."

Here, indeed, was indication of business enough. Of the
"farces " "York and Lancaster " was printed many years
later, but the comedy has, so far, eluded identification.
Despite this busy-ness Hood seemed prepared to undertake other work too. In November he was down at
Brighton again, contemplating an " unserious " guide to
that watering place, as we gather from a letter which he
addressed to Sir Thomas Lawrence, then President
of the Royal Academy, to whom he had probably
been introduced by the Balmannos. The letter is
dated " 31, King's Road, Brighton, Sunday morning,
November 16, 1828," and runs—

" MY DEAR SIR,—There are some sketches of
Brighton (in Cooke's copper), and I have undertaken to
scribble some notes on the margin of the sea. To this

Early Home Life (1825—1829).

end, I am enjoying the breezes which I inh-*ale* like a
sea-*sider*, looking over a prospect that, in its calm,
reminds me of a sea-*peace* by Vandervelde, and in its
shingles, of *Beechey*.   It is now like royal Bessie in
its *rough* : and the wind, that great *raiser* of waves, is
accompanied by a suitable *lather* on Neptune's face.   It
is besides, high water—or more properly high *waiter*, for
the tide *serves at the Bar*, and there is a great influx of
the weeds that grow 'in the garden of the gull,' *i.e.*,
Sea Gull.   Afar off, a lonely vessel is tumbling about,
and observe there the goodness of Providence, that the
rougher the storm, the better the vessel is *pitched*, while
here and there in the foreground, may be seen what
Molière with his French inversion would call a *Tar-
tough*.   The skeleton of a lost Brig, like the bones of
a sea monster, lies at the extreme left.   I am told by
the Brighton people that ship disasters are not uncommon here.   They have often had *Georgius Rex*.
You will understand, Sir, from this sample, that my
guide will be unserious chiefly ; but I contemplate a
graver description of the Pavilion, provided I can gain
entrance to the interior, which I understand is more
difficult than aforetime.   In a conversation with
Mr. Balmanno, it occurred to me, however, that you
could put me in the way, for I do not even know the
proper quarter to apply to amongst the *Chain Piers*, but,
of course, not Captain Brown's.   I have spent some time
in making up my mind to trouble you on this *subject* or
head, considering how many better ones engage you.
But pray *frame* some excuse for my freedom, which
originates in my reliance on your kindly feelings
towards me.   I have no doubt but that you can, at any
rate, direct me how to get access, and even that will
accessively oblige, My dear Sir, yours very respectfully,

"THOMAS HOOD."

Thomas Hood :

Whether he got the requisite permission to visit the Pavilion and whether he ever perpetrated his humorous guide to Brighton has not proved ascertainable.

In the following year the Hoods removed from their house in the Adelphi, where they had been visited by the many friends they had made, thanks to their both possessing that gift for friendship which is one of the happiest that a fairy godmother can bestow. Of the Robert Street home-life we have unfortunately no intimate particulars beyond the following account of an evening there written by Mary Balmanno thirty years later :—

" Bound in the closest ties of friendship with ' The Hoods,' with whom we also were in the habit of continually associating, we had the pleasure of meeting Charles Lamb at their house one evening, together with his sister and several other friends, amongst whom was Miss Kelly, that most natural and unrivalled of English comic actresses.

" In outward appearance Hood conveyed the idea of a clergyman. His figure slight, and invariably dressed in black ; his face pallid ; the complexion delicate, and features regular : his countenance bespeaking sympathy by its sweet expression of melancholy and suffering.

" Lamb was of a different mould and aspect. Of middle height, with brown and rather ruddy complexion, grey eyes expressive of sense and shrewdness, but neither large nor brilliant ; his head and features well shaped, and the general expression of his countenance quiet, kind, and observant, undergoing rapid changes in conversation, as did his manner, variable as an April day, particularly to his sister, whose saint-like good-humour and patience were as remarkable as his strange and whimsical modes of trying them.

" But the brother and sister perfectly understood each other, and ' Charles ' as she always called him would not have been the ' Charles ' of her loving heart without

242

Early Home Life (1825—1829).

the pranks and oddities which he was continually playing off upon her, and which were only outnumbered by the instances of affection, and evidences of ever watchful solicitude with which he surrounded her.

" Miss Lamb, although many years older than her brother, by no means looked so, but presented the pleasant appearance of a mild, rather stout and comely lady of middle age.

"Dressed with quaker-like simplicity in dove-coloured silk, with a transparent kerchief of snow-white muslin folded across her bosom, she at once prepossessed the beholder in her favour by an aspect of serenity and peace. Her manners were very quiet and gentle, and her voice low. She smiled frequently, and seldom laughed, partaking of the courtesies and hospitalities of her merry host and hostess with all the cheerfulness and grace of a most mild and kindly nature.

" Her behaviour to her brother was like that of an admiring disciple; her eyes seldom absent from his face. And when apparently engrossed in conversation with others, she would, by supplying some word for which he was at a loss, even when talking in a distant part of the room, show how closely her mind waited upon his.

" Mr. Lamb was in high spirits, sauntering about the room with his hands crossed behind his back, conversing by fits and starts with those most familiarly known to him, but evidently mentally acknowledging Miss Kelly to be the *rara avis* of his thoughts, by the great attention he paid to every word she uttered.

"Truly pleasant it must have been to her, even though accustomed to see people listen breathless with admiration while she spoke, to find her words have so much charm for such a man as Charles Lamb.

" Miss Kelly (charming, natural Miss Kelly, who has drawn from her audiences more heart-felt tears and smiles than perhaps any other English actress) with quiet good humour listened and laughed at the witty sallies of her host and his gifted friend, seeming as little an actress as it is possible to conceive.

" Once, however, when some allusion was made to a comic scene in a new play, then just brought out, wherein she had performed to the life the character of a low-bred lady's maid, passing herself off as her mistress, Miss Kelly arose, and with a kind of resistless ardour repeated a few sentences so inimitably, that everybody laughed as much as if the real lady's maid, and not the actress, had been before them; while she who had personated the part, quietly resumed her seat without the least sign of merriment, as grave as possible.

" This little scene for a few moments charmed everybody out of themselves, and gave a new impetus to conversation. Mrs. Hood's eyes sparkled with joy, as she saw the effect it had produced upon her husband, whose pale face, like an illuminated comic mask, shone with fun and good humour. Never was happier couple than ' The Hoods '; ' mutual reliance and fond faith ' seemed to be their motto.

" Mrs. Hood was a most amiable woman—of excellent manners, and full of sincerity and goodness. She perfectly adored her husband, tending him like a child, whilst he, with unbounded affection, seemed to delight to yield himself to her guidance. Nevertheless, true to his humorous nature, he loved to tease her with jokes and whimsical accusations which were only responded to by, ' Hood, Hood, how can you run on so ? ' ' Perhaps you don't know,' said he, ' that Jane's besetting weakness is a desire to appear in print and be thought a Blue.'

" Mrs. Hood coloured and gave her usual reply; then observed laughingly : ' Hood does not know one kind of material from another, he thinks this dress is blue *print*.' On looking at it I saw it was only a very pretty blue *silk*. The evening was concluded by a

Early Home Life (1825—1829).

supper, one of those elegant social repasts which Flemish artists delight to paint; so fresh the fruit, so tempting the viands, and all so exquisitely arranged by the very hand of taste. Mrs. Hood has frequently smiled when I have complimented her on setting out 'picture suppers,'—this was truly one.

"Mr. Lamb oddly walked round the table, looking closely at any dish that struck his fancy before he would decide where to sit, telling Mrs. Hood that he should by that means know how to select some dish that was difficult to carve, and take the trouble off her hands; accordingly, having jested in this manner, he placed himself, with great deliberation before a lobster salad, observing *that* was the thing.

"Mr. Hood, with inexpressible gravity in the upper part of his face, and his mouth twitching with smiles, sang his own comic song of 'If you go to France be sure you learn the lingo'; his pensive manner and feeble voice making it doubly ludicrous.

"Mr. Lamb, on being pressed to sing, excused himself in his own peculiar manner, but offered to pronounce a Latin eulogium instead. This was accepted, and he accordingly stammered forth a long stream of Latin words; among which, as the name of Mrs. Hood frequently occurred, we ladies thought it in praise of her. The delivery of this speech occupied about five minutes. On inquiring of a gentleman who sat next me whether Mr. Lamb was praising Mrs. Hood, he informed me that was by no means the case, the eulogium being on the lobster salad! Thus, in the gayest of moods, progressed and concluded a truly merry little social supper, worthy in all respects of the author of 'Whims and Oddities.'"

One more of Hood's amusing letters to his sister-in-law, Charlotte Reynolds, may well close this chapter. It was evidently written when the Hoods were returning from a stay in the country somewhere; possibly it

marks the close of their visit to the Lambs, for it is
postmarked July 11, 1828 :—

" MY DEAR LOT,
There's a blot !—
This is to write
That Sunday night
By the late
Coach at eight,
We shall get in
To Little Britain,—
So have handy
Gin, rum, Brandy,
A lobster,—may be—
Cucumbers, they be
Also in season
And within reason—
Porter, by Gum !
Egainst we come—
In lieu of Friday
Then we keep high day
And holy, as long as
We can.   I get strong as
A horse—*i.e.* pony
Jane tho keeps boney.
How is your mother,
Still with your brother,
And Marian too—
And that good man too
Call'd your papa, Miss
After these ah Miss
Don't say I never
Made an endeavour
To write you verses
Tho this lay worse is
Than any I've written—
The truth is I've sitten
So long over letters
Addressed to your betters
That—that—that
Somehow—
My pen,
    Amen,
        T. HOOD."

CHAPTER X.

SOME time in 1829 the Hoods gave up their house in the Adelphi and removed to what was then the rural district of Winchmore Hill. Rose Cottage, the pleasant house in which they made their new home, stands in a nice garden bowered by shrubs and trees, and, but for some enlargement, remains to-day much as it was in Hood's time. It is quite likely that in the choice of neighbourhood Hood was influenced by the fact that Winchmore Hill is within an easy walk of Enfield, and that thus he became a neighbour of Charles Lamb. Of the actual particulars of the removal we have no details beyond a story that, a large hamper of china and glass having been unpacked, the contents were put on a newly erected dresser which could not support them and fell with a crash. Hood, after surveying the *débris*, sent the maid to his wife to say that " The china which *came up* in the morning had *come down* in the evening." Few letters written during the years spent at Winchmore Hill remain to us, but it seems to have been a happy and busy time with Hood, for he was popular with his friends, his work was popular with the public, and much of it was in demand. It was at Rose Cottage, too, that in 1830 his second daughter, named Frances Freeling, was born, happily to survive.

In 1829 Thomas Hood made fresh attempts to write for the theatre, and at the end of February there was produced at the Surrey Theatre his farce of " Mr. Sims "—a piece of which no particulars

have proved recoverable beyond the identification of its
name and time of production. It is to this farce
that he evidently refers in his "Ode to Perry"—"O!
Patent, Pen-inventing Perrian Perry"—where, after
enlarging upon the nervousness of dramatic authors on
the production of their pieces, he says :—

> "To clench the fact,
> Myself, once guilty, of one small rash act,
> Committed at the Surrey
> Quite in a hurry,
> Felt all this flurry
> Corporal worry,
> And spiritual scurry.
> Dram-devil—attic curry !
> All going well,
> From prompter's bell,
> Until befell
> A hissing at some dull imperfect dunce—
> There's no denying,
> I felt in all four elements at once !
> My head was swimming, while my arms were flying,
> My legs for running—all the rest was frying !"

Hood also wrote about this time entertainments for
Mathews, notably songs and patter for "The Spring
Meeting," in which were embodied "The Ship Launch"
and "The Lord Mayor's Show." It was reported at
the time that Mathews's entertainments were the joint
productions of Thomas Hood and W. T. Moncrieff, but
the extent of Hood's contributions is not definable.
He wrote also, for the Adelphi, a farce entitled "York
and Lancaster, or a School without Scholars," and the
first rehearsal of the piece took place one Sunday morning at his home at Winchmore Hill. A merry gathering,
we may be sure, though no letter-writer or diarist has
left us details. Remembering, perhaps, his nervousness
at the Surrey when this farce was produced, the author
remained outside, walking up and down the Strand,

while its fate was decided. In 1832, too, Hood seems to have written for Mr. Yates of the Adelphi an untraceable " Pantomime of Harlequin and Mr. Jenkins."

A brief note to Hood from Allan Cunningham suggests that the removal from Robert Street did not take place until after the summer of 1829, for the note is dated June 25 and was evidently an invitation to dinner that evening :—" I have this moment got your kind invitation —never mind short notices or long—pitch idle ceremony between honest fellows into the lake of darkness and there let it lie. I am yours at six o'clock with a clear conscience and a clearer appetite."

In 1829 Hood published his most sustained punning effort in ballad metre when he issued as a tiny volume, with half a dozen engravings by George Cruikshank, his " Epping Hunt." The verses, which set off in parody of Cowper's diverting history of John Gilpin—

> " John Huggins was as bold a man
> As trade did ever know,"

tell how this worthy provision-monger attended the old Epping Hunt. The story, set forth with an amazing succession of puns simple and puns recondite, was immediately popular, and when a fresh edition was called for in the following year the author wrote a prefatory letter to the publisher (Charles Tilt) in the course of which he said:—

" I attended the last Anniversary of the Festival, and am concerned to say that the sport does not improve, but appears an ebbing as well as Epping custom. The run was miserable indeed ; but what was to be expected ? The chase was a Doe and, consequently, the Hunt set off with the *Hind* part before. It was, therefore, quite in character, for so many Nimrods to start, as they did, before the hounds, but which, as you know, is quite contrary to the *Lex Tallyho-nis*, or Laws of Hunting.

Thomas Hood :

" I dined with the Master of the Revel, who is as hale as ever, and promises to reside some time in the *Wells* ere he *kicks the bucket*. He is an honest, hearty, worthy man, and when he dies there will be ' a cry of dogs ' in his kennel."

The success of the " Epping Hunt " was such that Hood contemplated and probably partly wrote a similar piece of extravagance dealing with the Epsom Races, but for some reason or other the scheme fell through.[1]

Belonging to the summer of this year (1829)—though he presumably added to them again in 1834—are a series of " Comic Composites for the Scrap Book," which were published by W. B. Cooke. To the earlier set I have not been able to refer, so may give the following notice of them from a contemporary journal :—

" Figures composed of household, gardening, and other utensils : droll enough ; but we have had almost sufficient of such things. The lines by Mr. Hood afford additional proof of his extraordinary facility in adapting expressions to purposes to which they certainly were never before applied. For instance, under a figure, the supporters of which are a mop and a broom, are these lines :—

> " ' Like fleet Camilla
> In the poet's strain
> A pair of legs well form'd
> To *scour* the plain.'

" Another figure (by Cruikshank) formed of guns, pistols, swords, etc., has this subscription :—

> " ' The rise of Wellington was on this plan :
> For *arms* have been *the making of the man.*' "

The four of these " Comic Composites " which I have, and of which two copies are here given, are

[1] Charles Clark (1806—1880) published a very poor imitation of Hood's work, entitled " Epsom Races," and signed it " Thomas Hood the Younger."

Winchmore Hill and Wanstead.

dated 1834 and present "The Artist," "A Chymist," "The Dairy Maid," and "The Grocer," their respective couplets running :—

> "On mind and matter there has been great schism,
> And here's the doctrine of *Materia*lism."

> "A Chymist this !—your shoulders do not shrug—
> Why not—when Malthus proves mankind a *Drug ?*"

> "Some antique Pedestal this used to be on ?
> She has at least, a look of the *Pan*theon."

> "Frankenstein wanted to make man, and so, Sir,
> He tried this first attempt upon a Grocer."

The comic pictures are unsigned, but they are such pictorial puns as might well have been designed by the writer of the accompanying jingles. The writing of verses for Charles Mathews's entertainments probably led to Hood's being invited to write words for music, for in 1830 there was published in three parts, each giving two songs, "Comic Melodies : a series of Humorous Ballads, Duetts and Trios. The words (written expressly for this work) by Thomas Hood, Esq. The music consisting of Original Airs by J. Blewitt." The cover of each part gave a series of musical notes depicting faces, with beneath the Hoodian couplet :—

> "A doleful Song a doleful look retraces
> But merry music maketh merry Faces."

The half-dozen songs—including the two already mentioned as written for Mathews—are to be found in Hood's collected works ; the most characteristic piece is "Lieutenant Luff," with his unanswerable puns against temperance :—

> "If Wine's a poison, so is Tea,
> Tho' in another shape
> What matter whether one is kill'd
> By *canister* or *grape !*"

The success of the "Comic Melodies" was apparently such that Jonathan Blewitt also composed music to " John Trot," " Nelly Gray," and "Sally Brown (to Wapping Time)," and issued them as numbers of the *Ballad Singer.*

Late in 1828 we have seen that Charles Lamb mentioned the fact that Hood was contemplating a " Comic Annual." During 1829 the project took shape and was probably well in hand before the removal to Winchmore Hill, for the late W. J. Linton recorded in his reminiscences that he saw Hood at his chambers in the Adelphi when going thither to fetch his drawings for the "Comic Annual" : " Queer pen-and-ink drawings to be cut in facsimile, some by myself. I recall him only as a spare man of fair stature, grave but not ungenial. But I most regarded his tools. Beside pencil and pen there lay on his desk an old graver, a reminiscence of his early time as an engraver in copper, a penknife, and a nail, with which it appeared he cut or scraped out any wrong lines in his drawings."

Another youthful engraver who saw something of Hood in the days when " Comic Annuals " were preparing was William Tegg, who was apprenticed to Wright and later became well known as a publisher and compiler of books. Wright, who engraved many of the drawings in the earlier volumes of the annual and controlled all the engraving of the later ones, became one of Hood's close friends. Says Tegg, in some interesting scraps of reminiscences contributed towards the end of his life to *Notes and Queries* : " Hood was a frequent visitor at New London Street, and from Hood I learned all that was doing, besides having often to see Hood about all work in progress. I always received the greatest kindness from him." Once to his youthful visitor he remarked : " Yours is a curious name ; I don't remember or know of any man but you who takes an ' egg ' after his ' T.' "

Arrangements for publication of the " Comic Annual "

had been made with Messrs. Hurst, Chance & Co., and towards the end of the year the work made its appearance, dedicated to Sir Francis Freeling, "the great Patron of Letters," in his capacity of Postmaster-General. In his preface Hood said that he had contemplated a third series of " Whims and Oddities," but had thrown its materials into the new venture. Though mostly written, prose and verse, by Hood himself, there were several contributions from other writers—Reynolds, Horatio Smith, and Miss Isabel Hill, and it also included Keats's " Sonnet to a Cat" (written for Jane Hood's mother). In the illustrations, too, Hood had some assistance from a " Miss A. K." (not identified), from George Cruikshank, F. Branston, and in one instance from J. H. Reynolds. In later issues almost the whole of the work, letterpress and illustrations, was done by Hood himself. The annual was a success from the first, perhaps in no small measure because it was something quite new. " The work indeed, at present is like the celebrated Elephant that had no rival but himself. If, however, others of the kind should spring up, all the Editor wishes for is an open field and fair play." Each autumn the annual for the following year was announced by a comic letter or " protocol " in the *Athenæum*.

Others did spring up at once, and in the preface to the annual for 1831 Hood had to point out that he was not altogether getting fair play. His arrangement with Hurst, Chance & Co. fell through, and the " Comic " was taken to Charles Tilt, who published it for the next four years ; but the publisher of the first volume was revenged by bringing out the " New Comic," and advertising it along with one of Hood's own books so that book-buyers might well be misled. In illustration of the extent to which others sought to trade on Hood's success in his peculiar field it may be well to cite the greater part of the preface to the second issue of the

Thomas Hood :

annual in which he deals playfully but seriously with his rivals.

"Now, I do not intend, like some votaries of freedom to cast mud on the muddy, or dirt on the dirty,—but while I am on the hustings, I will ask the Committee of that Uncandid Candidate, 'The New Comic,' whether it was quite honest to canvass against me under my own colours, and to pass off the enemy's poll-book as mine? The Code of Honour should be a kind of Coade's Cement between man and man,—but to speak technically some seem bound by it and some unbound. Mr. Hurst gave me his word and shook hands thereon, that the delusive title should be altered ; and yet that bad title to a good name, 'The New Comic,' is still retained. Surely he feels both the brand and the blush, in what Byron called 'that red right hand.' Were there no other and fitter labels extant than such close parodies of mine? For example, The Laughing Hyæna—or the Merry Unwise ;—or The Main-Chance? The Old Brown Bear in Piccadilly is bearish perhaps—but he is Original.

"The Editor of the *Edinburgh Literary Journal* was actually induced to swallow what Izaak Walton would call the *Cad*-bait,—and after a jolt in the 'New' concern, was induced to criticise it as a ride in the old.

"Fain would I drop the Steel Pen for a softer quill, to speak of an Editress who—distinguishing fair from unfair—has acted the perfect brunette towards me, and has brought a heavy charge against me 'for work done.' In the Announcement of 'The Comic Offering' —a little book chiefly remarkable for a coat of damson cheese, seeming equally fit, like Sheridan's poor Peruvians, for 'covering and devouring,'—it is insinuated that I am an author unfit for female perusal :—I, who have never had that respect infringed which, with me, dwells 'like fringe upon a petticoat.' Miss Sheridan

Winchmore Hill and Wanstead.

and modesty compel me to declare, that, many Ladies have deigned to request for their albums some little proof of ' the versatility ' or prosatility of my pen :—yet what says the Announcement, or rather Denouncement : ' But shall we permit a Clown or Pantaloon to enter the Drawing-room or Boudoir ; no, *not even under a Hood !* '

" Putting Pantomimic people on a par,—was Clown Grimaldi so very unfit for the Drawing-room of Mrs. Serle,—or Pantaloon Barnes for the Boudoir of Miss Barnet ? Is it vulgar to go to Margate by the *Harlequin,* but genteel by the *Columbine*—to read ' The Comic ' instead of the ' Offering to be Comic ' ? To put the Screw of Comparison into my Cork Model, have I made any drawing less worthy of the drawing-room than ' Going it in High Style ! '—any verse more perverse to gentility than,—

" ' Old Bet crying ' Ma-ca-rel ! ' happened to meet—'

Gad - a - mercy ! Did Miss Sheridan never read or see a Comedy called *The School for Scandal ?* If she has heard of my indelicacy or vulgarity, it must have been from Sir Benjamin Backbite. Mrs. Candour compels me to confess that I am not guilty of either. Joseph Surface would give me credit for morality ; and even those Crabtrees, the reviewers, have awarded me the praise of propriety,—confessing that though I am merry, my spirits are rectified. Like Sir Peter Teazle, I would willingly resign my character to their discussion,—but little Moses has a post obit on my reputation, and forbids my silence. I confess, besides, that on being so attacked by a perfect stranger, I did at first think it rather hard of her ; but having now seen her book, I think it rather soft of her, and shall say no more."

The imitators had no staying power, and, indeed, the imitation was mostly so poor that lasting success could

Thomas Hood :

scarcely have been expected. For some years the " Comic Annual " was Hood's chief literary performance, the medium through which he made most of his comic offerings to the public that had accorded him the first place among humorous writers of the day. It is not necessary to refer particularly to the successive volumes, but it may be said that the first four were—in accordance with the fashion of the time—dedicated to notable people, the first, as we have seen, to Sir Francis Freeling, and the succeeding ones to the Duke of Devonshire, King William IV., and Viscountess Granville. The later volumes were issued without any dedicatory introduction, and it was only in the first two or three that Hood received contributions from other writers. Year by year, sometimes in difficulties owing to financial embarrassments and sometimes owing to ill-health, he managed to produce his always bright and original miscellany of wit and fun, the Annual forming the chief part of his year's work, though he probably was also engaged in much unidentified journalistic work.

In January, 1828, James Silk Buckingham, a well-known traveller and miscellaneous writer, founded the *Athenæum*, but did not continue long to control it, for in the same year he parted with his interest in the journal to John Sterling, and shortly afterwards the paper became the property of a small company, consisting of Charles Wentworth Dilke, Thomas Hood, John Hamilton Reynolds, Allan Cunningham, and Holmes (the printer).[1] Change of proprietorship marked the early years of the journal, but early in the thirties it became the property of Dilke. The extent of Hood's contributions is not ascertainable.[2]

[1] " Papers of a Critic."
[2] The list of his contributions given in "John Francis: a Literary Chronicle of Half a Century," is by no means a complete one.

Winchmore Hill and Wanstead.

It may be taken for granted that he wrote in the paper
when he was one of the owners of it, and it is known
that he was an occasional contributor from the time
that Dilke became proprietor until near the end of his
life. With Dilke himself Hood was for many years on
terms of closest friendship, visiting him and, when
abroad, keeping up a lively correspondence with him.

The establishment of the " Comic Annual " may be
said to have clinched Hood's position as a comic writer.
He was hailed as such publicly, though there were not
wanting lovers of the more serious side of literature who
sought to keep him in the austerer and less profitable
paths. In *Blackwood's Magazine* for April, 1830, there
appeared in thirty-four quatrains a series of " Poetical
Portraits," " signed A Modern Pythagorean." The series
opened with Shakespeare and closed thus with Hood—

> " Im*pugn* I dare not thee
> For I'm of *puny* brood
> And thou would'st *puni*sh me
> With *pun*gent hardiʜooᴅ."

An admirable instance of the pun as commonly understood and not as used by Hood himself. The common
punster—pythagorean or otherwise—is carried away by
mere similarity of sound, but the punster of genius—and
he stands *sui generis*—contrives by his words a double debt
to pay, the duplicity being in the significance and not
—or else as well as—in the sound. Among the writers
who did not view with favour the constant identification
of Hood's name with things comical was Hartley
Coleridge, who wrote to him about this time: " I wish
you would write a little more in the style of ' Lycus the
Centaur,' or ' Eugene Aram's Dream.' In whatever
you attempt you excel. Then why not exert your best
and noblest talent, as well as that wit, which I would
never wish to be dominant." Hood's serious work was
newly brought before the public the same year by the

Thomas Hood :

issue in book form of "The Dream of Eugene Aram," with a series of illustrations by his friend William Harvey, the last to survive of Bewick's pupils. A copy of the first issue of the "Comic Annual" having been sent to the Duke of Devonshire was acknowledged by a letter in which the Duke asked for Hood's help in devising inscriptions for "unreal folios, quartos and 12mos" forming a door of sham books for the entrance of a library staircase at Chatsworth :—

"One is tired of the 'Plain Dealings,' 'Essays on Wood,' and 'Perpetual Motion' on such doors,—on one I have seen the names of 'Don Quixote's Library,' and on others impossibilities, such as 'Virgilii Odaria,' —'Herodoti Poemata,'—'Byron's Sermons,'—etc., etc.; but from you I venture to hope for more attractive titles—at your perfect leisure and convenience."

Hood readily responded with a series of witty titles, some of which have become widely familiar—

"On the Lung Arno in Consumption. By D. Cline.

Dante's Inferno; or Description of Van Demon's Land.

The Racing Calendar, with the Eclipses for 1831.

Ye Devill on Two Styx (Black letter). 2 Vols.

On cutting off Heirs with a Shilling. By Barber Beaumont.

Percy Vere. In 40 Volumes.

Galerie des Grands Tableaux par les Petits Maîtres.

On the Affinity of the Death Watch and Sheep Tick.

Lamb's Recollections of Suett.

Lamb on the Death of Wolfe.

The *Hop*tician. By Lord Farnham.

Tadpoles; or Tales out of my own Head.

On the connection of the River Oder and the River Wezel.

Malthus' Attack of Infantry.

258

Winchmore Hill and Wanstead.

McAdam's Views in Rhodes.

Spenser, with Chaucer's Tales.

Autographia; or Man's Nature, known by his Signature.

Manfredi. Translated by Defoe.

Earl Grey on Early Rising.

Plurality of Livings, with regard to the Common Cat.

The Life of Zimmermann. By Himself.

On the Quadrature of the Circle; or Squaring in the Ring. By J. Mendoza.

Gall's Sculler's Fares.

Bish's Retreat of the Ten Thousand.

Dibdin's Cream of Tar—.

Cornaro on Longevity and the Construction of 74's.

Pompeii; or Memoirs of a Black Footman. By Sir W. Gell.

Pygmalion. By Lord Bacon.

Macintosh, Macculloch, and Macaulay on Almacks.

On Trial by Jury, with remarkable Packing Cases.

On the Distinction between Lawgivers and Lawsellers. By Lord Brougham.

Memoirs of Mrs. Mountain. By Ben Lomond.

Feu mon père—feu ma mère. Par Swing."

Posting these to the Duke in April, Hood said that he would call upon him with others on the 14th of that month, and again sent the following batch at the close of 1832 :—

" Boyle on Steam.

Rules for Punctuation. By a thorough-bred Pointer.

Blaine on Equestrian Burglary; or the Breaking-in of Horses.

Chronological Account of the Date Tree.

Hughes Ball on Duelling.

Book-keeping by Single Entry.

John Knox on ' Death's Door.'

Thomas Hood :

Designs for Friezes. By Captain Parry.

Remarks on the Terra Cotta or Mud Cottages of Ireland.

Considérations sur le Vrai Guy, et le Faux.

Kosciusko on the right of the Poles to stick up for themselves.

Prize poems in *Blank* verse.

On the Site of Tully's Offices.

The Rape of the Lock, with Bramah's Notes.

Haughty-cultural remarks on London Pride.

Annual Parliaments ; a Plea for Short Commons.

Michau on Ball-Practice.

On Sore Throat and the Migration of the Swallow. By T. Abernethy.

Scott and Lot. By the author of ' Waverley.'

Debrett on Chain Piers.

Voltaire, Volney, Volta. 3 Vols.

Peel on Bell's System.

Grose's Slang Dictionary ; or Vocabulary of Grose Language.

Freeling on Enclosing Waste Lands.

Elegy on a Black-Cock, shot amongst the Moors. By W. Wilberforce.

Johnson's Contradictionary.

Sir T. Lawrence on the Complexion of Fairies and Brownies.

Life of Jack Ketch, with Cuts of his own Execution.

Barrow on the Common Weal.

Hoyle's Quadrupedia ; or Rules of All-Fours.

Campaigns of the British Arm :. By one of the German Leg :.

Cursory Remarks on Swearing.

On the Collar of the Garter. By Miss Bailey of Halifax.

Shelley's Conchologist.

Recollections of Bannister. By Lord Stair.

Winchmore Hill and Wanstead.

The Hole Duty of Man. By I. P. Brunel.
Ude's Tables of Interest.
Chantry on the Sculpture of the Chipaway Indians.
The Scottish Boccaccio. By D. Cameron.
Cook's Specimens of the Sandwich Tongue.
In-i-go on Secret Entrances.
Hoyle on the Game Laws.
Mémoires de La-porte."

Some of these titles may have lost their point by lapse of time, but most of them are as irresistibly funny as when first penned. Some of them, too, suggested work to their deviser, for "The Life of Zimmermann. By Himself," duly appeared in the "Comic Annual" (1832), while "Cursory Remarks on Swearing" had already been used in a quaint article in the *London Magazine* for May, 1824, "Observations on the 'Ghost-Player's Guide' and on the Invariable Tendency to Corpulence in Shakespeare's Ghosts: Together with Cursory Remarks on Swearing." That article is signed "Horrida Bella," and *may* have been written by Hood himself; a footnote stating that the swearing in "Hamlet" is natural in one descended from *Oatho* the Great suggests that it was written by an ingenious user of the pun.

Between the sending of these two lists of amusing titles of *biblia-a-biblia,* the "Comic Annual" for 1832 was published with its dedication to William IV., and His Majesty subsequently expressed a desire to see Hood, who accordingly called on the King by appointment at Brighton, and was received in a "cordial and hearty manner." On backing out of the royal presence Hood forgot the way he had entered, but "the King good humouredly laughed, and himself showed him the right direction, going with him to the door."

Owing to disagreement with his landlord over the subject of repairs, Hood, late in 1831, or in the early part of the following year, gave up the pleasant cottage at Winchmore Hill and removed to the quaint Lake House at Wanstead, a step to which he is said to have been persuaded by injudicious friends, and one which he came later to regret. When Hood took the house there seems to have been thirty acres of land attached to it, for a letter of Lamb's to Moxon—with various inaccuracy dated " 1833," " May, 1833," and " ? Christmas, 1830," by Lamb's editors—says : " Only think of the new farmer with his thirty acres. There is a portion of land in Lambeth Parish called Knaves Acre. I wonder he overlook'd it. Don't show this to the firm of Dilke & Co. . . . . A pert half chemist half apothecary in our town, who smatters of literature, and is immeasurably unlettered, said to me ' Pray, Sir, may not Hood (he of the acres) be reckon'd the Prince of Wits in the present day ? ' To which I assenting, he adds, ' I had always thought that Rogers had been reckon'd the Prince of Wits, but I suppose that now Mr. Hood has the better title to that appellation.' To which I replied that Mr. R. had wit with much better qualities, but did not aspire to the principality."

The opening portion of this has an un-Elia-like bitterness about it that seems to hint at some unpleasantness between the friends, but such can only be conjecture, and there is no mention of such in Hood's unqualified tribute to Lamb, written a few years later.

Lake House, even as this book is passing through the press, is in the hands of the house breakers, and its acres are mostly to be given over to the builder. The house stood on Wanstend Flats loooking to the south with a distant view of Shooter's Hill. The place was known as Lake House, and had been formed by wooden additions out of an old summer house or hunting lodge belonging to the Wanstead House, which had been demolished a few years earlier. Wanstead

LAKE HOUSE, WANSTEAD.

[*To face p.* 262.

Winchmore Hill and Wanstead.

House had been erected in 1715 by Sir Richard Child, afterwards Earl Tylney, and was during the early part of the 19th century the residence of Louis XVIII. and other of the Bourbons in exile. It was the old house which provided Hood with the title and some of the materials of his long novel, published, as we shall see, towards the close of his tenancy of the converted summer house. The chief room of Lake House—going out on to the portico—had four great wall paintings in the French style still (when I visited it seventy years after Hood's tenancy) in a good state, excepting that one had a large rat hole through it. From the portico, flanked by two sycamores and two smooth-leaved hollies, the ground sloped downwards to the shrub-grown gardens, where fine old rhododendrons, overgrown with blackberry brambles, met closely over the path leading to the small tree-surrounded pond or lake on which Hood used to keep a little model frigate. Further to the north, on a slight rise at the extreme end of the Lake House grounds (whereon now stands a small châlet), Hood used to go to look down upon the gipsies who camped there.

At Lake House the Hoods passed a few happy years, though the end of their time there was overshadowed by trouble. The poet's last surviving nephew (Mr. W. A. Longmore), who stayed there as a boy of eight or nine, tells how towards evening his uncle would sit on the steps of the portico with a gun and pop at the scuttling rabbits that came into the garden foraging from the neighbouring parkland. Procter has recorded that Hood's pastimes were making puns and shooting sparrows. He had indeed a boyish fondness for guns and shooting, and kept at Lake House a miniature cannon for firing " salutes." Mr. Longmore remembers how, when he and some little friends and the four-year-old Fanny Hood were seeking for cherries from some of

Thomas Hood :

the old trees standing by the house Hood set his gardener-factotum with a rake to climb and knock the fruit down to the expectant youngsters, and how the little party was spoiled by the rake falling and badly wounding one of the children.

For some years Lake House was used as a kind of refreshment pavilion for cyclists, tennis players, and other pleasure-seekers drawn into the vicinity. It stood at the south-west point of Wanstead Park, which may be looked upon as the southern extension of Epping Forest, and it seems a pity that with all its old associations it could not have been preserved.

At Wanstead the home life seems to have been a happy one, though Hood can scarcely have been well advised, with his recurring attacks of rheumatic fever and other ailments calling for a dry climate, in going to reside on the "flats," and the latter part of his stay there was to have few but unpleasant associations. His daughter—who must have depended upon family tradition, for she was but about two years old on going to and but about five on leaving Lake House—has told some pleasant stories illustrative of Hood's love of boyish fun, his taste for practical joking. On one occasion some boys were found robbing the orchard, and with the assistance of the gardener were dragged trembling into the house.

"My mother's father (George Reynolds), of Christ's Hospital, happened to be staying there, an imposing-looking old gentleman, who had not forgotten his scholastic dignity when looking on anything in the shape of a boy. A hint to him sufficed, and he assumed an armchair and the character of a J.P. for the county. The frightened offenders were drawn up before him and formally charged by my father with the theft, which was further proved by the contents of their pockets. The judge, assuming a severe air, immediately sentenced them to instant execution by

Winchmore Hill and Wanstead.

hanging on the cherry tree. I can recollect being prompted by my father to kneel down and intercede for the culprits, and my frightened crying, and the solemn farce of the whole scene had its due effect on the offenders. Down on their knees they dropped in a row, sobbing and whining most piteously, and vowing never ' to do so no more.' My father, thinking them sufficiently punished, gave the hint, and they were as solemnly pardoned, my father and grandfather laughing heartily to see the celerity with which they made off."

Practical jokes took the form of painting Fanny's doll with pink spots so that the child did not dare to touch it, thinking that the poor thing was suffering from measles. On another occasion, having been made the victim of a practical joke which took the form of upsetting him out of his boat in the little lake, Hood turned the tables neatly on his jocular visitors. Having got out of the water,

"he presently began to complain of cramps and stitches, and at last went indoors. His friends getting rather ashamed of their rough fun, persuaded him to go to bed, which he immediately did. His groans and complaints increased so alarmingly, that they were almost at their wits' ends what to do. My mother had received a quiet hint, and was therefore not alarmed, though much amused at the terrified efforts and prescriptions of the repentant jokers. There was no doctor to be had for miles, and all sorts of queer remedies were suggested and administered, my father shaking with laughing, while they supposed he had got ague or fever. One rushed up with a tea kettle of boiling water hanging on his arm, another tottered under a tin bath, and a third brought the mustard. My father at length, as well as he could speak, gave out in a sepulchral voice that he was sure he was dying, and detailed some most

Thomas Hood :

absurd directions for his will, which they were all too
frightened to see the fun of. At last he could stand it
no longer, and after hearing the penitent offenders beg
him to forgive them for their unfortunate joke, and
beseech him to believe in their remorse, he burst into
a perfect shout of laughing, which they thought at first
was delirious frenzy, but which ultimately betrayed
the joke."

Another of his jokes, in the concoction of which he
must have taken some delight, was the writing of
an illiterate letter to Mrs. Dilke. This was a form of
fun in which he indulged more than once—on one
occasion sending a letter in severe condemnation of his
own work (probably in parody of something actually
received) to the editor of the *Athenæum*. The letter to
Mrs. Dilke may be quoted in illustration of this
playfulness.

" MADAM,—By having seen some Benevolent recum
mendations in the *Athenium* and supposing their by the
Editor too be humain disposed and Having no othe
Means of Publishing my own case which is as follows
I humbly Beg leav to say I am left with Eleven offspring
the yougest off whom But a munth old none so Much as
taste Butchers Meat and nothing in the World to lay on
xcept straw winter and summer owing to my Family
am unabel to get or do ether nedle work or charing and
there father am sorry to say not willing if he could get
work but peple wont employ Him on account of
caracter to Be sure he was Born to verry different
Prospects in life my mane object being to get sum of
the children of my hands am intending to send one up to
you by the Saturdays carryer hoping you will excuse the
offence and if approved of god willing may be the Means
of getting him into sum sittiation in London witch is
very scarce·hearabouts and the Allmity Bless and

Winchmore Hill and Wanstead.

prosper you for such and as the well noon gudness of Hart of you and Mr. Dilke will I trust exert in Behalf of our deplorible states and am begging your Humbel pardin for trubling with the distresses of a Stranger But not to your gudness your humbel servant L P."

The little stranger thus characteristically announced proved to be a sucking pig! With the Dilkes at this time the Hoods seem to have been on a footing of the friendliest intimacy, and many scraps of letters from the poet are included in the memoir of his grandfather which Sir Charles W. Dilke prefixed to the " Papers of a Critic." Hood was probably a fairly regular contributor to the *Athenæum* at this time, though he apparently still maintained his friendly relations with William Jerdan of the rival critical journal, the *Literary Gazette*, for there were several kindly references to him in the *Gazette* at a time when the writers on that paper let pass few opportunities of jeering at Lamb and other writers of his set. Verses signed " W.," for example, were prefaced with the apologetic " Everybody writes like Tom Hood now "; while a few months later appeared the following unstinting tribute : " We have often said to ourselves, there may be another Milton, another Pope, another Scott, another Byron,—as the wheel of time revolves the earth may again witness genius like and equal to these; but if we were to lose Tom Hood it is *un*possible for Nature herself to reproduce such another." Jerdan and Hood seem to have had a mutual liking, and there are two or three letters from the poet to the editor acknowledging friendly notices ; as he says in one of these, " friends ought to be friends, whether in Long Island or the Inch of Perth."

While at Winchmore Hill and at Wanstead Hood took several opportunities of visiting the sea-coast. In

Thomas Hood :

February, 1831, he was at Brighton with his brother-in-law, and they joined in protesting—shortsightedly as events proved—in Dilke's lowering the price of the *Athenæum* from eightpence to fourpence. In May, 1833, having again been ill, he went to Ramsgate to recuperate, journeying there by steamer and expressing surprise that there was no illness on board, "at least human sickness. The only symptom I saw was the *heaving* of the lead." Inviting his friend Wright the engraver to join them at Margate, Hood included the following, saying that though prose he defied a poet to write lines better descriptive of the sea—

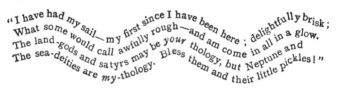

"I have had my sail—my first since I have been here; delightfully brisk; What some would call awfully rough—and am come in all in a glow. The land-gods and satyrs may be your thology, but Neptune and The sea-deities are my-thology. Bless them and their little pickles!"

The preparation of the "Comic Annual" took up a good part of the summer and autumn, and even then publication was sometimes a little late. For, quite apart from matters of health, which sometimes hindered his progress, Hood seems to have had something of that not uncommon facility for putting off work until the last moment. On one occasion he describes the Annual as riding on his back "like a centipede spurred on each foot." But in 1833 he was busy over an undertaking of a more ambitious character than he had before attempted, the writing of a full-sized novel. In August of this year he wrote to the Duke of Devonshire asking permission to dedicate the new work to him, and acknowledging assistance which that nobleman had rendered him. What special difficulties had arisen at this time is not ascertainable, but it may be surmised that they were not unconnected with Hood's illness in the spring. Whatever they may have been, the Duke volunteered a loan to assist the author in his troubles,— to what purpose we may gather from this extract from Hood's letter:—

"I hesitate to intrude with details, but I know the goodness which originated one obligation will be gratified to learn that the assistance referred to has been, and is, of the greatest service in a temporary struggle—though arduous enough for one of a profession never overburthened with wealth, from Homer downwards. Indeed the Nine Muses seem all to have lived in one house for cheapness. I await, hopefully anxious, Your Grace's pleasure as to the new honour I solicit, fully prepared, in case of acquiescence, to exclaim with the Tinker to the 'Good Duke' of Burgundy, in the old ballad,

> "'Well, I thank your good Grace,
> And your love I embrace,
> I was never before in so happy a case!'"

The dedication was duly accepted, though some months were to elapse before the novel was published. Indeed a year passed after it was completed before it was issued, and the delay may have been consequent upon the difficulties which beset Hood in 1834. The "Comic Annual" for that year was the last to be published by Tilt, that for 1835 bearing the imprint of A. H. Baily.

On October 12th, 1833, Hood wrote:—

"With regard to my novel, 'Tylney Hall' is completed, and the whole building, in one story, is expected to be printed and papered very early in December. You can treat in the meantime with parties who may be disposed to occupy themselves with the premises; and a reading lease for a term of ninety-nine years will not be at all objected to."

Thomas Hood :

An•ther note written about the same time says, "The novel is printing, and christened Tylney Hall." Things seemed to be prospering, but anxious times were close ahead. He was, however, unaware of this, and was able for a while to indulge in riding exercise, in which he delighted, and to start a chaise, for an undated note runs : "If you should feel disposed for a day or two to relax here, Wright will drive down my new shay (your old friend Bob is out of office, and a bay mare is premier) Saturday evening or Sunday morning, which you like, and let him know where to meet you."

Periodical difficulties with his publishers mark the story of Hood's literary career so persistently that it is impossible to refrain from thinking that there must have been in him an unbusinesslike readiness to enter into unsatisfactory engagements, or a quarrelsomeness in business matters of which we have no indications in his other relations of life. With Charles Tilt he had however kept on publishing terms for some years, had perhaps even acquired some interest in the business, for during this year of 1834 he had to change his publisher while his novel was printing, and at the close of this year it was financial troubles said to be consequent on the failure of a publishing firm which necessitated a complete change in the conditions of his life. In the summer, however, the difficulties did not appear insuperable, as we find from a letter (July 21) to William Dilke at Chichester, in response to an invitation thither to attend the Goodwood Races :

" MY DEAR DILKE,—You will surely suppose that we have some insurmountable old grudge against some one, some where in Chichester or its neighbourhood—or that we are unusually timid on the subject of earthquakes, when so many kind invitations fail to bring us under

Winchmore Hill and Wanstead.

your roof—for we must again regretfully give up the pleasure of seeing you this year. I did hope last year to visit you this season at your race time, but with us ' The course of *Goodwood* never did run smooth.' The change of a publisher, and the delay and difficulty of finding another, honest and responsible, delayed me so this spring, with my novel, that as soon as that is launched I must put my annual on the stocks. So your other friends must enjoy the bed, and your hospitality, which we must take for *granted*.

" I will not dilate on the enjoyment we thus lose. Jane and I are equally disappointed :—for she does not like my racing against time in lieu of yours for a cup. She unites with me in kindest regards to yourself and Mrs. Dilke, with which my inexorable printer warns me to conclude and write myself, my dear Dilke, Yours very truly,

" Thos. Hood."

"Tylney Hall" was not "launched" until October 20, though a premature review of the novel had appeared on October 4 in the *Athenæum*, but as late as that the "Comic Annual" was still far from finished, for it was on October 16 that the Houses of Parliament were destroyed by fire and suggested fresh material for inclusion in that miscellany. Writing to Dilke shortly after, Hood said :—

"I am fagging hard at the comic. It's an ill fire that bakes nobody's bread, and the Great Conflagration will make an excellent subject. I was up all last night, bright moonlight, drawing cuts and writing, and watching a gang of gipsies encamped just out of my bounds. I saved my fowls, and geese, and pigs, but they took my faggots. However, I shot two cats that were poaching. As Scott says, ' My life is a mingled yarn.' To-day the man's missing, I'm afraid he's scragged."

Thomas Hood :

The publication of "Tylney Hall" should have marked a new stage of prosperity in Hood's life; for he had the popularity which assured it a welcome, and it affords very entertaining reading though it did not in any way add to the author's literary reputation. The book was on the whole well received, and among his friends received such praise as made Hood declare that it revived in him "the delights of young authorship," for he was, as he added, young in the path which he was treading. He confessed that he felt that some of the characters were failures because he could not write love scenes—"as a fellow said at my piece at the Surrey, 'I can act the part, but I forget the words.'" It is not necessary here to enlarge upon the story, for it has maintained some measure of popularity and is easily obtainable; but it is pertinent to draw attention to the views of the book expressed by some of the most notable of Hood's contemporaries. Charles Lamb, in a note which I have the privilege of printing for the first time, wrote to the author in his usual kindly strain :—

"DR. H.,—I have been infinitely amused with 'Tylney Hall.' 'Tis a medley, without a confusion, of farce, melodrame, pantomime, comedy, tragedy, punchery, what not ? if not the best sort of novel, the best of its sort, as how could it fail being the only one ? 'The Fete' is as góod as H[ogarth]'s 'Strollers in the Barn.' For the serious part, the warning Piece shot over Raby's head is most impressive. Only Luckless Joe should not have been killed; his fates were teazers, not absolute inexorable Clothos; and the Creole should have been hang'd. With kind remembrances to Mrs. Hood, Yours,

"C. LAMB.

"The puns are so neat, that the most inveterate foe

Winchmore Hill and Wanstead.

to that sort of joke, not being expectant of 'em might read it all thro' and not find you out.

" My sister I hope will relish it by and by; as it is she tries to make it out, and laughs heartily, but it puzzles her to read above a page or so a day."

This was probably the last letter which Hood ever received from Lamb, whose life, clouded by the death of Coleridge in the previous July, was drawing towards its close. Charles Dickens, writing some years later to John Forster, said :—

" I have been reading poor Hood's ' Tylney Hall ' : the most extraordinary jumble of impossible extravagance, and especial cleverness I ever saw. The man drawn to the life from the pirate bookseller is wonderfully good; and his recommendation to a reduced gentleman from the university, to rise from nothing, as he, the pirate, did, and go round to the churches and see whether there's an opening, and begin by being a beadle, is one of the finest things I ever read, in its way."

Lamb and Dickens were justified in describing the novel as a medley; yet it is a medley full of humour and observation, and provides pleasant entertainment for those readers who can find pleasure in the words of the author as well as in the scenes and episodes which he presents. The story is most successful where the author is describing scenes and people in which his humorous ability is able to find expression ; it is least successful where he has to deal with the tragic and emotional. Some of his characters are quite Dickensian —and before Dickens had published a book—as presentations of quaint individualities. In the style of his storytelling, however, the author was too fond of playing upon words, for though this is often elusive it is also frequently too obvious, and it is curious to find that Charles Lamb,

Thomas Hood :

who had resented the puns in the " Odes and Addresses,"
where they formed an integral and essential part of the
scheme, should applaud them here, where they are at
times annoyingly redundant. Though refraining from
any discussion of the novel in detail, it may be interesting to give some passages from the preface which Hood
wrote for the story a few years later on its re-issue in
single volume form.

" ' Tylney Hall ' was the first attempt of the Author
in what some military writer has called the ' three-volley
line,' from the number of *tomes* assigned to such performances. There was no popular predecessor, therefore, to bespeak for it a public welcome ; but in the
absence of any particular expectations elsewhere, a
certain degree of local interest was excited in favour of
the book in the county of Essex,—an interest curiously
illustrative of the common relish for a condiment which
is often looked for, and is sometimes found in a novel.
It pleased some of those ingenious persons who pique
themselves on putting this and that together, to discover
a wonderful resemblance in ' Tylney Hall ' to Tylney
Long ; and to associate the author's then residence,
Lake House, with a celebrated mansion formerly standing in the vicinity. From these *premises* it was inferred
that, as sundry structures had been indebted for their
building materials to the wreck of Wanstead House,
even so the private histories of the Wellesley and Long
families had furnished matter for this novel. Some
domestic secrets, whether overheard by the rooks in
their nests, or underneath by the rabbits in their burrows,
or repeated by the echo in the Park, were supposed to
be in the possession of the author, who was conceived
to be equally incapable of retaining them in his own
bosom. Accordingly, not a few copies travelled east-
ward, through Stratford-le-Bow, but, of course, to
the signal discomfiture of the speculators, who must

Winchmore Hill and Wanstead.

have been infinitely puzzled to identify the fictitious characters with the real personages. One of the conjectures which transpired was quite as wild as the coneys in Wanstead Park, or the herons on its island.

"The truth is, the figures were not drawn, after the Royal Academy fashion, from living models. My friends and acquaintances will forgive me for saying that none of them had *character* enough—in the artistic sense of the word—to make good pen and ink portraits. Indeed, it has been my bad fortune through life (for a novelist) to know intimately but one original ; and his originality consisted in having stockings made for him expressly, with a separate stall for each toe."

After referring to some of the criticisms to which his story had been subjected, the author made fun of the reviewer who "boldly declared, in defiance of the Law List, that ' Hood was an attorney ' " ; and went on to say that through a natural misgiving on his part the manuscript had been submitted to a legal friend who pronounced that the law of the book was quite bad enough to be good enough for a rural justice, adding that " it had not yet been ruled that the Laws of Fiction were subject to the Fictions of the Law." He then cited a sentence from the letter of Lamb's appealing against the fate of " unlucky Joe," and continued :—

" Finally, an objection of a serious nature has been urged against the book by critics of the fairer sex. A certain naval officer of a bad figure was once pointed out in company, to a lady, as a lieutenant just made— ' and not *well made* either,' was the feminine remark. The same fault has been found with the love making in this novel, and it has even been hinted, that in his next work of the kind, the author ought to introduce none but married people. But in reality, the sentimental

part of the passion was purposely shirked, not that I
was exactly in the predicament of the innocent Adonis,

> "'Quoth he, I know not Love,
> Unless it be a Boar, and then I chase it,'

but because that, to my taste, with very rare exceptions,
Love reads as badly in prose as Piety in verse. To be
candid, the perusal of what is termed Religious Poetry
always exercises a deadening influence, rather than
otherwise, on my devotional feelings ; and we all know
the effect of reading even genuine love letters in a court
of justice—that the tenderest effusions of the tenderest
of passions, written in the softest of hours, with the
softest of pens, seldom fail to elicit a roar of laughter,
from the Bar to the Bench. In short, rather than risk
that my lovers should say too much, I have made them
say too little—but it was erring on the safe side ; and,
moreover, a great deal of love may be made in one
word ; for example, when Charlotte laid her hand upon
Werter's arm, and said, ' Klopstock ! ' "

The "celebrated house" was Wanstead House, and
the name of the novel being taken from the Tylney
family which had resided there was sure to make the
curious in such matters think that the story was one
with a "key." In Horace Walpole's letters is an
account of a visit to Wanstead House in 1755, and his
account of dragging a gold-fish pond for my Lady F.
and Lord S., may well refer to the shrub-shaded pond—
in which until quite recently gold fish disported
themselves—in the garden of Lake House.

To the troubles which had fallen on Hood there was
added a certain family anxiety : as he wrote to Dilke
towards the end of the year, "every day I am a step
father to being a parent." The year closed, too, with
the loss of a dear old friend, his "literary father,"
Charles Lamb, and Hood was one of the small band
of friends who stood on that winter's day in Edmonton

ROSE COTTAGE, WINCHMORE HILL.

[*To face p.* 276.

Winchmore Hill and Wanstead.

Churchyard "beside a grave in which all that was mortal of Elia was deposited." Hood has recorded that — though it seemed a dangerous confession to make—he shed no tear; scarcely had a sigh at the painful ceremony. There were, as he recognised, many sources of comfort. "He had not died young. He had happily gone before that noble sister, who not in selfishness, but the devotion of a unique affection, would have prayed to survive him but for a day, lest he should miss that tender care which had watched over him upwards from a little child. Finally he had left behind him his works, a rare legacy!—and above all, however much of him had departed, there was still more of him that could not die — for as long as Humanity endures and man owns fellowship with man, the spirit of Charles Lamb will still be extant!" Hood's admiration of, his love for, Lamb was so great that it may be permissible to give one or two further passages from his reminiscences of Elia, and more especially as those very qualities in Lamb which struck his friend were also such as belonged to Hood himself. The following descriptions might be applied to the writer of them : " If he was intolerant of anything, it was of intolerance. He would have been (if the foundation had existed, save in the fiction of Rabelais) of the Utopian Order of Thelemites, where each man under scriptural warrant did what seemed good in his own eyes. He hated evil speaking, carping, and petty scandal. On one occasion, having slipped out an anecdote, to the discredit of a literary man, during a very confidential conversation, the next moment, with an expression of remorse, for having impaired even my opinion of the party, he bound me solemnly to bury the story in my own bosom. In another case he characteristically rebuked the backbiting spirit of a censorious neighbour. Some Mrs. Candour telling him, in expectation of an ill-natured comment, that Miss ——, the teacher at the Ladies' School, had married a publican. ' Has she so ? ' said Lamb, ' then I'll have my beer there ! . . .'

" Such was Charles Lamb. To sum up his character, on his own principle of antagonism, he was, in his views of human nature, the opposite of Crabbe ; in criticism, of Gifford ; in poetry, of Lord Byron ; in prose, of the last new novelist ; in philosophy, of Kant ; and in religion, of Sir Andrew Agnew. Of his wit I have endeavoured to give such samples as occurred to me ; but the spirit of his sayings was too subtle and too much married to the circumstances of the time to survive the occasion. They had the brevity without the levity of wit—some of his puns contained the germs of whole essays. Moreover, like Falstaff, he seemed not only witty himself, but the occasion of it by example in others. ' There is M——,' said he, ' who goes about dropping his good things as an ostrich lays her eggs, without caring what becomes of them.' It was once my good fortune to pick up one of Mr. M.'s foundlings, and it struck me as particularly in Lamb's own style, containing at once a pun and a criticism. ' What do you think,' asked somebody, ' of the book called " A Day in Stowe Gardens " ? ' Answer—' A Day ill-bestowed.' "

Of the extent to which Hood's position in the literary world of the time was recognised at this critical point in his life, we get an idea from the series of articles giving a survey of British Literature which Allan Cunningham contributed to the *Athenæum*. In these articles, which were reprinted in Paris, Cunningham wrote : " Thomas Hood is, perhaps, better known to the world as a dexterous punster than as a true poet ; in his ' Little Odes to Great Folks ' (*sic*) he dallied with words till he made them wanton, and, by the force of a

Winchmore Hill and Wanstead.

peculiar fancy, compelled the language to bear the burthen of meanings alien to its nature. Yet no one could read these sprightly and laughable things without perceiving the spirit of a true poet ; his 'Dream of Eugene Aram' places him high among the bards who deal in dark and fearful things, and intimate rather than express deeds which men shudder to hear named. Some others of his poems have much tenderness, and a sense of nature animate and inanimate ; but he has left the company of the serious Muse for the society of her with the light foot and the merry eye—and the world has smiled on his choice."

It was probably during the stay at Wanstead that the portrait of Hood which hangs in the National Portrait Gallery was painted. Mr. Longmore remembers the artist visiting Lake House for the purpose and recalls his name as Hilton. The picture has long been "attributed to Masquerier," but was, there seems little doubt, really the work of William Hilton, R.A. (1786—1839), a notable historical painter who became Keeper of the Royal Academy in 1827. There are several slight references to Hilton in Hood's writings. At the same time the artist painted the portrait of Jane Hood, and also one of her mother Mrs. Reynolds (now in the possession of Mr. Longmore).

CHAPTER XI.

LIFE IN GERMANY (1835—1837).

*" A brave knight who went laughingly to battle, but still went
to battle, against giant falsehoods and follies and giant wrongs
and giant misbeliefs, and with his smooth round stones of song
did smite them."*—DR. T. U. DUDLEY.

ON January 19th, 1835, at Lake House, Wanstead,
Jane Hood gave birth to a son, who was duly named
Tom—to the confusion of many subsequent writers.
After the birth of her child, Mrs. Hood was so seriously
ill for a time that her life was despaired of, but fortunately the period of grave anxiety on her behalf came
to an end, and Hood had then to decide upon the future
course of his life, that he might live economically and
quietly while his creditors were being paid, for he refused
to avail himself of the protection of the bankruptcy laws.
In a letter written in the third person he described the
whole course of his affairs, but unfortunately the passages
from that letter presented in the " Memorials " do not
give us any particulars of the reason for or the extent
of his embarrassments, though they suggest that the
extent was not very considerable :

" For some months he strove with his embarrassments, but the first heavy sea being followed up by
other adversities, all hope of righting the vessel was
abandoned. In this extremity had he listened to the
majority of his advisers, he would at once have absolved
himself of his obligations by one or other of those sharp
but sure remedies, which the legislature has provided for
all such evils. But a sense of honour forbade such a course,

Life in Germany (1835—1837).

and, emulating the illustrious example of Sir Walter
Scott, he determined to try whether he could not score
off his debts as effectually and more creditably, with his
pen, than with the legal whitewash or a wet sponge.
He had aforetime realised in one year a sum equal to
the amount in arrear, and there was consequently fair
reason to expect that by redoubled diligence, econo-
mising, and escaping costs at law, he would soon
be able to retrieve his affairs. With these views,
leaving every shilling behind him, derived from
the sale of his effects, the means he carried with
him being an advance upon his future labours, he
voluntarily expatriated himself, and bade his native
land good-night."

The expatriation would appear to have been a great
mistake, for Hood's health had become too uncertain a
factor to make it advisable to change the whole conditions of his life. He might well have economised
and lived quietly at some resort on the English coast
by that sea which he ever loved, and the neighbourhood
of which had never failed to give him renewed health
and strength. He decided, however, on going to one of
the Rhine towns, and on Dilke's recommendation
thought of settling in Coblenz. His wife being convalescent, he left her in the hands of the kind friend
whom her illness had given to the little family, Dr.
William Elliot, of Stratford, and set out early in March,
1835, for Rotterdam, *en route* for the Rhine, in the
steamer *Lord Melville*. The passage was a terrible
experience, including as it did a violent storm (March
4th and 5th), in which eleven vessels, including a large
Indiaman, went down off the Dutch coast. The first
letter written home to his wife may be quoted not only
as giving his account of the storm, but also as indicating
the cheerfulness of spirit which he maintained in his
troubles and in the ill-health which was more or less

Thomas Hood :

constant after this, but also as an illustration of his unfailing devotion to his true helpmate.

"COBLENZ, *March* 13*th* [1835].

"At last, my own dearest and best, I sit down to write to you, and I fear you have been looking anxiously for news from me.

"In truth, I wrote a long letter at Nimeguen which I suppressed, having nothing certain to say. I will now tell you first that I am *safe* and *well*—which is the very *truth*—and then I may relate how I got on. I had a dreadful passage to Rotterdam : Wednesday night was an awful storm, and Thursday morning was worse. I was *sea-sick* and *frightened* at sea for the first time : so you will suppose it was no trifle : in fact, it was unusually severe. I went up at midnight and found *four* men at the helm, hint enough for me, so I went down again, and in the morning a terrific sea tore the whole *four* from the helm, threw the captain as far as the funnel (twenty paces), and the three men after him. Had it not come *direct aft*, it would have swept them into the sea, boat, skylights, and everything in short, and have left us a complete wreck. Eleven others miscarried that same night, near at hand, so you may thank the cherub I told you of : but such a storm has seldom been known. It was quite a squeak for the Comic for 1836. But when you come the weather will be settled, and such a sea comes but once in seven years. When you see four at the helm you may be frightened, but mind, not till then. Steam, I think, saved us ; you ought to offer up a golden kettle somewhere. You were given over and I was given under—but we have both been saved, I trust, for each other, and Heaven does not mean to part us yet. But it made me very ill, for it was like being shaken up in a dice box, and I have had a sort of bilious fever, with something of the complaint Elliot cured me of, and could not eat, with pains in my side, etc., which I nursed myself for as well as I could.

" I made two acquaintances on board—one gave me an introduction to a doctor at Coblenz, whom I have not seen; the other gave me an introduction to his father here, where I took tea to-night; their name is Vertue, so you see my morals are in good hands.

" I got to Rotterdam only on Thursday night, and I supped there very merrily with the young Vertue and two of his friends.

" On Friday night I stopped at Nimeguen, which is in a state of war, and could proceed no further till Saturday, which night I passed abroad, and on Sunday arrived and slept in Cologne. Here I was detained on Monday by the steamer having broken a paddle, but made myself agreeable to an old general, Sir Parker Carrol, who took me with him to see the lions. I gave him a bulletin to carry to Dilke. Strange to say, the general once lived at their house. Also made acquaintance with a Rev. Mr. Clarke, a gentlemanly young man, and we started on Tuesday for Coblenz, where we slept; again, on Wednesday to Mayence, slept there, and to-day he set off for Frankfort, and I returned here. At all these starts I have had to rise at five, and was too worn out and weak to undertake the walking plan I had concerted with Dilke, so I went up and down by the boat instead. Luckily, I got better on Tuesday, and that day and Wednesday and to-day being fine, I enjoyed it very much. From Cologne to Mayence is all beautiful or magnificent; I am sure you will enjoy it, especially if, as I will try, I meet you at Cologne.

" I want you to see the cathedral. I am going to-morrow on foot to look among the villages; but my impression is, from what Mr. Vertue says, there will be some difficulty in finding anything there; but at all events there are lodgings to be had in Coblenz, which is a place I admire much. I therefore think you might start for Coblenz at once, without hearing further from me, when you feel able, letting me know, of course, your day of sailing, for in case of my getting anything at Bingen, etc., you would have to stop *here*, and unless I meet with something to my taste above, I shall make this our fixture.

"Consult Dilke. For my part, if well enough, I think you may safely come on the chance, as it would take you five days: one to Rotterdam, one to Nimeguen, two to Cologne, and one to Coblenz. I am writing but a business letter, and you must give me credit, my own dearest, for everything else, as I wish to devote all the space I can, to describing what will be for your comfort. You must come to Rotterdam by *Der Batavier*, which has female accommodations and a stewardess. You may tell the steward I was nearly swamped with him in the *Lord Melville*, for he was with us, and will remember it. . . . You must expect some nuisances and inconveniences, but they will do to laugh at when we meet, and *Der Batavier* is a splendid and powerful steamer. . . . With my dear ones by my side, my pen will gambol through the 'Comic' like the monkey who had seen the world. We are not transported even for seven years, and the Rhine is a deal better than Swan River. I have made a great many notes. My mind was never so free—and meaning what is right and just to all, I feel cheerful at our prospects, and in spite of illness have kept up. This will not reach you for four or five days, and then it would take you as much more to come, during which I should be sure to get a place, so do not wait to hear from me again. . . . You may reckon, I think, upon settling at Coblenz: it is a capital and clean town, and does justice to Dilke's recommendation. I have already begun some 'Rhymes

Life in Germany (1835—1837).

of the Rhine,' of which the first is justly dedicated to
your own self. But to-night is my first leisure. I have
been like the Wandering Jew. How my thoughts and
wishes fly over the vine-covered hills to meet yours; my
love sets towards you like the mighty current of the
great Rhine itself, and will brook no impediments.

" I grudge the common-place I have been obliged to
write; every sentence should claim you, as my own
dear wife, the pride of my youth, the joy of my manhood,
the hope of all my after days. Twice has the shadow
of death come between us, but our hearts are preserved
to throb against each other. I am content for your
sake to wait the good time when you may safely undertake the voyage, and do not let your heart run away
with your head. Be strong before you attempt it.
Bring out with you a copy of 'Tylney Hall,' which I
shall want to refer to. I want no others, but the last
'Comic.' If you are likely to be some time, treat me
with one letter. Dilke will tell you how to send it.
I long to be settled and at work; I owe *him* much, and
wish to do C. Lamb while it is fresh. I hope Reynolds's
spasms are gone. *They* could not do better than come
up the Rhine this summer, it would not cost so much
as Brighton—and such a change of scene. I have
had some adventures I must tell you when we meet. I
bought this paper all by telegraph of a girl at Cologne.
We could not speak a word to each other, and the
whole ended in a regular laugh throughout the shop,
when she picked out of the money in my hand. Was
not I in luck to meet the only two or three English that
were out, and make such friends with them. But I
really am getting a traveller, and am getting *brass*, and
pushing my way with them. I forgot to say at Coblenz
the men frequent the Casinos, and the women make
evening parties of their own, but I do not mean to give
up my old domestic habits. We shall set an example

of fireside felicity, if that can be said of a stove, for we have no grates here—the more 's the pity. God bless you ever. Your own,

"T. H."

Another and longer letter followed this, explaining that Hood had taken furnished rooms at 372, Castor Hof, just at the junction of the Rhine and the Moselle, almost the corner house of Coblenz, as he put it; "there are three little rooms, one backward, my study as is to be, with such a lovely view over the Moselle. My heart jumped when I saw it, and I thought, 'There I shall write volumes!'" He had, however, already realised that there might be some amusing difficulties in that neither he nor his wife spoke German. He was impatient for them all to arrive, and looked forward confidently to a happy future; "our own little home, though homely, will be happy for us, and we do not bid England a very long good night." There is more advice to Mrs. Hood as to her journey, a message or two to Fanny, a promise to meet them at Cologne, and a few characteristic lapses into levity, as when he says that Mrs. Dilke had told him to have his linen well-aired, having been misled by the word *Dampschiffe* on the river boats—"not an unnatural mistake," he adds. He closes by saying, " I am become quite a citizen of the world; I talk to every one in broken English, broken French, and bad German, and have the vanity to think I make friends wherever I go."

In the course of this letter Hood shows that he was still contemplating an " Epsom " successor to the Epping Hunt, for he asked that his wife should bring with her a sufficiency of wood blocks for the drawings for the annual and some for the other purpose.

Jane Hood set out with her baby boy and Fanny on March 29, and after a somewhat trying trip they were

Life in Germany (1835—1837).

duly met by Hood at Cologne. His cheerful letters had, however, apparently belied his state, for his wife, in writing home, said that he looked so ill she scarcely knew him. They stayed for a day in the town, of which Hood said that if a certain place is paved with good intentions then Cologne must have been paved with the bad ones, and then proceeded to the new home in Coblenz. Then, unfortunately, Hood's health broke down, and he had one of the bouts of serious illness which marred the whole of his stay on the Rhine. He suffered, too, mentally from worry consequent upon the interruption of his work, and, having to call in medical aid, found it " based on Sangrado's practice, bleeding, blistering, and drastics." In the middle of a long letter to Dilke he continues after a break—

" I was going to resume this, but was prevented by what soldiers call a night attack. On going to bed I was seized with violent spasms in the chest, which after some time compelled me to send for the Dr. at midnight. I could only breath when bolt upright, and rarely then at the expense of intense pain ; I thought every breath would be the last."

Still he gets much fun from his wife's attempts to make broken English do duty for German with the maid of the house, and describes at length some features of their life, but regrets the slow progress made with the next year's " Comic," while recognising that in his new surroundings he is finding much fresh material. The month of May seems to have been particularly bad, for though his wife's health happily improved, he had a second severe " attack of the spasms " in the chest, which left him so weak that he could hardly walk, but he seems rapidly to have recovered his power of making fun, even out of his own ailments, and the long letters home are crowded with pleasantries. He suggests to Dilke that the *Athenæum* might like a weekly letter from

Thomas Hood :

Coblenz, and hints that he could make it *very foreign;* or, as the Germans translate his works, he thinks some *free* translations from the German might be acceptable, and proposes making a first experiment on Kant's "Transcendentalism!" adding that he has been to the Hotel of an evening and got a good notion of German philosophy, which is laid on with *pipes*—"like the gas in London!"

A chance meeting in Coblenz with Lieutenant de Franck, an officer, of partly English parentage, attached to the 19th Polish Regiment at Ehrenbreitstein, introduced Hood to a very good friend of whom he saw much and to whom he later wrote long and amusing letters. De Franck hearing English spoken, introduced himself to the Hoods, and his companionship proved a source of much pleasure. In the summer the Elliots visited the Hoods on a holiday and brought a whiff of the home from which they had exiled themselves. Dr. Elliot found Hood so much improved in health that he growled at feeding time if dinner was not punctual! By mid-September work on the "Comic Annual" was getting well advanced, and to John Wright, who engraved most of his woodcuts and who had undertaken the arrangement of materials in the annual, correcting proofs, etc., during the author's absence, Hood wrote in a pleasant strain, suggesting that he was well and busy :—

"You will be glad to hear that I cannot write at great length to you, because I am busy, and able to be busy. You may imagine what a delight it was to us to see the Elliots,—they are so very kind and friendly. Besides, it was a comfort to have his opinion about me, though I am much better. I almost growl at feeding-time if the dinner is not ready. We dine at a very genteel hour—two o'clock—which is also the Governor's time. The universal people take it at one. But I find

Life in Germany (1835—1837).

the difference more striking mentally than corporeally even; and ideas now come of themselves without being laboured for—and *in vain*. In fact, I know that I have a mind, or according to the famous form, ' *Cogito, ergo sum.*' I believe that's something like the Latin for it, but I forget, for *I had a Latin prize at school!* As I find a positive pleasure in the power, its exercise must be equally pleasant, and I think I shall get on rapidly; indeed, some evenings I have been quite delighted with my comparative fertility of thought. I have got some good stories, or hints for stories, from De Franck, whose loss I fear I shall shortly have to regret, for I really like him. How odd his knowing C—— and H. D——; there must have been some mysterious animal magnetism in his accosting me. A joke with him has led to my writing a poem of some 700 lines, which you will soon receive. My own impression is, if good enough for the ' Comic' it had better be there to advance; but consult with Dilke, who will judge better than I can. I have been so unwell, I am down, and diffident as to what I do. I shall have some more Sketches on the Road, and some German stories, so I have not been quite idle even in bed. I did hope to be earlier this year, but, as all philosophers must say when it comes to be impossible, ' it can't be helped.' I am only too happy to exclaim, like the poor scullion in ' Tristram Shandy,' ' I'm alive.' But some day I hope to make my account even with the storm; for there were some Eugene Aram-like verses rambled through my brain as I lay for the first night alone here—I believe a trifle delirious—but I remember something of their tenour, and I have a storm by me to work them up with. You see I am cutting out work for the winter. I went, the day the Elliots left, to Metternich, and in a wood at the top of a hill I found a large patch of wild purple crocuses in full bloom. I suppose they, too, had suffered a storm,

Thomas Hood :

and could not bud as they ought to have done in the
spring. To-morrow I dine on game!—'Think of that,
Master Brooke!' for it will make me think of you. I
am sorry about Gilston Park. It would have turned all
my hares white in one night, and then such a herd of
deers. I have only three here, Jane, Fanny, and Tom ;
but they make a strong ring fence about me. What a
lot of Tremaines he must write to get it back again.
We authors are an unlucky set—freehold, copyhold, or
copyright !

" Kind regards to all. God bless you, and send you
bright days, that we may meet in 1855 like two Roth-
schildren just come of age and into our fortunes. Yours
ever truly,

"THOMAS HOOD.

" P.S.—' Vallnuts is in, and thrippins an underd, and
will be lowerer !' Think of that ! "

Who the friends or acquaintances were whom
De Franck and the Hoods had in common cannot be
recognised. The "poem of some 700 lines" was evidently
the farcical romance of " Love and Lunacy," which
duly found its place in the " Comic Annual " for the
following year. Gilston Park was the seat of R. Plumer
Ward, politician and man of letters, author of
"Tremaine," " De Vere," and other novels of a past
day. A week or two later De Franck left with his
regiment for Posen, and at the end of October Hood
wrote him a whimsical, quizzing letter, full of all sorts
of wild and wilful mistakes, apparently making fun of
his correspondent's bad memory for names. Recalling
the old note from Lamb to himself, Hood wrote as to
" My dear Mr. Wood," and subscribed himself " Philip
De Franck." When De Franck had gone Hood was left
but with one acquaintance, a M. Ramponi, a teacher of
languages, who dropped in every Sunday for a talk.

Life in Germany (1835—1837).

There was the further entertainment of writing long letters to friends in England, with however the chance that they might go astray, for some of his correspondence addressed to Wright never reached its destination, and so made him anxious for the fate of batches of copy sent to England. Then, too, was a disquieting delay in delivery of the wood blocks on which Hood had drawn his pictures for the " Comic," as these seem to have excited some suspicion at the frontier between Prussia and Holland. A lengthy letter, full of amusing flippancies, was written to Mrs. Dilke—dating from " 372 Cast-him-off, God Bless "—because Hood declared that all Dilke replied to " huge letters full and crossed " was " a little letteret that cannot do anybody any harm "—" I suppose some day I shall come to, ' T. H. is received ' at the fag end of the *Athenæum*, amidst the miscalled Answers to Correspondents." The Dilkes had gone to Margate, and Hood made much fun of that popular watering place—though, truth to tell, he would probably have preferred the Isle of Thanet to the banks of the Moselle. The letter runs to about sixteen pages of type, but from it may be taken a bit of characteristic banter in which Hood supposes Dilke discussing Margate with his wife :—

" ' Upon my soul, Maria, this is a delightful place ! So like Coblenz ! So you call this Margate, do you, my beauty ? Well—' (a grunt like a paviour's) ' and I suppose you call that the fort—humph ! Considering we might have stood before Ehrenbreitstein instead of it—hah ! ' (a sigh like an alligator's). ' My God !—that we could be so insane !—how any Christian being could stay a month in it !—why I should hang myself in ten days, or drown myself in that stinking sea yonder ! There is not one thing worth looking at—not one ! I know what you are going to say, Beauty ; but because the Crosbys and the Chatfields are such donkeys, and the

Thomas Hood :

Lord knows who besides, is it any reason because they don't act like common rational beings—— ? But come along ! ' (no offer to stir though) ' let's go up to the market and look at the fish, for I suppose you know there is none to be had here, because it is so near the coast. To be sure, says you, there is whiting—and so there is at Billingsgate ! If ever I go again to a watering-place—I believe that's what you call it, Maria—it shall be Hungerford Market. My God ! it is a madness —a perfect madness—to leave home and come down here and see—what ? a parcel of yellow slippers and pepper-and-salt dressing-gowns.' Here he draws down his mouth, and hoists up his shoulders, till his coat-collar hides his ears. ' Well, it's too late now to listen to common sense. It serves me right for being such an ass. By the time my holidays are over, I shall know how to spend them ! But perhaps *you* like it better than I do, for there's no disputing of tastes.

" ' There may be something to recommend even Margate, though an angel from heaven couldn't find out what it is. I know *I* can't, unless it's having a drunken noisy vagabond overhead to keep you awake all night long. But I forget, my darling, you don't sleep so light as I do—so much the better for you ! Then there's his sister that Mrs. —— what d'ye call her, Tops-and-Bottoms, with her infernal bobbings and curtesyings and over-civility. Damme if I know how to answer the woman ! I suppose according to Margate manners, we ought to ask her to Grosvenor Place. But mind, Maria, when she calls, I'm at Somerset House ! Come along ' (not a stump stirred yet). ' I suppose we must see what isn't to be seen in our salt-water Wapping. All *I* have seen is " London butter,"—just think of that, Maria,—" London butter may be had here." Why so it may in London without going sixty miles by sea for it ; and you, my darling, as sick as a dog ! Spasms ! I

Life in Germany (1835—1837).

don't wonder you've had spasms; I've almost had them
myself. It's the cursed negatives, and the place, rather
than anything positive,—the utter bleakness and desola-
tion of the country against the stinks of the sea-shore.
Lord! that a man with a nose on his face should come
here; and here too one has to remember that there are
such places as Coblenz; and such a river as the Rhine.
I'll tell you what, Maria!' Here he tells you nothing;
but stooping over his base, like the leaning tower at
Bologna, he takes a very long pinch of snuff, and then
anathematising, shakes the dust off his fingers against
all Margate and all its inhabitants, present and future.

"There! isn't that a portrait of him to the life—a
cabinet picture—a gem! Pray take care of it, to be a
comfort to you when you are a widow. Perhaps I shall
send him a sketch of you as a companion picture, for I
can fancy you quite as vividly. If I recollect rightly,
you were at Margate before and liked it amazingly.
Between your raptures and his disgusts I suppose you
got up a quarrel, for I observed you say in your letter
that 'you are both getting a little more *reconciled.*'"

His lengthy letter he winds up with an amusing
parody of the peroration used by certain writers of
books:—

"If these pages should be the happy means of
exciting one virtuous impression, or confirming one
moral or religious principle, or lightening one moment
of human suffering, or eradicating one speculative error,
or removing one ill-founded prejudice, the writer will
have his reward, and will not have written in vain."

On Christmas Day Lieutenant De Franck, who had
returned to Coblentz "for good," joined the Hoods at
dinner, and they introduced him to plum pudding,
while he initiated little Fanny into the mysteries of the
Christmas tree, then quite unknown in England. The
tree was such a success that Hood said he should

introduce the custom when he returned home ; while De Franck enjoyed the plum pudding so much that Mrs. Hood promised to make one for him. Jane Hood's own account of it and of the practical joke which her husband played may be given in her own words as she wrote it to her friend Mrs. Elliot :—

" Hood threatened to play some trick with it—either to pop in bullets or tenpenny nails ; and I watched over my work with great vigilance, so that it was put in to boil without any misfortune.

" I went to bed early, telling Gradle to put it, when done, into the drawing-room till the morning. Hood was writing, and says, it was put down smoking under his very nose, and the spirit of mischief was irresistible. I had bought a groschen's worth of new white wooden skewers that very morning. He cut them a little shorter than the pudding's diameter, and poked them in across and across in all directions, so neatly, that I never perceived any sign of them when I packed and sealed it up the next day for De Franck's man to carry over to Ehrenbreitstein. He came to thank me and praised it highly. I find that while I was out of the room Hood asked him if it was not well trussed, and he answered ' Yes ' so gravely that Hood thought he meditated some joke in retaliation, and was on his guard. At the ball the truth came out—he actually thought it was some new method of making plum-puddings, and gave me credit for the woodwork. He had invited two of his brother officers to lunch upon it, and Hood wanted to persuade me that the ' Cardinal ' officer had swallowed one of the skewers ! Now was not this an abominable trick ? "

From Jane Hood's letter we learn that with brief outings in the neighbourhood of Coblentz, and with fairly constant work, the time of exile when health permitted did not pass unhappily. Hood had produced

Life in Germany (1835—1837).

more than sufficient matter for the Annual, so that there was some left over for the next one, and he was already contemplating making use of his German experiences in another book.

The year closed cheerfully, for, though living "as in a desert with one friend, De Franck, and one acquaintance, Ramponi the language master," Hood was on the whole better in health and was able to work. Writing on the last day of the year to his engraver friend, he said : "To-morrow I set in for a new year with many serious thoughts, a few sad ones, but some hopeful ones. I will make play and fight the good fight, never fear me. Remember me kindly to ——, but tell him I mean nothing short of payment in full—no composition ! The example of De Foe is before me. Somewhat widely is known, and honourably and honestly shall be known, if I live, the name of, yours, dear Wright, ever sincerely, Thomas Hood." That same evening Hood accompanied his friend De Franck to a New Year's Eve ball at the Casino— of which he later gave an amusing account in " Up the Rhine."

With De Franck's return Hood had some further opportunities of getting out, and had many fishing excursions with him ; this friendship was indeed one of the most notable features of the stay in Coblentz. Hood had mastered enough of the German language to get about with ease, but was moved to great indignation by the fact that the people of the town—making hay while the sun shone—took advantage of the Rhine tour having become popular with the English to devise special charges. In a lengthy letter to Dilke, he took occasion to point out how holiday visitors (and British residents) were treated. The very doctor who attended Hood charged him four shillings and sixpence a visit, while charging a German general only one shilling. The same treatment was meted out at restaurants and shops, while the servant whom they employed battened on their ignorance. There was no doubt sufficient grounds for the complaints that Hood made, but he was fond of whimsical exaggeration, and he seems to have possessed somewhat strongly the common belief of the traveller that he is being " done."

The long letter in which many of these grumbles against the unmannerly manners of the Germans in monetary matters were formulated was written from " Herr Deubel's, 752, Alten Graben, Coblentz," on June 20th. Shortly before that date the Hoods had left the Castor Hof for better lodgings at the same cost. The new address, which Hood translated as " at Mr. Devil's in the Old Grave," was of a house " near the Moselle bridge in a busy amusing street," but allowing them to get out of the town in a three minutes' walk. In September the Dilkes journeyed to Coblentz, and the Hoods had the pleasure of welcoming them, though their stay was marred by Dilke's illness. At the same time there were grand military manœuvres in the neighbourhood, and Hood took pleasure in following the sham fighting. The fact that his chief friend in the place was an officer in one of the participating regiments no doubt heightened his usual interest in such displays. A little later, too, De Franck's regiment was ordered to march to Bromberg, and the officers invited Hood to march with them. The Colonel, who had translated " Eugene Aram " into German, cordially seconded the invitation, and the Quartermaster was ordered to arrange that Hood should be quartered with De Franck. Hood purchased a horse, " with new saddle, bridle, and all, for seven pound ten shillings," as he was not equal to marching the fifteen or twenty miles a day which was the regiment's rule. The soldiers set out first, then Hood

Life in Germany (1835—1837).

and his wife followed, catching them up at Eisenach, whence Jane returned to her little family at Coblentz— having rough experience of "post-waggon" riding, including a spill in which she got badly shaken. "If you write of your journey faithfully to your mother" (said Hood), "the break-down and all, I suspect it will be 'Vardict, sarve 'em right. Hood and Jane are both gone mad together!'" Hood went on with the Polish Infantry to Berlin and returned by Dresden and Frankfort, having availed himself of the admirable opportunity of picking up fresh material for his projected book.

Writing to a friend, he gave the following slight sketch of his march :—

"Our start was a pretty one. We were to go at six, Jane and I, by the coach, and were to be called by four. Everything ready, but not all packed. I woke by *chance* at half-past five, our servant—hang her German phlegm! —being still in bed. Now, as all mails, etc., here are government concerns, you pay beforehand at the post-office, fare, postilions, turnpikes, and all, which makes it very pleasant to lose your place.

"By a miracle—I cannot imagine how—Mrs. Dilke helping, we somehow got Jane's bag and my portmanteau rammed full, and caught the coach just setting off. A fine day, and a fine view of the Rheingau, for we went round by the Baths to Frankfort-on-Maine, but 'dooms' slow, for it is hilly all the way, and they walked up, and *dragged* on slowly down.

"Started in the evening-coach from Frankfort for Eisenach. Myself taken very ill in the night; but had some illness hanging about me brought to a crisis by being stived up, all windows shut, with four Germans stinking of the accumulated smoke and odour, stale, flat, and unprofitable, of perhaps *two* years' reeking garlic and what not, besides heat insufferable. I was

Thomas Hood :

for some time insensible, unknown to Jane, and coming-
to again, let down the window, which let in a very cold
wind, but delicious to me, for it seemed like a breeze
through the branches and blossoms of the tree of life.
But it was the cause of a severe cold on the chest. We
slept at Eisenach; next morning posted to Langen
Seltzers, the head-quarters. . . . .

"I shall soon begin on my German book with
'wigger.' I have material prepared. Minor adventures on the march I have not given, as you will see
them there. I pique myself on the punctuality of my
brief military career. I was never too late, and always
had my baggage packed by my own hands ready for the
waggon. It was almost always dark at setting out, and
I had to lead my horse till I could see. After half an
hour, or an hour, we took generally a quarter's rest, for
a sort of after-breakfast; then made for the general
rendezvous, where we piled arms, and all fell to work
on our victuals,—a strange picnic, each bringing what
he could; and we made reports, and some showed
sketches of their last night's quarters. On the whole, I
was very fortunate. Some were regularly hovelled, in
pigeon-houses or anywhere. It was a lottery. On the
march I rode by turns at the head or the tail of the
company, talking with such of the officers as could
speak French. They were, one and all, very friendly, and
glad of my company. I almost wondered at myself, to
find that I could manage my horse so well, for we had
queer ground sometimes, when we took short cuts.

"I assure you sometimes I have almost asked myself
the question, whether I was I, seeming to be so much
out of my ordinary life,—for example, on horseback,
following, or rather belonging to, a company of soldiers:
the bugle ringing through a vast pine wood to keep us
together, or the men perhaps singing Polish songs in
chorus, for this is a Polish regiment chiefly.

Life in Germany (1835—1837).

"About a year ago I had a military cloak, at the contractor's price, from Berlin, but without any idea of a march. Thanks to it, and my horse, having been a captain of engineers', with its saddle-cloth, etc., I cheated the king of all the road-money, for they let me pass all the toll-houses as an officer. I was taken alternately for the chaplain and doctor of the regiment. It did me a world of good, but the finish marred all again. I was disappointed at not going to the end with them, but as De Franck stays, I could not well proceed; and I have since heard he has been stopped three weeks more to go on a grand hunting party into Austria."

The full story of the march is told in a series of tender letters from which but a few extracts can be given here. The first letter, evidently written shortly after they had parted, after Hood had "joined his regiment," shows that he had not been well, but that his indisposition was merely that of fatigue.

"GOTHA, 18th October, 1837.

"MY OWN DEAREST AND BEST,—I send you a packet for Baily: the 'Love Lane' is longer by some verses, so send the present copy: so much for business, and now for the pleasant.

"We parted manfully and womanfully, as we ought. I drank only half a bottle of the Rhine wine, and only the half of that, ere I fell asleep on the sofa, which lasted two hours. It was the re-action, for your going tired me more than I cared to show. Then I drank the other half, and as that did not do, I went and retraced our walk in the Park, and sat down in *the same seat*, and felt happier and better. Have not you a romantic old husband?"

The march was full of pleasure and interest to Hood, and the officers whom he met were extremely friendly, but his time must have been very fully occupied, for he

Thomas Hood :

was still working on the " Comic Annual " for the coming
year; indeed, with the letter just cited he sent, besides
" Love Lane," that admirable essay in anti-climax, " The
Desert Born." While he journeyed he sent his manuscript from time to time to Coblentz that his wife might
send on copies to the publisher in case of their mis-
carrying. Incidents of the march made him revise some
of his strictures on the Germans:—"At the inn at
Kremnitz, I had dinner, supper, bed and breakfast for
7 good groschen, about 11 pence! Think of that, ye
Jewish Rhinelanders. . . . . I like the Saxons much."
He showed all his old love of hoaxing in his intercourse
with the people he met on his journey :—

" Our second quarters were at Nichel near Truen-
britzen. We arrived after a march of eight hours and
a half; think of that for me! and I came in all alive
and kicking. We got at it over wide barren heaths,
and plenty of deep sand. Our billet was on the Burgomaster, or schultze, and his civic robe was a sheepskin
with the wool inward, the usual wintry dress in those
bleak parts. The lady mayoress a stout, plump, short-
faced *mutterkin*, with a vast number of petticoats to
make amends for shortness. I told my host I was an
English burgomaster, so we kept up a great respect and
fellowship for each other. . . . .

" Thence we went to Schlunkendorf (what a name!)
near Belitz: quartered at a miller's, very clean and
wholesome, but only two beds, so Franck was littered
down again. I wanted the host to give him corn instead
of straw by mistake, and then come and thrash them
both out together. I forgot to say the little captain
called on me at Pruhlitz to see how I was, and took tea
with us. Last night I called on Bonkowski, who was
opposite to us; I found him flirting with the Frau. I
told her I had come 50,000 miles, was married at 14,
and had 17 children ; and as I was in yellow boots, and

Life in Germany (1835—1837).

Mrs. D.'s present of a robe, and really looked a Grand Turk, she believed me like Gospel. We made a Welch rabbit for supper, and then played loo till bed-time for pfennigs; I had a young officer for our third instead of Bonkowski. This morning I rode over from Schlunkendorf to Belitz, Heilman taking back the mare, where I found your welcome letter, and started my diligence to Potsdam, where I am, having just eaten a capital dinner—chiefly a plate of good English-like roasted mutton—and a whole bottle of genuine English porter. I am to brush up here to see them parade before the king to-morrow morning.

"Then a day's rest here, and then to Berlin. After the parade, a party of us are going to Sans Souci, and so forth, sight seeing. Franck hopes to introduce me to the Radziwills at Berlin; I have no pain, and really wonder how I *march*. But I had made up my heart and mind to it, and that is everything; it keeps me, I think, from falling off my horse, I am so determined to stick to him, and keep my wits always about me: in fact I quite enjoy it, and only wish I could return so, 'tis so much better than being jammed up in a diligence, and, says *you*, 'less dangerous!'

"Pray tell my dear *good* Fanny that at Schlunkendorf, there was a tame robin, that killed all the flies in the room, hopped on the table, and the edges of our plates, for some dinner. I am delighted with her keeping her promise to me.

"My project is to go with the 10th Company to Custrin, and then home by Frankfort on the Oder, Breslau, Dresden, Frankfort on the Maine, Mayence, Coblenz, where God send I may find you all well."

Before the end of October Hood was in Berlin and well satisfied with his jaunt.

"When I find myself on horseback, riding through a

long wood with the regiment, it seems almost like a dream; your mother will no more believe it than your upset. You have subjects enough now for the Elliots with a vengeance, and so shall I have! I wish I *could* wish the Dilkes may be comfortably in Coblenz by my return. As they are not wanted, they would see the vintage; God bless them any way, and say everything kind for me. I really think they might stay longer in Coblenz, quiet and cheap enough, and recover thoroughly, against their winter campaign of company; I long to see them again ere they cross the sea.

"I have rambled on to amuse you, and left little room to say all I could wish to yourself; but you will find in your own heart the echo of all I have to say (rather an Irish one, but a truth-teller). . . . .

"I seem to have scarcely had an inconvenience, certainly not a hardship and it will ever be a pleasant thing for me to remember. I like little troubles; I do not covet too flowery a path. By the by I have some dried flowers for my flower-loving Fanny, gathered at odd out-of-the-way places; I will show her where on the map when I return.

"It was singular in the sheepskin country, whilst the men were all so warmly pelissed, to see the women in their short petticoats, their legs looking so cold. I suspect I pass for very hardy, if not fool-hardy, I slight the cold so; but it seems to me a German characteristic, that they can bear being sugar-bakers, but can hardly endure what I call a bracing air.

"Bless you, bless you, again and again, my dear one, my only one, my one as good as a thousand to Your old Unitarian in love,

"T. H."

In Berlin Hood had a busy time sight-seeing at Sans Souci and elsewhere, and visiting the people from whom

Life in Germany (1835—1837).

De Franck procured invitations. On the last day of October he was invited to dine with Prince William Radziwill, most of whose family spoke English, and several of whom were acquainted with his writings— "they had even read 'Tylney Hall!'" A visit to the Musée delighted him so that he expressed a wish to be one of the attendants for a month—"altogether I have had a most happy time of it, and in health and every respect have reason to be highly gratified ; . . . . and here I am writing to you with the spirits of a lark, in the hope that after a couple or three days, every hour will bring me nearer to all that is dearest to me on earth."

The return to Coblentz was unfortunately marred by mishaps and by the taking of a chill which more than negatived all the good that the holiday had done. The story may best be given in Hood's own words as written to De Franck. The opening words were a reminiscence of a droll old Irish story, of which there are several versions. The story gives a dialogue between an Irishman and his servant. The former having some money, thinks he would like to spend it ; the latter hints that wages might first be paid :—

"Tim," says he ;
"What ? " says he ;
"Fetch me my hat," says he,
"For I will go," says he,
"To Timahoe," says he,
"To buy the fair," says he,
"And all that's there," says he ;
"Arrah ! *pay what you owe !*" says he,
"And *then* you may go," says he,
"To Timahoe," says he,
"To buy the fair," says he,
"And all that's there," says he.
"Well, by this and by that ! " says he,
"Tim, *hang up my hat*," says he.

303

Thomas Hood :

"752, Alten Graben, Coblenz, *Dec. 2nd*, 1836.

" Tim, says he,—It was odd enough I should have
my accident too as if to persuade me that German
eilwagens are the most dangerous vehicles in the world
—but about four o'clock on the third morning, after a
great ' leap in the dark,' the coach turned short round,
and brought up against the rails at the roadside ; luckily
they were strong, or we should have gone over a
precipice.   There we were on the top of a bleak
hill, the pole having broken short off, till we were
fetched by *beiwagens*, to the next station, where a new
pole was made ; but it delayed us six hours.   Here I
got the first of my cold, for the weather and wind were
keen ; the night journey from Frankfort to Mayence in
an *open* coupé confirmed it.   I could not help falling
asleep in it from cold.   So I came home looking well,
and as ruddy as bacon ; but the very next day turned
white with a dreadful cough, which ended in spitting
blood ; but I sent for the doctor, was bled, and it was
stopped : but I am still weak.   To make things better
I had not sent enough for the ' Comic,' and was obliged
to set to work again, willy-nilly, well or illy.   I have
not been out of doors yet since I came home, but shall
in a day or two.   The Rhine and Moselle are very high
—the Castor Street is flooded—the weather being very
mild—but I guess cold is coming, for I saw a fellow
bring into the town to-day a very large wolf on his
shoulders.   He was as fat as a pig.   I found all well at
home.   Tom stared his eyes out at me, almost, and for
two days would scarcely quit my lap.   He talks and
sings like a parrot.   I should have liked to see your
Grand Hunt (a Battue), but for sport I would rather
take my dog and gun and pick up what I could find.
The night procession must have looked well.   Poor
Dilke went away very unwell, but the last account of

Life in Germany (1835—1837).

him was better. I did not get home soon enough to see him. I am going to give him a long account of my march. I think the horse sold very well, but I cannot fancy what you will do with the saddle, unless you put it on a clothes-horse when you want to ride. Don't forget in your next to let me know the fate of the cheese. I guess it got ' high and mity ' enough to deserve a title. Oh ! I do miss the porter at Berlin ! Schumacher's is to let again, and the beer we get is ' *ex-crabble !* ' I hope next winter to taste it in London, but can form no plans till my health clears up more. I must beg you in your next to give me the list of the officers. I was to have had it before we parted, as I begin my German book with the march. How do you find your quarters ? Are there any Miss A——s at Bromberg ? By the bye, I undertook a letter from Lieutenant B—— to deliver here, and sent it by Katchen, who says the mother came in and made a bit of a *row*. But I cannot well understand what she said in German. Perhaps there has been a cat let out of the bag, the young lady having left the letter lying on the table in view of the mamma.

" How is Wildegans ? and do you ever see him and Carlovicz ? My kind regards to both, and most friendly remembrances to all you see, not forgetting *my* captain. How you will delight in settling down to your drill duties and parades after so much gaiety ! I quite envy you : a few raw recruits would be quite a treat ! You do not tell me whether you had any trolling with Prince Boguslaff : all our old fishing-stands by the Moselle are under water. I hope to get you out a ' Comic ' early in the spring, and the books for Berlin ; but I shall not know how to get anything over before, as I guess land-carriage cometh very dear, and they must come *viâ* Ostend till the Rhine-boats run again. Perhaps my painter will come out early ; as Jane has told you I am to

be 'done in oil.' I have now no news—how should I
have? for I have at least been *room*-ridden. I shall
take to my rod again as soon as the season begins; but
I shall miss you, Johnny, and your 'wenting in.' I must
promise you a better letter next time. This is only a
brief from, Dear Johnny, Yours ever truly,

" JOHNNY."

Already the Hoods were contemplating a return to
England, were discussing what they would do when
they returned—he thinking of a visit to an *à la mode*
beef shop in the Old Bailey, she of being able to get
hold of any number of English books again. From
this time, however, the state of his health seems to
have been a serious set-back. He probably looked to
the proceeds of his German book to go far towards
setting him straight with the world, and the completion
of this was delayed. His letters home—mostly to the
Dilkes and to Wright—are pathetic blendings of fun
and gravity. The illness that followed on his return to
Coblenz meant "a touch on the lungs, which were
never touched before, being indeed my strongest point."
There was probably a predisposition to lung trouble,
and neither the conditions of his life nor the medical
attendance at command were such as to tend to the
minimising of it. As he puts it in a note in one of his
letters about the draughtiness of German houses: " I
have a stiff neck that goes all down my back, and then
comes up the other side, thanks to their well-staircases
and drying lofts in the attics."

Towards the end of April a long letter to De Franck
told of a winter that had been bad in every way. The
weather had been severe, and Hood's health so bad that
since his return from Berlin in November he had not
been out of doors half a dozen times. Trouble with the
customs officers over a box of things from England

Life in Germany (1835—1837).

seems to have clinched the resolve to move at least nearer home, and already Ostend was provisionally fixed upon. He sends on to his friend fishing tackle, and speaks woefully of his chest being so bad as not to permit him to cast a fly. There is a sad note for a young man of thirty-eight about this letter, though his irrepressible fun comes out even in speaking of his own illness. A few days later, and the removal is decided upon for the first of June, or a week earlier if possible, the whole family seeming to welcome the proposed change, for all had suffered from the *grippe* during the spring.

Though Hood had grown tired of Coblenz and its people, it was largely owing to the difficulties inherent in his being so far from London, packages from which took a month in transit, so that punctuality in the production of the " Comic Annual" had become well nigh impossible. No sooner was Ostend decided upon for the next camping ground than he could write, " I fancy already that I sniff the sea, and feel it bracing me. . . . The sea is *life* to me." There is, however, despite its associations, which the past few months had made particularly unpleasant, a touch of regret over leaving the town that had been a two-years' home: "And yet, oh yet, when I look at the Rhine, it *is* a lovely country, and I love the beautiful. I shall see all I can before I go, as I can carry all the scenery vividly in my mind."

From Coblenz Hood wrote to the *Athenæum* a series of lively and well-reasoned letters on " Copyright and Copywrong," which attracted a goodly share of attention and may have had their influence in bringing about the legislation of a few years later, though we seem still as far as ever from the ideal, to which Hood looked forward, of perpetual copyright. The " Letters " have been reprinted in his works, but the closing passages may be cited as showing that despite disappointments, despite the knowledge of the injustice which governed the rights of literary property, he had the highest regard for the calling to which he belonged.

"And now, before I close, I will here place on record my own obligations to Literature : a debt so immense, as not to be cancelled, like that of nature, by death itself. I owe to it something more than my worldly welfare. Adrift early in life upon the great waters—as pilotless as Wordsworth's blind boy afloat in the turtle shell—if I did not come to shipwreck it was, that in default of paternal or fraternal guidance, I was rescued, like the ancient mariner, by guardian spirits, 'each one a lovely light,' who stood as beacons to my course. Infirm health, and a natural love of reading, happily threw me, instead of worse society, into the company of poets, philosophers and sages— to me good angels and ministers of grace. From these silent instructors—who often do more than fathers, and always more than godfathers, for our temporal and spiritual interests — from these mild monitors — no importunate tutors, teasing Mentors, moral taskmasters, obtrusive advisers, harsh censors or wearisome lecturers —but, delightful associates—I learned something of the divine, and more of the human religion. They were my interpreters in the House Beautiful of God, and my guides among the Delectable Mountains of Nature. They reformed my prejudices, chastened my passions, tempered my heart, purified my tastes, elevated my mind, and directed my aspirations. I was lost in a chaos of undigested problems, false theories, crude fancies, obscure impulses, and bewildering doubts— when those bright intelligences called my mental world out of darkness like a new creation, and gave it 'two great lights,' Hope and Memory—the past for a moon and the future for a sun."

Life in Germany (1835—1837).

It was a beautiful recognition of the debt which intelligence owes to Literature.[1]

Leaving Coblenz Hood likened to a farce, and as such described it as a fitting end. A pleasant journey down the Rhine, with a two days' stay at a M. Nagelmacher's, near Liège, and so on, *viâ* Brussels and Ghent, to Ostend, which was reached on the 23rd of June. There the family settled down at 39, Rue Longue, after a trying journey, "poor wretched travellers that we are," and Hood looked forward to carrying on his work. "I have moved only just in time, for I feel convinced the Rhine was killing me: between hurry, worry, delay, tedium, disgust, the climate, and the diet, and the consciousness, with all these disadvantages, of no very great improvement besides in health. I write a long letter by this same post to Dr. Elliot, with further particulars that I may have the benefit of his advice, how to live and keep alive."

[1] Five years later he took up the theme again in two further letters to the editor of the *Athenæum*, the final paragraph summing up the matter thus :—

"So much for the distinctions bestowed on a literary man during his life. Now for the honours paid to him at his death. We all know how he lives. He writes for bread, and gets it short weight; for money, and gets the wrong change; for the Present, and he is pirated ;—for the Future, and his children are disinherited for his pains. At last he sickens, as he well may, and can write no more. He makes his will, but, for any literary property, might as well die intestate. His eldest son is his heir, but the Row administers. And so he dies a beggar, with the world in his debt. Being poor, he is buried with less ceremony than Cock Robin. Had he been rich enough, he might have bought a 'snug lying in the abbey' of the Dean and Chapter of Westminster, who even then, true to the same style of treatment, would put him, were he the greatest and best of our poets, as the mother puts the least and worst of her brats—into a corner!"

"Distinctions" have been bestowed on men of letters since Hood's time, but we seem still far from the justice of perpetual copyright.

Thomas Hood :

The last winter in Coblenz seems really to have sealed Hood's fate, for though, as we shall see, he made a good fight of it, kept ever cheerful in spite of recurring illness, and valiantly continued his work, yet the record as it is pieced together from his and his wife's letters suggests that it was a prematurely aged man who had returned so far homewards from the exile to which he had devoted himself from the noblest of motives. The full letters, with their blent record of fun and illness, written from Coblenz and Ostend, form so large a portion of the " Memorials " that it is only necessary here to give such portions of them as help to keep the whole of Hood's life-story in perspective and to indicate the character of the man.

THE COMMON LOT.

CHAPTER XII.

LIFE AT OSTEND (1837—1840).

> " Jealous, I own it, I was once—
> That wickedness I here renounce
> I tried at wit . . . it would not do;
> At tenderness . . . that failed me too—
> Before me on each path there stood
> The witty and the tender Hood! "
> WALTER SAVAGE LANDOR.

AT Ostend, with four London mails in each week, Hood felt that he was in much easier communication with Wright over his work, and it would even be possible to see proofs; he felt at once in good spirits as to his writing, and hopeful as regards his health. He asked Wright—who, much to his delight, contemplated a visit to Ostend—to bring books and papers with him, said that he was contemplating an ode to Queen Victoria for the *Athenæum*, and added whimsically : " Why can't the Queen make me Consul here ? I don't want to turn anybody out, but can't there be nothing-to-do enough for two ? " Wright and the Dilkes were at Ostend during the autumn, so that, though they found few people of whom to make friends in the place, Hood and his wife did not feel so cut off as at Coblenz. The "Comic" was got through more rapidly than before, and Hood was already contemplating something of a periodical nature for the following year that should not clash with the annual. An outburst on political matters in one of his letters is unusual. " For my part, I say, hang party ! There wants a true *country party* to look singly to the good of England—retrench and economise, reduce taxes, and make it possible to live as cheap at home as abroad. *There* would be patriotism, instead of a mere struggle of Ins and Outs for place and pelf. Common sense seems the great desideratum for governors, whether of kingdom or family. I suspect the principles that ought to guide a private family would bear a pretty close application to the great public one ; their evils are much of the same nature—extravagance, luxury, debt, etc."

The projected work, possibly at the suggestion of Wright, was to mingle the contents of the various " Comic Annuals " and reissue them in monthly parts, a plan which was subsequently decided upon, with the idea that it might be followed by another periodical publication the nature of which was to be considered later. The great success of Dickens's "Pickwick Papers,' the monthly issue of which was just completed, had no doubt something to do with the idea, though both Hood and Dilke were inclined to think that the success of " Boz " would be more likely to militate against the success of a similarly planned venture unless something very novel could be hit upon. He was feeling ready for and equal to work. "I do not think I fall off, and have no misgivings about over-writing myself ; one cannot do too much if it be well done ; and I never care to turn out anything that does not please myself. I hear a demon whisper—I hope no lying one—I can do better yet, or as good as ever, and more of it ; so let's look for the best. Nobody ever died the sooner for hoping."

A long letter to Dr. Elliot continued the hopeful strain to the close of this year.

The first important work undertaken at Ostend was the stinging " Ode to Rae Wilson, Esq.," which appeared in the *Athenæum* for August 12. Hood, whose nature was a serious and even devout one, was frequently misunderstood by those who were incapable of appreciating

Life at Ostend (1837—1840).

this fact and who chose to think that when he was attacking cant he was attacking that which cant pretended to represent.   Rae Wilson, a moneyed traveller who wrote uninteresting books, had more than once attacked Hood, and in his " Ode " the poet not only took revenge but wrote one of the finest pieces of satire of its kind in our language.

At the beginning of 1838 the monthly publication of " Hood's Own," a medley of prose, verse, and pictures made up out of the " Comic Annuals," with fresh additions, was commenced and met with some measure of success, Wright again proving the best of friends in arranging matters for the distant author.   Writing to thank him for his help and to congratulate him on the birth of a daughter, Hood suggests that the child should be named " Mary Wollstonecraft," as the supporter of " *Female Wrights*," and concludes " God bless you and yours, including Miss Wright—only think of a *mile* of daughters !   There is a family of Furlongs coming to live here, whereof *eight* are daughters—8 furlongs = 1 mile." The " Hood's Own ; or Laughter from Year to Year : being Former Runnings of His Comic Vein, with an Infusion of New Blood for General Circulation," met with considerable success, though the arranging of it month by month, even from the nearer distance of Ostend, proved very trying at times.   The publisher had large sheets of the comical cuts illustrating the work printed for hanging in the booksellers' and newsagents' shops, and these proved effective advertisements.

Bad weather and continuous sedentary work militated against Hood, but his first sail did him so much good that he longed to go to sea again, and he had perhaps on the whole a happier time—despite various set-backs—at Ostend than at Coblenz.   His long letters show his irrepressible tendency to make fun of troubles—though at times there is a feeling of sadness in the fun to the reader who realises that it was the surface play of a deeply serious and suffering man.

At the end of December 1837, or early in 1838, Hood crossed over to England and spent three weeks in London—staying with the Dilkes—that he might consult Dr. Elliot as to the advisability of staying for another year or two at Ostend. The place suited him in many ways, and he felt unequal to a return to England.

"It will be some time before I shall be strong enough to live a London life ; and being rather popular in that city, I cannot keep out of society and late hours [during his three weeks' stay he was never in bed before one or two in the morning]. At all events I am close at hand if wanted for a new ministry. Jane says she should not like me to be a *place*-man, for fear of red spots. . . . .

"Since the above I have been to England. I spent there about three weeks, and am just returned, full of good news and spirits. Elliot came to me, and after a very careful examination, and sounding every inch of me by the ear, and by the stethoscope, declares my lungs perfectly sound, and the complaint is in the liver. He altogether coincides with my doctor here, both as to the case and its treatment, and my own feelings quite confirmed their view ; so that at last I seem in the right road. But what long and precious time I have lost—I only wonder I have survived it ! "

It was perhaps during his stay in England, when he went out so many evenings, that he met Samuel Carter Hall, the maker of many books, who has left this description of him : " His countenance had more of melancholy than of mirth ; it was calm even to solemnity. There was seldom any conscious attempt at brilliancy in his talk ; and so far from sharing in that weakness, with which wits are generally credited, a desire to monopolise the conversation, he seemed ever ready in society to give way to any who would supply talk." Another acquaintance—Charles Knight—said on the same theme: "I have witnessed the irresistible joke come slowly and demurely off the tongue of Hood, he perfectly grave and silent after the effusion, whilst his hearers are bursting again and again into peals of laughter."

Hood was reassured somewhat by the verdict of the friendly Elliot, and on going through three years' accounts with his publisher found them satisfactory, establishing as they did the fact that the "Comic Annual" kept up a steady sale though all the other annuals were dead or dying.

The portrait painter Lewis—presumably, for there were two or three contemporary artists of the name, George Robert Lewis, 1782-1871—journeyed to Ostend to paint a portrait of Hood, and the result was the best portrait of him that we have,[1] one in which about the brow and eyes we seem to see the seriousness and about the flexile mouth something of the ever-ready humour of the subject. When it was first proposed that the portrait painter should visit him Hood had said: "I shall be very happy to see Mr. Lewis and show him all the *countenance* I can . . . by letting him take my own; but, for my own part, I never got any good of my face yet, except that it once got me credit for eighteenpence at a shop, when I had gone out without my purse." He thought that people would scarcely see the "comic" in his pale, thin face, but it may be said, on the contrary, that the face distinctly suggests the character of the man. One who knew him slightly wrote about the same time that "the countenance of Mr. Hood is more solemn than merry:

[1] When shown at the Exhibition of National Portraits at South Kensington, in 1868, Lewis's portrait of Thomas Hood was the property of Dr. William Elliot. A photograph of it was published by the Arundel Society.

there is nothing in his appearance to indicate that wit and humour for which he is so eminent." The judge in this case can, however, have known Hood but indifferently well, for in a biographical sketch he declared that Hood had been intended for the sea, but could never get over his distaste for the water. A ridiculous misstatement of which the subject duly made much fun in " Hood's Own." Lewis's portrait of the author was included with the July part of " Hood's Own," and later took its place as frontispiece to the completed work.

Ever jealous of the recognition of men of his profession, Hood wrote that he hoped to write a verse or two about the coronation of Queen Victoria (June, 1838), and asks: " I want to know if any distinction was shown to Art, Science and Literature on the occasion. Was the P. R. A. there? Had the live Poets admission to the Corner?"

Further letters to De Franck tell how the family passed their time, having " an undiminished liking for the place which suits our quiet 'domestic habits,' though it is notorious as dull, amongst the *notoriously* gay." He was lucky enough to come across an old English shipmaster who had a capital little boat built under his own charge, and the use of this boat he could have whenever he liked, or rather whenever he was able to make use of it, for, though it is not necessary repeatedly to emphasise the fact, he was doomed to be a man of broken health. After his wife had paid a flying visit to England he wrote with a philosophic resignation possible only to that tragic compound the man of humour: " I shall never be strong again—Jane got the verdict of our friend Dr. Elliot, that the danger of the case was gone, but that as I had never been particularly strong and sturdy, I must not now expect to be more than a young old gentleman. But I will be a boy as long as I can in mind and spirits, only the troublesome bile is apt to

Life at Ostend (1837—1840).

upset my temper now and then. We are all a little rabid at present, for after having fires far into June, the weather has just set in broiling hot, and the children do not know what to make of it."

The fact that brief journeys to England and the visits of friends were now possible helped to make life pleasanter. The promised visit of one of Jane's sisters, with her child, and other holiday-makers, moved him to enthusiasm. More friends, too, were made at Ostend, though he found that many of the English domiciled in the place belonged to the " genus scamp," and there were casual acquaintances to temper the monotony of exile : " In fact in spite of keeping quiet, I am a little sought after here, now I am found out. A friend of Byron's wanted to know me the other day, but I was laid up in bed ; and now Long Wellesley (Duke of Wellington's nephew), my old landlord [at Lake House], is here, and asking after me." The weather continued unpropitiously variable : " What an abominable swindling season ! The winter embezzled the spring, and the summer has absconded with the autumn."

By the end of the year most of the rearranging and additions for " Hood's Own " had been done and the " Comic Annual " completed, and Hood looked forward to finishing the slowly produced book on Germany ; the getting the " Comic " done, he said, always seemed " a long miracle," as indeed it well might seeing the circumstances in which it was produced during these last two years. But with all his work he still managed occasional letters to the Dilkes and other friends. For Mrs. Dilke he jotted down a sketch of the amenities of life at the Belgian watering place : " We go on as usual at Ostend. Tell Dilke there are some other 'friends' staying at Harrison's, a Captain B., *alias* K., and Sir W. J., said to be of large fortune. But what a residence to choose !

Thomas Hood :

"I heard also of two young men obliged to fly from the troubles at Hanover; but it turns out that they have robbed or swindled a Chatham bank. So we don't improve. A Colonel B. has done W. out of 100*l.*, and an English lady, in passing through, did the banker here out of 78*l.* Then an Englishman shot at his wife the other day with an air-gun; and Mrs. F. will not set her foot in our house again, because I gave her a lecture on scandal-mongering; and the doctor has done Captain F. in the sale of some gin; and the Captain talks of calling out the doctor for speaking ill of his wife; and the De M.'s are gone;—a fig for Reid and Marshall, and their revolving hurricanes! We Ostenders live in a perpetual round of breezes. . . . . I forgot to mention that I had a little duel of messages with my 'scandal-mongering' acquaintance the other day. 'Pray tell Mr. Hud,' says she, 'that I have no doubt but his complaint is a *scurrilous* liver!' (schirrous). So I sent her my compliments, and begged leave to say that was better than a 'cantankerous gizzard!'" To that same scandal-monger it is said that Hood in mischievous mood sent a 'peace offering' of some *medlars.*

After the return from London to Ostend Hood set to work, having "as much to do as a strong person could get through." He did not contemplate another visit to England, with the exception of trips to Dover for the sake of the Channel breezes, for another year. As he wrote to his medical friend : "As I learned when in town, I am far from fit yet for a London life. Summer is before me, and I do not mean to throw it away by late hours and dissipation, but to try, by a regular system, to get a little ahead in health." The beginnings of photography are indicated in another passage in the same letter. "Have you read the account of Photogenic drawing or Lightography? Moore saw 'History *write* with *pencil*

Life at Ostend (1837—1840).

of *light*,' but now light itself draws without any pencil at all. 'Tis a mercy light does not write; but perhaps even that will be done hereafter, and Phœbus will not only be a patron of poets, but a poet himself, and deal, like me, in light literature. Jane, who has some maternal vanity, when she heard of the sun drawing pictures, said, 'So does *my* son!'"

On his fortieth birthday (May 23, 1839) Hood wrote to De Franck:—

"Tim, says he, I am only able to write at short length, having more work for my pen and less time to do it in than ever. I have had a sad nine or ten months of it, almost always ill, and then having to do everything in haste by day and night. I think my liver complaint is tolerably cured, and I have not spit any blood for a very long while, but the *curing* has half killed me. I am as thin as a lath and as weak as plaster. Perhaps I have no blood left to spit.

"As to my leanness, look at the portrait. Tim, says he, I was over in England about three months ago at Dilke's, where I spent three weeks; but though I am quite at home there, I came back to Ostend very willingly; late hours and company do not agree with me yet. Will they ever? God knows.

"Another year will set me up, or knock me down,— the wear and tear of my nerves, etc., cannot last longer. By the bye, this very day I am forty,—and you will have to drink my health out of a certain Bohemian goblet, given to me on a certain birthday. As you cannot pledge me in it yourself, I will cheerfully be your proxy, provided the wine be good. As Béranger sings—

"'Dans un grenier qu'on est bien à vingt ans!'

But then I am two score, and sometimes am ready to call them the Forty Thieves, having stolen away all my youth and health.

Thomas Hood :

" Look at the picture, Tim, I do not quite look so ill as then, but I am as weak as gin-and-water without the gin.

" Since Jane wrote, I have found your list and procured what tackle you wanted. But, moreover, I have had the good luck to meet with some *here*, which I jumped at, and send, good or bad, with some flies and hooks I had by me. For fear of plunder, I send a list signed by me, in the box.

" All the tackle you will be so kind as to accept from me—with my best wishes towards the fisherman, and the worst towards the fish—except the gentle-boxes, which Tom junior (I will not call him my ' son and heir,' as you have neither son nor hair) is desirous of sending you. He says, ' The gentles have not only a little house, but a yard to walk about in.' I did not expect an improvement in a gentle-box, but you see there is a little tray to roll them into and select from. I guess you will enjoy the Pickwick—it is so very English."

De Franck had had an illness as a result of which he lost his hair, and this afforded many opportunities for fun to his lively correspondent.

In October most of " Up the Rhine " was actually in the printer's hands—it was to be announced for publication on December 10—and Jane Hood visited England to arrange some of her husband's business. While she was away he had a severe attack for a short while, of which he wrote her particulars, his letter being a medley of affection for her, accounts of his illness, asking for little commissions to be executed on behalf of various friends, and particulars of the good behaviour of the children, with other matters to set the housewife's heart at rest as to the manner in which her little household was getting along in her absence.

" I do beg you will see Elliot, it is of as great concern

THOMAS HOOD.

From the Painting in the National Portrait Gallery, attributed to Masquerier.

[*To face p.* 320.

Life at Ostend (1837—1840).

as anything else, and you are apt to forget *yourself*, dearest, when other matters are in hand. . . . Come back to me well, and you will find me so, or make me so, my best. We shall do well yet, and weather the point, if my health keeps as it promises. I shall go out to sea again. Trolling is over, and long-line fishing begun. Backer does not stay out all night, but goes one day and puts down his lines, returns, and goes and takes them up the next day. That would suit me very well. . . .

"God bless you, my own, enjoy yourself as much as you can, you may be easier about me now this is over than before. It was CRUEL suffering; but I could not describe, without laughing, that cramp, for I was pirouetting about on one leg, and the other drawn up in such a twist, as only Grimaldi used to effect. Or remembering I was only in my shirt, I must have been like Oscar Byrne in his short tunic, and making as many grimaces. Luckily I was alone, for I must have bundled out of bed, had Hannah More been present! Don't tell Mrs. Dilke, or she will never lend me a spare bed again. Mary has brought me up a two-fold supper on one plate; on one side a roasted apple, on the other some nondescript strips (tripe). I ate the apple, and looked at the tripe, *Verbum sap.* She is very attentive, so bring her something. God bless you again; I am going to settle, it's half-past ten. . . . (Bulletin) Huzza! I can move my toes!"

In another letter he says, "My poor legs! I must go and stick them in the sands, as the piles are, to get *mussels* to 'em!"

A letter to Dilke, written in this autumn of 1839, is interesting as affording one of Hood's tributes to the great merits of the newly "arrived" Charles Dickens, whose "Oliver Twist" had just been published in volume form.[1]

[1] Elsewhere Hood referred to Oliver Twist as a slave of circumstances, and added, "There are few authors whom one would

Thomas Hood :

" As regards Boz, his *morale* is better than his material, though that is often very good; it is *wholesome* reading : the drift is natural, *along with the great human currents, and not against them.* His purpose sound, with that honest independence of thinking, which is the constant adjunct of true-heartedness, recognising good in low places, and evil in high ones, in short a manly assertion of Truth *as* Truth. Compared with such merits, his defects of over-painting, and the like, are but spots on the sun.

" For these merits alone, he deserves all the successes he has obtained, and long may he enjoy them ! As for Jack Sheppard, the test of its value is furnished by the thieves and blackguards that yell their applause at its slang songs, in the Adelphi. Can the penny theatres so unceremoniously routed, produce any effects more degrading and demoralising ? From what I have heard of *their* pieces they were comparatively mere absurdities to such positive Moral Nuisances."

Just before Christmas " Up the Rhine " was published by A. H. Baily & Co., and within a fortnight the first edition of 1500 copies had been sold. Unfortunately its publication synchronised with the discovery that Hood's publisher had not been treating him fairly, and also at the same time Hood's friend and engraver, Wright, who had acted throughout the part of a good friend for him, died. Worry and anxiety, added to other troubles, made it a particularly painful winter. In January Hood visited London, staying again with the Dilkes in Grosvenor Place, and having with him " Tom Junior," aged five —" a fine healthy fellow, very good and almost reads." The trip was made necessary by the unsatisfactory position of his business affairs with Baily : " Throughout

care to see running two heats with the same horse. It is intended, therefore, as a compliment that I wish Boz would re-write the history in question from p. 122, supposing his hero not to have met with the Artful Dodger on his road to seek his fortunes."

322

Life at Ostend (1837—1840).

I have been obliged to puzzle through very ill-kept and tardily rendered accounts—a harassing job enough—and I know its ill effects on me ; but *necessitas non habet!*" The return to Ostend meant a return of bad health, and the conviction on Hood's part that it was the incessantly damp climate of the place that was working such constant mischief. He contemplated removal to Dieppe, "or some other such place answerable to our own coast, on a chalk cliff." Ordered to speak as little as possible he said " I will try to be as dumb as I can ; but then I have as many impediments to silence as there are sometimes to speech."

" I perfectly understand your description of my case, and have not the slightest doubt of your being right. What I mean to say is, there is no lung disease, *i.e.* original. This mischief is in the stomach or liver ; and I can imagine how that may affect the lungs, or any other neighbouring part, as an embarrassment or stoppage in the Strand would affect bridges or any other laterals." This was in reply to a letter of advice from Dr. Elliot, who sent an invitation to the invalid[1] to visit him at Stratford, which he did in April. After having spent a week with the Dilkes his arrival at the house of his doctor-friend was marked by a further attack of blood-spitting ; the first time that he had found himself in such a sad case in England, a return to which he was looking forward to with some confidence as a return to his old health. He had to write from a sick bed to his wife :—

" It will be a comfort to you, dearest, to know I am here with all skill and help at my hand, and every comfort and care. A brother and sister could not be kinder

---

[1] " I one day overheard a dispute between Tom and Fanny as to what I was. ' Pa's a literary man,' said Fanny. ' He's not ! ' said Tom : ' I know what he is.' ' What is he, then ? ' ' Why,' says Tom, ' he's not a literary man—he's an invalid.' "

to me than they are; only *one* other *could* nurse me more tenderly and affectionately. So pray do not be anxious on my account. I am now better, body and mind. The doctor says he has now no doubt on my case, that I am as he expected to find me, and the affection is what he supposed it to be, aggravated by the largeness of my heart. The more to give to you, love ! . . . .

"I quite regret that I was prevented from bringing Tom here; he would have been so happy. There is a little fellow, full of fun, about his own age, and a little girl, so like what Willie was, it struck me in an instant. They are all very well. I am a sort of melodramatic mystery, I suspect, to some of the boys, associated with many basons and blood ! The two little ones have visited me in my room, and this morning brought me in the Comic Annual to *amuse* me."

The doctor, who urged that Hood should refrain from all mental worry, and that he should return finally to England, wrote a frank statement of his condition to Jane Hood, pointing out that the attacks of disease were caused or aggravated in a peculiar degree by anxiety and depression of mind. The removal of mental worry was unfortunately impossible in the troubled state of his affairs and the return to England was finally resolved upon during the summer. Anxious as to her husband's state, Jane Hood crossed over to England in the middle of May, and it was nearly two months later before they returned to Ostend to fetch the children home. Mrs. Hood's arrival was a great comfort to her husband, for though he was made at home at the Elliots' house—then 10, Vicarage Terrace, now renamed 82, Romford Road, Stratford—he felt the separation keenly, and she was also of great service to him in business matters. The trouble with Baily had resulted in entering an action against him, which meant

Life at Ostend (1837—1840).

the stoppage of any sale of his books until the winter, and the obtaining of no money except from current work which he was so little fit for undertaking.[1] He arranged, however, to contribute to Colburn's *New Monthly Magazine*, then edited by Theodore Hook.

The trip to Ostend was made pleasant by the fact that the loved children were to be seen after a painful absence and by the fact that it was but a trip. Hood's intense affection for Fanny (or Tibbie, as he nicknamed her) and Tom Junior, indeed, his whole-hearted devotion to the domesticities, is shown all through his letters, but he was indeed always a lover of children, always able to make himself a child in their company. There are probably but few people now living who had personal experience of his way with small people, but one such is Mrs. Hood's nephew, Mr. W. A. Longmore, who as a boy of about twelve or fourteen visited his relatives at Ostend. He journeyed thither in the steam packet "Liverpool," and on the day after his arrival an official came to the Hoods' house enquiring for "Mr. Longmore." Wondering for what he could be wanted he went to the door and was presented by a gendarme with a formidable document headed "Police." This document notified that as he had arrived without a passport he must forthwith repair to a certain house in the "Rue Poisson d'Avril," and must further pay for one month's permit to stay in Ostend the sum of two and a half francs. The payment was promptly made, and the

[1] In the *Sporting Magazine* this summer he had an amusing plea for the old sport of ass racing, and also a further prose article in the form of an extravaganza in "Praise of Fishing," introducing some of his friend De Franck's experiences at Bromberg. Before returning to Ostend, too, he had probably written the first of his "Rhymes for the Times," "An Open Question," which appeared in the *New Monthly* for August, and begun "Miss Kilmansegg," which commenced its appearance in the same magazine a month later.

Thomas Hood :

boy was preparing to seek out the Rue Poisson d'Avril when he was told that the whole thing was an elaborate hoax of his uncle's and that he had been made a nice "April Fool!" The same visitor recalls Hood's liking for boating, and the readiness with which he entered into the children's games, even inventing one in which he seated the children round him, giving to each the name of some bird or animal and then telling them a story. In the course of the story the names of these animals would be artfully introduced, and as each one was mentioned the child representing it had to rise and bow—or pay a forfeit. Mr. Longmore was generally the ounce, a word which in the hands of the punning tale-teller let the boy in for many forfeits. Another game was that of "Merchantmen," in which boxes rigged with paper sails represented the traders, and were freighted with different articles of commerce to be bartered at various "ports," in different parts of the room, and duly executed bills of freight and merchants' accounts had to be made out. He was, too, a ready teller of stories for children, illustrating them with his pencil as he went on, and would further amuse them by the cutting out of paper animals. The "Memorials" give several reminiscences of his son and daughter illustrating this trait of his character.

"While in Germany, he bought a small toy theatre for us, and then (and subsequently at Camberwell, during an illness) drew, painted, and cut out the characters and scenery for a tragedy (Paul and Virginia), a spectacle (St. George and the Dragon), and a pantomime. The figures were very clever, the groups and processions capitally arranged—and the dragon *was* a dragon! Some of the scenes, such as the planter's house, and the cottages of Margaret and Madame de la Tour, are gems of effect and colour. Two moonlight scenes are very good too—the grave of Paul and Virginia, and the

Life at Ostend (1837—1840).

Palace in St. George, where a (tinsel) torchlight procession by water wound up the play. The whole, however, cannot be described, and must be seen to be appreciated. On high days and holidays this theatre used to be brought out, and my father used to perform the pieces to the delight of the little friends (and big ones too) who were present. He used to extemporise the dialogue, which was considered by the elders, who were better judges than we children could pretend to be, very lively and apt. His stage management, properties, and machinery were capital, and I can still remember the agony with which I used to see the wreck in Paul and Virginia break up by degrees, and the bodies of the lovers washed in over the breakers. In addition to these means of evening entertainment, he had a magic lantern, for which he painted a number of slides, some humorous and some pretty ones—a flight of doves and swallows with a hawk and a little cottage in the snow, with a 'practicable' regiment marching over a bridge."

" This review (the one he had witnessed at Coblenz), no doubt, was the origin of a game of military manœuvres my father subsequently made for us. He got some common wooden toy soldiers, and painted them proper colours, putting feathers, epaulettes, and all other necessary accoutrements for officers, band, and privates, with colours and tents for each regiment. The whole formed two armies, which acted against each other by certain rules, not unlike chess, and the game was won by the general who took the best position. The two armies were supplied with cannon and caissons, baggage-waggons, and all requirements. The field was supplied with bridges, churches, villages, and forts— all little models. The game was a most ingenious one, and afforded us much amusement, and was greatly admired by my father's friends who saw it. This is another instance of the trouble and time he spent in finding amusement for his children."

Of the stories and jingles which he wrote for his own children and his little friends unfortunately little remains. His " Precocious Piggy" was, however, published many years after his death (in 1859), with illustrations by his son, who had inherited a small share of facility in using both pen and pencil. Having sent Dilke some of his essays in painting,[1] Hood was complimented upon them, and in reply gave an amusing anecdote about his little boy, then about five years old : " You talk of my being meant for a painter,—Tom *is ;* t'other day he cut a great notch out of his hair. ' How came you to do that ? ' asked his mother. Says Tom, as grave as a judge, ' for a *paint-brush !* ' There's early bias for you ! "

It is probable that his friendship for various small children led to the writing of many letters, but of these only four seem to be recoverable, and though those belong to a date nearer the end they may well find a place here. The little correspondents were children of Dr. Elliot, at the time spending a summer holiday at Sandgate.

"17, ELM TREE ROAD, ST. JOHN'S WOOD,
" *Monday, April,* 1844.

" MY DEAR MAY,—I promised you a letter, and here it is. I was sure to remember it ; for you are as hard to forget, as you are soft to roll down a hill with.[2] What fun it was ! only so prickly, I thought I had a porcupine in one pocket, and a hedgehog in the other. The next time, before we kiss the earth we will have its face well shaved. Did you ever go to Greenwich Fair ?

---

[1] Still in the possession of Sir Charles Dilke.
[2] He and the little girl had rolled down a bank in Epping Forest and landed in a furze bush.

Life at Ostend (1837—1840).

I should like to go there with you, for I get no rolling at St. John's Wood. Tom and Fanny only like roll and butter, and as for Mrs. Hood, she is for rolling in money.

"Tell Dunnie that Tom has set his trap in the balcony and has caught a cold, and tell Jeanie that Fanny has set her foot in the garden, but it has not come up yet. Oh, how I wish it was the season when 'March winds and April showers bring forth *May* flowers!' for then of course you would give me another pretty little nosegay. Besides it is frosty and foggy weather, which I do not like. The other night, when I came from Stratford, the cold shrivelled me up so, that when I got home, I thought I was my own child!

"However, I hope we shall all have a merry Christmas; I mean to come in my most ticklesome waistcoat, and to laugh till I grow fat, or at least streaky. Fanny is to be allowed a glass of wine, Tom's mouth is to have a *hole* holiday, and Mrs. Hood is to sit up to supper! There will be doings! And then such good things to eat; but, pray, pray, pray, mind they don't boil the baby by mistake for a *plump* pudding, instead of a plum one.

"Give my love to everybody, from yourself down to Willy, with which and a kiss, I remain, up hill and down dale, your affectionate lover,

"THOMAS HOOD."

"DEVONSHIRE LODGE, NEW FINCHLEY ROAD, ST JOHN'S WOOD,
"*July* 1st (1st of Hebrew falsity).

"MY DEAR DUNNIE,—I have heard of your doings at Sandgate, and that you were so happy at getting to the sea, that you were obliged to be flogged a little to moderate it, and keep some for next day. I am very

Thomas Hood :

fond of the sea, too, though I have been twice nearly
drowned by it ; once in a storm in a ship, and once
under a boat's bottom when I was bathing. Of course
you have bathed, but have you learned to swim yet ?
It is rather easy in salt water, and diving is still easier,
even, than at the *sink*. I only swim in fancy, and
strike out new ideas.

" Is not the tide curious ?   Though I cannot say
much for its tidiness ; it makes such a slop and litter
on the beach. It comes and goes as regularly as the
boys of a proprietary school, but has no holidays. And
what a rattle the waves make with the stones when
they are rough ; you will find some rolled into decent
marbles and bounces : and sometimes you may hear
the sound of a heavy sea, at a distance, like a giant
snoring. Some people say that every ninth wave is
bigger than the rest. I have often counted, but never
found it come true, except with tailors, of whom every
ninth is a man. But in rough weather there are giant
waves, bigger than the rest, that come in trios, from
which, I suppose, Britannia rules the waves by the rule
of three. When I was a boy, I loved to play with the
sea, in spite of its sometimes getting rather *rough*. I
and my brother chucked hundreds of stones into it, as
you do ; but we came away before we could fill it up.
In those days we were at war with France. Unluckily,
it's peace now, or with so many stones you might have
good fun for days in pelting the enemy's coast. Once
I almost thought I nearly hit Boney ! Then there was
looking for an island like Robinson Crusoe ! Have
you ever found one yet, surrounded by water ? I
remember once staying on the beach, when the tide
was flowing, till I was a peninsula, and only by running
turned myself into a continent.

" Then there's fishing at the seaside. I used to catch
flat fish with a very long string line. It was like swim-

Life at Ostend (1837—1840).

ming a kite! But perhaps there are no flat fish at Sandgate—except your shoe-soles. The best plan, if you want flat fish where there are none, is to bring codlings and hammer them into dabs. Once I caught a plaice, and, seeing it all over red spots, thought I had caught the measles.

"Do you ever long, when you are looking at the sea, for a voyage? If I were off Sandgate with my yacht (only she is not yet built), I would give you a cruise in her. In the meantime you can practise sailing any little boat you can get. But mind that it does not flounder or get squamped, as some people say instead of 'founder' and 'swamp.' I have been swamped myself by malaria, and almost foundered, which reminds me that Tom junior, being very ingenious, has made a cork model of a diving-bell that won't sink!

"By this time, I suppose, you are become, instead of a land-boy, a regular sea-urchin; and so amphibious, that you can walk on the land as well as on the water —or better. And don't you mean, when you grow up, to go to sea? Should you not like to be a little mid-shipman? or half a quarter-master, with a cocked hat, and a dirk, that will be a sword by the time you are a man? If you do resolve to be a post-captain, let me know; and I will endeavour, through my interest with the Commissioners of Pavements, to get you a post to jump over of the proper height. Tom is just rigging a boat, so I suppose that he inclines to be an Admiral of the Marines. But before you decide, remember the port-holes, and that there are great guns in those battle-doors that will blow you into shuttlecocks, which is a worse game than whoop and hide—as to a good hiding!

"And so farewell, young 'Old Fellow,' and take care of yourself so near the sea, for in some places, they say, it has not even a bottom to go to if you fall in. And

331

remember when you are bathing, if you meet with a shark, the best way is to bite off his legs, if you can, before he walks off with yours. And so, hoping you will be better soon, for somebody told me you had the shingles, I am, my dear Dunnie, your affectionate friend,

"THOMAS HOOD.

"P.S.—I have heard that at Sandgate there used to be *lob*sters; but some ignorant fairy turned them all by a *spell* into *bol*sters."

"DEVONSHIRE LODGE, NEW FINCHLEY ROAD, *July 1st*, 1844.

"MY DEAR JEANIE,—So you are at Sandgate! Of course, wishing for your old playfellow, M—— H——, (he *can* play,—it's work to me) to help you to make little puddles in the Sand, and swing on the Gate. But perhaps there are no sand and gate at Sandgate, which, in that case, nominally tells us a fib. But there must be little crabs somewhere, which you can catch, if you are nimble enough, so like spiders, I wonder they do not make webs. The large crabs are scarcer.

"If you do catch a big one with strong claws—and like experiments—you can shut him up in a cupboard with a loaf of sugar, and you can see whether he will break it up with his nippers. Besides crabs, I used to find jelly-fish on the beach, made, it seemed to me, of sea-calves' feet, and no sherry.

"The mermaids eat them, I suppose, at their wet water-parties, or salt *soirées*. There were star-fish also, but they did not shine till they were stinking, and so made very uncelestial constellations.

"I suppose you never gather any sea-flowers, but only sea-weeds. The truth is Mr. David Jones never rises from his bed, and so has a garden full of weeds, like Dr. Watts's Sluggard.

Life at Ostend (1837—1840).

" Oysters are as bad, for they never leave their beds willingly, though they get such oceans of ' cold pig.' At some sea-sides you may pick up shells, but I have been told that at Sandgate there are no shells, except those with passive green peas and lively maggots.

" I have heard that you bathe in the sea, which is very refreshing, but it requires care; for if you stay under water too long, you may come up a mermaid, who is only half a lady, with a fish's tail,—which she can boil if she likes. You had better try this with your Doll, whether it turns her into half a ' doll-fin.'

" I hope you like the sea. I always did when I was a child, which was about two years ago. Sometimes it makes such a fizzing and foaming, I wonder some of our London cheats do not bottle it up, and sell it for ginger-pop.

" When the sea is too rough, if you pour the sweet-oil out of the cruet *all over it,* and wait for a calm, it will be quite smooth,—much smoother than a dressed salad.

" Some time ago exactly, there used to be, about the part of the coast where you are, large white birds with black-tipped wings, that went flying and screaming over the sea, and now and then plunged down into the water after a fish. Perhaps they catch their sprats now with nets or hooks and lines. Do you ever see such birds? We used to call them ' gulls,'—but they didn't mind it! Do you ever see any boats or vessels? And don't you wish, when you see a ship, that Somebody was a sea-captain instead of a Doctor, that he might bring you home a pet lion, or calf elephant, ever so many parrots, or a monkey, from foreign parts? I knew a little girl who was promised a baby whale by her sailor brother, and who *blubbered* because he did not bring it. I suppose there are no whales at Sandgate, but you might find a seal about the beach; or, at least, a stone for one. The sea stones are not pretty when they are dry, but look beautiful when they are wet,—and we can *always* keep sucking them!

"If you can find one, pray pick me up a pebble for a seal. I prefer the red sort, like Mrs. Jenkins's brooch and ear-rings, which she calls 'red chamelion.' Well, how happy you must be! Childhood is such a joyous, merry time; and I often wish I was two or three children! But I suppose I can't be; or else I would be Jeanie, and May, and Dunnie Elliot. And wouldn't I pull off my three pairs of shoes and socks, and go paddling in the sea up to my six knees! And oh! how I could climb up the downs, and roll down the ups on my three backs and stomachs! Capital sport, only it wears out the woollens. Which reminds me of the sheep on the downs, and little May, so innocent, I daresay, she often crawls about on all fours, and tries to eat grass like a lamb. Grass isn't nasty; at least, not very, if you take care, while you are browsing, not to chump up the dandelions. They are large, yellow star-flowers, and often grow about dairy farms, but give very bad milk!

"When I can buy a telescope powerful enough, I shall have a peep at you. I am told with a good glass, you can see the sea at such a distance that the sea cannot see you! Now I must say good-bye, for my paper gets short, but not stouter. Pray give my love to your Ma, and my compliments to Mrs. H—— and no mistake, and remember me, my dear Jeanie, as your affectionate friend,

"THOS. HOOD.

"The other Tom Hood sends his love to everybody and everything.

"P.S. Don't forget my pebble:—and a good *naughty-lass* would be esteemed a curiosity."

Life at Ostend (1837—1840).

"DEVONSHIRE LODGE, NEW FINCHLEY ROAD, *July 1st*, 1844.

" MY DEAR MAY,—How do you do, and how do you like the sea ? not much perhaps, it's ' so big.' But shouldn't you like a nice little ocean, that you could put in a pan ? Yet the sea, although it looks rather ugly at first, is very useful, and, if I were near it this dry summer, I would carry it all home, to water the garden with at Stratford, and it would be sure to drown all the blights, *May*-flies and all !

" I remember that, when I saw the sea, it used sometimes to be very fussy, and fidgetty, and did not always wash itself quite clean; but it was very fond of fun. Have the waves ever run after you yet, and turned your two little shoes into pumps full of water ?

" If you want a joke you might push Dunnie into the sea, and then fish for him as they do for a Jack. But don't go in yourself, and don't let the baby go in and swim away, although he *is* the shrimp of the family. Did you ever taste the sea-water ? The fishes are so fond of it, they keep drinking it all the day long. Dip your little finger in, and then suck it to see how it tastes. A glass of it warm, with sugar, and a grate of nutmeg, would quite astonish you ! The water of the sea is so saline, I wonder nobody catches salt fish in it. I should think a good way would be to go out in a butter-boat, with a little melted for sauce. Have you been bathed yet in the sea, and were you afraid ? I was, the first time, and the time before that ; and dear me, how I kicked, and screamed—or, at least meant to scream, but the sea, ships and all, began to run into my mouth, and so I shut it up. I think I see *you* being dipped in the sea, screwing your eyes up, and putting your nose, like a button, into your mouth, like a button-hole, for fear of getting another smell and taste ! By the bye did you ever dive your head under water with your legs up in the air like a duck, and try whether you could cry

Thomas Hood :

'Quack?' Some animals can! I would try, but there is no sea here, and so I am forced to dip into books. I wish there were such nice green hills here as there are at Sandgate. They must be very nice to roll down, especially if there are no furze bushes to prickle one at the bottom! Do you remember how the thorns stuck in us like a penn'orth of mixed pins at Wanstead? I have been very ill, and am so thin now, I could stick myself into a prickle. My legs, in particular, are so wasted away that somebody says my pins are only needles: and I am so weak, I dare say you could push me down on the floor, and right thro' the carpet, unless it was a strong pattern. I am sure if I were at Sandgate, you could carry me to the post office, and fetch my letters. Talking of carrying I suppose you have donkeys at Sandgate, and ride about on them. Mind and always call them 'donkeys,' for if you call them asses, it might reach such long ears! I knew a donkey once that kicked a man for calling him Jack instead of John.

"There are no flowers I suppose on the beach, or I would ask you to bring me a bouquet as you used at Stratford. But there are little crabs! If you would catch one for me, and teach it to dance the Polka, it would make me quite happy; for I have not had any toys, or play-things for a long time. Did you ever try, like a little crab, to run two ways at once? See if you can do it, for it is good fun; never mind tumbling over yourself a little at first. It would be a good plan to hire a little crab, for an hour a day, to teach baby to crawl, if he can't walk, and, if I was his mamma, I *would* too! Bless him! But I must not write on him any more—he is so soft, and I have nothing but steel pens.

"And now good bye; Fanny has made my tea, and I must drink it before it gets too hot, as we *all* were

Life at Ostend (1837—1840).

last Sunday week. They say the glass was 88 in the shade, which is a great age! The last fair breeze I blew dozens of kisses for you, but the wind changed, and I am afraid took them all to Miss H——, or somebody that it shouldn't. Give my love to everybody, and my compliments to all the rest, and remember, I am, my dear May, your loving friend,

"THOMAS HOOD.

"P.S. Don't forget my little crab to dance the Polka, and pray write to me soon as you can't, if it's only a line."

"HAVE I A WOTE FOR GRINNAGE?"

CHAPTER XIII.

CAMBERWELL—ST. JOHN'S WOOD—"THE NEW MONTHLY" (1840—3).

"'Poor Hood!' for whom a people wreathes
  The heart-born flowers that never die.
'Poor Hood!' for whom a requiem breathes
  In every human toil-wrung sigh."

ELIZA COOK.

IT was late in July or early in August, 1840, that the Hoods returned finally to England after over five years of ill-advised exile. The motives that prompted leaving England were of the noblest, but the step seems to have been a mistaken one, for though it cannot be supposed that he would have escaped all the illness to which his poor body was subjected, he would no doubt have been easier in his mind and been able to work the better had he not gone so far; had he contented himself with migrating to Hastings or Brighton or some other healthful place by his well-loved sea. From his return he seems to have been doomed to an invalid's life, though his closing years were fruitful of some of his best work. The connection with the *New Monthly Magazine* seems to have inspired him freshly, and he began a series of " Rhymes for the Times and Reason for the Season," with discussion of "An Open Question"—concerning the closing of the *Zoological* Gardens on Sundays. The spirit was that in which he had retorted on Sir Andrew Agnew, on Rae Wilson, and others, who would make repression rather than recreation the dominant note of

338

Camberwell, &c. (1840—1843).

Sabbath conduct, who would not recognise as religion that which was not manifested in gloom.

"In spite of all the fanatic compiles,
  I cannot think the day a bit diviner,
Because no children, with forestalling smiles,
  Throng, happy, to the gates of Eden Minor—
It is not plain, to my poor faith at least,
  That what we christen 'Natural' on Monday,
The wondrous history of Bird and Beast,
  Can be Unnatural because it's Sunday—
But what is your opinion, Mrs. Grundy? . . . .

"Spirit of Kant! have we not had enough
  To make Religion sad, and sour, and snubbish,
But Saints Zoological must cant their stuff,
  As vessels cant their ballast—rattling rubbish!
Once let the sect, triumphant to their text,
  Shut Nero up from Saturday till Monday,
And sure as fate they will deny us next
  To see the Dandelions on a Sunday—
But what is your opinion, Mrs. Grundy?"

It could not but be gratifying to Hood to find that his return to England and his reappearance in one of the most popular of the magazines was hailed with pleasure both by those who knew him personally and by the wider world of readers. The dropping of the issue of the " Comic Annual " was probably helpful; instead of working towards that miscellany he was able to devote himself to such subjects as were suggested by current affairs without having the hampering considerations of keeping a certain balance between prose and verse, a proper variety of themes, and of appropriate lengths for the annual. In September the chief of the works in which he combined wit and humour, " Miss Kilmansegg and Her Precious Leg,"[1] was begun in the

[1] H. F. Chorley wrote to the *Athenæum* in 1869, referring to a dinner which he had had at Lake House, when he had

magazine, and during the following year he was represented in nearly every issue of the periodical. In the
autumn of 1840, too, " Tylney Hall "—the sale of the
copyright enabling him to bring over his family and
settle in England—was re-published as one of Bentley's
Standard Novels, with a new preface to which
reference has been made on an earlier page. In the
Athenæum, also, shortly after Hood's return, appeared
some unsigned verses which must surely have come
from his pen—" The Sailor's Soliloquy (with inter-
ruptions) "—

> " The Land ! the Land ! that cheering cry
>   Brings rapture to my heart ;
>   Thank Heaven ! this trip is at an end——
>   [We're just upon ' the Start ! ']"

The new home was set up in modest lodgings at
Camberwell, but after a few months these were changed
for more comfortable rooms in the same neighbourhood, where the author was able to indulge in
the luxury of a room to himself, a necessary luxury
indeed, for he had reached the stage when little dis-
concerted his nerves—"I am a little Job in afflictions,
but without his patience." Perhaps in the latter clause
Hood rather maligned himself, for he seems to have
borne his trials with uncommon fortitude. His action
against Baily (apparently for the restitution of copyrights belonging to the author) dragged slowly on, and
was not to be decided in his lifetime, so that his family
was dependent upon his immediate exertions. The
lawsuit, it may be said, was finally successful and that
without any cost to the plaintiff, for, as Hood's children
have recorded, Mr. Hook, his legal adviser, firmly and

told Hood of a childish game, " Give me my Golden Leg," and
thought that in it might have lain the suggestion of the later
tragic satire.

340

Camberwell, &c. (1840—1843).

consistently declined all remuneration for his labours. Other friends, too, came forward in this time of trial: the Committee of the Royal Literary Fund made frequent enquiries of Dilke as to Hood's health and the progress of the "Baily business," and then, without any knowledge on his part, and waiving the personal application usually necessary, unanimously voted him a sum of fifty pounds. While admitting to a friend that the money would have afforded him some ease and relief, Hood, for many and well-weighed reasons, decided to return it, feeling, however, all the better for the offer, as he says with pardonable pride: " I am the first who has said ' no.' But I am in good spirits and hope to get through all my troubles as independently as heretofore." The letter in which he acknowledged the proffered money is strongly characteristic of the man. There is no shamefaced minimising of his troubles, merely a sturdy assertion of his preference for independence, however hard won.

"2 UNION STREET, HIGH STREET, CAMBERWELL.

"GENTLEMEN,—I have to acknowledge the receipt of a letter from your secretary, which has deeply affected me.

" The adverse circumstances to which it alludes are, unfortunately, too well known from their public announcement in the *Athenæum* by my precocious executor and officious assignee. But I beg most emphatically to repeat that the disclosures so drawn from me were never intended to bespeak the world's pity or assistance. Sickness is too common to humanity, and poverty too old a companion of my order to justify such an appeal. The revelation was merely meant to show, when taunted with ' my creditors,' that I had been striving in humble imitation

Thomas Hood :

of an illustrious literary example to satisfy all claims upon me, and to account for my imperfect success. I am too proud of my profession to grudge it some suffering. I love it still, as Lord Byron loved England, ' with all its faults,' and should hardly feel as one of the fraternity, if I had not my portion of the calamities of authors. More fortunate than many, I have succeeded not only in getting into print, but occasionally in getting out of it, and surely a man who has overcome such formidable difficulties may hope and expect to get over the commonplace ones of procuring bread and cheese.

" I am writing seriously, gentlemen, although in a cheerful tone, partly natural and partly intended to relieve you of some of your kindly concern on my account. Indeed my position at present is an easy one, compared with that of some eight months ago, when out of heart and out of health, helpless, spiritless, sleepless, childless. I have now a home in my own country, and my little ones sit at my hearth. I smile sometimes, and even laugh. For the same benign Providence that gifted me with the power of amusing others has not denied me the ability of entertaining myself. Moreover, as to mere worldly losses, I profess a cheerful philosophy, which can jest, ' though China fall,' and for graver troubles a Christian faith, that consoles and supports me even in walking through something like the Valley of the Shadow of Death.

" My embarrassment and bad health are of such standing that I am become as it were seasoned. For the last six years I have been engaged in the same struggle without sinking, receiving or requiring any pecuniary assistance whatever. My pen and pencil procured not only enough for my own wants, but to form a surplus besides—a sort of literary fund of my own, which at this moment is ' doing good by stealth ' to a person, not exactly of learning or genius, but

Camberwell, &c. (1840—1843).

whom, according to the example of your excellent society, I will forbear to name.

"To provide for similar wants there are the same means and resources—the same head, heart, and hands—the same bad health—and may it only last long enough! In short, the same crazy vessel for the same foul weather; but I have not thought yet of hanging out my ensign upside down.

"Fortunately, since manhood I have been dependent solely on my own exertions—a condition which has exposed and inured me to vicissitude, while it has nourished a pride which will fight on, and has yet some retrenchments to make ere its surrender.

"I have now, gentlemen, described circumstances and feelings, which will explain and must excuse my present course. The honourable and liberal manner in which you have entertained an application—that a friendly delicacy concealed from me—is acknowledged with the most ardent gratitude. Your welcome sympathy is valued in proportion to the very great comfort and encouragement it affords me. Your kind wishes for my better health—my greatest want—I accept and thank you for with my whole heart; but I must not and cannot retain your money, which at the first safe opportunity will be returned. I really do not feel myself to be yet a proper object for your bounty, and should I ever become so, I fear that such a crisis will find me looking elsewhere—to the earth beneath me for final rest—and to the heaven above me for final justice.

"Pray excuse my trespassing at such length on your patience, and believe that I am, with the utmost respect, Gentlemen, your most obliged and grateful servant,

"Thos. Hood.

"*January 19th*, 1841."

Thomas Hood :

Bryan Waller Procter has recorded in his brief
reminiscences of Hood that "just before his death, when
consumption had mastered him, and the caprice of
public favour had much diminished his means of living,
he bore himself very independently." There is in the
closing words a suggestion of resentment, as though
Procter had perhaps been a member of the Literary
Fund Committee, and as though the rare "independence" of the author was resented. Procter was
evidently unaware of the circumstances, for it may be
safely said that the "caprice of public favour" had
nothing to do with Hood's diminished means of living;
it was rather the unhappy nature of his relations with
some of his publishers. Looking back over his life, it
is impossible to refrain from regretting that Hood did
not make some arrangement with Edward Moxon when
that *protégé* of Samuel Rogers and friend of Lamb's
set up publishing, a decade or so before.

Shortly after the writing of his letter to the Literary
Fund came the interrupted finishing of "Miss Kil-
mansegg," and the final tragedy was announced to
Dilke in the following manner :—

"You will be glad to hear—that I have kill'd her at
last, instead of her killing me. I don't mean Jane, but
Miss Kilmansegg ; and as she liked pomp there will be
twelve pages at her funeral. She is now screwing in at
Beaufort House ; and being a happy release for all
parties—you will conclude it is a relief to me, especially
as I come in for all she is worth. Love to all and no
more news from—Yours very truly,

"T. Hood."

To the Camberwell lodgings came gratifying testimony
to the continued popularity of his work in Germany, in
the shape of copies of a German translation of " The

Camberwell, &c. (1840—1843).

Dream of Eugene Aram" made by his friend De Franck and Herr von Rühe. One of these copies was sent by Hood at the request of the translators to Prince Albert. A long and amusing letter to Franck, full of the usual quizzing in which Hood indulged with this friend acknowledged receipt of the volumes. "For your sake I will not regret Germany." From this letter we learn that Hood worked quietly at home at Camberwell, rarely going into town oftener than once a month :—

"We are about three miles from St. Paul's, so that it is a walk for the children, and then we buss back, after a stroll to look at the shops, which are as good as an Exhibition. Very rarely I dine out—they dine too late for me at seven, and a cold ride through night air lays me up for a month. I am grown, Tim, quite an old man, and an invalid for good. . . . . And for all my temperance nobody gives *me* a medal. One hot evening last summer as I walked home I could have murdered an old fish-woman who stood drinking a pot of porter *out of the cool pewter!* why couldn't she drink it in the tap-room, or at the bar, out of my sight ? I fully expect next dog-days to have the Hydrophobia."

Anecdotes of the children, a description of Jane Hood in the more comfortable housekeeping of "Lunnon," with recollections of their companionship in Germany, lead up to an amusing account of the German translation of "Eugene Aram" as it appeared to the English author :—

"How can I express my delight at knowing the whole truth ? Jane says I looked as if I was turned to red and white with pleasure! I am sure she turned from red and white to all red, and looked as happy as if I had been transported instead of translated. But the next moment I was horrified, for I saw your name, 'Von Franck,' as one of the translators ! No fear had I on account of my friend Mr. Rühe, his habits qualified

him for the work, but 'odds triggers, and blades!' (as
Bob Acres says) a Lieutenant of the 19th Infanterie
regiment!   Oh! Jane! (here I fairly groaned to think
of it), Oh! Jane! We know from Dr. Weitershausen's
book what sort of work a *Prussian soldier* will make of
poetry!   Zounds! he will put Eugene Aram into
'parade breeches.' Yes, he will make him *march* up
and down (see verse 7) '*rechtsum und linksum,*' the
bludgeon will be the stick of a *heerpauk,* and the booty
regularly packed in the *tornistor.* Confound him! it
will be no more like Eugene Aram than Commis-brod
to muffins and crumpets,—all Brown Tommy and
Brown Bess!   I actually cried *dry,* for I was too
shocked to shed tears at the picture.

" But this comes, said I, of your young whiskered
Sword-Blades that sigh so for war, and because it is
peace, and no other butchery stirring, they must go and
murder Eugene Aram, as well as Daniel Clarke! For
he knows, the *Blut Egel,* that in spite of all his swagger
and curling his moustachios, there is not going to
be any '*Krieg,*' except, perhaps, between the New
Zealanders and the Esquimaux. And sure enough
when I looked into the German version, in the very
beginning, I found the game of cricket turned into *Ball
Spiel;* which I suppose means playing with bullets or
cannon balls, or as we call it, Ball-Practice. . . . .
Such were my misgivings when I saw your name in the
muster-roll (I beg your pardon, the title page), though
Jane, from her dealings with French money in Belgium,
thought at first it was the price of the book in francs.
When I explained it, she literally screamed with
surprise, and exclaimed, 'What, Franck turned literary!
Then take my word for it, Hood, he has married
Bettine the authoress.' And she was as frightened as
I was for Eugene Aram, though for a different cause,
namely your extravagant passion for fishing. 'Franck

Camberwell, &c. (1840—1843).

must be very much changed,' she said, alluding to the first verse, ' if he leave you one of the " troutlets in the pool." ' And in point of fact, on referring to your German, you do make them jump *here* and *there* as if, at least, you had *hooked* them. Lord knows what you have made of my ' Calm and Cool Evening,' but I suppose instead of one solitary beetle as in ' Gray's Elegy,' there is a whole flight of cockchafers, *because they are such good baits for chub*. Of one thing I can judge, for I have measured with a straw, and some of the lines are rather long, as if you had thrown them as far as you could. Moreover, I asked Fanny, who is the best German scholar in the family, to give me an account of the thing, and she said, that Eugene Aram ' played ' with the old man before he killed him, and then struck till he broke his *top-joint*. That when the body was full of *gentles* it was thrown into the stream for *ground-bait*, but unfortunately the water dried up, and so the body was put into a heap of bran, and the wind blew away the bran, etc. But I cannot depend enough on Fanny's acquaintance with the German language to feel sure of such a translation ; perhaps it may not turn out quite so fishy as she represents. Mind, however, that should it not prove to be full of ram-rod and fishing-rod I shall attribute that merit to your coadjutor, for even Tom asked when he heard that you had been translating it, ' Did Mr. Franck do it with his sword, and his schako, and his moustachios on ? ' (as if the last ever took off !) "

In the same letter, referring to Charles Dickens, Hood says, " Boz is a very good fellow and he and I are very good friends." Though he went out but little his work had made him many friends among his fellow authors, and it is curious when *Punch* was started in July, 1841, that he was not enlisted in the service of that journal to which his genius was so admirably suited.

Thomas Hood :

In the opening number there appeared, however, a quizzing paragraph which stated that " Mr. T. Hood, Professor of Punmanship, begs to acquaint the dull and witless, that he has established a class for the acquirement of an elegant and ready style of punning, on the pure Joe Millerian principle. The very worst hands are improved in six short and mirthful lessons. . . . . A good laugher wanted." This mild jest should not have annoyed Hood but it did, and he "could only express his amazement that his name should be paraded with apparent authority in a paper of the very existence of which he was not aware." Certainly, Hood, from his very position as a humorist and satirist, offered no fair game to a paper setting out to attack the very things which he had himself been attacking. The jest had but little point and was perhaps in all the circumstances wanting in good taste. It was to be two years later before Hood was himself to be numbered among the "*Punch* men."

On August 24th, 1841, Theodore Hook died, and within a week an emissary from the publisher, Colburn, visited Hood to offer him the succession to the editorship of the *New Monthly Magazine*. The prospect of a regular and assured income seemed too good to be true to poor Jane Hood, who wrote to her friend Mrs. Elliot that she seemed in a "mizzy maze" after the visit of the messenger of good—"Hood, with all the proper dignity of his sex is more calm and sedate upon the subject." Colburn wished to secure Hood's services at a salary of £200 a year, but the author refused to accept the position on anything less than the salary which Hook had received £300, and at length, in the middle of September, the matter was settled on those terms, and the position accepted. There is something pathetic in brave Mrs. Hood's joy over the small turn of prosperity —"the prospect of a certainty makes me feel 'passing rich.' Poverty has come so very near of late, that, in the words of Moore's song, 'Hope grew sick as the witch drew nigh.' "

Hood took up the editorship of the *New Monthly* with its October number, and set off with a whimsical account of "A Tête-à-Tête with the Editor," in which he described Advice personified as a talkative old woman come to indicate the nature of his duties and the way he should perform them. At first he is in doubt as to the personality of his visitor :—

" ' I've been a friend to you ever since you were born.'

" ' You, Madam ! '

" ' Yes, for I recommended your nurse—and I was the cause of your being vaccinated instead of inoculated— and of your going to Alfred House instead of Eton ; and of your visit to Scotland, and your residence in Germany ; and that you wore flannel next your skin, and shoes with cork soles ; and have left off fermented liquors. In short, it is through me that you are what you are. My name is Ad—— '

" ' Vice,' said I, recollecting her features in a moment. But if she had been called Gorgon, her presence could not more have embarrassed me. Such a variety of associations, pleasant and unpleasant, rushed upon me at the name, as made it impossible for me to adopt any certain course of behaviour.

" My first impulse, to be candid, was to turn my visitor out of the room by the shoulders—the next to embrace her like a near and dear relation. For oh ! what desperate scrapes, messes, puckers, dilemmas, disasters, losses, crosses, bothers, bubbles and troubles—what law suits and jaw suits,—hang her !—had she brought on me ! But then—bless her !—what comforts, and cures, and profit, and fleecy hosiery, and happiness, had she not wheedled me into ! Never was there such a complicated account current, since the one which the Irishman declared had ' a balance on both sides.' "

Work on the *New Monthly Magazine* with its assurance of a regular income enabled the Hoods to remove to pleasanter lodgings than those at Camberwell, and before the close of 1841 they left that neighbourhood for St. John's Wood. While still at Camberwell, however, Hood received a visit from one of those impertinent people who are so assured of their own goodness that they delight in pointing out to others the evils of their ways; he had known the lady some years before, and had before resented her manner of obtruding her religious views on those with whom she came in contact. On visiting Hood she was " unintentionally accompanied by a young friend and so did not feel free to say the things which she wished to say." In an unhappy moment for her on returning home she wrote to him to this effect, sending him some tracts, attacking his religious opinions and his writings and enquiring with seeming grim satisfaction what good his " Whims and Oddities " would do his soul, and how he would recall his literary levities when on his death-bed. Used as he was to attacks from those who worshipping the letter cannot recognise the spirit, Hood was moved once more to retaliation. It took the form of a stinging letter to which he gave the title of " My Tract." The letter is too long to give as an interruption of the narrative of his life, but so thoroughly represents the outlook of the man on serious matters that it is given fully in the appendices (*see* p. 403). Hood was not a church-goer, but that he was essentially a religious man is plain to anyone who reads his work with understanding, and the whole story of his life goes to enforce the fact.

From Camberwell the family removed at the beginning of 1842 to pleasanter lodgings at 17, Elm Tree Road, St. John's Wood, their landlady being

Camberwell, &c. (1840—1843).

ludicrously portrayed as the heroine of " Mrs. Gardiner, a Horticultural Romance "; her " large and personal love" of flowers, her jealous care of her garden, affording Hood a pleasant theme. The new rooms overlooked Lord's Cricket Ground, and Hood said that this was a drawback, as when he was at work he could so often see others at play; and himself, only able to walk short distances, was made envious by witnessing from his windows an occasional foot-race. The new life began auspiciously, health was better, and regular employment meant lessened anxieties; congenial visitors came to Elm Tree Road to simple dinner parties, and Hood got away to visit friends in the country. After a week at Twickenham, where the Dilkes had a summer cottage, Hood and Tom junior returned home " as brown as gipsies." The magazine business seemed prospering, and at the beginning of 1842 the " Comic Annual " was revived—its contents being made up of the editor's own contributions to the *New Monthly*. With some measure of success things certainly seemed to have taken a turn for the better, and this year to have been a happy contrast to many of those immediately preceding it. The letters written by both the Hoods to their good friend De Franck are full of hopefulness and liveliness—Jane's letters being " corrected " by her husband, who in playful fashion wrote over some of her words what he chose to think she meant: "muzzy" over " merry," " damd " over " dear," " pasty " over " party," and so on, to the combined mystification and amusement of the German officer. In one such letter which Hood got hold of he inserted this "rigmarole":—

" Hood will copy at the end the direction to be sent on the box. I am pretty well, much the same as Hood, but my wife is not over strong, neither is Jane, and Mrs. Hood seems to be no better than she is, but I hope she will mend and so does Hood. As to Johnny,

Thomas Hood:

he is as well as can be expected, but Hood does not expect he shall ever be very strong again; so we must all make the best of it, the Editor and all, who seems to sympathise in his ailments with me, and Hood, and Johnny; but he cannot expect to be better than we are, for he and we have the same complaint, a sort of monthly eruption which we think is better 'out' than in; my wife, Jane, and Mrs. Hood call it the 'Magazine.' It is a sort of black and white literary rash of a periodical nature, chiefly affecting the head; as yet none of the children have caught it."

With the playfulness of a boy, Hood seemed never to tire of such tricks with his wife, not only altering her letters, but giving the most extravagant accounts of her sayings and doings. Well might a friend say that strangers would think Jane a most extraordinary person from the odd stories Hood told of her.

In the summer of 1842, Hood was one of the party of friends who gave Charles Dickens on returning from his American tour a welcoming dinner at Greenwich. Describing it in a letter to Mrs. Elliot, Hood said:—

"You will be pleased to hear that, in spite of my warnings and forebodings, I got better and betterer, till by dining *as the physicians did* on turtle soup, whitebait, and champagne, I seemed quite well. But I have always suspected the doctors' practice to be better than their precepts; and particularly those which turn down *Diet* Street. The snug one dozen of diners however turned out to be above two (in fact twenty-seven)—two others, Talfourd and Macready being prevented. Jerdan was the *Vice*, and a certain person, not very well adapted to *fill* a Chair, was to have occupied the opposite *Virtue*, but on the score of ill-health I begged off, and Captain Marryat presided instead. On his right, Dickens, and Monckton Milnes, the poetical M.P.; on his left, Sir John Wilson, T.H., and for my

Camberwell, &c. (1840—1843).

left-hand neighbour Doctor Elliot*son*, which seemed considerately contrived to break my fall from Stratford. The Kelso man was supported by Foster, and Stanfield the painter. Amongst the rest were Charles and Tom Landseer. Tom two stone deafer than I am, and obliged to carry a tube. Father Prout and Ainsworth; these two men at paper war,—therefore some six, including a clergyman, were put between them. Procter, *alias* Barry Cornwall, and Barham, otherwise Ingoldsby, Cruikshank, and Cattermole, a Dr. Gwynne, or Quin, and a Rev. Mr. Wilde, who greatly interested Dr. Elliotson and myself: a tall, very earnest-looking man, like your doctor, only with none of his Sweet-William colour, but quite pale; and the more so for long jet-black locks, either strange natural hair, or an unnatural wig. He was silent till he sang, and then came out such a powerful bass voice, fit for a Cathedral organ— to a song of the olden time, that between physiognomy, costume, vox, and words, the impression was quite black-letterish. I had never seen him before, but seemed to know him, *traditionally*, somewhere about Cromwell's time. Nevertheless some of his reading had been more modern and profane, for when we broke up, he came and shook hands with me, to my pleasant surprise, for I seemed to have ascended to antiquity, whilst only aiming to descend to posterity.

" Well, we drank 'the Boz' with a delectable clatter, which drew from him a good warm-hearted speech, in which he hinted the great advantage of going to America for the pleasure of coming back again; and pleasantly described the embarrassing attentions of the Transatlantickers, who made his private house, and private cabin, particularly public. He looked very well, and had a younger brother along with him. He told me that two American prints have attacked me for my copyright letters in the *Athenæum*, so I shall procure

Thomas Hood :

them as a treat for 'Jane.' Then we had more songs. Barham chanted a Robin Hood ballad, and Cruikshank sang a burlesque ballad of Lord H——; and somebody, unknown to me, gave a capital imitation of a French showman. Then we toasted Mrs. Boz, and the Chairman, and Vice, and the Traditional Priest sang the 'Deep deep sea,' in his deep deep voice; and then we drank to Procter, who wrote the said song; also Sir J. Wilson's good health, and Cruikshank's, and Ainsworth's; and a Manchester friend of the latter sang a Manchester ditty, so full of trading stuff, that it really seemed to have been not composed, but manufactured. Jerdan, as Jerdanish as usual on such occasions—you know how paradoxically he is *quite at home* in *dining out*. As to myself, I had to make my *second maiden speech*, for Mr. Monckton Milnes proposed my health in terms my modesty might allow me to repeat to *you*, but my memory won't. However, I ascribed the toast to my notoriously bad health, and assured them that their wishes had already improved it—that I felt a brisker circulation—a more genial warmth about the heart, and explained that a certain trembling of my hand was not from palsy, or my old ague, but an inclination in my hand to shake itself with every one present. Whereupon I had to go through the friendly ceremony with as many of the company as were within reach, besides a few more who came express from the other end of the table. *Very* gratifying, wasn't it? Though I cannot go quite so far as Jane, who wants me to have that hand chopped off, bottled, and preserved in spirits. She was sitting up for me, very anxiously, as usual when I go out, because I am so domestic and steady, and was down at the door before I could ring at the gate, to which Boz kindly sent me in his own carriage. Poor girl! what *would* she do if she had a wild husband instead of a tame one."

354

Camberwell, &c. (1840—1843).

The pleasant outing had no harmful effects. Return-ing home Dickens suggested calling on the Hoods with his wife, but Jane Hood had to remind her husband—he described her as his "flapper, not a young wild duck, but a Remembrancer of Laputa"—that he was already engaged to go down into Berkshire for three or four days' rabbit shooting with the reverend "Peter Priggins" at Letcombe Regis, near Wantage. "Peter Priggins," who was the Rev. James T. J. Hewlett, was a contributor to the *New Monthly*, and with him Hood seems to have passed a few days of happy holiday. As he wrote to Dilke: "Dined every day with a regular old English squire—Goodlake—the famous breeder of greyhounds. Lounged delightfully, and had what I have been longing for : a lie on the grass. No such green Turkey carpets abroad, Dilke. Then, for company, a Mrs. *Smiley* of *May Fair*. What isn't there in a name? God bless, T. H."

In this same year came a pleasant tribute of recogni-tion from a fellow man of letters, when Douglas Jerrold dedicated his two volumes of "Cakes and Ale" "To Thomas Hood, Esq., whose various genius touches alike the springs of laughter and the source of tears."

The Dickens's visit was apparently long post-poned. Hood, asking for an early copy of the "American Notes" for review in the *New Monthly* in mid-October, suggests as a motto for the new book, "I wish I was in A-me-ri-ca !" which he gravely states Coleridge frequently exclaimed in his Pantisocracy days; he wishes for Dickens that he may "live, fatten, prosper, write, and draw the mopuses wholesale through Chapman and *Haul*." On December 6, Dickens, with his wife and her sister, paid their promised visit to the Hoods, taking with them Daniel Maclise, "a very unaffected and ardent admirer of your genius, who has no small portion of that commodity in his own right." Dickens had asked permission to take Miss Hogarth and Maclise, and Hood promptly responded : " Many thanks for your friendly additions to our little edition of a party ; as to Maclise, I would rather be introduced to him—in spite of ' Mason on Self-knowledge '—than to myself." With the cordial note was enclosed a card with a white vehicle on a black ground—a characteristic interpretation of *carte blanche*. Other visitors, too, came to 17, Elm Tree Road, and on one occasion, perhaps more, the Hoods were able to welcome their old friend Mary Lamb, for Crabb Robinson has recorded that having called on Mary Lamb, who had but recently recovered from one of her melancholy attacks, and found her " quite in possession of her faculties, and recollecting everything nearly," he walked with her to St. John's Wood and left her at the Hoods.

It was a time of pleasant friendships, and of working hard with pen and pencil, with occasional reminders in the way of ill-health ; once his foot is so swelled and tender with rheumatism that he can hardly put it to the ground, and he refuses, therefore, to believe that he can be suffering from a *long-standing* complaint like the gout. When Southey died, in March, 1843, Hood wrote to Dilke asking if it was supposed that he would have any chance for the Laureateship. As a comic poet he was little likely to have any chance—though there have been some comic appointments to the post—but had the vacancy occurred a couple of years later, the momentum of his newer popularity might have made his chance a better one. There is no record of Dilke's reply, but presumably no steps were taken to put Hood's name forward on the occasion ; indeed, almost immediately on Southey's death the Laureateship was first offered where it was first due, to the veteran who most fully represented the poetic spirit of his age—to William Wordsworth.

A letter written during this spring to one of Dr.

Camberwell, &c. (1840—1843).

Elliot's sons, who was being educated as a civil engineer and to whom Hood had sent a book on the Steam Engine, may be given in further illustration of his readiness to find amusement himself in amusing his correspondents.

"DEAR WILLIE,—You owe me no thanks, the book is in better hands than mine. I have not the organ of constructiveness, and made sure that by the help of the sledges at the foundry, you would hammer more out of the volume than I could.

"Till lately, such was my ignorance, I thought the Engineers were the Fire Brigade.

"And even yet I do not rightly understand what you make at those factories along the river-side, except a noise, enough to render the Thames fishes deaf, as well as dumb. Of what use then could such a book be to me, who have no more notion of engineering than a *Zoological monkey* of driving piles? I hastily read a few pages, but understood little, except about fastening cross beams with two ties, which being like a counsellor's wig, seemed to me the legal way. The railroad matter was quite beyond my comprehension, especially the necrological mode of laying down sleepers, which I should have thought belonged to medical practice. I hope you have no hand or finger in the construction of the Flying Fly at Blackwall; some people insist rather inconsistently, that it will never ascend because it is a bubble, but you engineers know best. By the bye, your operations at Dover do the profession great credit, you beat the Doctors hollow. Give your father as much Dover's powder as he pleases, and see if he can mine into a gouty foot, and blow out its chalk. I rather think I have an engineer amongst my correspondents. He signs himself *Screw*-tator, constantly quotes from Dr. Lever, and speaks of carrots and turnips as

357

*wedge*ables. He even dines, I am told, at a French house, that he may ask for a *pully* instead of a chicken.

" Good night ! I would write more, but I have scientifically lighted my candle, and am going mechanically to bed, yours, dear Willie, very truly,

" Thos. Hood.

" Talking of Engineering, it is strange that Brunel never calculated on one great use of the Thames Tunnel, namely, to give the Cockneys at Easter a *hole* holiday. I forget how many thousands of Londoners had a *dry dive* under the river. Some day, I predict, the tunnel will become a great waterpipe. And I'm a prophet.

" I foretold, in last month's Magazine, that *the Comet would blow up the Waltham Abbey Powder Mills*."

In the summer of 1843, with Douglas Jerrold and John Forster, he attended the dinner of the Printers' Pension Fund, in support of Dickens's chairmanship and then came an invitation to Hood to allow his name to be used as patron of a great Bazaar arranged for the benefit of the Manchester Athenæum—an institution which also gained the support by voice and pen of his friends Charles Dickens and Douglas Jerrold. Hood's reply, which newly asserted his debt to literature and was printed and sold at the Bazaar for the benefit of the funds, ran as follows :—

" (From my bed.)   17, Elm Tree Road, St. John's Wood,
" *July 18th*, 1843.

" Gentlemen,—If my humble name can be of the least use for your purpose, it is heartily at your service, with my best wishes for the prosperity of the Manchester Athenæum, and my warmest approval of the objects of that Institution.

" I have elsewhere recorded my own deep obligations to Literature—that a natural turn for reading, and

Camberwell, &c. (1840—1843).

intellectual pursuits, probably preserved me from the moral shipwreck, so apt to befal those, who are deprived in early life of the paternal pilotage. At the very least my books kept me aloof from the ring, the dog-pit, the tavern, and the saloons, with their degrading orgies. For the closet associate of Pope and Addison, the mind accustomed to the noble, though silent discourse of Shakspere and Milton, will hardly seek, or put up with low company and slang. The reading animal will not be content with the brutish wallowings that satisfy the unlearned pigs of the world. Later experience enables me to depose to the comfort and blessing that Literature can prove in seasons of sickness and sorrow : how powerfully intellectual pursuits can help in keeping the head from crazing, and the heart from breaking; nay, not to be too grave, how generous mental food can even atone for a meagre diet; rich fare on the paper, for short commons on the cloth.

" Poisoned by the malaria of the Dutch marshes, my stomach for many months resolutely set itself against fish, flesh, or fowl; my appetite had no more edge than the German knife placed before me. But luckily the mental palate and digestion were still sensible and vigorous ; and while I passed untasted every dish at the Rhenish table d'hôte, I could still enjoy my ' Peregrine Pickle,' and the Feast after the manner of the Ancients. There was no yearning towards calf's head à *la tortue,* or sheep's heart ; but I could still relish Head à *la Brunnen,* and the ' Heart of Mid-Lothian.' Still more recently it was my misfortune, with a tolerable appetite, to be condemned to Lenten fare, like Sancho Panza, by my physician, to a diet, in fact, lower than any prescribed by the Poor-Law Commissioners, all animal food, from a bullock to a rabbit, being strictly interdicted, as well as all fluids, stronger than that which lays dust, washes pinafores, and waters polyanthus. But the feast of reason and the flow of soul were still mine !

" Denied beef, I had Bulwer and Cowper; forbidden mutton, there was Lamb; and, in lieu of pork, the great Bacon, or Hogg. Then as to beverage; it was hard, doubtless, for a Christian to set his face, like a Turk, against the juice of the grape. But eschewing wine, I had still my Butler, and in the absence of liquor, all the Choice Spirits from Tom Browne to Tom Moore. Thus though confined physically to the drink that drowns kittens, I quaffed mentally, not merely the best of our own home-made, but the rich, racy, sparkling growths of France and Italy, of Germany and Spain; the champagne of Molière, the Monte Pulciano of Boccaccio, the hock of Schiller, and the sherry of Cervantes. Depressed bodily by the fluid that damps everything, I got intellectually elevated with Milton, a little merry with Swift, or rather jolly with Rabelais, whose Pantagruel, by the way, is equal to the best gruel with rum in it.

" So far can literature palliate, or compensate, for gastronomical privations. But there are other evils, great and small, in this world, which try the stomach less than the head, the heart, and the temper; bowls that will not roll right, well-laid schemes that will ' gang aglee,' and ill-winds that blow with the pertinacity of the monsoon. Of these Providence has allotted me a full share; but still, paradoxical as it may sound, my *burthen* has been greatly lightened by *a load of books*. The manner of this will be best understood by a *feline* illustration. Everybody has heard of the two Kilkenny cats, who devoured each other; but it is not so generally known, that they left behind them an orphan kitten, which, true to its breed, began to eat itself up, till it was diverted from the operation by a mouse. Now the human mind, under vexation, is like that kitten; for it is apt to *prey upon itself*, unless drawn

Camberwell, &c. (1840—1843).

off by a new object, and none better for the purpose than a book. For example, one of Defoe's; for who, in reading his thrilling ' History of the Great Plague,' would not be reconciled to a few little ones ?

" Many, many a dreary weary hour have I got over —many a gloomy misgiving postponed—many a mental and bodily annoyance forgotten by help of the tragedies, and comedies, of our dramatists and novelists! Many a trouble has been soothed by the still small voice of the moral philosopher; many a dragon-like care charmed to sleep by the sweet song of the poet! For all which I cry incessantly, not aloud, but in my heart, ' Thanks and honour to the glorious masters of the pen, and the great inventors of the press!' Such has been my own experience of the blessing and comfort of Literature, and intellectual pursuits; and of the same mind, doubtless, was Sir Humphry Davy, who went for ' Consolations in Travel' not to the inn, or the posting-house, but to his library and his books. I am, Gentlemen, yours very truly,

" THOS. HOOD."

The day after that letter was written the *Pegasus* was wrecked on a rock near Holy Island, and Edward William Elton, the popular actor, was drowned, leaving an insane wife and five young children. The case appealed strongly to the public imagination, and Dickens, who started a fund with very general support, wrote for help to Hood, who replied, " Make any use you can of my name, or me, for the purpose you mention. I would add my purse, but unluckily just now there is nothing in it, thanks to B." Dickens asked for his friend's pen as a means of reaching the purses of others, and Hood responded with a pathetic " address," which was spoken by Mrs. Warner at a benefit performance (August 2nd, 1843) at the Haymarket Theatre.

Thomas Hood:

In mid-August a whimsical letter to De Franck—
"you who have half-pay for doing nothing, whereas I
am only half-paid for doing everything"—tells of the busy
life being led by the invalided author. At the end of
the month as magazine day draws near Hood says he
has sometimes to sit up three nights successively, Jane
sitting up with him; "then we are obliged to visit and
be visited, which we shun as much as we can, but must
to some extent go through, as I am a sort of public
man. Mind, this does not mean keeping a public house,
as you may think from the sound, and your oblivion of
English." The routine of editorial work was also
worrying him: "but of all, the hardest work is writing
refusals to literary ladies, who *will* write poetry, and
won't write it well. I wish you would come and marry
a few of them, which would perhaps reduce them to
prose."

Early in September came the sudden resolve to
revisit Scotland by way of a short holiday, and taking
"Tom Junior" with him Hood set out for Dundee, going,
as he had gone nearly thirty years earlier, by boat.
They made a very good passage and arrived at Dundee in
the early morning of September 15th, the only "incident"
of the voyage being the attempt of a lunatic to inspire
panic on board the evening before the arrival in the Tay.

"While finishing our dinner, down came into the
cabin a gentleman we had never seen before, announcing,
' Ladies and gentlemen, I don't know whether you are
aware of it, but we are all in imminent danger: the fires
are out, and the captain don't know where we are; the
ship is sinking, and you will all be at the bottom in a few
minutes.' At first I was a little alarmed, not hearing
what he said, for I had left Tom on deck, who was too
squeamish to come below, but thinking, when I heard
better, that he was some fool who had got frightened,
I went up, brought Tom down, and said with a laugh

Camberwell, &c. (1840—1843).

to the passengers, 'then my boy shall go down in good company!'—for some looked scared. Luckily the prophet of ill-luck did not go into the ladies' cabin, where many of them were sick, or we should have had screams and hysterics. It turned out that he was insane.

"I remembered seeing the man rather mysteriously brought on board at Gravesend, and shut into the captain's private cabin on deck. It seems, after a day there, he got violent, and insisted on coming out. All the rest of the evening he did nothing else but go about addressing everybody, and particularly the captain, in a style that shocked weak nerves:—'We are all going (throwing up his hands), you will be all at the bottom in a few minutes, and no one left to tell the tale. She is settling fast forwards! Captain, captain, do you know where you are? Are you aware that the fire is out? Look, look forward there, she is going down. Good Heavens! and nobody seems aware of it, and *you* (to me) won't care about it, till you are making a bubble in the water! Good Heavens! what day is it, sir? (to another), Thursday! no such thing, sir, it is Saturday, but no matter, it is your last day! And what a destruction of property, this fine vessel and all her cargo.'

"He harped a good deal on this, for it was said he had lost his own property. The steward meanwhile dogging him all over the ship, lest he should jump overboard; but in the evening they got him in again, and locked him up, and he is safe landed."

From Dundee Hood crossed over to Tayport to visit his aunt, Mrs. Keay, and Tayport he made his head-quarters during his week's stay though he was in Dundee each day visiting old scenes and looking up such old friends as remained. He determined to banish " all thoughts of bookery," to take his swing of idleness, adding, however, " I shall finish the article on Temperance by the help of whiskey-toddy, but that need not be put in the

363

paper." After a pleasant week in Dundee feeling very much the better, Hood set off with his boy for Edinburgh, and there he passed another week. Several of the people to whom he had letters of introduction from Dickens and other friends were out of town, but he dined with Lord Jeffrey, and visited William Chambers, and D. M. Moir ("Delta" of *Blackwood's Magazine* and other periodicals), with whom he had frequently corresponded. He found himself able to walk about all day visiting and sight-seeing, but looked longingly up at Salisbury Crags and Arthur's Seat and sighed "who can tell how hard it is to climb."

Hood returned to London looking and feeling well and ready to take up his "bookery" again with renewed zest. He was to gather his contributions of the *New Monthly Magazine* into a couple of volumes "with tedious waitings on Colburn." This last phrase suggests that Hood was finding something irksome in his relations with the publisher and proprietor of the *New Monthly*. He had already nearly reached breaking point with Colburn in September, and on consulting Dickens with regard to his position with that publisher the novelist wrote, "there can be no doubt in the mind of any honourable man, that the circumstances under which you signed your agreement are of the most disgraceful kind in so far as Mr. Colburn is concerned. There can be no doubt that he took a money-lending, bill-broke, Jew-clothes-bagging, Saturday-night-pawnbroking advantage of your temporary situation." Probably the consciousness that his reputation ought to be productive of a better income than he was making led to Hood's entertaining the idea of starting a magazine of which he should be a part proprietor. Negotiations were entered into, and early in December he was able to tell his friend Elliot that the new magazine was practically decided upon.

Camberwell, &c. (1840—1843).

"Negociations about to close for a new periodical—'Hood's Magazine'—to come out on 1st January!!! So, I cannot keep the news from you, but write to tell you at once what is likely to be.

"My fortunes seem subject to *crises*, like certain disorders. On or about Christmas, I am to dine with you, turn out, and get a new house, come to issue with B——, and start with a periodical under my own name. N.B.—There are folks with money to back it. I shall have a future share if the thing becomes a property.

"Yesterday I had an offer to write for 'Jerrold's Magazine'[1] on my own terms, the project having got wind. This looks well: so do I, people say, for Scotland did me good in various ways. I think, if I could live in a monument on the Calton Hill, I should keep pretty well."

A notable "crisis" was about to happen in his fortunes. On November 18th, "A Drop of Gin" appeared in *Punch*, a journal to which he was but for a very brief but significant period to be a contributor. This was, apart from some conundrums and a sketch, his first appearance of any importance in *Punch*. The poem, while having more than the forcefulness of a temperance tract, pointed out the provocations which led to drink—

> "Let Anger be mute
> And sweet Mercy dilute,
> With a drop of Pity, the Drop of Gin."

In the closing lines, too, we have what is perhaps the first use of the now commonly used words : the "gin palace."

In the Christmas Number of *Punch*—for December 16th, 1843—appeared "The Song of the Shirt." On

[1] The *Illuminated Magazine*, which Douglas Jerrold edited May, 1843, to October, 1844.

Thomas Hood :

October 25, a wretched woman named Biddell was charged at the Lambeth police office with having pawned articles belonging to her employer. It was shown that she made trousers for sevenpence a pair and that the utmost she could make was seven shillings a week, which her employers looked upon as "a good living for a woman who had herself and two infant children to support." This case attracted immediate attention. Two days later the *Times* had "a powerful leader" on the incident. *Punch* quoted from this leader with stinging additions—probably by Douglas Jerrold—in the following week. Hood, whose sympathies were ever stirred by suffering, as by cant, penned his "Song" and sent it to *Punch*, his wife saying as the package was done up, "Now mind, Hood, mark my words, this will tell wonderfully! It is one of the best things you ever did!" Mark Lemon, who was at the time *Punch's* editor, recalling receipt of the manuscript in later years, said that the author accompanied it with a note saying that the lines had already been rejected by three papers, that he feared it was not suited to *Punch*, and leaving it to Lemon's discretion whether to put it in the paper or in the waste-paper basket. Hood was at the time putting together materials for his own magazine to be commenced in the New Year, and had "The Song of the Shirt" been voted unsuitable for *Punch* there can be little doubt that he would have used it there. I am inclined to think that the story of its rejection by various journals is inaccurate, because Hood does not appear to have been in the habit of sending his work round to different papers, and the fact that he had recently commenced contributing to *Punch* —through the jesting pages of which ran a strong vein of seriousness in its earlier years—would suggest that paper as the most obvious medium for the publication of the impressive verses.

Camberwell, &c. (1840—1843).

Jane Hood's confidence was justified. The poem
" told " in the most emphatic fashion. It was copied
into the *Times* and other journals, and, as Mr. M. H.
Spielmann has put it in his sympathetic appreciation
of Hood as contributor to *Punch*, it " went through the
land like wild-fire." And not only in England, for it
appeared in translations in various foreign journals,
Hood wondering how the French and German writers
would render " Stitch, stitch, stitch ! " and " Seam and
gusset and band ! " It was printed on cotton pocket-
handkerchiefs and made use of in many ways that
must have brought it to the attention of every reader
in the land. Many were the enquiries as to who *could*
have written it. Dickens, aided perhaps by the knowledge that Hood had recently become a writer on
Punch, was one of those who ascribed it rightly, but in
truth the ascription should not have been difficult to
those with any intimate knowledge of Hood's work, and
especially of such a later manifestation of his genius
as " Miss Kilmansegg " ; the woman singing " The Song
of the Shirt " might have been own sister to that
Peggy in the longer poem who

> " Hawks flowers from street to street,
> Till, think of it ye who find life so sweet,
> She hates the smell of roses ! "

" The Song of the Shirt " was one of those pieces
that, touching the conscience and appealing to the
sentiment of a people, took its place at once as something of a folk song.[1] It was sung about the streets by
poor people " to a rude air of their own adaptation in a
way that cannot fail to have touched the author."
When Hood's name came to be mentioned as writer

---

[1] In May, 1906, it was read as the second lesson at the West
Hampstead Unitarian Church, the sermon dealing with sweated
labour.

Thomas Hood :

of the " Song " there were not wanting people to dispute it ! Indeed it was definitely claimed for some unknown person, and a journal which referred to it as Hood's was asked to contradict that statement. Fortunately, however, there was incontestable proof, but over a year after its publication the author was compelled to reassert that he was the author.

" As I have publicly acknowledged the authorship of the 'Song of the Shirt,' I can have no objection to satisfy you privately on the subject. My old friends Bradbury and Evans, the proprietors of *Punch*, could show you the document conclusive on the subject. But I trust my authority will be sufficient, especially as it comes from *a man on his death-bed*."

We have it on authority of the historian of *Punch* that the publication of " The Song of the Shirt " *trebled* the circulation of that journal. It may be said also to have trebled Hood's fame and popularity at the time and so have made it a most auspicious moment for starting his new venture, for with the December number his editorship of the *New Monthly Magazine* came to a close. It was natural that the author should wish to make provision for his small family by forming something in the nature of a property, though it may be believed that Colburn deeply resented Hood's defection. The post of editor had been neither an easy nor a very remunerative one, but to the *New Monthly* the editor had contributed some very characteristic work from his own pen, both in prose and verse, including in the former a very able essay on Shakespeare by way of a review of the national poet's works as edited by Charles Knight. This essay is marked by true critical feeling and insight, illustrating a side of Hood's literary talent not generally known. On its publication the writer received a gratifying note from Laman Blanchard, a poet-critic of less but not dissimilar genius. Said

Camberwell, &c. (1840—1843).

Blanchard, "It is rather an odd thing to do, but I have only this minute read your 'Shakespeare,' and as I never happened to read anything that I enjoyed more, I take the pen simply to tell you so at once. . . . You will feel why I thank and congratulate you when I say that the disgust produced by some commentaries is hardly greater than the delight with which I read yours —so thoroughly does the spirit to comprehend both the Divinity and the Dunces pervade and elevate it all."

Colburn's resentment of his editor's leaving him was such that he returned three letters which arrived at his office addressed to Hood and endorsed them "not known to Mr. Colburn." Presumably one of the letters was from Dilke, for to that friend Hood sent the following lines on the subject :—

> "For a couple of years in the columns of Puff
> I was rated a passable writer enough;
> But, alas! for the favours of Fame!
> Since I quitted her seat in Great Marlborough St.
> In repute my decline is so very complete
> That a Colburn don't know of my name!

> "Now a Colburn I knew in his person so small
> That he seemed the *half*-brother of nothing at all,
> Yet in spirit a Dwarf may be big;
> But his mind was so narrow, his soul was so dim,
> Where's the wonder if all I remember of him
> Is—a suit of Boy's clothes and a wig!"

"In the columns of Puff" is a reference to Colburn's well-known methods of advertising as publisher, those methods having been made fun of in the *London Magazine* and other places. Miss H. Lawrance, the author of "Historical Memoirs of the Queens of England" and other works, apparently wished to do some reviewing on the magazine, and Hood's reply suggests that he had not altogether a free hand as editor, for he said: "I undertook to review all books

Thomas Hood.

except Colburn's own, with the puffery of which I of course desired to have no concern. They are *done* by the persons of the Establishment, Patmore, Williams & Shoberl. If you see the Magazine you will know what wretched things these reviews are. As to mine they are few and far between. I get few books and those appear to be the *refuse*, what it is not worth the while of somebody else to keep."

It was about this time that Charles Cowden Clarke met Hood at the house of a friend and recorded his impressions of the man whose " worn, pallid look strangely belied the effect of jocularity and high spirits conveyed in his writings. He punned incessantly, but languidly, almost as if unable to think in any other way than in play upon words. His smile was attractively sweet : it bespoke the affectionate-natured man which his serious verses—those especially addressed to his wife or to his children—show him to be, and it also revealed the depth of pathos in his soul that inspired his 'Bridge of Sighs,' 'Song of the Shirt,' and 'Eugene Aram.'"

Confidential.   17. Elm Tree Road
                    Friday.

My dear Miss Lawrance.

        I write in haste a few
lines to put you on yr. guard,
by telling You of the arrangements
for reviewing in the Magazine.
I undertook to review all books
except Colburn's own with the
puffing of which I of course de:
sired to have no concern. They
are done by the persons of the
establishment, Patmore, Williams
or Shoberl. If you see the Mag.
you will know what wretched
things these reviews are.

        I do not mind your saying
You have understood from me afore
time, or have detected from the style
that I write the reviews, except of
C's books. If he would give you
to yr. a sheet to review his generally
(not one only) I should rejoice for I
am ashamed of them at present or
should be were it not pretty well
known that I have no hand in them.
Pray give my complts to your Mama
& believe me My dear Miss Lawrance
        Yours very truly Thos Hood

FACSIMILE LETTER TO MISS LAWRANCE.

[To face p. 370.

CHAPTER XIV.

DEVONSHIRE LODGE—" HOOD'S MAGAZINE "—
THE END (1844—1845).

" Here lies a poet. Stranger, if to thee
　His claim to memory be obscure
If thou would'st know how truly great was he
　Go, ask it of the poor."

JAMES RUSSELL LOWELL.

THE year 1844 opened in the most auspicious fashion.
The new venture, *Hood's Monthly Magazine and Comic
Miscellany*, started on January 1, and the family had
left their lodgings in the Elm Tree Road and returned
to the joys of a house of their own after eight years
of moving from lodgings to lodgings abroad and at home.
The house, taken for three years, was in the New
Finchley Road, St. John's Wood—"just beyond the
'Eyre Arms,' three doors short of the turnpike," and to it,
in remembrance of the generosity and kindness of the
Duke of Devonshire, Hood gave the name of Devonshire Lodge.   The removal to a house of her own again
must have been a great comfort to Mrs. Hood, and her
husband entered on his fresh undertaking with renewed
heart and every promise of success—promise unfortunately to be marred almost from the outset.   The plan of
the magazine was described in the approved fashion in
the following prospectus :—

" Whatever may be thought of Dr. Dickson's theory,
that the type of Disease in general is periodical, there
can be no doubt of its applicability to Modern Literature,
which is essentially Periodical, whether the type be long

primer, brevier, or bourgeois. It appears, moreover, by the rapid consumption of Monthlies, compared with the decline of the Annuals, that frequent fits of publication are more prevalent and popular than yearly paroxysms.

"Under these circumstances, no apology is necessary for the present undertaking; but Custom, which exacts an Overture to a new Opera, and a prologue to a new Play, requires a few words of Introduction to a new Monthly Magazine.

"One prominent object, then, of the projected Publication as implied by the sub-title of 'Comic Miscellany,' will be the supply of harmless 'Mirth for the Million,' and light thoughts, to a Public sorely oppressed—if its word be worth a rush, or its complaints of an ounce weight—by hard times, heavy taxes, and those 'eating cares' which attend on the securing of food for the day as well as a provision for the future. For the relief of such afflicted classes, the Editor, assisted by able Humourists, will dispense a series of papers and woodcuts, which it is hoped will cheer the gloom of Willow Walk, and the loneliness of Wilderness Row—sweeten the bitterness of Camomile Street, and Wormwood Street—smoothe the ruffled temper of Cross Street, and enable even Crooked Lane to unbend itself! It is hardly necessary to promise that this end will be pursued without raising a Maiden Blush, much less a Damask, in the nursery grounds of modesty—or trespassing, by wanton personalities, on the parks and lawns of Private Life. In a word, it will aim at being merry and wise, instead of merry and otherwise.

"For the Sedate there will be papers of a becoming gravity; and the lover of Poetry will be supplied with numbers in each Number.

"As to politics, the Reader of *Hood's Magazine* will vainly search in its pages for a Panacea for Agricultural Distress, or a Grand Catholicon for Irish Agitation; he

Devonshire Lodge, &c. (1844—1845).

will uselessly seek to know whether we ought to depend for our bread on foreign farmers, or merely on foreign sea-fowl; or if the Repeal of the Union would produce low rents, and only three Quarter-days. Neither must he hope to learn the proper Terminus of Reform, nor even whether a Finality Man means Campbell's Last Man or an Undertaker.

"A total abstinence from such stimulating topics and fermented questions is, indeed, ensured by the established character of the Editor, and his notorious aversion to party spirit. To borrow his own words, from a letter to the Proprietors—'I am no Politician, and far from instructed on those topics which, to parody a common phrase, no gentleman's newspaper should be without. Thus, for any knowledge of mine, the Irish Prosecutions may be for pirating the Irish Melodies; the Pennsylvanians may have "repudiated" their wives; Duff Green may be a place, like Goose Green; Prince Polignac a dahlia or a carnation, and the Duc de Bordeaux a tulip. The Spanish affairs I could never master, even with a *Pronouncing* Dictionary at my elbow; it would puzzle me to see whether Queen Isabella's majority is or is not equal to Sir Robert Peel's; or if the shelling the Barcelonese was done with bombs and mortars or the nutcrackers. Prim may be a quaker, and the "whole civil war about the Seville oranges." Nay, even on domestic matters nearer home, my profound political ignorance leaves me in doubt on questions concerning which the newsmen's boys and printers' devils have formed very decided opinions; for example, whether the Corn Law League ought to extend beyond three miles from Mark Lane—or the sliding scale should regulate the charges at the Glaciarium—what shares the Welch whigs have had in the Welch riots, and how far the Ryots in India were excited by the slaughter of the Brahmin Dull. On all such public subjects I am

Thomas Hood :

less *au fait* than that Publicist, the Potboy, at the public house, with the insolvent sign, The Hog in the Pound.' Polemics will be excluded with the same rigour; and especially the Tractarian Schism. The reader of *Hood's Magazine* must not hope, therefore, to be told whether an old Protestant Church ought to be plastered with Roman Cement; or, if a design for a new one should be washed in with Newman's colours. And most egregiously will he be disappointed, should he look for Controversial Theology in our Poet's Corner. He might as well expect to see Queens of Sheba and divided babies, from wearing Solomon's Spectacles.

" For the rest, a critical eye will be kept on our current Literature, a regretful one on the Drama, and a kind one for the Fine Arts, from whose Artesian well there will be an occasional *drawing*.

" With this brief explanatory announcement *Hood's Magazine and Comic Miscellany* is left to recommend itself by its own merits to those enlightened judges, the Reviewers; and to that impartial jury—too vast to pack in any case—the British Public."

Offices for the magazine were taken at 1, Adam Street, Adelphi, and with a notable list of promised contributors the periodical promised to make a good bid for popularity. The contributors who responded to the editor's request to allow him to enrol them under his banner included writers of good standing with the reading public of the time, and others who were yet to win their widest fame. They included Charles Dickens, Robert Browning, Sir E. Bulwer Lytton, R. Monckton Milnes, Samuel Lover, G. P. R. James, William and Mary Howitt, the Hon. Mrs. Norton, " Barry Cornwall," " Peter Priggins " (J. T. Hewlett), "Delta " (D. M. Moir), and Mrs. S. C. Hall. The last named lady wrote, offering to send occasional sketches for the magazine, stipulating to name her own terms, the payment to be " the pleasure she will

374

Devonshire Lodge, &c. (1844—1845).

feel in assisting however humbly, in the success of his periodical : as a tribute of veneration to the author of the Song of the Shirt." Hood accepted the offer of contributions, "but it must be on more equitable terms than those you have so liberally proposed."

With all this promised array of helpers, the editor realised that with his name on the forefront of the magazine he would be expected to supply a goodly quantity of his own peculiar work, and of the opening number he wrote more than half—nearly sixty pages being from his own pen—including " The Haunted House,"[1] which was accompanied by an engraving from a picture by Thomas Creswick. To be " out of the bustle of moving," as his wife put it, Hood stayed in the Adelphi; and thence on the 1st of January, when his first number was newly out, he wrote a letter to one of the contributors, Samuel Phillips, who had just lost his wife. In this letter we see something of the faith and philosophy of the writer who, having won through many troubles, was to have but breathing space before being plunged into fresh ones.

" I cannot tell you how much your letter shocked and grieved me; for being strictly a domestic man myself, finding my comfort for many evils in the bosom of my family, I can the better imagine and sympathise with such a bereavement.

" The only comfort I can offer to you, is the one which I have found most consolatory under the loss of dear relatives, the belief that we do not love in vain ; that so surely as we must live, having lived, so must we love, having loved ; and that after some term, longer or shorter, but a mere vibration of the great pendulum of eternity, we shall all be reunited. In the meantime let us *endure* as bravely as we can for the sake of others.

[1] " The Haunted House" and "Eugene Aram" were both translated into Latin by the Rev. G. P. A. Longmore.

Thomas Hood :

. . . . I would earnestly recommend you, from my own experience, to resume your pen. I have had my share of the troubles of this world, as well as of the calamities of authors, and have found it to be a very great blessing to be able to carry my thoughts into the ideal, from the too strong real."

Of the first number of the magazine 1,500 copies were sold—*then* considered a remarkable sale for the first issue of a new venture—but before January was out the trouble had begun. The man with whom Hood had entered into a sort of partnership was a man of no means. When the February number was printing there was a quarrel with the printers about payment. Another printer undertook the work early in February, and could not manage, so that yet another had to be got, and he, engaged on February 12, had to buy the necessary type, so that he could not start setting up until the 16th, and " this in the shortest month of the year." The worry and anxiety was such that Hood was laid up and the magazine was late in getting out, but still the report was that it was " doing well." Hood seems to have entered into partnership without any business-like enquiries as to the financial standing of his partner, and had already to look around for some one else to join him in the enterprise. Writing to tell her sympathetic friends the Elliots of the posture of affairs, Jane Hood added : " Hood dines to-day at Dr. [Sir John] Bowring's, in Queen's Square. He knew him well years ago on the *London Magazine ;* and he wrote a few days ago to ask Hood to meet Bright and Cobden on business. *I* think to engage him to write songs for the League. I augur good from it. This comes of the ' Song of the Shirt,' of which we hear something continually."

Of the dinner at Bowring's, the meeting with Cobden and Bright, there is, unfortunately, no record. " The

Devonshire Lodge, &c. (1844—1845).

League " was, of course, the Anti-Corn Law League, but there is nothing to show that Hood was ever asked to undertake the work that his wife suggested.

Knowledge of the trouble about the magazine soon got abroad. Writing early in the year, John Blackwood, the Edinburgh publisher, said:—

" I dined on Friday last with Phillips. Thomas Hood was there, a very quiet fellow, evidently in the most miserable health. He is in a dreadful fix with the man who is associated with him in the unhappy magazine, so I daresay it will speedily come to a close. He has applied to Phillips to arbitrate. P. says the other fellow deluded Hood with the notion that he had money ; it turns out that he had only £100, which he has never produced, and grabbed the money received at the office as it came in. Do not say anything about this.

" Phillips himself is the most extraordinary character. I begin to think he is the Wandering Jew. You cannot name any human being but he knows all about him or has had something to do with him." [1]

In May came a serious breakdown of health, consequent no doubt in great part on the troubles attendant upon the magazine. On the 22nd, Jane Hood wrote that on the previous night he had had to give up any hope of getting the magazine out at all, and, as she put it, it really seemed quite a sin to let what might be so good fall to the ground. It was too late to get a publisher to undertake the publication and leave Hood to contribute while keeping his name on it and leaving the more active work of editing to an assistant. He kept up as long as possible, and when the decision was finally come to, his wife wrote, " Last night he fretted dreadfully, and, at one this morning, was seized so

---

[1] " William Blackwood and His Sons," by Mrs. Oliphant, in which is no mention of the fact that Hood had been a contributor to *Blackwood's Magazine.*

Thomas Hood :

suddenly with short breathing, and fullness of the chest, I thought he could not live. . . . . What can be done to relieve his poor mind, which feels cruelly this failure of a work he has laboured at night and day, and which would have been a good property if carried on."

Poor Mrs. Hood! Added to their common anxieties, she had the additional one of a husband calling for constant nursing, and the change from the time of hopefulness must have been a great blow. The next day was Hood's forty-fifth birthday, and on the day after Dr. Robert Elliot was giving a party at which the Hoods had hoped to be present, instead of which came a note from the patient ending: " A pleasant party to you. To-day is my birthday—forty-five—but I can't tell you how old I *feel;* enough to be your grandfather at least, and give *you* advice! viz., don't over-polka yourself.

> " 'Whatever Doctor Robert's skill be worth,
>   One hope within me still is stout and hearty,
> He would not *kill* me till the 24th,
>   For fear of my *appearing* at his party!' "

The writing of this letter—in bed—was followed by attempts to do some sketches and writing—the spirit was ever willing even when the flesh was at its weakest —but the effort was too much for his strength and was followed by the wandering delirium of nervous exhaustion. " Next morning his medical attendants declared that the repetition of any such attempt, at that critical period of his illness might cost him his life."

The magazine was not, however, dropped. F. O. Ward, one of the contributors, " installed himself as unpaid sub-editor " and got the June number out with a note explaining the critical condition of the editor.

Devonshire Lodge, &c. (1844—1845).

Dickens, Browning,[1] Landor—great names all—came to the help of the magazine. The first named contributed his " Threatening Letter to Thomas Hood, from an Ancient Gentleman." In the same number (that for May) appeared Hood's " Bridge of Sighs " to appeal to the public sympathies with a forcefulness second only to that of the " Song of the Shirt " of a few months earlier. It has been declared that "in all the wide range of the poetry of our own country, and of all other countries, there is nothing more profoundly pathetic" than these lines on the poor suicide, which have taken their place among our familiar quotations. Browning hailed the poem as "alone in its generation." A reference in Dickens's " Threatening Letter " to a young woman who, "though she was in full work (making shirts at three halfpence apiece)," having been robbed of her earnings, attempted to drown herself and her child, and being herself rescued, was promptly tried and sentenced to death, evidently moved Hood to the writing of another "part" to the poem, in which should be told the story of the mother who threw her illegitimate child into the river and was then "legitimately" done to death; among his papers after his death were found these fragments, entitled " Bridge of Sighs.—Part II." :—

> " Weary with troubles
> The Death must deliver
> Once more life bubbles
> Away in the river—

> .   .   .   .   .

---

[1] Joseph Arnould wrote to Alfred Domett : " Do you remember F. O. Ward ? He is now sub-editor of *Hood's Magazine*, and in this capacity has acted well in wrenching from our Robert [Browning] several little morceaux, sketches by a master, which have appeared in said magazine, and being more exoteric than even his *sketches* generally are, may do him some further service with the public."

Thomas Hood :

"The moon in the river shone
And the stars some six or seven—
Poor child of sin, to throw it therein
Seemed sending it to Heaven.

.   .   .   .

"Cover her, cover her,
Throw the earth over her—
Victim of murder inhumanly done;
With gravel and sod—
Hide—hide her from God,
And the light of the sun!"

With Thackeray, as well as with Charles Dickens and Douglas Jerrold, Hood appears to have been on terms of cordial friendship during these closing years when he had taken his position in London among the literary figures of the time. The only scrap of correspondence between them is the following short note written on August 4 [1844] :—

"MY DEAR THACKERAY,—I am grieved to hear of your ill-health, and sincerely trust that before many days intervene you will have thoroughly recovered. I fear that so far as I myself am concerned King Death will claim me ere many months elapse. However, there's a good time coming, if not in this world, most assuredly in the next. Always yours,

"THOS. HOOD."

Having recovered somewhat from his illness in the summer of this year, Hood went for change of air to Blackheath, where he stayed at Vanbrugh House for a couple of months, to return much better than had been hoped. There was already, it would seem, a movement on foot to get him a pension on the Civil List, for in a note to Elliot appointing a meeting at Greenwich—"I was going to say amongst the other Pensioners, but as yet I only know the pen part of it"—he adds

Devonshire Lodge, &c. (1844—1845).

that he is getting to work again. "I have had a little more spinning material in me, the last few days, and have nearly done three chapters[1]; but you needn't tell Sir Robert." Sir Robert was, of course, Sir Robert Peel. Returning to Devonshire Lodge in September, one of the first things Hood had to do was to write to one of his new friends, Samuel Phillips, who had recently become tutor to a nobleman's son, and who had had a fall when out riding.

"MY DEAR PHILLIPS,—What the devil do you mean? Have you no concern for the nerves of editors—the nourishment of magazine readers? It may be horse-play to you, but death to us. What business had you in the saddle at all? Have I not said in print, that sedentary persons never have a good seat? Is it not notorious that authors from Coleridge down to Poole are bad riders? And you must go proving it again by being run away with; not by vanity, in a very writer-like way, but by the brute quadruped, never well pick-a-backed by seamen and the literati. Do you want a hole in your head as well as in your lungs?[2] And are you not contented with the *Neck*, crying 'lost, lost,' but you must break your own? Is your head no better than a common pumpkin, that you must go pitching on it, and grazing the 'dome of thought and palace of the soul?' I think I see you getting up—not content with expectorating blood—spitting mud! And, plague take you, all through trotting on an earthly roadster, when you might have been soaring so celestially on Pegasus, after his feed of 'husk and grain.' Do you really expect, though you die of riding, that you will get an equestrian statue for it at Trafalgar Square, Cockspur Street, or in front of the new Exchange? Not a bronze

---

[1] Of his unfinished story, "Our Family."
[2] Phillips died of consumption in 1854, aged 40.

Thomas Hood :

poney! Nor will you get a shilling a sheet the more
from *Hood's* or *Blackwood's*, no, nor from any of
the *Sporting Magazines*, for going at a gate without
hounds or fox! And a father too, with a baby and a
boy, and a young lord to bring up! And a friend, with
such friends as a Blair, a Salomans, and a Hood, and
all the Pratts, to expose himself to be kicked out of
such society by a hoof. Oh! Philippus, you deserve a
Philippic—and here it is! Seriously, I am glad you
escaped, and hope 'you will not do so any more.' If
you must run risks, do it as I do, on two legs, and at a
walk—for such invalids, a damp clothes-horse is danger
enough—or if you *must* go pick-a-back, get acquainted
with some sheriff that can lend you a quiet nag.

"I am come back here from Vanbrugh House for
good—much better; and have resumed the driving of
the Magazine. I am sorry to have had the last of the
'Sea-side Lore': but your beautiful poem was some
consolation. It has been much admired by my friends.
Don't get too proud with your Marchionesses for the
muses. My bust is modelled and cast. It is said to
be a correct likeness: two parts Methodist, to one of
Humourist, and quite recognisable in spite of the Hood
all over the face.

"To-morrow I take a trip to Calais, for a day only,
with Fanny, for the sake of the voyage and sea air.
We are a brace in need of bracing, as you know. If
I can catch a sea-horse, I will, for you to ride in the
Race of Portland. Ward accompanies to edit the
main sheet, and return the whole Packet if unsuitable. I only hope he won't be sick without 'Notice
to Correspondents.'

"Pray for us, and for peace, for if a war breaks out
while we are there, the Magazine will be as bad as
blown up, and I might as well be cased *full*-length in
plaster of Paris.

Devonshire Lodge, &c. (1844—1845).

" By the bye, have you read the ' Mysteries of Paris'?
Very bad! Or the 'Amber Witch,' which is very good?
Or do you read nothing but Burke and Debrett to the
young Peerage? Do you like my novel? or do you
prefer 'Rookwood' for the sake of the ride to York?
—— advertises 'Revelations of London,' in imitation
of the Parisian mysteries, of course! Won't they be
very full of the slang of the Rookery? The mere idea
gives me the *Back-Slumbago!*

" Write soon, and tell me how you like your new
position, and how you live. Aristocratically enough I
guess, and spitting nothing under high blood. Your
stomach a mere game bag, or pot for the preserves, eh?
And some fine day you will come and triumph over us
with your corpulence, and ' Phillips me like a three-man
beadle.' For you drink the choicest of wines of course
—your smallest beer old double X ale. What a change
for an author! And then you lie I warrant in a down
bed, with such sheets! every one equal to forty-eight
pages of superfine cambric, margined with lace and
hot-pressed with a silver warming-pan! Nevertheless
come some day and see us—some day when you
are ordered to live very low, and then perhaps our
best holiday diet may be good enough for you. We
are very poor and have only seventy-two thousand
a-year (pence mind, not pounds), and our names not
even in the Post-office Directory, much less the Court
Guide!

" Well, if it isn't too great a liberty, God bless you!
Mrs. Hood hopes you will forgive her offering her
kind regards; and Fanny and Tom presume to join
in the same. And if you would condescend to present
my kind regards and respects to Mr. Salomans, it
would exceedingly oblige, dear Phillips, yours very
truly, and hoping no offence,
                                        " THOS. HOOD."

Thomas Hood :

The bust which had been modelled was that by Edward Davis. In it we see the face as Procter described it—"a quiet face, the laughter lying hid behind the gravity."

In September came an invitation to Hood to attend a soirée at the Manchester Athenæum, at which Benjamin Disraeli was to preside, but he had to write, "For me all long journeys are over save one," and that, as for Mr. Disraeli, he might as well hope for an introduction to Ben Ledi or Ben Nevis! The trip to Calais with Fanny and Ward mentioned in the letter to Phillips had shown that he was barely equal to water-carriage. Again he expressed the delight to be found in the companionship of books—"Forbidden to walk, there is the run of the library"—and offered healthy advice which was, no doubt, duly read to the members of the Manchester Athenæum :—

"As age and accidents to the human machinery will impair the strongest horse-power of health, whilst the fairest mercantile endeavour may fail to secure a fortune, I would earnestly forewarn all persons within reach of my counsel—especially the young—to provide against such contingencies by the timely cultivation and enrichment of that divine allotment, which it depends on ourselves to render a flower-garden or a dead waste— a pleasure-ground visited by the Graces and frequented by the Fairies, or a wilderness haunted by Satyrs."

Again came a period of serious illness, the poor worn body lying for three weeks in extreme danger, the three doctors—"three doctors could not kill me"—in attendance almost giving him over. The clay soil of the neighbourhood in which he was living was thought to be bad, and the very pretty house which they had taken for three years was to be given up, if a sub-tenant could be found, and the family move into London lodgings once more, to be nearer Dr. Elliot, who journeyed daily ten miles to see his friend. To a letter of Jane Hood's telling De Franck the news her husband added a postscript in his indomitably cheerful fashion, saying that he had almost gone "a-fishing in Lethe for forgotten fishes." To Bulwer Lytton, thanking him for a contribution to the November number of the magazine, Hood said that though ordered not to work he was compelled to do so, "and so it will be to the end. I must 'die in harness,' like a hero—or a horse." In that number of the magazine appeared the editor's "Lay of the Labourer," another of those powerful poems of social reform which mark his closing years. In the spring of 1844 a young Huntingdon labourer of eighteen was tried for sending a letter threatening incendiarism on the local farmers if he could not get work. He pleaded guilty, was convicted and sentenced to—transportation for life! A newspaper cutting containing the record of this case Hood put in a prominent position on his study mantelpiece, and the subject, to which he would recur again and again, seemed literally to haunt him. At length he wrote the "Lay" and set it in a stirring prose appeal on behalf of the Starving Unemployed, an appeal more cogent if less rhetorical than his poems, and concluded by directly asking the Home Secretary to inquire into the case of Gifford White, and saying that if the appeal should meet with any success it would be one of the dearest deeds of the writer's pen. A marked copy of the magazine was at once sent to the Home Secretary; the poet had relieved his heart, appeased his conscience and absolved his soul, and all the effect, so far as the Minister was concerned, was the writing of the following note:—

"Sir James Graham presents his compliments to Mr. Hood, and begs to acknowledge the Magazine accompanying his letter of the 30th instant."

Thomas Hood :

Though Hood had written whole-heartedly on the subject, he scarcely hoped to make any impression on the Minister, for, as he said in referring to this formal acknowledgment, " I fear he will do no more; they say he is a cold, hard man, bigoted to the New Poor Law." A few days later, from another Government Department, came a semi-official notice desiring that he should name a female relative on whom Her Majesty might be recommended to confer a pension. He responded by naming his wife and at the same time wrote privately to the Prime Minister, Sir Robert Peel, to the following effect :—

"November, 1844.

" SIR,—In your comparative leisure at Brighton, if a Prime Minister has even *comparative* leisure, you may find time to accept and taste the grateful acknowledgments of one whom you have served from motives rarely attributed to such Patrons.

"Complaints have been often made of the neglect of literature and literary men by the State and its ministers. I have joined in them myself, but with reference to authors in general—I am quite aware of my own unfitness for any of those posts alluded to by Mr. Smythe in his speech, especially for those official employments, which, if I had any ambition that way, I should be physically unable to fulfil. Almost too thin to represent myself, I should make a very indifferent ambassador, consul, or attaché. You may therefore rely, Sir, on my entertaining no such gratitude for ' favours to come.'

" Such impressions have occasionally received confirmation from unlucky oversights, such as I suppose to have caused the omission of ' Literature ' from the Queen's answer to the Civic address, in which it was inserted. An unlucky omission I presume to say ; for whatever differences may obtain in society, that will

386

Devonshire Lodge, &c. (1844—1845).

be an unlucky one, which distinguishes a Sovereign from a reading public, rapidly becoming a reading people.

"As an Author I cannot but think it a good omen for the cause, that this mark of your favour has fallen on a writer so totally unconnected with party politics as myself, whose favourite theory of Government is, 'An Angel from Heaven, and a Despotism.'

"As a Man, I am deeply sensible of a consideration and kindness, which have made this 'work-a-day' world more park-like to me, as well as to the people of Manchester, and will render the poor remnant of my life much happier, and easier, than it could be with the prospect that was before me.

"My humble name has sufficiently occupied your thoughts already, yet may it, with its pleasanter associations recur to you, whenever you meet with a discontented partisan, or a political ingrate!

"Lord F. Egerton having kindly offered to convey my acceptance and choice to you, I have forwarded them, but could not resist the direct expression of my sentiments as to a '*Premier pas*' which, instead of 'costing,' enriches me.

"I have the honour to be, &c., &c.,
"THOMAS HOOD."

Sir Robert Peel's reply, including as it does a warm appreciation of Hood's literary work, may fittingly be given as showing that the Prime Minister had personal knowledge of the services to literature rendered by the man whom he was aiding.

"BRIGHTON, *November 10th*, 1844.

"SIR,—I am more than repaid by the personal satisfaction, which I have had in doing that, for which you return me warm and characteristic acknowledgments.

"You perhaps think that you are known to one, with

Thomas Hood :

such multifarious occupations as myself, merely by general reputation as an author; but I assure you that there can be little, which you have written and acknowledged, which I have not read; and that there are few, who can appreciate and admire more than myself, the good sense and good feeling, which have taught you to infuse so much fun and merriment into writings correcting folly, and exposing absurdities, and yet never trespassing beyond those limits, within which wit and facetiousness are not very often confined. You may write on with the consciousness of independence, as free and unfettered, as if no communication had ever passed between us. I am not conferring a private obligation upon you, but am fulfilling the intentions of the Legislature, which has placed at the disposal of the Crown a certain sum (miserable, indeed, in amount) to be applied to the recognition of public claims on the Bounty of the Crown. If you will review the names of those, whose claims have been admitted on account of their literary or scientific eminence, you will find an ample confirmation of the truth of my statement.

" One return, indeed, I shall ask of you,—that you will give me the opportunity of making your personal acquaintance.

" Believe me to be, faithfully yours,
" ROBERT PEEL."

Six days later, on returning to Whitehall, Peel sent an official communication by special messenger saying that the Queen had approved of his proposal that a pension of one hundred pounds per annum should be granted to Mrs. Hood for her life, the grant to take effect from the preceding June. Hood at once announced the news to his unfailing friend, Dr. Elliot, and also recorded that "The Lay of the Labourer" had made a great hit and was going through most of the papers like " The Song of the

Devonshire Lodge, &c. (1844—1845).

Shirt," and added that though he had again been unwell, " my well is not yet dry. I have pumped out a sheet already of Christmas fun, am drawing some cuts, and shall write a sheet more of my novel." Acknowledging Peel's letter, Hood said :—

" I am so inexperienced a pensioner (unlike the father of a friend of mine, who was made in his infancy a superannuated postman), as to be quite ignorant of the etiquette of such cases; but, in the absence of know-ledge, I *feel* that it would be quite proper to thank the Queen for her gracious approval. May I request of your goodness, at a fit opportunity, to lay my humble and grateful acknowledgments at Her Majesty's feet, with the respectful assurance, that a man, who has lived, conscious of his good name being the better part of his children's inheritance, will never disgrace the royal favour.

"Your letter of the 10th inst., which is deposited amongst my literary heir-looms, I hesitated to answer, partly because it gave rise to feelings, which would keep without congealing, and partly from knowing editorially, the oppression of too many ' Communica-tions from Correspondents.' But I may say here how extremely flattered I am by your liberal praise and handsome judgment of my writings; nearly all of which you must have seen, if you have read the acknowledged ones. The anonymous only comprise a few trifles and reviews; and even against these as a set-off, I have had my name affixed to some pieces I had not written; for example, a poem on the Sale of the Stud of the late King William." [1]

Though he was at this time much bedridden, there were efforts that he *must* make, as he put it, and so he

[1] These verses, which appeared in the *Torch*, September 9, 1837, with a disclaimer a fortnight later, have occasionally, but of course wrongly, been reprinted as Hood's.

Thomas Hood :

went on working for the magazine, though the fact that the fun had to be "pumped out" shows that it was only indomitable will that was keeping him at work, but it was will so compelling that the readers of his monthly budget could not have realised that much of it was written on a sick-bed. Before Christmas, 1844, he may be said to have taken to his bed finally. Occasionally afterwards he would sit propped up in an easy-chair, and on Christmas Day, for the sake of the children more than for his own, as his daughter pathetically recorded, he allowed himself to be moved for a few hours into the room next to his bedroom, "but it was a painful mockery of enjoyment." His wife, her nerves sadly tried by long-continued nursing, feared that he was in great danger before the close of the year, but again he rallied and wrote further for the magazine.

Long aware that his hold on life was but slight, early in 1845 he realised that a few weeks, at the most months, must see the end; though he had several times, as he put it, "been so near Death's door that he could almost fancy he heard the creaking of the hinges," he knew now that there could be no lasting rally. With characteristic thoughtfulness and courage he wrote a few touchingly simple farewells, sending copies of his portrait to several of his friends, of which but one or two appear to have been kept.

To Bryan Waller Procter, one of the first friends he had made on joining the *London Magazine* nearly a quarter of a century before, he wrote :—

"DEAR PROCTER,—I feel so *sure* that you do not know of my state, or you would come and see me, that I do not hesitate to ask it. I have been three months in bed, and am given over; but, as I have never been quite alive for some years, was quite prepared for such a verdict.

Devonshire Lodge, &c. (1844—1845).

"As one of my earliest literary friends, come and say good-bye to yours, ever truly,

"THOMAS HOOD."

To Dr. Moir, the "Delta" of *Blackwood's Magazine*, whom he had met during his second visit to Scotland, he wrote:—

"DEAR MOIR,—God bless you and yours, and good-by! I drop these few lines, as in a bottle from a ship water-logged, and on the brink of foundering, being in the last stage of dropsical debility; but though suffering in body, serene in mind. So without reversing my union-jack, I await my last lurch. Till which, believe me, dear Moir, yours most truly,

"THOMAS HOOD."

Another of these letters was addressed to the statesman who had lessened the anxiety of his closing days by assuring some provision for his wife and children. The letter is in Jane Hood's handwriting, signed by her husband:—

"DEVONSHIRE LODGE, NEW FINCHLEY ROAD.

"DEAR SIR,—We are not to meet in the flesh. Given over by my physicians and by myself, I am only kept alive by frequent instalments of mulled port wine. In this extremity I feel a comfort, for which I cannot refrain from again thanking you, with all the sincerity of a dying man,—and, at the same time, bidding you a respectful farewell.

"Thank God my mind is composed and my reason undisturbed, but my race as an author is run. My physical debility finds no tonic virtue in a steel pen, otherwise I would have written one more paper—a forewarning one—against an evil, or the danger of it, arising from a literary movement in which I have had

Thomas Hood :

some share, a one-sided humanity, opposite to that Catholic Shaksperian sympathy, which felt with King as well as Peasant, and duly estimated the mortal temptations of both stations.[1] Certain classes at the poles of Society are already too far asunder; it should be the duty of our writers to draw them nearer by kindly attraction, not to aggravate the existing repulsion, and place a wider moral gulf between Rich and Poor, with Hate on the one side and Fear on the other. But I am too weak for this task, the last I had set myself; it is death that stops my pen, you see, and not the pension.

"God bless you, Sir, and prosper all your measures for the benefit of my beloved country. I have the honour to be, Sir, your most grateful and obedient servant,

"THOMAS HOOD."

To his Dundee relatives he wrote on March 12th:—

"MY DEAR UNCLE AND AUNT,—With this you will receive a magazine with the portrait of me which I promised.

"I little thought to have been alive at this date— but some strong point in my constitution has made a desperate struggle to recover, though in vain. I am now helpless in bed, dreadfully swollen by dropsy from weakness, and have suffered very much:—but only

---

[1] Writing to Dilke in 1838, Hood had made one of his rare references to his political views. After referring to Rowland Hill's postage scheme and the use of franks by rich men, he went on: "But I'm a low-lived, ungenteel, villainous, blackguard Radical. There is a deep stigma on the Have-nots trying to take from the Have-some-things, but what ought to be the stigma on the have-every-things trying to take from the Have-nothings? Chorley has proclaimed me a 'Liberal'; I don't mind being called at once a Moderate Republican."

Devonshire Lodge, &c. (1844—1845).

bodily—for my mind has been calm and resigned, as Mr. Nicholson would inform you. I was glad he came, on that account, for I have been a good deal pestered by Betsy,[1] who, you know, has some peculiar religious notions of her own, and would very likely describe me to you, as dying a pagan, or infidel, because I do not conform to her views.

"God bless you both—we shall soon meet I hope in a better world.

"Let it comfort you to know that I die beloved and respected and have met with unexpected kindness and distinction from very many strangers as well as friends. These are probably the last lines I shall write. Your affectionate nephew,

"THOMAS HOOD.

"24th. Still alive—but cannot last long. God bless you and again a last farewell.—T. H."

This was probably the last letter he ever wrote though he lingered on for some weeks.

F. O. Ward, who had self-sacrificingly undertaken the work connected with the monthly production of the magazine, wrote: "He saw the oncoming of death with great cheerfulness, though without anything approaching to levity; and last night when his friends, Harvey and another, came, he bade them come up, had wine brought, and made us all drink a glass with him 'that he might know us for friends as of old, and not undertakers.' He conversed for about an hour in his old playful way, with now and then a word or two full of

---

[1] Elizabeth Hood was one of those obtrusively pious persons whose actions cannot but jar on those who possess their religion less demonstratively ; she sought to influence her brother's household by furtively leaving prayer-books and tracts under the sofa cushions, etc. Hood said that she was so pious that every time she sat down she hatched out a prayer-book.

Thomas Hood :

deep and tender feeling. When I left he bade me good-
bye, and kissed me, shedding tears, and saying that perhaps
we never should meet again." In the magazine for March
the critical state of the Editor's health was referred to,
and the April number announced his approaching death.
From friends and strangers came offers of help of all
kinds; an anonymous correspondent sent a bank-note
for twenty pounds, with a slip of paper inscribed—
" A Shirt! and a sincere wish for health." Another
anonymous writer sent touching verses " To T. Hood,
on Hearing of His Sickness," beginning—

> " Were I in Heaven my song would be of mirth
> When wings like thine are upward spread to fly;
> But ah! my brother, would upon the earth,
> Hearts good and true might beat eternally! "

All these testimonies of friendship and popularity
touched the dying man very deeply. He enjoyed as
much of the beautiful spring as could be seen from his
bedroom window, from the violets and other flowers
which he loved and which were sent by country
admirers, and speaking of it, said in one of his last
recorded utterances : " It's a beautiful world, and since
I have been lying here, I have thought of it more and
more; it is not so bad, even humanly speaking, as
people would make it out. I have had some very happy
days while I lived in it, and I *could* have wished to stay
a little longer. But it is all for the best, and we shall
all meet in a better world! "

The whole story of his lingering death showed the
true nature of the man, the sincere devotion which had
informed his outspoken attacks on cant and humbug,
and the fact that he was essentially a religious man,
though always impatient of ostentatious religion and
lip-service. During the many weeks that he lay dying
he was generally clear in mind, calm and collected in

Devonshire Lodge, &c. (1844—1845).

intellect, expressing his wishes and hopes with quiet tranquillity. On one occasion, in half delirium, his watching family heard him repeating the words of the pathetic song—poignantly pathetic to the listening wife —"I'm fading awa', Jean." On May 1st, knowing himself to be dying, he called his family round him —the patient, loving wife of twenty years, the daughter of fifteen, and the son of ten—and spoke tender words to all, then added " Remember, Jane, I forgive all, *all*, as I hope to be forgiven." Shortly after he sank into apparent slumber, and after remaining apparently unconscious for about thirty-six hours, passed peacefully away at noon on Saturday, May 3rd.

On his death-bed he wrote stanzas which beautifully express his faith in a hereafter, the swan-song of a suffering man possessed of unconquerable optimism :—

> "Farewell, Life ! My senses swim ;
> And the world is growing dim ;
> Thronging shadows cloud the light,
> Like the advent of the night,—
> Colder, colder, colder still
> Upward steals a vapour chill—
> Strong the earthy odour grows—
> I smell the Mould above the Rose !

> "Welcome, Life ! the Spirit strives !
> Strength returns, and hope revives ;
> Cloudy fears and shapes forlorn
> Fly like shadows at the morn,—
> O'er the earth there comes a bloom—
> Sunny light for sullen gloom,
> Warm perfume for vapour cold—
> I smell the Rose above the Mould ! "

It had been a long and severe battle with ill-health during Hood's later years, but he had borne himself manfully throughout, had worked at his appointed calling as long as the hand could guide the pen, had written

Thomas Hood :

not a line which dying he could wish to recall, and
though misunderstood and misinterpreted by those who
had moved his indignation, had worked ever for the
amelioration of the condition of the suffering, for
sympathy with those unhappily situated, and for the
increase of that healthful laughter which, as another
wit had put it, enlivens the days of man's pilgrimage
and charms his pained steps over the burning marl.

There was some talk, his daughter has recorded, of the
burial of Thomas Hood in the Poets' Corner of Westminster Abbey, but the idea, if seriously entertained,
was soon abandoned, and the funeral took place on
May 10th at Kensal Green Cemetery.

Poor Jane Hood—that "pleasant and very lovable
woman," as Procter describes her—after her long and
anxious time, was left with the value of her husband's
copyrights and her civil list pension, with some debts
to clear off and two children to bring up. Her own
health was sadly broken, and within a fortnight of her
husband's death she learned that her mother was in a
serious state from which she was little likely to recover.
Six months later Mrs. George Reynolds was again
seriously ill, and Jane Hood and John Hamilton
Reynolds met and were reconciled at their mother's
bedside, after a quarrel of some years' standing, the
occasion of which is not known. Again the old lady
rallied, and Jane Hood was to pre-decease her mother,
dying in November, 1846, eighteen months after her
loved husband. Mrs. Reynolds died in May, 1848, and
her husband on July 29, 1853, aged 88.

.   .   .   .   .

After Hood's death a number of his friends and
admirers banded together to get up a public subscription to ensure the comfort of those he left. Thomas
Reseigh, one of his later friends, confidential clerk to

THE THOMAS HOOD MEMORIAL, KENSAL GREEN CEMETERY.

[To face p. 396.

Devonshire Lodge, &c. (1844—1845).

a city firm of solicitors, took much of the active work on his shoulders, and with F. O. Ward and Samuel Phillips, and a committee representing the literary men of the day, started a Hood Memorial Fund. In Hood's own desk, which was given to Reseigh, that gentleman kept all the documents concerning the Fund. That desk and those papers have come into my possession, and from them we learn that the amount realised was £1,386 15s. 6d., representing sums from all sorts and conditions of men and women. The full list of the subscribers shows amounts ranging from the half-crown sent by "A Few Journeymen Tailors" to the fifty pounds contributed by Sir Robert Peel. One correspondent wrote with his remittance a reminiscence of the poet's own jest, that he had to be a lively Hood to earn a livelihood :—

> "To cheer the widow's heart in her distress,
> To make provision for the fatherless,
> Is but a Christian's duty—and none should
> Resist the heart appeal of *Widow Hood.*"

The many letters connected with the Fund show that Thomas Carlyle, Richard Monckton Milnes (afterwards Lord Houghton), Charles Cowden Clarke, John Britton, William Harvey and others interested themselves in the matter. A Mr. Joseph Ellis, while objecting to be on the committee, wrote a letter which is interesting as an unliterary contemporary appreciation of Hood :—

"SIR,—When I received your letter on the subject of the Hood Committee I had only time to request a friend to call on Mr. Ward and withdraw my name. I now trouble you because I would not willingly be misunderstood by one who has so high a feeling in common with me as love for Thomas Hood. I have no leisure, and therefore no power, in such a cause; hence to permit my name on the committee would have

Thomas Hood :

been to indulge something like vanity where all should be sincerity. You will oblige me by handing my mite (enclosed) to Mr. Ward, and by entering the same 'Joseph Ellis.'

" From schooldays I have been a thoughtful admirer of Hood's writings, and it was an early (abiding) hope to be one day in a situation to know that man. Hood has always appeared to me a remarkable example of the evenly balanced, perfect intellect. In his mental constitution there was nothing of what is called 'idiosyncrasy of talent.' The common acceptation was that he had 'a turn for the humorous,' but it was the perfection of the perceptive faculty which enabled him to see humour in all things human. Else we should not have found that subtle pathos (often how deep!) in what seemed fun. Although himself so sadly subject to 'the ills which flesh is heir to,' he never could believe in the reality of pain and trouble. These were to him the defects of a high nature, shadows on a bright surface, spots on the sun. He was an intellectual entity, a great psychological fact—soul with a body rather than body with a soul. This is why those who were not with him 'in the body' can hardly believe him dead—the portion of him which could die was so insignificant! His wit was the exemplar of all examples. The caustic and burr-like property of a Rabelais, the dry humour of a Bayle or a Voltaire, the broad farce of a Butler, the touching tone and smile of a Sterne, the ringing meaning laugh of Lear's 'poor fool,' yet imitating none. He saw comparatives where other men perceived only positives—the type of the small in the great, of the jocular in the grave. Thus he was sometimes a punster, not because he wished to pun but because he could not escape from the coincidences of words and things. This came from the perfection (humanly speaking) of his intellect, which

398

often permitted him to see 'consequences yet dormant in their principles and effects yet unborn in the womb of their causes.' I will not apologise to you for thus allowing myself to dwell on the uncommon gifts of your lost friend. Such were my opinions of him.—I am, with respect, Sir, your obedient servant,

"JOSEPH ELLIS.

"BRIGHTON, *May* 28, 1845."

Carlyle, whose personal nature and literary genius were far removed from those of Thomas Hood, wrote:—

"CHELSEA, *May* 30, 1845.

"DEAR SIR,—I am unfortunately still far too busy to be of the smallest help on your committee, but if you think my name can be of any service to you at all, there can be no objection to your using it (with this understanding) for so entirely laudable a purpose.—Yours very truly,

"T. CARLYLE."

The promoters of the Fund did not apparently raise as large an amount as they had hoped, and when Dickens was consulted as to whether the subscription list should be closed, he took a very sensible view of the position in a letter to F. O. Ward:—

"DEVONSHIRE TERRACE, *August* 14, 1845.

"DEAR SIR,—My impression decidedly is that all that can be done has been done in the matter of Mrs. Hood's Subscription. The appeal, as a general claim on public sympathy, is greatly weakened by the existence of the pension, and I do not think more money is to be got.

"In the case of the Elton Fund we received two

thousand three or four hundred pounds. But it was a very peculiar case. There were six children—all females, and without a mother. It was a particularly distressing accident in which Elton lost his life, and one to which public attention was very strongly attracted. Moreover, the managers of theatres and actors in theatres had a lively interest in the catastrophe and the endeavour to mitigate the severity of its pressure on the unfortunate children; and free benefits were had in diverse parts of the kingdom, from which a good deal of the money came.

"Such practical knowledge as I have of these matters leads me distinctly to the conclusion that it is not advisable to press Mrs. Hood's appeal to any greater extent. I think it would be useless to her, and would be tortured into an unpleasant association with the memory of our deceased friend. I express this merely as my individual opinion, of course, and not expecting you to attach any greater weight to it than as it may seem to you on consideration to be reasonable and well founded. My estimate of the great genius of poor Hood is as high as it is possible for man to form, and always has been, consequently I set her case on very lofty grounds indeed. But in turning the question in my mind I separate myself, or you, from the crowd who are addressed. Faithfully yours,

"CHARLES DICKENS."

When Jane Hood died, so soon after her husband, their children would have been in a poor position had it not been for the Fund, for the pension lapsed. It was, however, renewed for £50 in their interest. Many of the documents in Hood's desk are connected with the education and upbringing of his children. Fanny Hood, in 1849, married the Rev. John S. Broderip, and died in 1878; and Tom Hood after being educated at University College, London, and Pembroke College, Oxford, was for a time in the War Office before taking wholly to a literary life. He was the author of many amusing stories and verses, and edited *Fun* for some years. He died in 1874. As he is frequently confused with his father through being referred to as Thomas Hood, and his father confused with him by being referred to as Tom Hood, the following postscript from a letter of his in the MS. Department of the British Museum may be quoted: " My name, given at christening, is Tom, though as a beginner I could never get publishers to let me use it for obvious reasons. It luckily aids in distinguishing everything I write as my father *always* signed Thomas." In the British Museum Catalogue, the " Dictionary of National Biography," and elsewhere he is erroneously styled Thomas Hood the Younger.

    .   .   .   .   .

Seven years after the death of Thomas Hood—just about the time that John Hamilton Reynolds died in the Isle of Wight—a movement was started to place a fitting memorial over his burial place. Many prominent writers joined, though Dickens protested against anything other than " a simple and plain record over the remains of a great writer that should be as modest as he was himself." One of the last letters written by Thackeray before setting out for America was a letter to Monckton Milnes, saying, " give £1 for me to Hood's Tomb, please "; while Longfellow in sending his contribution said, " Poor Mrs. Hood and the children, who have lost him! They will have forgotten the stranger who called one October morning, with Dickens, and was hospitably entertained by them. But I remember the visit, and the pale face of the poet, and the house in St. John's Wood." Longfellow was not aware that Jane Hood had so soon followed her husband into the

Thomas Hood.

great silence. When the fund was completed the commission for designing the monument was given to Matthew Noble. The monument, surmounted by a bust of the poet, was duly unveiled at Kensal Green on July 18, 1854, by Monckton Milnes, who delivered an address on the subject of Hood's contribution to the literature of his country.

APPENDICES.

———◆———

I.

MY TRACT (p. 350).

MADAM,—I have received your pious billet-doux, but have little leisure, and less inclination for a religious flirtation, and what (according to our Law and Police Reports) is its usual issue—a decidedly serious intrigue. How else, indeed, am I to interpret the mysterious "object" of your late visit, which you significantly tell me was defeated by your being unintentionally accompanied by a friend?—how answer for her designs on a man's person, who can take such liberties with his soul? The presence of a companion could not of course stand in the way of you giving me a tract or a letter or anything proper for a modest woman to offer; but where can be the womanly modesty, or delicacy, or decency of a female, who intrudes on a man's private house, and private correspondence, and his most private affairs, those of his heart and soul, with as much masculine assurance as if she wore Paul Pry's inexpressibles under her petticoats? Perhaps I have to congratulate myself, as Joseph Andrews did on the preservation of his virtue from that amorous widow, Lady Booby! But whatever impropriety you intended to commit has been providentially frustrated, it appears, by the intrusion of the young lady in question, to whom, therefore, I beg you will present my most grateful and special thanks. I am, as you know, a married man, and do not care to forget that character, only that I may be able to say afterwards,

Appendix I.

as you suggest, "*I have gone astray*, but now I have learned thy righteous law."

The cool calculations you have indulged in on my desperate health, probable decease, and death-bed perturbations must have afforded you much Christian amusement, as your ignorance must have derived infinite comfort from your conviction of the inutility of literature, and all intellectual pursuits. And even your regret over the "Whims and Oddities, that have made thousands laugh" may be alleviated, if you will only reflect that Fanaticism has caused millions to shed blood, as well as tears; a tolerable set-off against my levities. For my own part, I thank God, I have used the talents He has bestowed on me in so cheerful a spirit, and not abused them by writing the profane stuff called pious poetry, nor spiritualised my prose by stringing together Scriptural phrases, which have become the mere slang of a religious swell mob. Such impieties and blasphemies I leave to the Evangelical and Elect; to the sacrilegious quacks, who pound up equal parts of Bible and Babble, and convert wholesome food, by their nauseous handling, into filthiest physic; to the Canters, who profane all holy names and things by their application to common and vulgar uses; and to the presumptuous women, who, I verily believe with the Turks, have no souls of their own to mend, and therefore set themselves to patch and cobble the souls of the other gender.

It is, I know, the policy of your faction to decry literature, which they abhor as the Devil hates Gospel. And for a similar reason. For all the most celebrated authors, the wisest, and most learned in the ways of mankind, Scott, Fielding, Smollett, Sterne, Crabbe, Addison, Butler, Pope, Moore, Burns, Byron, Molière, Voltaire, Boileau, and a host of others, have concurred in denouncing, and exposing Tartuffes, Maw-worms, Cantwells, Puritans, in short sanctimonious folly and

Appendix I.

knavery of every description. Such writers I know would be called scoffers and infidels; but a Divine Hand, incapable of the injustice, has drawn a full length picture of a self-righteous Pharisee; and Holy Lips, prone to all gentleness and charity, have addressed their sharpest rebukes to Spiritual Pride and Religious Hypocrisy. Are the sacrilegious animals aware that in their retaliations they are kicking even at *Him ?*

In behalf of our literature I will boldly say that to our lay authors it is mainly owing, that the country is not at this hour enthralled by Priestcraft, Superstition, and, if you please, Popery, which, by the bye, has met with more efficient opponents in Dante, Boccaccio, and Rabelais (profane writers, madam), than in all the M'Neiles, M'Ghees, and Macaws, that have screamed within Exeter Hall.

As for literature "palling on my soul in my dying hour,"—on the contrary it has been my solace and comfort through the extremes of worldly trouble and sickness, and has maintained me in a cheerfulness, a perfect sunshine of the mind, seldom seen on the faces of the most prosperous and healthy of your sect, who, considering that they are as sure of going to Heaven as the " poor Indian's dog," are certainly more melancholy dogs than they ought to be ! But what else can come of chanting " pious chansons " with hell-fire burthens, that to my taste, fit them particularly for contributions to the Devil's Album ? Some such verses you have sent me, and I could return you others quite as religious— but unfortunately written by a minister, who, after being expelled in disgrace from a public foundation in London, went and robbed a poor Savings Bank in the country.

Such literature may indeed appal the soul at the hour of death, and such an author may justly dread an Eternal Review. Again, therefore, I thank God that

Appendix I.

my pen has not been devoted to such serious composi-
tions, that I have never profaned His Holy Name with
common-place jingles, or passed off the inspirations of
presumption, vanity, or hypocrisy, for devout effusions.
My humble works have flowed from my heart, as well
as my head, and, whatever their errors, are such as I
have been able to contemplate with composure, when,
more than once, the Destroyer assumed almost a visible
presence. For I have stood several times in that serious
extremity both by land and sea—yet, for all my near
approaches to the other world, I have never pretended
to catch glimpses of its heaven, or of its hell, or to have
had intimations of who, among my neighbours, were on
the road to one place or the other. Such special revelations are reserved, it seems, by a Wisdom, certainly
inscrutable, for the worst or weakest of the weaker sex,
such cackling hen-prophetesses as its Southcotes, its
G——s, and its L——s.

And verily if they be the Righteous, I am content
to be the Lefteous of the species.

It has pleased you to picture me occasionally in
such extremities as those just alluded to,—and, no
doubt, with regret that you could not, Saint-like, beset
my couch, to try spiritual experiments on my soul, and
enjoy its excruciations, as certain brutal anatomists
have gloated on the last agonies of mutilated dogs and
rabbits. But we will now turn, if you please, from my
death-bed to your own—supposing you to be lying there
at that awful crisis, which reveals the depravity of the
human heart as distinctly as the mortality of the human
frame! And now, on that terrible, narrow isthmus
between the past and the future, just imagine yourself
appealing to your conscience for answers to such solemn
questions as follow. And first, whether your extreme
devotion has been affected or sincere,—unobtrusive or
ostentatious,—humble to your Creator, but arrogant to

406

Appendix I.

His creatures,—in short, Piety, or Mag-piety? Whether
your professed love for your species has been active and
fruitful, or only that flatulent charity, which evaporates
upwards in wind, and catechises the hungry, and
preaches to the naked? And finally, how far, in
meddling with the spiritual concerns of your neighbours, you have neglected your own; and, consequently,
what you may have to dread from that Hell and its
fires, which you have so often amused yourself with
letting off at a poor Sinner,—just as a boy would squib
a Guy? These are queries important to your "eternal
destiny," which ought to be considered in time; whereas
from the tenor of your letter, it appears to me that you
have never entertained them for a moment, and I am
sorry to add that, judging from the same evidence,
whatever may be your acquaintance with the *letter* of
the New Testament, of its *spirit* you are as deplorably
ignorant as the blindest heathen Hottentot, for whose
enlightenment you perhaps subscribe a few Missionary
pence.

I implore you to spend a few years, say twenty, in
this self-scrutiny, which may be wholesomely varied by
the exercise of a little active benevolence; not, however,
in sending tracts, instead of baby-linen, to poor lying-in
sisters, or in volunteering pork chops for distressed
Jews, or in recommending a Solemn Fast to the
Spitalfields weavers, or in coddling and pampering
a pulpit favourite, but in converting rags to raiment,
and empty stomachs to full ones, and in helping the
wretched and indigent to " keep their souls and bodies
together ! "

And, should you ever relapse and feel tempted to
write religious Swing letters, such as you have sent to
me, let me recommend to you a quotation from a great
and wise writer, and moreover a namesake of your pious
mother. It runs thus—" *I find you are perfectly qualified*

Appendix I.

to make converts, and so, go, help your mother to make the gooseberry pie."

Still if you will and must indite such epistles, pray address them elsewhere. There are plenty of young single "men about town" (and of the very sort such saints are partial to—namely, "*precious*" sinners) who no doubt would be willing to discuss with you their "experiences," and to embrace you and your persuasion together. But on me your pains would be wasted. I am not to be converted, except *from* Christianity, by arrogance, insolence, and ignorance enough, as Mrs. Jarley says, "to make one turn atheist." Indeed the only effect of your letter has been to inspire me, like old Tony Weller, with a profound horror of widows, whether amorous or pious, for both seem equally resolute that a man shall not "call his soul his own."

And now, Madam, farewell. Your mode of recalling yourself to my memory reminds me that your fanatical mother insulted mine in the last days of her life (which was marked by every Christian virtue), by the presentation of a Tract addressed to Infidels. I remember also that the same heartless woman intruded herself, with less reverence than a Mohawk Squaw would have exhibited, on the chamber of death; and interrupted with her jargon almost my very last interview with my dying parent. Such reminiscences warrant some severity; but, if more be wanting, know that my poor sister has been excited by a circle of Canters like yourself, into a religious frenzy, and is at this moment in a private mad-house. I am, Madam, yours with disgust,

THOS. HOOD.

II.

TO THE EDITOR OF THE *Athenæum*.

SIR,—The extraordinary latitude taken by Mr. Baily compels me to sue for a little more longitude, seeing

408

Appendix II.

that, as my Ex-Publisher cannot obtain anything from my pen, he has commenced the publication of my private affairs. The charge of unfairly using my name has, by his own help, been fully established; and his own advertisement in your Journal, has proved the justice of the terms applied by me to the transaction. I shall not retort any others, for it is not in the power of Mr. Baily to upset my philosophy :—the notion in Physics, that "Nature abhors a vacuum," always excepted. As regards my interference,—seeing a very kind o d friend to me—the Public—being lured to the purchase of second hand novelties,—not in Monmouth Street, but on Cornhill,—common gratitude might or might not induce me to hint that the Eagle over the shop-door was the appropriate sign of an establishment where old articles "renewed their youth." But when my own name is used in such transactions, all the Bailys old or new, cannot controvert my claim to intervene. And, just to assert my " right of remark," I will observe, that on such a system, the Bishop of Exeter himself might some day be advertised as an eminent contributor to a Socialist's Oracle, or the Non-Intrusive Dr. Chalmers as a communicant to a Paul Pry Gazette. The papers in the *Sporting*, for which, according to Mr. Baily, he paid much too large a sum, were written at his own request and on terms he offered. I remember that the papers pleased the Editor (Nimrod) and the reviewers, but cannot recollect even thinking of thinking if they would, or could, hit the taste of Mr. Baily. His retrospective review of them is therefore only amusing—especially when in the canine, not wisdom, teeth of his own critique, he has proved, by reproducing one of the papers in the "Oracle," that he thought it worthy of a second perusal ! On a point of more importance below this and amongst menials than anywhere else—the " Who gave warning first ? "—my

Appendix II.

Ex-Publisher is so peculiarly sensitive, that he circumstantially describes an elaborate letter of dismissal—which, however, he must have put into the same post with Sheridan's famous "double letter from Northamptonshire." As a test of veracity, the point is worth deciding,—and here are the facts, from documents now before me. So far from a positive refusal to discontinue the connexion on account of my declining popularity, Mr. Baily formally accepted my terms for a new work on the 13th of last March. On the 18th he attempted to substitute other conditions—which were peremptorily rejected—and, moreover, a letter giving him my candid opinion of him as a publisher and a man, left him no alternative but to acquiesce and consider the end as the end. *He*, therefore, was the discharged; and, instead of his pretended thunder went off as follows, with a report ridiculously like pop :—" In your announcement that the terms proposed by me are absolutely declined, I distinctly acquiesce, and, having no further proposal to make, consider the negotiation between us for future publications as decidedly at an end.—(Signed) A. H. Baily." And now to a graver matter. In his desire to wound me, Mr. Baily has thought proper to partly expose my private circumstances,— he has partially dared to raise a veil which any man of common feeling, and, in his case, of common sense, would have held sacred. The disclosure so rashly and wantonly begun, must, for my own vindication, be completed. The task is eminently painful,—but one pang is spared me. A man who has so long borne his burthen in secret and silence, and with so cheerful a spirit—bear witness for me my humble works !—will not be confounded with a suppliant for the world's pity or assistance. One who seeks his happiness in the domestic affections, and who has a home and a family circle,—whose favourite pursuits are his profession,—

Appendix II.

can neither be poor nor feel so,—and least of all if he happen to have before his eyes some signal example of poverty, nay, utter destituion, of all enjoyments, moral or intellectual. Be it known, then, to the world—since such is Mr. Baily's *pleasure*—that, self-banished, I have been struggling abroad to retrieve my affairs, and to acquit myself honourably of all claims upon me—a consummation once quite in the foreground of my prospects, but rendered remote by the sudden breaking up of my health, after a stormy passage to Rotterdam. I can adduce medical testimony that my literary exertions have been fully as great as could be expected under the circumstances of my case, indeed, I will venture to say in my own behalf, that, taking both effusions together, no gentleman alive has written so much comic and spitten so much blood within six consecutive years. The property thus acquired is at this hour in the hands of the same individual who taunts me with my misfortunes — a taunt, nevertheless, quite delicious from the intense assurance it gives me that such a person is not my friend. It is true, as he states, that my property was attached ; though not " by my creditors," but by *a* creditor—and not "lately," but above four months ago. Two significant mis-statements which, without any of the innocence, have all the weakness of the babe that cannot stand. It is also true, though Mr. Baily never mentions it, that the property was not attached till legal proceedings were commenced to wrest the " heavy stock of my last works" from a Publisher who was no creditor at all. Finally, it is true, that the attachment *was kept secret by Mr. Baily,* although as a Paid Agent he was undoubtedly bound to communicate the fact to the proprietor ! After these disclosures, may I not justly say, that the " Suppressio Veri " affects his moral constitution and not mine ? I put aside the

Appendix II.

allusion to the respectable publishers who " got rid of me one after the other," a statement as correct as Mr. Baily's circumstantial account of his own sending me adrift. The present is not a Faction Fight between Authors and Booksellers, and, if it were, most assuredly the respectable publishers would not elect a Champion who not only gives his head, but exposes his heart to the severest punishment. The infliction, however, is so like helping a man to commit suicide that I forbear —and besides I want to read over again that chapter in " Count Robert of Paris," where the Knight, in the very extremity of his distress, is so brutally set upon by a creature whose chief resemblance to humanity is in his shape.—I am, yours, &c.,

THOMAS HOOD.

INDEX.

Index.

Index.

Index.

416

Index.

Index.

Index.

Index.